THE MAKING OF A
CHRISTIAN ARISTOCRACY

Michele Renee Salzman

The Making of a Christian Aristocracy

Social and Religious Change
in the Western Roman Empire

Harvard University Press

Cambridge, Massachusetts, and London, England   2002

Library of Congress Cataloging-in-Publication Data

Salzman, Michele Renee.
    The making of a Christian aristocracy : social and religious change in the western
    Roman Empire / Michele Renee Salzman.
       p.   cm.
    Includes bibliographical references (p.) and index.
    ISBN 0-674-00641-0 (alk. paper)
      1. Christian converts—Rome.   2. Aristocracy (Social class)—Religious life—Rome.
   3. Sociology, Christian—History—Early church, ca. 30–600.   I. Title.

BR195.C6 S35   2002
270.2'086'21—dc21   2001047075

To my husband, Steven,
and my children, Juliana and Ben

Contents

Preface

Every student of the later Roman empire will, at one time or other, confront the subject of this book: What did it take to make the Roman aristocracy in the later western empire change its ancient religious traditions, turning from paganism to Christianity, in the century of Constantine?

My answer to this question would not have been possible without the work of generations of scholars, whose advances and missteps have challenged and taught me. Although, in the end, dissatisfaction with their solutions and approaches led me to write this book, I have learned much from my predecessors and the frameworks they used. Hence it seems only fitting to outline in brief the approaches and advances that led me to write this book as I did.[1]

Many scholars in the late nineteenth and early twentieth century studied Christianization by interpreting the experiences of individuals. The classic study of conversion by Arthur Darby Nock is emblematic of this approach. Nock sees the process as "the reorientation of the soul of the individual, his deliberate turning from indifference or from an earlier form of piety to another, a turning which implies a consciousness that a great change is involved, that the old was wrong and the new is right." Nock emphasized the individual's decision and the appeal of the message of Christianity to the individual.[2]

Implicit in the work of many who, following in Nock's footsteps, study the lives of individual converts is the notion that conversion is a response to a felt need. For a time, scholars were much influenced by the modern concept of cognitive dissonance, a theory that assumes that people who are attracted to a different religion feel in some measure conflict in their present state and gravitate naturally toward a "message" of some sort that soothes that inner turmoil.[3] This focus on the personal side of conversion fits easily with modern notions of individualism, and it is reinforced by the nature of the extant evidence, for what survives most strikingly are texts by and about the conversions of individuals.[4]

However, such studies rely on a convert's reinterpretation of his own past in terms of his present perspective and goals.[5] Moreover, the story of any particular individual might be more idiosyncratic than typical. While approaching Christianization through the mindset of the individual aristocrat may tell us much about the way in which that individual wishes to be perceived, this approach will not allow historians to assess the transformation of the aristocracy as a class—which is precisely what is necessary for analyzing a religious change like the Christianization of the Roman aristocracy.

Similar problems arise from an approach that would explain the spread of Christianity on the basis of its ideological or theological message. Some scholars believed that Christianity's doctrine was simply superior; this implicit theological understanding explains why the influential religious scholar Adolf Harnack and his circle used the term "expansion" as a virtual synonym for the "triumph of the gospel message over its environment."[6] Thus some historians and theologians isolated aspects of fourth-century Christianity that were notably distinctive and hence, in their view, led to its triumph over paganism. Some have seen its promise of salvation as especially appealing in troubled times.[7] Others have focused on the radical conceptualization of Christian love with its concomitant ideas of mercy and compassion, which developed into a notion of social welfare new to the Roman empire.[8] Still others have theorized that Christianity offered a new and broader form of community in which all were "equal in Christ," stripping its adherents of ethnicity and other social distinctions.[9]

Relatively few scholars, however, have attempted to explain the spread of Christianity among the senatorial aristocracy on ideological grounds alone. This may well be the result of a view that aristocrats were among the least likely people to be sympathetic to the ideas of Christianity. Only a handful of scholars have focused on the inherent attraction Christian ideology held for aristocrats, and then mostly in terms of the individual's intellectual growth.[10] This motive appears, too, in the work of those who see Christianity as uniquely offering elite women the freedom to pursue the study of biblical texts.

Some idea-based explanations have clearly fallen out of favor. The notion that the doctrine of Christianity is somehow better than all others is at odds with what comparative religionists tell us about the ways that very divergent religious doctrines can satisfy spiritual needs. There is no good way of proving or disproving such claims other than to point to the success of Christianity, a tautology out of which we cannot progress.

In any case, explanations grounded in Christian ideas suffer by presupposing that people act primarily on the basis of belief. Beliefs matter, but to have broader historical impact they need to interact with wider social and political forces and institutions. A strictly theological or idea-based approach cannot answer why some groups of aristocrats found Christianity intellectually and emotionally compelling while others did not, nor why some groups were more likely to convert earlier than others.

Historians of the last fifty years who have emphasized the political and social forces surrounding this change have taken a more fruitful approach. Those examining the political forces involved in the religious transformation of the aristocracy have focused on the role of the emperor.[11] Constantine and the pro-Christian policies that he and his successors advanced are viewed as having been the direct cause of the conversion of the aristocracy and the population at large.[12] Historians who share this assumption differ on how the emperors Christianized the aristocracy. In the aftermath of World War II some scholars emphasized the conflictual aspects of this process, seeing the struggle between emperor and aristocracy as a power play between two opposing religious camps.[13] A generation of scholars in the 1950s and 1960s, perhaps influenced by Cold War politics, emphasized more subtle methods. They focused on the impact of imperial appointments to high office or changes in the duties of certain magistracies as more indirect avenues for affecting religious change.[14]

The dominant political interpretive model by and large sees religion spreading from "top to bottom," with an aristocracy following the religious lead of powerful Christian emperors. Some have diligently examined the number of pagan or Christian appointees by individual emperors as a demonstration of this influence. Since assessing the religiosity of one or another individual can depend on differing analyses of the evidence, this approach has led to differing conclusions. R. von Haehling analyzed imperial appointments in the East and West and found a gradual change, with an emphasis on the reign of Gratian as a pivotal time. But when T. D. Barnes reanalyzed von Haehling's evidence, he came up with different statistics, which he then used to argue that the Christianization of the aristocracy was fast and generally noncontroversial, reflecting a rapid adjustment of aristocratic behavior to fit imperial policy.[15]

I do not reject the notion that emperors had an impact, yet emperors had to work against an entrenched and considerably autonomous aristocratic culture. Hence imperial influence was more diffuse and, as this study will show, the conversion of its aristocracy slower than Barnes and certain scholars have argued. The fourth-century Christian emperors who developed Constantine's initial policies are of importance in this process. Indeed, considering only imperial appointments provides too limited a gauge of late Roman political life. Politics also worked outside of the formal channels of appointment, through the building of patronage obligations, friendships, family ties, and the like.

Recognition of the numerous avenues of late antique politics has led some to widen their study of imperial influence. John Matthews showed the importance not only of the emperor but of the imperial court and its courtiers in setting policy after 364.[16] Others have traced the imperial laws that privileged Christians (particularly bishops) and penalized pagans or the role of emperor as patron.[17]

Yet such political analyses have not gone far enough, for Christianization is still construed essentially in terms of the emperor's influence on the aristocracy. The late Roman political world was more complicated and less centrifugal than this top-down interpretive model suggests. There were other sources of political power and influence than that of the emperor. The imperial court, the church, the *collegia,* the senate, the military, and the provincial elites all exercised power and influence. Individual aristocrats had ties to one or other of these political groups. Even emperors desired to maintain their ties with the aristocracy. Thus, to comprehend the political dimension of religious change, we need a deep understanding of the aristocrats who faced these political forces in their daily lives.

But to understand the aristocracy in their daily lives we need to analyze the social and cultural world in which they lived. Some historians have moved in that direction, notably A. H. M. Jones and Peter Brown, who saw Christianity as spreading horizontally, largely as the result of interactions among aristocrats or due to changes within the aristocracy itself. Jones emphasized the changing composition of the aristocracy, seeing in the social mobility of new men a primary force for change, religious and social.[18]

Subsequent scholars have modified Jones' observations on specific aspects of compositional and institutional changes within the senatorial aristocracy, but neither Jones nor his successors have demonstrated their precise influence on Christianization. The idea that compositional changes, like the rise of new men, encouraged Christianization remains more an assertion than an established fact.

Other scholars have highlighted the spread of religion through friendship and kinship networks. Peter Brown's work has been most influential in this regard.[19] Following Brown, some have studied the role of kinship and friendship ties on the religious affiliations of one or another aristocratic family.[20] Others, also influenced by Brown, have emphasized the important role played by aristocratic women in conversion.[21]

These studies have advanced our appreciation of the social and cultural influences important in religious change, but they represent only the beginning of a synthetic understanding. Most of the empirical studies have focused on a small number of families. The difficulties involved in unraveling family ties and religious affiliations make studies of selected families understandable. But such studies can also be misleading if they are centered on atypical families. Nor have such studies considered the full range of social and cultural influences at play in the Christianization of the aristocracy. Many sorts of social considerations—such as bonds between aristocrats involved in similar career paths or between aristocrats from the same geographical area—may also be important for conversion.

No study has yet taken what seems to me the most fruitful approach, that is, to place the senatorial aristocracy at the center of analysis. Only by looking at religious change from the perspective of the senatorial aristocracy, its style of life and values, can we hope to understand how the Roman aristocracy became Christian in the fourth century. Hence I will focus on the culture and institutions of the aristocracy and the key differences among aristocrats.

My debt to the community of scholars extends beyond those noted above. I want to thank those who have been my constant interlocutors and who have so willingly read and critiqued my work. Emily Albu, Alan Cameron, Hal Drake, Susanna Elm, Hugh Elton, Judith Evans-Grubbs, Sandra Joshel, Michael Maas, John Matthews, Claudia Rapp, Teresa Shaw, Karen Torjesen, and Dennis Trout have read the manuscript, in part or whole, at various stages of its development. My debt to them for their time, criticism, and encouragement is great and heartfelt. Works by Peter Brown, Elizabeth Clark, and John Matthews were constant companions, and they have each, in their ways, been special sources of inspiration for me. I also want to thank the two anonymous reviewers for the Press for their incisive and intelligent comments on the manuscript. The book is better for their contributions.

This study would not have been possible without the resources of several research institutions and granting bodies. I want to thank the American Academy in Rome for granting me a Mellon Fellowship in the Humanities that allowed me the time to pursue my research and gave unlimited access to its library. Research grants from Boston University and the University of California, Riverside have enabled me to continue that work. I owe the Inter-Library Loan Department at UC Riverside a special thanks for their help. I wish to thank, too, the research assistants who have helped me in the preparation of the manuscript and in tracking down sources: Debbie Ahlberg, Daniel Christensen, and Tim Watson have been resourceful and diligent aids in this process. Rebecca Li's statistical assistance has been invaluable; her calm manner eased my distress at the numerous computer-related problems that arose. I want to thank, in particular, the editorial staff at Harvard University Press, led by Peg Fulton, for their help in preparing the manuscript for publication.

My deepest debt goes to my family. My husband, Steven Brint, has been my best supporter and loving companion through the genesis and growth of this book. He has had the patience and willingness to make the world of statistics comprehensible to me, no easy task. He has been willing to listen to my ideas and critique them, orally and in writing, as I worked through the many problems and drafts of the manuscript. I thank him for his wit and loving patience, traits exhibited too by my two children, Juliana and Ben, who have put up with my many hours at my desk. Their pride in my accomplishments has taught me much about the generosity of the human spirit.

In the end I take responsibility for this book—both its advances and its missteps. It is the product of many years of thought and research on a question that, I confess, I still find fascinating. The possibility of such large-scale social and religious change as the Christianization of the Roman aristocracy and the drama of dying and rising religions are still meaningful to me, for in many ways we live with the consequences of those events. I hope others will find these processes as compelling as I have in writing this book.

CHAPTER 1

Approaches to a Paradox

It was the Jew who with frightening consistency, dared to invert the aristocratic value equations good/noble/powerful/happy/favored-of-the-gods and maintain, with the furious hatred of the underprivileged and impotent, that "only the poor, the powerless, are good; only the suffering, sick, and ugly, truly blessed. But you noble and mighty ones of the earth will be, to all eternity, the evil, the cruel, the avaricious, the godless, and thus the cursed and damned." We know who has fallen heir to this Jewish inversion of values . . . Jesus of Nazareth.

—F. Nietzsche, *The Genealogy of Morals* (trans. Francis Golffing)

There is a story, told by the fourth-century Christian poet Prudentius and the fifth-century pagan Greek historian Zosimus, that in the year 394 C.E. the emperor Theodosius came to Rome fresh from his victory at the River Frigid. He called the senators to the senate house and urged them to "cast off their previous error," paganism, and adopt Christianity "which promises deliverance from all sin and impiety."[1] According to Prudentius, the senate, of its own free will and without coercion, voted for Christianity.[2] Zosimus, however, claims the opposite occurred: "no-one obeyed his summons or abandoned their ancestral rites . . . the observation of which had allowed them to live in a city unconquered for almost twelve hundred years."[3] Modern historians may wonder if this story is true, if Theodosius visited Rome in this year or made any such request.[4] Yet Prudentius and Zosimus both recount the visit for polemical ends, the former to proclaim the triumph of Christianity, the latter to blame Christianity for the woes of the fifth-century empire. Their narratives encapsulate a more fundamental truth about late Roman society, namely the importance of the Christianization of the senatorial aristocracy to emperors and contemporaries in the late Roman world.

Although their military and political preeminence had been shaken by civil wars and invasions in the third century, many of the old Roman senatorial aristocratic families had reemerged in the West in the fourth century to reassert leadership in civic and social life. Many of these men were among the wealthiest landowners in the empire. Their position was further enhanced by Constantine, who reincorporated senatorial aristocrats into political life and carried out reforms in state government.[5] The men from old aristocratic families were joined by a large number of "new men," relatively recent arrivals into the senatorial aristocracy from the provinces and beyond, many of whom served the imperial bureaucracy in capitals that now eclipsed Rome as political centers. The senatorial aristocracy—the upper-class holders of the senatorial rank of *clarissimi* or "most outstanding"— that emerged in the West in the fourth and early fifth centuries thus encompassed a number of elite groups who enjoyed wide-ranging social, economic, legal, and political influence.

Given their prestige and resources, it is not surprising that the senatorial aristocracy was also viewed as being of central importance in the Christianization of the empire. The Romans had never separated the secular from the sacred. For centuries the same men who held high state office also held the most important priesthoods in the pagan state cults. These positions were traditionally much sought after as a means of manifesting and reinforcing a man's social status.[6] Indeed, winning the religious affiliation of the aristocracy would be especially significant to Constantine who, after a bloody civil war, made public his support for Christianity. This was, after all, a hierarchical society. Once an emperor had declared his religious preference, the object of his veneration would generally receive cult support from the upper classes and the public at large. But would this be the case for Christianity? What would the senatorial aristocracy do?

There could hardly have been a more unlikely candidate for Christianity; the senatorial aristocracy of Rome and Italy, with its deeply entrenched pagan and civic traditions, held values that were fundamentally at odds with Christianity. A religion whose texts taught love for one's neighbor and humility, with strictures on wealth and notions of equality, did not, generally speaking, appeal to aristocrats. Nietzsche's view of Christianity as a "slave religion" would have been appreciated by many a late Roman aristocrat. Affirmation of status and privilege motivated all members of this order, the newly arrived senatorial aristocrat as much as one with a prestigious family tree. It made narrative sense to both Prudentius and Zosimus that an emperor would personally appeal to the senatorial aristocracy since this act acknowledged even as it augmented this group's prestige. Zosimus' history suggests, too, that the senatorial aristocrats of Rome and Italy were the most resistant of their class to religious change. Yet both authors present the conversion of the aristocracy as key. Once the aristocracy—in Rome and throughout the West—had converted, the empire could be proclaimed Christian.

It would be wrong to assume that polytheism was a dead issue in the late third and fourth centuries. On the contrary, polytheism was very much alive in the daily lives of late Roman senatorial aristocrats. The virulence of the antipagan polemics that emerge at the end of the fourth century (to which Prudentius' narrative can be attached) is but one of many indicators of its continued existence.[7] Thus we can no longer see the end of polytheism as Edward Gibbon did, that is, "almost exclusively in terms of the impact of a formidable moving body upon an inert and static mass."[8] Gibbon's vision is at odds with what we now know about the vitality of late Roman polytheism.

The success of Christianity was by no means a foregone conclusion in 312. At the beginning of the fourth century, before Constantine, there were very few attested Christian senatorial aristocrats.[9] Yet, somehow, over the course of the fourth and early fifth centuries these two forces—Christianity and the aristocracy—met and merged. This conjunction—the process by which pagan aristocrats became Christian and Christianity became aristocratic—is the subject of this book.

A New Approach to the Problem

Scholars, confronted with the seeming paradox of a conservative and proud pagan senatorial aristocracy turning to the religion of "the poor and powerless" over the course of the fourth and fifth centuries, have come to this phenomenon using different interpretive frameworks. This book draws selectively on their contributions, particularly those who have focused on political dynamics and changes in the social structure of the Roman empire.[10] Yet no scholarly work has yet approached Christianization in the most fruitful way—by putting the senatorial aristocracy at the center of the discussion. Only by examining the world of the aristocracy, its values and style of life, its institutions and resources, can we determine how and why aristocrats converted. This book is based on just such an approach. While this analysis seeks to take into account the political influence of the emperor and the bishops, and of changes in the religiosity of the population at large, it argues that these influences are important insofar as they intersect with the interests and views of aristocrats.

The senatorial aristocracy, I will argue, was united by a shared status culture. Every aristocrat, be he a Roman of ancient lineage, a Gallic man new to the senatorial aristocracy, or a Spaniard of the imperial entourage, felt a deep concern about his status in the world. His lifestyle, values, and manner aimed at demonstrating to his peers that he was truly a member of the senatorial aristocracy. Proper aristocratic behavior extended to religious rites and duties; these were traditionally in the service of the pagan cults. Only by meeting the expectations of his peers could an aristocrat expect to gain the acceptance that was the primary guarantee of aristocratic standing. This was true for women as well as men. As J. Lendon has rightly observed, to be a member of the aristocracy meant "membership in a co-opting club, and fundamentally it was membership in this club which distinguished the unquestionably aristocratic . . . from the enormously rich but (to aristocratic opinion) déclassé freedman."[11]

This sense of shared values and the esteem aristocrats felt for these qualities justify calling the senatorial elite of the late Roman world an "aristocracy." Consequently, I use the term "senatorial aristocracy" throughout this book to refer to all holders of the senatorial rank of *clarissimus*.[12] Above all, to fully understand the sociocultural forces involved in the Christianization of the senatorial aristocracy, we must take into account the form and content of the shared status culture of this group.

The western senatorial aristocracy of the fourth and fifth centuries had tremendous resources. Many were rich landowners; with wealth came power and influence. Many were holders of high civic or imperial administrative office; with office came opportunities for financial gain and personal prestige. When underestimating the vitality of the senatorial aristocracy, historians have overestimated imperial influence on the conversion of this group. Neither emperors nor their entourages could force religious change on the aristocracy, even if they wanted to. The same is true of the church and its bishops. Rather, the position of the senatorial aristocracy was such that emperors and churchmen alike had to appeal to the aristocracy on its own terms, speaking in a style and invoking concepts that aristocrats would find attractive; we now find traditional senatorial aristocratic values, such as friendship and patronage, addressed with a renewed emphasis.

At the same time, significant differences existed among senatorial aristocrats. These differences were rooted, above all, in provenance (and therefore the landholdings of families) and in careers. New divisions follow the trajectory of empire. As new regions of the empire developed homegrown elites and as new career paths opened to handle the business of the empire, members of the senatorial aristocracy began to live more independently from one another. Such differences fueled rivalries between aristocrats from different regions and milieux: Spaniard versus Gaul, imperial courtier versus civic administrator. These differences must be understood and weighed in analyzing religious change.

By placing the senatorial aristocracy at the center of the discussion, this study tries to avoid the missteps that have caused previous scholarly approaches to falter, chief among them the persistent tendency to underestimate the autonomy and resources of the aristocracy in facing imperial and episcopal influence. The dominant model of change is problematic precisely in this regard, for it sees religion spreading from "top to bottom," as it were, with an aristocracy accepting the religious example set by enthusiastic and powerful Christian emperors out of ambition or greed, or simply indifference to religion. Hence many have argued that Constantine's conversion in 312 and the pro-Christian policies that he and his successors promulgated explain the conversion of the aristocracy and the population at large.[13] Indeed, the importance of the emperor is greatly reinforced if, as scholars following Gibbon have argued, "the Christians before 312 were a small, persecuted and insignificant minority of the population of the Roman empire, small clusters of believers obliged to conceal their religion in an alien society."[14] While some have advanced the view that Christians made up a larger percentage of the population than suggested by this description, few believe that Christianity included many aristocrats until after the reign of Constantine.[15] Hence scholars have focused on the role of the emperor to explain the conversion of the aristocracy.

This study does not reject the idea that emperors had an impact on the aristocracy. However, because emperors were working against an imbedded and considerably autonomous senatorial culture, the emperor's influence was more limited and more diffuse than many have argued. I suggest a more gradual process, with a shift toward a predominance of Christians only under Gratian in the late 360s. A string of fourth-century Christian emperors continued and improvised upon Constantine's initial policies, and their efforts are of importance in understanding this process. Focusing on imperial influence over appointments to high public office provides too narrow a measure of imperial influence.[16] Politics also worked outside of the formal channels of appointment, through loose-knit patronage, the granting of privileges, and the forging of family ties.

Aristocrats, too, had powerful ties not only to other aristocrats and the emperor but to other elites in Roman society, namely to provincial elites, courtiers, and the military.[17] Aristocrats used these ties and their considerable resources to reinforce their positions within society. I will show that emperors were constrained by both the traditions of Roman political life and their need for senatorial aristocratic support. Emperors could not and did not pursue policies that would threaten their legitimacy.

Only by examining the world of the senatorial aristocracy and the interconnection of its parts can we see what role religion played in that world and how aristocrats came to change from polytheism to Christianity over the course of the fourth and early fifth centuries C.E. This book offers a new interpretation of a key transition in western history, based on an understanding of the status culture of the aristocracy, the changing composition of that group, and the lines of social division that emerged with its expansion. My analysis of the Christianization of the Roman senatorial aristocracy reads the lives of some four hundred aristocrats against all the available evidence about the religious choices of aristocrats, including literary, archaeological, prosopographical, and epigraphic sources and studies. I have also drawn selectively from comparative social science and social theory. Only by incorporating all the available evidence and theory can we reach a sound understanding of religious change.

Examining the Evidence

One new source of evidence in this book is the short biographies I have assembled of 414 aristocrats who lived or held office of senatorial rank in the western empire between 284 and 423 C.E. These biographies represent but a small proportion of a stratum that must have included at least 36,000 members during the time period.[18] Yet these are the only people about whom we have certain evidence of religious affiliation and rank, and this is the largest group of senatorial aristocratic men and women ever studied in relation to the full range of their life activities.

These short biographies are based on the existing evidence found in extant texts, material remains, inscriptions, and the work of modern prosopographies or reference works that collect information on individuals. They play a dual role in this study. First, taken together with the other sources, they have informed my understanding of the culture and institutions of the later Roman aristocracy in the western empire and the patterns of division among aristocrats. Second, they have provided a source for considering ideas about religious change in the years before and after Constantine.

Although these short biographies are one important part of the study, I want to emphasize that the weight of the argument in this book does not rest on the evidence drawn from the lives of these 414 senatorial aristocrats. My interpretation of Christianization is based primarily on many years of study of Roman history and institutions and on a close reading of the literary and archaeological record. I also draw selectively on social theory to help understand the process of change in the lives of aristocrats. It is to this larger mosaic of evidence and theory that I have added quantitative evidence on 414 senatorial aristocrats.

Unfortunately, statistically valid inferences cannot be drawn from the quantitative evidence in this study. Because the quantitative evidence is not based on a random sample of aristocrats, it lacks representativeness. However, analysis of the study population can be used as one additional piece of evidence among others. If the quantitative evidence is evaluated critically in relation to everything else we know about the Roman aristocracy, it can suggest patterns of change and the effect of those patterns on other aristocrats. Everything else that we know about the aristocracy comes from textual and material remains.

Short Biographies of 414 Senatorial Aristocrats

The men and women whose biographies I have assembled include senatorial aristocrats who lived or held high office in the western empire between the reign of Diocletian, 284 C.E., and the death of Honorius, 423 C.E.[19] An aristocrat was defined on legal grounds as any man or woman who held the rank of *clarissimus,* the rank indicating senatorial standing.[20] The men and women in this study population did, therefore, meet certain social and economic criteria and enjoyed senatorial legal privileges. Moreover, using rank to define senatorial aristocrats ensured the inclusion of individuals from diverse elite circles within the aristocracy, even as it bestowed a uniform standard for admittance. This legal definition for an aristocrat is not totally satisfactory; it can, for instance, overlook the important role played by peer approval in constructing aristocratic society, which I discuss in Chapter 2. But given the difficulties of defining an aristocracy solely by social standards (knowing who was and was not "socially acceptable" could fluctuate greatly), a legal definition provided at the least the outer boundaries of the group in which I am interested.

In the late Roman empire, a major division existed between eastern and western aristocrats. Indeed, in the 350s, Constantius II divided the senatorial order on purely geographic grounds.[21] Any assessment that joins together the aristocracies of the eastern and western empire does not adequately account for the very real differences in social and economic position these two groups held in their respective areas. In the West, the aristocracy had centuries of tradition, tightly knit friendship and family ties, as well as considerable landholdings that reinforced their social and political position. In the East, many were relative newcomers to senatorial status, dependent more upon imperial and state dispensations than their western peers. A number of eastern senators were from the wealthy landowning elite or curial class, but they did not have the traditions of senatorial service of their western peers. And those eastern senators who arose via the imperial bureaucracy lacked the old, inherited economic and social resources of their western counterparts. Certainly the senate at Constantinople did not have the symbolic authority or social status of the senate at Rome; although it did rise in standing over the century, in the 350s it still included members who could be derided for their "new" status regardless of their wealth.[22] The social position of aristocratic women was also distinctly different in the East and West, with expectations for appropriate feminine comportment differing by region; wearing a veil, for instance, was part of expected dress for married women in certain areas in the Greek-speaking eastern empire but not in the Latin-speaking West.[23]

Since the western aristocracy lived in markedly different social and economic conditions than its eastern counterpart, I decided to draw geographical as well as temporal limits, examining only those aristocrats who lived or held high office in the western empire.[24] And, most important for this study, I included only those individuals for whom there was certain or near-certain explicit evidence of religious affiliation.[25] Moreover, I did not question to what degree a person was a Christian or a pagan; religious identification by self or others was taken at face value, and all varieties of Christian belief—heretical or not—were subsumed under a more general term, Christian. In determining if a man or woman met my criteria for inclusion in the study population, I took a consistently conservative approach. This degree of certainty for religious affiliation explains, in part, the size of the database; hundreds more senators are listed by name in prosopographies. But for many of these we have no explicit or certain indication of religious affiliation. For many others we lack attestation of rank, date, or geographic origin. Hence they were not included in my study population. This reduced the number of pagans as well as the number of Christians.[26]

As a group, this study population reflects certain realities of the Roman world. I found far more information for men than for women. This is understandable given the prominence of men within Roman society. The study population has more than three times as many men (315 out of 414, or 76% of the total) than women (99 out of 414, or 24% of the total). Information for Christians was also more abundant than for pagans, no doubt reflecting the eventual "triumph of Christianity," which enabled the Church to preserve Christian texts and artifacts. Thus, in my study population, Christians (230 out of 414, or 56%) occurred in greater numbers than pagans (166 out of 414, or 40%). Converts were rarely attested in the sources and hence were relatively infrequent in the population. Only 14 out of 414, or 3%, were converts from a pagan cult to Christianity; only 4 out of 414, or 1%, were converts from Christianity to a pagan cult.

For individuals who fit my established criteria, I gathered information about what they did in their lives that might elucidate their religious identification. Thus I noted the offices they held, the career paths they followed, the places they lived, the people they married, their spouses' religion, their children's religions, and other information. The fullness of these biographies varied considerably, depending upon survival of information as well as prominence. Yet even for some of the most prominent individuals, key information is lacking; we do not know, for example, the name of the daughter of Symmachus, one of the most prominent pagan aristocratic senators of the late fourth century.

My goal in creating these biographies was to examine propositions, my own and those of other scholars, concerning which social factors were linked to religious change by viewing these factors against the behavior of an actual population of case studies. In particular, I looked for social differences associated with a higher proportion of Christians or pagans, or with earlier and later conversion to Christianity. For instance, to investigate whether intermarriage was a means of spreading Christianity, I gathered information about the intermarriage of pagans and Christians and calculated whether the children of intermarried couples were more likely to convert than the children of two pagan parents.

In studies of large-scale historical change, analysis of many cases is generally preferable to intensive study of particular individuals or families (although these latter studies also clearly have value). We can assume a greater social and historical significance when fifty aristocrats of a particular type, as compared to one, can be shown to be doing the same thing. And when fifty aristocrats start doing something, that in turn affects what other aristocrats do.

In discussing the behavior of aristocrats within this population of 414, I will at times talk of numbers and percentages. For example, among those who held high offices, I will note the percentage of pagan and Christian aristocrats in Gaul and compare these percentages to those for pagan and Christian aristocrats in Italy. Such quantitative analyses can be useful because they can help to compare patterns of behavior in a population and suggest reasons for differences among groups. However, based as they are on the extant evidence, quantitative analyses are subject to the vagaries of survival.[27] The patterns in the population studied here did not come from a randomly chosen sample and cannot be evaluated through the use of inferential statistics.

As with all evidence, I approach the quantitative evidence critically, weighing it against the other evidence and theoretical ideas. In many cases I have decided not to use particular findings from the quantitative study population because the findings seemed to me to be based either on very small numbers or potentially unrepresentative cases or, most important, to run counter to the weight of the other evidence and theory that I have used to study Christianization. For example, the quantitative evidence for converts in this study population was so weak that it had to be omitted. Similarly, the evidence for the religious choices of military aristocrats is inconclusive. In cases like these, I have relied on the full weight of all the evidence, not on the findings from the study population.

Textual Remains

The extant texts from the fourth and fifth centuries take many forms—letters, sermons, histories, personal narratives, poems, and polemical treatises. The relevant texts have to be read critically since the written remains are often quite problematic to historians. Some of these texts are simply biased, making claims to favor one or other religious group. So, for example, statements by Ambrose claiming a majority of Christians in the Roman senate may have greater rhetorical force than reality.[28] There is also a bias in favor of the religion that succeeded; that, too, makes these texts problematic for the historian trying to understand the aristocracy as a whole since certain groups are not well represented by the textual remains. It is difficult, for example, to understand the perspectives of pagan aristocrats confronting Christianity because most of the surviving texts are by Christian men. Almost all of the texts by women are by Christians. The texts that survive thus tend to favor the notion that Christianity was more attractive to aristocratic women; yet the absence of pagan women's texts is an argument *ex silentio* about their perspectives on conversion.

Nonetheless, textual remains are critical for the historian trying to reconstruct the realities of aristocratic life and the behavior and values that were relevant for religious change. For example, friendship ties often cited as a key to relation between aristocratic men are given substance if we read closely the letters of the pagan Symmachus or those of the Christian Ambrose. In the extant correspondence of these men, recommendations for friends and clients abound, with detailed information about the kinds of favors that were done, such as a simple letter of introduction or help in getting a client cleared of a criminal charge.[29] The fact that so many of Symmachus' letters were recommendations underscores the real impact of friendship ties.

Some of the details of aristocratic life survive only in texts. We would not know, for instance, that merely acknowledging a friendship by sending a formal note of greeting was seen as an important way of sustaining friendships if it were not for the survival of certain of Symmachus' letters that do only this.[30] Sometimes the textual evidence provides the only secure information about the religious affiliation of an aristocrat; the letters of Jerome, for instance, are particularly valuable for identifying female Christian aristocrats not otherwise known.

One methodological note is necessary concerning the textual remains that would seem to offer us the most compelling evidence for aristocratic religious choice. These are individuals' accounts of their own conversions. These accounts exist only in retrospective memory, so that the individual's past is shaped to fit present concerns.[31]

Perhaps the most influential conversion account is Augustine's narrative in Book VIII of the *Confessions,* written around 400 C.E. As he tells it, Augustine focuses on the importance of sin and grace, and is heavily influenced by the words of Paul in *Romans*. But if we turn to Augustine's own words just after his conversion in 386, he was concerned not with sin and grace but with the problem of evil philosophically conceived.[32] Over time, Augustine's theological opinions changed, as did his view of Paul and, consequently, his view of himself and his own conversion.

Augustine's text underscores the simple fact that conversion narratives are never disinterested; they are shaped by the concerns at the time they are told as the convert, in the present, tries to explain his past self to himself and to his or her audience. In such accounts converts adopt the rhetorical norms accepted by the new community into which they are entering. Modern social scientists have observed this phenomenon and have, consequently, come to stress the social dimensions of conversion, seeing in a convert a subject who actively develops a new world of meaning by conversion and entrance into a new community. In this, the community itself has an enormous effect on the meaning of conversion.[33] This dynamic, observed in modern religious groups, may help to explain the formulaic quality of the conversion literature from the later Roman empire, but it strongly undercuts reading conversion narratives as a (or the) primary source for understanding Christianization. Rather, these accounts are only one sort of evidence for the process.

Material Remains

To bring texts into closer contact with the real lives of aristocrats, I also turned to material remains. Fragments of the lives of aristocrats—their houses, their silverware, their artwork, even their drinking cups—provide intriguing scraps of evidence to draw the contours of aristocratic existence and religious belief. So, for example, the countless mosaics from villa floors attest to the central role that hunting still played in an aristocrat's life. Indeed, the actual methods of hunting as carried out are almost exclusively known because of material remains, again mostly from mosaics depicting aristocratic hunts.

Similarly, we know of many details of the aristocrat's life only through material remains. So, for example, the substitution of semicircular couches for rectangular ones in the dining rooms of certain villas in the western provinces in the fourth century is a stylistic change that may suggest an increased focus on the aristocratic patron; the significance of this detail may be still argued, but it is evidence that is only known due to material remains.[34]

And a rich, albeit often fragmentary, source of evidence exists in the numerous inscriptions that have survived from the late Roman empire. Thus we would not know that sacrifices continued to the cult of Saturn in Africa Proconsularis were it not for the chance survival of a votive stele dated to November of 323 c.e..[35] A chance inscription to a certain Maternus from a richly decorated villa in Spain may allow us to identify the kind of villa establishment and lifestyle of one of the most prominent Spanish supporters of the emperor Theodosius.[36] And the funerary inscription on a Christian sarcophagus in Arles by the consul of 328, Flavius Ianuarinus, provides the only evidence for this man's religiosity.[37]

Archaeologists have provided regional studies of the material remains of certain areas or provinces. These have been very useful since they have provided evidence for patterns of behavior for entire regions. So, for example, the analysis of mosaics and the material remains of church buildings in Italy indicated the relative wealth of Christian congregations in different cities.[38] Since the aristocratic elites would be financing some part of such building, a regional analysis of the material remains for basilica construction also elucidates their conversion.

The Major Themes of This Study

The evidence leads me to focus on several major themes that I believe explain the process of religious change in the western empire. In my view an understanding of the role of status concerns is a most important key to unlocking the process by which senatorial aristocrats became Christian. Max Weber's views on status aptly describe the situation of the late Roman senatorial aristocrat who, in "every typical component" of life, was influenced by "a specific, positive or negative, social estimation of *honor*."[39] Roman aristocrats were actively engaged in asserting and maintaining their honor, hence their status in society.[40] But religion—traditionally polytheism—was tied to social esteem; hence polytheism was tied to personal status. The difficulty that Christianity presented to senatorial aristocrats was how to incorporate this new religion as a status-confirming aspect of their social identity. This was harder for some aristocrats than for others. A senatorial aristocrat from Rome whose family was strongly associated with paganism, who had strong public ties as patron or participant in certain cults or rituals, would have had a more difficult time assimilating Christianity than a senatorial aristocrat from a new family or one from certain of the provinces. The former would, understandably, be more likely to become Christian later than the new, provincial aristocrat.

Constantine did influence the senatorial aristocracy by, among other things, increasing its size and adding new opportunities for men in imperial service and in the provinces to advance to senatorial rank. The resulting compositional changes offer another key to understanding religious change among the late Roman aristocracy. Constantine's actions led to a certain repositioning within the senatorial aristocracy that made some within the elite concerned about the public recognition of their status in an expanding class. As early as the reign of Constantine's son, Constantius II (337–361), we find some aristocrats distinguishing themselves by adding to their titles *illustris* and *spectabilis* in order to publicize their status.[41] Such a ranking system reflected and further sharpened differences emerging within the senatorial aristocracy, setting off a core of active, highly visible men from their less active, less connected peers. The growth and differentiation within the upper class fueled status concerns and contributed to a situation where certain segments of the aristocracy were more receptive to Christianity and others were far less so. In the population I studied, those aristocrats from Rome, the core area of senatorial strength, those tied to pagan institutions in Rome and Italy, and those actively engaged in traditional senatorial civic careers appear more resistant to Christianity than those from many of the provinces, and they were also more resistant than those engaged in military or imperial bureaucratic careers.

Christianity, by contrast, gained strength among those aristocrats not as completely influenced by these older families and traditionally pagan institutions. New aristocratic circles emerged in the provinces, and some of these were more open to Christianity. These social changes are associated with the rise of Christianity in the provinces of Gaul and Spain. Because they lacked the support of the older pagan families and institutions of Rome and Italy and were more dependent on imperial advancement, men from Gaul and Spain may have been more willing to convert.[42] Indeed, here the imperial court and imperial appointment to office were relevant factors in conversion.

Aristocrats were keenly aware of the necessity of maintaining status in the eyes of fellow aristocrats. Acceptance and recognition by one's peers were perhaps the most fundamental components of aristocratic status. The importance of peer approval has led some scholars to posit friendship and family networks as the key factors in conversion.[43] To support this view, some have

turned to modern studies of conversion that have focused on the importance of social networks in explaining the spread of new religions.[44] It is
a truism among certain historians of religion that "faith constitutes conformity to the religious outlook of one's intimates—membership spreads
through social networks."[45]

While it is in some ways appealing to apply modern network theory and
studies of contemporary religious cults to explain the spread of Christianity
in the ancient world, such an explanation must also take into account the
specific and particular contours of historical reality. For the post-Constantinian aristocracy, modern network theory is not the most helpful model.
Having Christians as friends or family members did not lead directly to conversion. The specific contexts within which aristocratic friendship and family networks functioned mediated the influence of both in spreading Christianity. While the importance of shared sentiments was a typical and oft-
expressed ideal of ancient friendship, by the end of the fourth century it had
become clear that the rules of friendship would ignore differences in religion
in favor of class and personal ties. The mutual favors exchanged between
the pagan Symmachus and the aggressively Christian bishop Ambrose on
behalf of their respective clients attest to the continuities of class ties across
the religious divide.[46]

Similarly, family relations had only a limited influence on conversion. In
the population I studied, pagans tended to marry pagans and Christians
tended to marry Christians. And in those few cases of intermarriage that I
did find, the influence of women on husbands or on sons appeared limited.
Only in terms of their daughters did aristocratic women seem to exercise influence on religious choice, and then only in circumscribed ways.[47]

Friendship and family networks were, however, important to the aristocracy because they served to maintain their position within society. The
ways in which Christians came to incorporate aristocratic ideals and institutions were far more critical, in my view, for understanding religious change.
Christianity spread among the aristocracy in part because it could assure
them that the new religion would not present a threat to their friendship
and family networks, institutions so critical to maintaining aristocratic status. Such guarantees of status were a significant factor facilitating conversion. Moreover, as it became clear over the course of the fourth century that
adopting Christianity would not undermine the esteem of their fellow aristocrats and family members, individuals found it easier to convert. Gradually, the very bases of social esteem would change. After a certain point,

depending upon the place, conversion to Christianity could even contribute positively toward personal status, a fact occasioning the caustic criticism of the pagan aristocrat Symmachus that at the time of Gratian some pagan senators were staying away from the pagan altars to advance their ambitions, presumably to ingratiate themselves with an increasingly Christian senatorial aristocracy and imperial court.[48]

The senatorial aristocrats studied here who served at the imperial court tended to be Christian more often than aristocrats actively engaged in other sorts of public office, such as those pursuing traditional civic magistracies.[49] The persistence of polytheism among senatorial aristocrats in certain spheres of public life is thus one visible indicator of the limits of imperial influence. While the fourth-century emperors were recognized as supreme, they could not successfully rule alone. And many western senatorial aristocrats, unlike many of their eastern counterparts, had tremendous resources at their disposal that gave them a marked degree of independence. They could (and many did) disregard the imperial religious model, preferring instead to continue following their patterns of behavior, living within their networks of friends and family.

The conversion of the senatorial aristocracy was a gradual process of change within which the encouragements of emperors and bishops were mediated by specific aristocratic institutions, ideas, and behaviors. The process of Christianization can be described as occurring in two stages. First was a stage of withdrawal of support by pagans from pagan institutions. We can see this development very clearly in the gradual turning away of pagans in this study's population from the holding of pagan priesthoods. This period of withdrawal is coupled with the gradual convergence of Christian and pagan aristocratic lives, a convergence that we can see in the career patterns of the aristocrats studied here. Christians and pagans tended, more and more, to follow similar patterns in their careers. In this convergence status concerns persisted and even bridged religious differences.

Although status concerns and structural changes contributed to religious change, so too did the larger cultural transformation that made possible an aristocratic Christianity. As emperors and church leaders promulgated support for Christianity, as they strove to assure aristocrats that changing religion would not deny them social esteem nor undermine the aristocratic institutions upon which their social position rested, they also tried to make Christianity appealing to aristocrats. In essence, they made Christianity conform in certain key ways to the status concerns and institutions of the aristocracy.

Christian emperors continued to appoint pagans to high office and to rec-ognize the prestige of the old senatorial families, but they also appointed Christians to high offices. Thus they bestowed upon coreligionists the kinds of honors that would lend Christians status within aristocratic society. Simi-larly, emperors built large, expensive places of worship for publicly celebrat-ing Christian holidays and granted the church and its officials the kinds of honors and privileges that formerly conferred prestige on the pagan cults. In these ways, emperors conformed to preexisting patterns of aristocratic and imperial patronage and bestowed upon their favored religion the status and prestige formerly associated with the pagan cults.

These imperial activities also show how the emperor was embedded within an aristocratic *mentalité*. Still regarded as the "most aristocratic of all aristocrats," the emperor, like aristocrats generally, desired honor from his peers and thus had to live in accord with the norms of this class in public and in private life. His adoption of Christianity did not end his identification with aristocratic attitudes and values, but it did require a new synthesis of the imperial role. As aristocrats and as Christians, the fourth-century emper-ors came to embody and promulgate an attractive, status-laden model that could also appeal to aristocratic sensibilities. In essence, the Christian em-peror offered a new symbolic option for aristocrats to follow, one that of-fered the prestige and honor so much desired by aristocrats.

Like the emperors, Christian leaders, too, appealed to aristocratic status concerns within a social and political context set by elite institutions. As their sermons and letters show, church leaders in the late fourth century modulated the message of Christianity in ways that soothed certain aristo-cratic sensibilities. Ambrose, one of the most influential western church fa-thers, informed priests and bishops under his sway to deliver sermons in the style appropriate to educated, elite listeners lest their audiences be deterred by the low-status manner in which the clergy spoke.[50]

But the efforts of Christian leaders like Ambrose to reach aristocrats ex-tended beyond stylistic concerns. In time, the discourse and sermons of Christian leaders came to incorporate not only the formal aspects of aristo-cratic status concerns but also the values and ideology of the late Roman up-per class. Such a fundamental aristocratic concept as *nobilitas,* an attribute derived from birth but joined in Roman thought to high public office, would appear directly at odds with Christian texts that claimed equality for all in Christ. And yet even the iconoclast Jerome incorporated standard notions of *nobilitas* in his vision of Christianity.[51] Jerome did not deny the value of no-ble birth; rather, he placed it within a Christian hierarchy of values within which his brand of Christianity, asceticism, emerged at the top. This approach was a successful one. By the middle of the fifth century in Gaul, the incorporation of the traditional aristocratic concept of nobility within a Christian value structure gave rise to the commonplace phrase "noble in birth, nobler in Christianity."[52] And by the end of the fifth century, noble birth had become a virtual qualification for a bishopric in Gaul.

Thus, in trying to bring senatorial aristocrats into the church, many Christian leaders appealed to the status concerns of this powerful group. In so doing, they made Christianity more aristocratic in certain respects. Nietzsche's view of this process, in the opening epitaph of this chapter, is not an accurate historical one. The sermons and letters of the fourth- and fifth-century western church fathers show clearly the extent to which aristocratic sociocultural values were incorporated into the emerging interpretations of Christianity.

The message of Christianity—its ideological content—would not have been enough by itself to make a Christian aristocracy. Rather, Christianity, as it emerged in its various fourth-century forms, must be understood in part as a response to aristocratic concerns with status and the traditional prerogatives of noble birth. The modulation of the message of Christianity was an effective strategy that facilitated the conversion of the senatorial aristocracy. Effective, too, were the Christian emperors who, following aristocratic norms, granted and augmented the prestige of the church and its officials.

Christianity made Roman senatorial aristocrats change certain patterns of behavior and thought. But, as the emperors and the western church fathers "Christianized" the traditional values of the aristocracy, they also influenced the ideology of Christianity and changed the ways in which Christianity would appear to subsequent generations. Christian leaders would be concerned with status in the secular world, with achieving *nobilitas*. Hence the importance of the Christianization of the late Roman senatorial aristocracy goes beyond a mere historical phenomenon to take on wide-ranging consequences for the history of medieval western Europe.

To gain a better understanding of the complex process of Christianization, I now turn to an analysis of the western aristocracy as a class and to its status culture in late antiquity.

CHAPTER 2

Defining the Senatorial Aristocracy

> Others [aristocrats] . . . assume a grave expression and greatly exag-
> gerate their wealth, doubling the annual yield of their fields . . . They
> are clearly unaware that their forefathers, through whom the great-
> ness of Rome was so far flung, gained renown, not by riches, but by
> fierce war, and not differing from the common soldiers in wealth,
> mode of life, or simplicity of attire.
>
> —Ammianus Marcellinus, *Res Gestae* (trans. John C. Rolfe)

The pervasive concern for status that marks the institutions, lifestyle, and values of the late Roman aristocrat that Ammianus complains about in the opening epigraph fits well the classic Weberian concept of a status group: "Every typical component of the life fate of men is determined by a specific, positive or negative, social estimation of honor. This honor may be connected with any quality shared by a plurality, and, of course, it can be knit to a class situation."[1] Status distinctions fostered feelings of shared membership in an elite community. Acceptance by other members of this elite community was itself the most important criterion for honor. This meant that aristocrats paid considerable attention to the expression of status and conformity with status-conferring practices, for these led to acceptance by other members of the group. In the western empire the senatorial aristocracy had spread its institutions, values, and lifestyle so thoroughly that, by the late third century, aristocrats from Spain and Africa can be said to have lived very similar lives and to have held many of the same values.

What were the contours and textures of these lives? From the moment the senatorial aristocrat awoke in the morning, he was concerned with status and its manifestation. He took care that his slaves dress him in fine cloth and jewelry; the purple border of his senatorial toga was one other indicator of rank, as were the codicils of appointment that he, as the holder of high office, would have prominently displayed in his house. The number and kinds of clients who attended him in the morning and who followed him through the streets were essential components of personal honor. In Rome such an entourage was as necessary as receiving public recognition or dining with the "right set" of friends. Wherever the aristocrat went, whether hunting with friends at his country estate or vacationing at a seaside retreat, he would be certain to express the public face of the elite: proud, identifiable by dress and manners, surrounded by slaves and clients, but at ease among his equals.

The aristocrat's concern for belonging to the right status group extended to religion. Senatorial aristocrats traditionally sought pagan priesthoods because they offered another arena in which to demonstrate and augment honor; pagan ceremonies, rituals, festivals, and holidays had for centuries allowed the aristocrat to assert preeminence in public. At home pagan family rites reinforced the patriarchal social order, conferring prestige on male aristocrats. In private cultic settings the aristocrat gained honor before his peers. To western aristocrats in the early fourth century, then, adopting Christianity presented a special sort of problem. How would changing religion affect their lifestyle and the institutions and values by which they lived? Most important from an aristocrat's perspective, would the adoption of Christianity entail a loss of status?

An understanding of the status components of aristocratic society should, then, be the first step in constructing any theory about the Christianization of the senatorial aristocracy, the clarissimate. This shared status culture—within which the late Roman elites lived, worked, and enjoyed their leisure—bestowed on senatorial aristocrats a continuity and communality even as this order grew and itself changed, incorporating new men from homegrown aristocracies in the provinces and those who had acquired senatorial standing by imperial or military service. Changes in the composition, recruitment, and political role of the senatorial aristocracy over the time period of this study encouraged divisions within the order, which had implications for the spread of Christianity. However, the status culture of the senatorial aristocracy, expressed in lifestyle, values, and institutions, remained a unifying force, more or less strongly embraced by its members, that had to be taken into account by emperors and bishops.

Criteria for Membership

From the perspective of the renowned orator Symmachus, the members of the senatorial aristocracy comprised "the better part of the human race."[2] The traditional criteria for membership included noble birth, distinction in public service, high moral character, intellectual culture, and sufficient wealth.[3] This was an ideal model, violated often enough in practice, but it had considerable and widespread force. Late Roman law put this ideal into reality by excluding those whose reputation or character was considered poor and those who were suspected or convicted of any crime.[4]

By the late third century and continuing into the fifth century, a man became a member of the senatorial aristocracy by attaining the lowest senatorial rank, that of *clarissimus*. One could attain this rank in a number of ways—by holding an office that conferred senatorial rank, by being granted honorary rank, or by being born into the rank.[5] Since the clarissimate was hereditary for men born after their father's promotion, the sons and grandsons of an original nonsenatorial office holder would be absorbed into the ranks of the senatorial class.[6] Although the laws only mention the passing of the clarissimate to male descendants, the clarissimate came to women as well, either through their fathers or their husbands; titles such as *clarissima puella* and *clarissima femina* indicate this but do not tell us if the title passed beyond one generation for women.[7]

In the early principate the senatorial order also included those men (mostly *equites* or *decurions*) who possessed the requisite qualifications and, although aspiring to a senatorial career, had not actually gained a senatorial magistracy but had been granted the right by the emperor of wearing the *latus clavus*, the distinctive broad stripe on the toga indicating senatorial status.[8] This procedure is not attested for the fourth and fifth centuries when the majority of men advanced by the emperor were introduced by adlection (nomination) into the senate; they received a rank in the senate but did not receive a magistracy. By the second half of the fourth century, admission by adlection also involved the approving nomination and vote of the senate (also referred to as cooptation). These adlected men were consequently considered as part of the senatorial order as well as members of the senate. The number of adlections, so far as we can tell, remained small during the principate and continued to be infrequent later, even when the procedure had changed in the fourth and fifth centuries.[9]

In discussing the senatorial aristocracy, a distinction must be made between aristocrats as the elite order in Roman society and the senate, the political institution that was in many ways a focus for the order. Criteria for membership in the Roman senate were different from those for membership in the senatorial aristocracy; admission to the senate had to be attained, according to the rule of the principate, upon election to the quaestorship or by nomination by the emperor to an office that entailed admission into the senate.[10] While there was some pressure for a senator's son to stand for the senate, he—or his parents—could obtain imperial permission to decline.[11] The distinction between being a member of the senatorial aristocracy and being a member of the senate widened considerably in the fourth and fifth centuries as the order grew. When referring to a senatorial aristocrat in this book, I am using the term to designate a member of the senatorial order who may or may not have been a member of the senate of Rome.

To become or remain a member of the senatorial aristocracy with the rank of *clarissimus,* it was necessary to possess a certain amount of income. We do not know the precise amount required, but it was apparently calculated on the basis of landholding. Both the new man adlected to the senate and the aristocrat by birth were required by law to make an official declaration *(professio)* stating their income, their acceptance of senatorial rank, and the province and city in which they claimed residency.[12] A law of 354 stipulates further that senatorial sons, about to give their first set of games, were required to come to Rome to make this declaration; presumably those adlected could make their declaration to the proper authorities at the imperial court or in the provinces, even though men adlected by the emperor directly into the senate *(inter praetores)* did not normally have to pay for a set of games.[13]

Within the senatorial aristocracy, certain distinctions were made on the basis of other, less formal, criteria. One category of continuing importance was the nobility *(nobilitas).* These were ancient senatorial families who still formed a special group within the senatorial aristocracy and enjoyed a marked position within society. Among the nobility were a small group of elite senatorial families, "patricians," whom emperors honored with religious and social privileges; the designation of elite families as patrician continued at least until the time of Constantine, when the title became a personal rather than an inherited distinction.[14] The criteria for *nobilitas* in the late empire were not at all clear-cut; in the view of T. D. Barnes, "in the fourth century, or at least after Constantine, a senator was a *nobilis* if he or a forebear had been either ordinary consul or prefect of the city or praetorian prefect."[15] However, testimony by late Roman authors raises doubts as to the strictness of these criteria and suggests, on the contrary, that the title *nobilis* is claimed on a variety of grounds. That said, considerations of birth were still of great import in determining *nobilitas.*[16]

Perhaps the most important nonofficial criterion for membership in the senatorial aristocracy is the one hardest to trace from a distance, namely acceptance by fellow aristocrats. Symmachus pointed to the weight placed upon peer approval in a speech delivered to the Roman senate concerning one Valerius Fortunatus who, upon reaching maturity, "vowed to recover that which he had sought on the grounds of his birth, perhaps at the instigation of good breeding, which always recognizes itself."[17] Symmachus argued that the young man ought to be admitted to the senate, despite his poverty, for his birth and good breeding made him easily recognizable as "one of us." The need for affirmation of inborn aristocratic status by his peers points to a key fact of aristocratic life: aristocrats needed mutual recognition and acceptance. In essence, they defined each other.[18] Recognition could compensate for even modest birth or inadequate wealth, as in the case of Valerius.

Although Symmachus claimed that senatorial aristocrats were immediately recognizable to one another, emperors felt it desirable and necessary to recognize who was and was not a senatorial aristocrat by laws that granted the rank and privileges of senator. Throughout this book I have used the attainment of the lowest senatorial rank of *clarissimus* or "most outstanding"—rather than purely social criteria—to define a senatorial aristocrat; unlike Symmachus, the modern historian cannot so easily discern the socially acceptable senatorial aristocrat from the unacceptable one. Moreover, acceptance might vary from one elite group to another; the man who attained senatorial status via a military career might not be welcomed as warmly by civic aristocrats as he would by others in the military elite. And over time the same person could lose or gain acceptability within any one group. Using the legal criteria of clarissimate rank, we can be certain, at least, that the person under discussion has met minimum legal, economic, and social qualifications. As such, this person also enjoyed the prestige, privileges, and protections long associated with the senatorial aristocracy. This legal definition allows us to draw the outermost boundaries of the senatorial order and to include members from various elite groups within this study.

The late Roman clarissimate, as it developed over the course of the fourth century, was a social stratum legally defined and requiring high social and economic status in one of several distinct sets of elites. One way of understanding this group is to see that Constantine and later emperors built on the outlines of a preexisting social and political order to bring together the major power elites in the western empire. Thus, in developing the clarissimate, Constantine and his successors evidently hoped to make this disparate set of elites a unified whole, conscious of one another as members of the same status group and, of course, aware of the preeminence of the emperor. The clarissimate was, then, in one sense at least a political construct that coopted potentially refractory elites. The emperors evidently expected the prestige and sense of belonging to the clarissimate would be built on consciousness of rank and privilege, but also on identification with the values of the established, wealthy senatorial families who formed the core of the old aristocracy. Whether emperors from Constantine on intended it or not, the clarissimate Romanized and aristocratized new men, and it is a mark of its success as a political construction that it did so, though, of course, to a greater or lesser degree depending upon the individual.

Obviously, applying the term "aristocracy" to this legally defined group is somewhat problematic. This term is typically used by modern historians to describe a legally privileged class of interconnected families whose position is based on the inheritance of large landed estates, and, as such, it is closely associated with historical studies of medieval or early modern European class relations.[19] The late Roman clarissimate does not comfortably fit that model, and the term itself did not exist among the Romans. Yet other terms for this group are even more problematic. Calling the clarissimate "the elite" is misleading; there were multiple elites at numerous levels of Roman society. Another possible term, "upper class," has a distinctly modern air and suggests a strongly economic interpretation of the criteria of membership. One could more accurately call the clarissimate the senatorial order, but that term, too, can suggest misleading continuities with the Roman republic or analogies with medieval society. Most important, however, none of these other terms capture the sense of shared values, culture, and privilege that the word "aristocracy" conveys.[20] Hence, while I will use these other terms occasionally, I will use "aristocracy" throughout this book to describe the clarissimate, although I will usually specify it further by adding the qualifying term "senatorial."

Resources of the Senatorial Aristocracy

Unlike a modern capitalist who sees wealth and property as ends in themselves, the Roman senatorial aristocrat viewed his resources as a means of asserting and augmenting his status and that of his family to relations, friends, clients, and, at times, emperors.[21]

Economic Resources

Maintaining an aristocratic lifestyle required significant economic expenditure. Clothes, slaves, houses, furnishings, hunting, cultural pursuits, clients—all were predicated on wealth. Political office also required wealth;

aside from money spent to win supporters, the primary responsibility of many of the lower civic officers was to finance public games and entertainments.[22] Moreover, when friends, family, or clients asked a favor, the aristocrat often required money to respond. This was true for all aristocrats, for men in the military elite as much as for those in civic office or imperial bureaucratic service.

Land was typically the basis of wealth. Senatorial aristocrats derived only a fraction of their wealth from moneylending, and they did not receive salaries from holding civic office. High-level imperial bureaucrats received salaries, but they were not a significant source of wealth.[23] Even some military families were landed.[24] Landowning was valued not only as a resource but as a visible sign of personal status; aristocrats associated rural estates, seaside retreats, and urban villas with the activities and values that marked the elite. After all, equestrians could be quite wealthy; it was how one used wealth that revealed status. Such status concerns explain why new senatorial aristocrats from the provinces and in the imperial bureaucracy as well as many senior military men invested in property when possible.[25]

The wealth of a senatorial aristocrat was measured in gold for accounting purposes. In an oft-cited passage, the early fifth-century historian Olympiodorus relates that the wealthiest Roman families obtained income from the rent of their property, approximately 4,000 pounds of gold. In addition to such rent, other sources of income included the sale of grain, wine, and other products, whose worth would equal on average a third of the gold from rent. The families at the next rung received an annual income from rent of approximately 1,000 to 1,500 pounds of gold.[26] Since a large proportion of income came from rents on land and from the sale of goods produced on the land in urban markets, aristocratic families could count on "a high degree of economic continuity."[27]

Landholding ensured the economic well-being of the aristocracy as a whole and provided the basis of wealth for its richest families. Generally, aristocrats owned several estates scattered across the provinces, and the older families held lands especially in central Italy, Campania, Sicily, and Africa.[28] Symmachus lists among his holdings some thirteen estates in central Italy as well as land in Samnium, Apulia, Sicily, Mauretania, and perhaps Lucania. He may have had other estates that he does not even mention.[29] Since the property of any one aristocrat was scattered over a province or over several provinces, his economic resources were protected from local political upheavals or natural disasters. Aristocrats used their influence to further protect their control of the markets for their goods. The Roman aristocrats, for example, who controlled the markets that fed Rome used their influence to manipulate prices and taxes.[30]

Although some estates were modest in size, most aristocratic landowners tried to increase their holdings through whatever means available—marriage, inheritance, purchase, or political influence.[31] Larger estates tended to become self-contained units; Palladius, a fourth-century writer, advises landowners to have craftsmen and artists on their estates so the peasants will not have to go to town. Here, the late Roman aristocrat could weather even the most troubled times. In times of war or uncertainty a villa could take on the aspect of a fortress; several villas appear in this form on mosaics.[32]

Property gave the senatorial aristocrat a controlling influence in local matters, especially in dealings with their *coloni* or tenant farmers. This was felt all the more after 332, when tenant farmers were technically bound to the land on which they were born.[33] Aristocrats appear in local communities as restorers of public buildings, as patrons of civic games or responding to local needs, and as legal advisers and protectors. In return, local communities honored senatorial aristocrats with titles and monuments and often conformed to their wishes.[34]

Senatorial aristocrats further enhanced their position in local communities by holding offices in areas in which they owned property. They used the numerous opportunities that office-holding gave them to do favors for friends and clients. Often they governed provinces that their fathers and uncles had previously governed; such inherited offices enabled the aristocrat to strengthen ties to his family's *clientelae*.[35] Aristocrats could also use office to buy land. Indeed, in the late empire patrons tended to become owners of property whose tenants were their clients, thus leading to the consolidation of estates and local influence.[36]

Compared to his economic resources, the financial obligations placed on senatorial aristocrats appear light. The most burdensome seem to have been the expenses incurred by holding public office, either in giving the requisite games or in gaining the support *(suffragium)* necessary to win public office since support was customarily obtained through financial favors.[37] The other monetary demands were minimal; senators paid an annual tax on the ownership of land *(gleba* or *follis)* and contributed to the gift of gold *(aurum oblaticium)* that the senate made to emperors on their accession and on successive quinquennial celebrations.[38] Until the time of Gratian, all senators were exempt from extraordinary levies and *sordida munera;* after Gratian, these privileges were limited to the uppermost senatorial ranks.[39]

Political Resources

By the late third century senatorial aristocrats did not generally hold positions with military authority, and they were therefore unable to use the ultimate political resource, armed conflict, independent of an emperor or a general. Aristocratic support did not save the usurper Eugenius in 394, and the only Roman aristocrat to become emperor, Petronius Maximus, lasted but six months. Nevertheless, by returning senatorial aristocrats to high public office, the emperors of the fourth and fifth centuries revived the traditional role played by the senatorial order and restored the notion that public office was a reflection of personal honor.[40] Public office once again became highly desirable as a means to manifest and augment status as well as for its economic benefits.

Through appointments, favors, and recommendations, a provincial governor or praetorian prefect could enlarge his patronage and add considerably to his prestige and fortune. The office holder could reduce his own taxes and those of his family, friends, and clients. He could protect and add to his own properties as well as theirs. It had long been true that governors and magistrates expected to reap significant financial benefits from their year in office; the gifts bestowed on them daily, and the numerous opportunities to turn public monies to private use, to say nothing of bribes and extortion, made high office financially advantageous.[41] The repeated legal prohibitions on magistrates purchasing land, houses, and slaves while in office indicate how widespread these practices were.[42] Aristocrats acquired connections and favors in public office that followed them into private life.

It is somewhat misleading to distinguish between the public and private life of the aristocrat, since no aristocrat was ever free from his public obligations.[43] These ties, as J. Matthews observed, "contributed cumulatively to the vast, spreading network of obligations and services by which the towns of Italy were linked with their residential aristocracy and those of Africa with the men who were the largest landowners in the province."[44] Senatorial aristocrats used their political connections to other aristocrats to achieve diverse private goals, including land purchases, marriages, and contracts.

Given these advantages, it can hardly be surprising that although some aristocrats chose to avoid the distractions and potential dangers of holding office, many did not.

Social Resources

To an aristocrat, friends and family were social resources. They provided the networks for getting things, be it office in the civic government or imperial service, land, marriage ties, or favors. Hence it was typical for a late Roman senatorial aristocrat to devote much of his time to asking for and receiving favors from his peers.

The social prestige of the aristocrat opened up numerous avenues to acquire further honors and to augment his position in society. The reputation (*gloria*) of the aristocrat made him the best candidate for high public office.[45] Similarly, towns and *collegia* sought aristocrats as patrons. The Roman noble Symmachus claimed to have left Beneventum because the local inhabitants were so preoccupied with feting him that he feared they would overlook necessary repairs on their city after an earthquake.[46]

Civil and criminal laws granting aristocrats special privileges attest to the very real benefits that came with clarissimate status. Aristocrats could expect to be judged by one of their peers.[47] Moreover, clarissimate standing released men from curial obligations and compulsory public services, with certain limitations.[48] Such privileges were a sort of social resource that aristocrats could use in a variety of ways to further themselves and their families.

In the religious arena, too, social resources helped the aristocrat; on the basis of his status, the aristocrat was chosen to organize and contribute to sacrifices, banquets, religious festivals, or games. Only those with the proper social standing could represent their city at the great public ceremonies of the state cults. Through such ceremonials an aristocrat manifested his position publicly and gained further honor.

Changes over Time

The senatorial aristocracy was not static throughout this period. The reforms of the late third-century emperors Gallienus and Diocletian, and those of the fourth-century emperors Constantine and Valentinian I, greatly increased the size of the aristocracy and accentuated divisions among aristocrats while encouraging still greater concerns about status. Such changes played into the religious transformation by creating faultlines in the aristocracy and by encouraging the development of an aristocratized Christianity.

The Third Century

The political upheavals of the mid-third century led to what many scholars have described as a reorientation within Roman society, bringing an increased professionalization of the military and state bureaucracy at the expense of senatorial traditions.[49] Many scholars assume the decline of the third-century senatorial aristocracy as a result of these changes; they emphasize the displacement of aristocrats by military men and state bureaucrats, many of whom were of lower, usually equestrian, rank.[50] On the basis of prosopographical studies, however, this model does not seem likely.

In an important study F. Jacques tracked certain aristocratic families from before the mid-third-century crisis to the end of the third and into the early fourth centuries. The number of clarissimate families that fall into this group are too many to appear as isolated remnants of a devalued elite, he argued, and the large number surviving provided evidence against a sharp break with the past.[51] The families who survived tended to be the elite of the senate, patrician families whose resources made them most able to resist economic disruptions. Many were from areas that suffered little military conflict.[52] The disappearance of some families and the advancement of some men new to the senatorial order indicated that its membership continued to evolve in ways not much different from that in the principate. Jacques found no evidence that the senatorial order or the senate was any smaller at the end of the third century than it had been at the beginning of the century.[53]

Jacques' study underscores not only the continuity but also the high prestige and entrenched position of the senatorial aristocracy into the early fourth century. The third-century emperors, including Diocletian, acknowledged the social and political influence of the ancient aristocratic families.[54] Indeed, historians who have seen Diocletian as "the hammer of the aristocracy"[55] because of his military origins and alleged hostility toward this group, are presenting a misleading view of this emperor and his relations with the aristocracy. Diocletian's appointments to ordinary consulships and urban prefectures indicate that he had no interest in destroying the aristocracy or, if he had entertained such an idea, could not act on it; of the fifteen known consuls under Diocletian (other than Caesars and Augusti), ten are from families attested as *clarissimi* before the third-century crisis. Only four of the praetorian prefects achieved senatorial status from equestrian backgrounds. Of those who were *clarissimi* from birth, eight belong to *gentes* attested under the Antonines. The same trend appears in Diocletian's appointments of urban prefects.[56] Moreover, the highest honor Diocletian conferred on his praetorian prefects was the ordinary consulship, which carried with it senatorial status.[57] Thus his civic appointments suggest an emperor eager to incorporate the old aristocratic families into government, a trend that is all the more striking because of the well-established fact that senatorial aristocrats after Gallienus (253–268 C.E.) did not hold military appointments and were removed from many administrative responsibilities in the provinces.[58]

The aristocracy's loss of certain administrative and all military duties did not suddenly cut off the senate collectively and most senators individually from the exercise of political power on behalf of the state.[59] In the first place, the offices held by the most elite senators were little affected by the changes of the third century. Even before Gallienus, the most prestigious senators had not engaged in highly demanding or confining military or administrative service.[60] Typically, they held the quaestorships and praetorships and stayed close to Rome and Italy. They were involved in administrative functions. They were curators of cities, legates of proconsuls (in Africa or Asia), and, rarely, of praetorian prefects. The pinnacle of a senatorial career was proconsul of the province of Africa or Asia, urban prefect, or consul.[61]

Less established senators, in contrast, did suffer from changes under Gallienus and Diocletian, for many of these men rose through service to the emperor or the state, and that service was transformed. These men faced fewer opportunities and more competition from equestrians who were filling the demanding military and civic administrative positions in the provinces that had once been the preserve of the less established aristocrats. For example, twenty-five posts as legates of legions and twelve posts as legates of the emperor disappeared from senatorial control.[62]

Judging from the number of diplomatic approaches, political decisions, and judicial and legal actions, the senate had greatly diminished duties, compared to its second-century counterpart. Its political role had been reduced over time. Even so, it retained great prestige as a corporate body, and it could display leadership in a crisis, as it did in defending Italy and in supporting candidates for emperor in 238 and after.[63] With frequent changes in emperor and with emperors rarely in Rome, the senate gained autonomy, especially in local matters. So, for example, when the emperor Gallienus was away fighting the Germans, the senate ordered levies and armed the people of Rome.[64] Diocletian could grant no greater honor than to adlect a man to the senate.[65]

In sum, over the course of the third century the senatorial aristocracy retained its role as the social and economic elite in the state, but the reduced number of military and administrative positions available to its members had altered the nature of its political leadership. Influence was exercised less by virtue of the office held and more by virtue of the wealth, prestige, and ties the individual and his family had to imperial and other aristocratic families. Yet the prestige of the aristocracy was such that emperors could grant no higher honor to the successful equestrian than senatorial rank.

Constantine and the Senatorial Aristocracy

Constantine evidently perceived an increasing tension between the high-status senatorial aristocracy and the low-prestige but powerful group of government and military functionaries. After winning the civil war in the West, he set out to resolve the problem by restoring the senate of Rome and the western senatorial aristocracy.[66] But his actions went further than a mere return of the *status quo ante* under Diocletian. Rather, he took steps to make office-holding a central activity of the senatorial aristocracy and integrated this group into the administration of his empire. At the same time, he made significant changes in the composition of the senatorial aristocracy.[67]

Constantine simultaneously increased the size of the senate at Rome and the senatorial order. How much and when the senate of Rome increased is disputed, but most likely it grew from about 600 members at the end of the third century to about 2,000 by 359, and some part of that increase may be attributed to Constantine.[68] This emperor's generosity in granting senatorial status came about in two ways. The first has been mentioned before, namely *adlectio*, nomination by the emperor into the senate. From the epigraphic evidence we know the names of four men adlected to the senate under Constantine.[69] The second way was far more frequent; the emperor advanced men into the senatorial order by granting them offices that carried clarissimate (i.e., senatorial) status automatically. There were many more possibilities for men to be advanced in this way since Constantine had increased the number of administrative posts reserved for senatorial aristocrats and upgraded many of the top posts traditionally occupied by equestrians into senatorial positions.[70] So, for example, the governorships of many provinces were changed from equestrian *praesides* to clarissimate *praesides* or *consulares.*[71]

Constantine also provided new avenues for advancement and honor, not only for those men aiming to become senatorial aristocrats but also for those who were senators or senatorial *clarissimi* already. He created the imperial companions *(comites)*, an honor open to senatorial aristocrats as well as to the highest order of equestrians. Those who actually served in the consistory *(comitatus)* were distinguished from those who held the title of companion *(comes)* merely as an honor at imperial discretion. The former were distinguished as the highest grade of imperial companion. Beginning with Constantine, imperial companions were employed on a variety of tasks outside the court, mostly juridical.[72] The same concern to award prestige to those who served loyally lies behind Constantine's revival of the term "patrician" as a title of distinction.[73]

While some positions rose in rank, others declined. From about 315 on, it became typical for aristocrats from Rome to hold the quaestorship and then the praetorship, but not the suffect consulship and to exercise instead the function of consular. Most likely, the suffect consulship had declined so much in status that it came to be viewed as a burden; its only duty was to stand in for the ordinary consul when he was not resident in Rome.[74]

Constantine's changes in government service encouraged the entry of new men into the senatorial order. These men usually came from two groups, either the equestrians or the provincial nobility.[75] Indeed, the equestrian class had been for centuries the seedbed of the senate. But Constantine's reforms so consistently advanced men from the highest equestrian posts into the senatorial order that by the second half of the century the equestrian rank virtually disappeared. The high civic administrative posts were now recruited from the *clarissimi.*

The provincial elites were encouraged to advance by the reforms that Constantine had made in residency requirements. Previously, provincials who joined the senatorial aristocracy were required to maintain at least a pied-à-terre in Rome, since it would be necessary for them to stay there for sessions of the senate. Senators were required to obtain a leave of absence *(commeatus)* to visit or reside in the provinces. Leave to reside in the provinces was in fact regularly granted, and in the third century more and more senators held "double domiciles."[76] It was Constantine, in all likelihood, who gave legal recognition to the primary domiciles of provincial sen-

ators outside of Rome.[77] Now certain provincial senators could merely send
a sum of money to Rome and have their games celebrated for them by government officials *(censuales)*.[78] Thus a man adlected to the senate or the son
of a senator could fulfill his duties and pursue a senatorial career in his own
province or at an imperial court, residing in Rome only briefly, if at all. A
grant of leave to reside in the provinces was still required, but it was a formality.[79]

Military men constituted a third nontraditional source for new senatorial posts. According to Ammianus Marcellinus, Constantine was the first
emperor to name even barbarians to the consulship, an office that would
have automatically granted them senatorial status.[80] This statement has con-
founded scholars, since no barbarians—meaning here non-Romans—are attested as ordinary consuls until Flavius Arbitio in 355.[81] Some scholars have
read this text as a recognition, however inaccurately stated, of Constantine's
willingness to advance military men. Many of these men were of barbarian
(i.e., non-Roman) or semibarbarian origin and rose through military service
to positions that conferred senatorial rank.[82] Soon after Constantine's death
we find military men distinguished as *comites rei militaris,* an honor that
Constantine had instituted and that most likely carried with it clarissimate
standing.[83]

With the defeat of Licinius in 324, Constantine established a senate and
aristocracy in his new capital, Constantinople.[84] His activities in this regard
are not directly relevant here, but it is worth emphasizing again that the
eastern aristocracy was quite different from that in the West. Constantinople
lacked a nucleus of ancient, large landowning, wealthy families such as that
at Rome, nor did it have the autonomy and traditions of Rome. The higher
prestige of the senate of Rome and the western senatorial aristocracy may
explain the reluctance of its members to transfer to Constantinople.[85] In the
350s Constantius divided the senatorial class on geographic lines, forcing
western senators living in the East to register at Constantinople.[86] During
the fourth century the senate at Constantinople did grow in influence and
prestige, incorporating wealthy landowners, formerly of curial status, alongside upwardly mobile courtiers and imperial bureaucrats who owed their
rank directly to the emperor and his service.[87] But composition, origin, and
dependency on the emperor made the eastern senate a somewhat more
fluid body than its western counterpart, and further differentiated the eastern and western aristocracies.

The last years of Constantine's rule, ca. 335–337, saw a significant reform in the adlection process. Senatorial cooptation of *adlecti*—an outgrowth of Constantine's first actions in restoring the senate after defeating Maxentius—was now publicly adopted.[88] Although these newly adlected men had to be confirmed by the emperor, the senate's ability to coopt new men for adlection indicates imperial recognition of senatorial autonomy. In the final years of his rule, we know of no one upon whom Constantine conferred senatorial rank who had not received the assent of the senate or had not first attained the office of praetor.

This last reform fits with Constantinian policy in general; earlier in his reign, Constantine had disengaged from the election of the lower magistracies (praetorships and quaestorships) that opened the way to membership in the senate.[89] With Constantine's reforms of 335–337 the senate now acquired the right to designate men for adlection to the senate,[90] with later laws stipulating that men should seek the "honor of adlection" actively and without bribery.[91]

By 359, laws indicate that the senate was being held fully responsible for the designation of the magistracies of praetor and quaestor.[92] Although these offices now entailed little in the way of administrative responsibilities, they were still important ceremonial moments in the lives of young aristocrats who made a name for themselves by giving lavish public games. These magistracies were important to the emperor too. They constituted an indirect tax on aristocrats and served to keep the good will of the urban populace. Imperial recognition of senatorial designation reinforced the senate's control over access to these offices and hence to entrance into the senate. In effect senators chose those who would become members of its most prestigious institution in late antiquity. By the end of the century we find senators recommending some men for inclusion in the senate without even attaining the lower magistracies or giving the games required of such positions.[93]

The institutionalization of these changes in adlection reinforced the prestige of senatorial aristocrats at Rome since through their efforts provincials, equestrians, and others could acquire senatorial status. The successful candidate for adlection would require a senator to swear to his suitability and to speak on his behalf.[94] Hence the reformed adlection process contributed toward the growing political and social influence of senatorial aristocrats as patrons.

Constantine's reforms had far-reaching effects; they encouraged the senatorial aristocracy to play once more a significant role in the actual administration of the empire. The prestige and wealth of these men added to the prestige of the clarissimate. The old senatorial aristocratic families were joined by increasing numbers of men from new families, for there was a proliferation of posts that carried senatorial standing. Equestrians and holders of positions with the most important responsibilities were incorporated into the senatorial aristocracy. The prestige of the governing class was augmented because all who were in the higher levels of government were now *clarissimi*. At the same time, Constantine established new honors and privileges to entice established senatorial aristocrats as well as new men into state service. Constantine's reforms augmented the influence of the senatorial aristocracy of Rome as well, for these men were given greater influence to act as conduits into the senate for new men from the equestrian class and the provinces.

Yet the reforms of Constantine also contributed toward making the newly expanded clarissimate a far more diversified group than before. It now included provincial aristocrats alongside Roman and Italian aristocrats, men from older and newer senatorial families, military men and imperial bureaucrats alongside courtiers. Provincial *clarissimi* could choose to remain in their home regions where they could dominate local matters, or they could choose to be active in nearby imperial courts or in the imperial bureaucracy, pursuing a senatorial career in state service outside of Rome before returning home. These Constantinian reforms encouraged the growth of regional aristocracies (the *honorati*), distinguished by their place of origin and local residency as much as by the careers that they followed.[95] The reforms also contributed toward the growth of a military elite distinct from those who pursued careers at the imperial court or in the imperial bureaucracy or via the traditional senatorial *cursus*. In essence, Constantine sought to strengthen his administrators, and hence his government, by conferring senatorial status on all who served him at the same time as he incorporated prestigious, traditionally wealthy elites of old senatorial families and landowners into the same social and legal stratum, the clarissimate.

The Senatorial Aristocracy after Constantine

With the exception of Valentinian I, emperors after Constantine largely followed the contours of his policies vis-à-vis membership in the senatorial aristocracy. Constantine's son, Constantius II, worked actively to reinforce the prestige of the senate of Rome, allowing only *clarissimi* to become senators and removing decurions.[96] Even Ammianus Marcellinus, hostile to Constantius in many ways, praised him for fighting against the inflation of offices that cheapened senatorial standing.[97] Moreover, Constantius emphasized the high level of literacy and rhetorical skill traditionally associated with senatorial aristocrats. So too did Julian who, in Libanius' words, ended the appointment of barbarians as governors and reinstated "men filled with poetry and prose."[98]

With the resurgence of the senatorial order in the fourth century, there are indications that the prestige and influence of the senate of Rome also grew. We find the senate acting independently at times, as when it exiled its own or when it refused to recognize the claim of Julian as Augustus.[99] We also find an indicator of its public honor; the *Victoria Senati,* a public celebration of the senate, is recorded in the *Codex-Calendar of 354.*[100] As far as we can see, and here the best source is the letters of Symmachus, fourth-century emperors continued to keep the senate informed of their actions, and the senate could vote to endorse formally any imperial policy. The senate could be consulted in councils of state, and its public support for imperial policy remained an element in creating and demonstrating that consensus existed between the ruler and the people.[101] By passing resolutions, it could, in certain cases, advocate a policy at odds with that of the emperor, as, for example, in protesting the removal of the altar of Victory from the senate house.[102] Since the minutes of the senate were passed on to the emperor, its discussions and resolutions were known and could affect imperial policy.

Despite its resurgence, however, the senate after Constantine had limited political powers as an institution. It was not required to vote on imperial policy nor would it generally advance its own initiatives. In setting policy, emperors consulted with the senate in conformance with traditions, not out of any constitutional necessity. Symmachus can only hope that the senate will be an equal to the military in the councils of state.[103] The senate seems most often reactive; it could express its wishes and did so, but largely in response to imperial initiatives. The senate could also send embassies of eminent men to the emperor to try to change policy or to inform the emperor of contrary senatorial views. A senatorial embassy, for instance, protested the torture of senators on trial for magic and forced the emperor Valentinian I to put an end to such actions.[104]

During the reign of Valentinian I and Valens (364–375), important changes were made in the system of senatorial precedence. Men in imperial or military service received the same distinctions and privileges as senatorial aristocrats in civic office. The ordinary consulship was still the highest honor, and former consuls took precedence over all other senators. Then came patrician status, the honorific title revived by Constantine, and, after that, those who had held the praetorian or urban prefecture or were masters of soldiers. After this came the principal palatine ministers. Next came proconsuls and vicars, with whom were equated military officers of the second grade, the *comites rei militaris* and *duces*. At the bottom were consulars of provinces, *praesides*, and tribunes of regiments.[105]

These rules formally incorporated new career paths and gave senatorial standing to men in important military and court posts. In some cases, a position in imperial service conferred that rank upon retirement; in others, it did so immediately.[106] But now *duces* (often barbarians of military origins), *comites,* and tribunes were included in the senatorial order and even exempted from the expense of praetorian games.[107] The reforms in the rules of precedence formalized under Valentinian I and Valens added many new positions of clarissimate rank and this further expanded the senatorial aristocracy. Nevertheless, the significance of the long-entrenched traditional criteria—birth, breeding, culture, education, wealth—still led to the expectation that aristocrats would be awarded office on these grounds rather than on the basis of service.[108] Thus, even during the "professionalizing" reign of Valentinian I and Valens, the old senatorial aristocracy still enjoyed its privileges. Nowhere was this more true than among the aristocrats of Rome and Italy.

The changing criteria for senatorial status could, however, lead to friction and hostility, as it did under Valentinian I. The prosecutions of some of the leading members of the aristocracy at Rome on charges of magic and adultery fueled the antipathy of the entrenched senatorial elite for the emperor and the men newly advanced by him. The trials, arising out of apparently trivial causes, revolved around issues of public safety and morality. The men in charge of the investigation were faithful imperial administrators, new men like the Pannonian *praefectus annonae,* Maximinus, men whom the nobility saw as rivals for the offices that they felt were theirs by birth.[109] The trials, whatever else they may be, reflect divisions within the senatorial aristocracy between career bureaucrats and the older, more established families of Rome and Italy. Ammianus' depiction of Valentinian as an uncultured, vicious upstart reflects, in part, the hostility of this segment of the aristocracy toward this ruler and his administrators.[110]

The promulgation of sharper distinctions of rank within the senatorial order is another sign of growing divisions and possible sources of tension within this body. Office holders in the upper echelons of power had already begun to differentiate themselves from ordinary senators—*clarissimi*—by adding to their titles *spectabiles* and *illustres* as early as the 350s. This use of titles became institutionalized under Valentinian I; the grade of proconsular began to be called *spectabilis* and this title eventually attached to all grades from proconsul to *dux*. Only consulars still ranked as simple *clarissimi*. Praetorian prefects, urban prefects, and masters of the soldiers were referred to as *illustres*. These titles were somewhat fluid until the end of the fourth century, when they became formalized.[111] The desire for such distinctions reflected the concerns of aristocrats eager to differentiate amongst themselves in their competition for honor and *dignitas* as their numbers and differences grew.

This evidence does not, however, fully support the view of Valentinian's reign as essentially antisenatorial. The legal recognition of the ranking system and increased prestige granted to military and administrative positions put into effect changes already under way since the time of Constantine or earlier. Moreover, these laws seem intended to ensure a more professional, loyal governing class over which the emperor could exercise greater control. Valentinian I's appointments to high office seem to show this; he chose loyal and experienced military leaders or imperial bureaucrats, and many came from nonsenatorial families. Nearly all the consulships of his reign went to such men, with the single exception of the western aristocrat, Sextus Petronius Probus.[112] Similarly, the senior administrative posts and the praetorian prefectures, with two exceptions, went to men of long service at the imperial court or in the military.[113] Valentinian even appointed bureaucratic officials to posts considered the preserve of senatorial aristocrats, including urban prefects, *praefecti annonae*, and consulars in Italy. The Pannonian, Viventius, for example, was made urban prefect of Rome, 366–367, and praetorian prefect of Gaul, 368–371.[114] Yet the appointment of experienced administrators does not necessarily reflect active hostility toward the senatorial order as much as an attempt to advance professional men on the basis of meritorious service and loyalty rather than on other criteria (i.e., family, wealth, influence, nobility).[115]

After Valentinian, Gratian and subsequent emperors returned to the policy of appointing senatorial aristocrats from the older established Roman circles to high civic administrative positions; the more entrenched senatorial aristocrats within the order breathed a collective sigh of relief. Valentinian's attempt to advance professional men on the basis of expertise and loyal service alone had not succeeded. Under Theodosius I, senatorial aristocrats from old Roman families even took palatine offices.[116] By 433 it looked as if the older aristocratic families had acquired administrative dominance in Italy; the ordinary consulship and city prefectureship were often filled by the great aristocratic families, as was the praetorian prefecture of Italy.[117] Yet Valentinian's legal reforms remained largely in place. Army officers, members of the imperial bureaucracy, and holders of high civic office all were brought together into one unitary system that culminated with senatorial standing.

Growth and Differentiation

As the administrative role of the senatorial aristocracy increased, so did its size. By ca. 400, it has been estimated that there were some three thousand positions in the West that conferred senatorial status, at least upon retirement.[118] Simultaneously, we see distinctions growing sharper over the century, as the senatorial aristocracy became increasingly less homogenous. Since growing numbers of men could achieve senatorial rank through very different trajectories—through the military, the imperial administration, or a traditional senatorial civic career—they entered the aristocracy possessed of very different experiences as well as different political and social connections, both inside and outside of the order.

There was a core of the older senatorial aristocratic families centered at Rome. These families remained deeply invested in Rome and Italy—economically, politically, and socially. In many respects their traditions and values remained unchanged. This was a conservative milieu. Many of these wealthy families achieved the highest rank *(illustres)* by holding the highest civic offices, thus maintaining their position as members of an inner aristocracy, and many were active in the senate at Rome as well. As *illustres,* they received greater privileges, fiscal and jurisdictional, than those of *clarissimi* and *spectabiles.*[119]

The distinctions between ranks within the aristocracy continued to increase so that eventually, between 450 and 530, membership in the senate was probably limited to only the most privileged, the *illustres.*[120] So, too, membership in the senate became more and more distinct from membership in the senatorial class. More of the provincial elite, newly advanced into the senatorial order, took advantage of the privileges of their status but did not participate in the senate at Rome or follow traditional senatorial civic careers. A law of 395 marks this distinction, requiring that gold payments of residents of Rome be made in the city, while allowing provincials to send their gold to Rome.[121]

Distinct from this core at Rome was the increasing number of provincials (the *honorati*) who became *clarissimi* but remained in or retired to their local cities and provincial estates.[122] Many of them rose through office in the imperial bureaucracy or at court. These provincial senatorial aristocrats could enjoy the leisured lifestyle and ideals of the Roman upper class, secure in their senatorial privileges. And as *clarissimi* they exercised greater influence in society than did the curials, the wealthy local men with heavy financial obligations to their cities. (Desire to escape curial duties led many a provincial to seek senatorial rank in the first place.) Thus, in a list from Numidia that records the order in which different groups were to greet the governor, the resident *clarissimi* come first.[123]

Some upwardly mobile and politically oriented provincials did devote themselves to careers, and most often these careers were pursued in the imperial bureaucracy or in palatine offices. Indeed, the growth of provincial aristocracies was aided by the presence of the emperor, whose court moved between cities in the West during this period, primarily between Milan and Trier and later Ravenna. The western imperial courts offered alternative foci for aristocratic activity. Service at court could bring office and honors, like the title "companion of the emperor." Such opportunities attracted men of diverse backgrounds, but upwardly mobile provincial elites especially. The Gallic circle of Ausonius, for example, advanced through imperial service in Trier; Ausonius never even visited Rome, while in North Africa Augustine also knew of many senators who had not been to Rome.[124]

The career opportunities for men in the late fourth and fifth centuries supported flourishing regional senatorial aristocracies. They are especially well attested for Gaul, Spain, and northern Italy. Many of these provincial senatorial aristocrats were not well integrated with the older aristocratic families of Rome and Italy.[125] Their backgrounds, experiences, and career paths were unlike those of the older senatorial elites. Moreover, dependency on the emperor for advancement made for a different sort of experience than that of the senator from older entrenched families. In the latter case, networks of patronage and family ties could offer a far greater measure of indifference to imperial influence.

Indeed, distance and independence from imperial favor also contributed to the growing differentiation within the aristocracy. The lives of members of the imperial consistory would differ greatly from those of senatorial aristocrats who focused on Rome and its senate. The former interacted with the emperor and his advisers as well as with senior military men. They were concerned with the imperial bureaucracy and policies from the perspective of the emperor and the empire. By contrast, the holder of a senatorial civic post often derived his influence from his wealth, prestige, and ties to networks of friends, families, and local communities.

The addition of titles like *illustris* and *spectabilis* signaled a growing desire among aristocrats to further distinguish themselves from one another. Over time these titles were conventionalized and came to reflect increasingly sharp differences in the levels of privilege and honor among senatorial aristocrats. By the mid-fifth century, emperors seeking to restrict the number of curials who attained senatorial status limited senatorial privileges so that only senators of the top grade, *illustres,* gained immunity from curial service. Since this rank could be generally obtained only through service in the highest state offices, the emperor thereby reinforced the distinction between the politically active senators and those who only held lower offices or resided on their estates.[126]

One segment of the aristocracy that grew, beginning with the reign of Constantine but especially after Valentinian's reforms, consisted of men who arose via military service. Some of these men came from backgrounds similar to other *clarissimi;* the military count Theodosius and his son, an army official *(dux)* under Valentinian, came from a Spanish family of landowners who also included civilian office holders.[127] But a good number of military men were of "barbarian" origins, that is, were non-Romans, from areas outside of or on the fringes of the empire. These men and their children were generally "Romanized" within a generation or two, and so military officers often appear as barbarians in our texts "only because we are told so or guess because of their names, not because of their behaviour."[128] Zosimus' description of the general Fravitta as "by birth a barbarian, but otherwise a Greek, not only in habits, but also in character and religion" could apply to many of the military men who held office high enough to acquire clarissimate standing.[129] These military leaders could, in certain cases, share in the aristocratic status culture associated with clarissimate rank.

At the imperial court military officers and imperial administrators rubbed elbows, "moved in the same circles," and shared many of the same interests.[130] Indeed, military and imperial bureaucrats both were said to be in *militia,* in service, and some imperial officials took to wearing the distinctive *cingulum,* the soldier's wide leather belt with metal fittings and an ornamental buckle as a visual status symbol.[131] Political alliances between high military officers and imperial bureaucrats throughout the fourth century suggest that the differences between the military and civic elites were not so great as some historians have suggested; the usurpation of the general Magnentius, for example, owed much to the palatine official, Marcellinus.[132] In 363 the military supported as candidate the civilian praetorian prefect, Secundus Salutius.[133] Military officers maintained friendship ties with senators outside of court; five of Theodosius' generals did so with the senatorial aristocrat Symmachus.[134]

Yet their training, experiences, and provenance did distinguish the military from other senatorial aristocrats. High army officers generally sought acceptance within their own elite circles and tended to make marriage ties with other military families or with imperial dynasties until the fifth century.[135] And in times of crisis or out of feelings of envy, other aristocrats denigrated military figures by calling them "barbarians" and "uneducated."[136] Such comments call into question how "Romanized" and "aristocraticized" the military elite were. While some generals were no doubt eager to live by senatorial aristocratic ideals, others did not. Moreover, the importance of the military aristocracy to the emperor and the state gave them influence and resources that made some emperors eager to reinforce the divide between the military and civic aristocracies.

It is one indication of the vitality of the established senatorial aristocracy that new men, whether at home on provincial estates, at court, in the imperial bureaucracy, or in the military, so often came to emulate its values and lifestyle. Levels of identification varied and may have been lowest among military men. However, over time many did adopt a positive attitude toward the traditional criteria for senatorial aristocratic membership and toward the culture and values associated with it, even if they did not themselves fully adopt them. Valentinian's father, for example, took care that his son was well educated, and Valentinian, in turn, took pains that his son Gratian receive the best classical education, a sign of aristocratic status; other military men apparently did the same for their sons.[137] For many, the old aristocratic families of Rome retained their aura; they stood at a pinnacle of wealth and honor, and other aristocrats were eager to make ties to them. A new man, like Ausonius, who rose to eminence in large measure through imperial support, strove to cultivate friendships with the more established, Rome-based aristocracy. Similarly, barbarian military officers, like Bauto and Richomeres, cultivated friendships with such men.[138]

Thus Rome, which had lost its prestige as the home of the emperor, remained into the sixth century a center for senatorial aristocratic society. As such, it continued to attract new senatorial aristocrats, competing successfully with imperial courts at Trier and Milan. Indeed, the senate of Rome and the western senatorial aristocracy retained their prestige even in the face of the growing eminence of Constantinople. In the 350s Constantius II, eager to augment the size and prestige of the eastern capital and its senate, required senators of Rome resident in the eastern Mediterranean to reregister in Constantinople; yet in his own day Libanius could still ridicule some eastern senators as sons of butchers, metalworkers, stenographers, and cloakroom guards in public baths.[139] Although Libanius' rhetoric may exaggerate, the senate of Constantinople did grow by incorporating upwardly mobile bureaucrats who owed their positions directly to the emperor, as well as many wealthy landowning elites, former curials. In contrast, Rome's senate was somewhat more stable, independent, and wealthy; in 384 only three praetorships were required to pay for the games at Rome as compared to eight at Constantinople.[140]

The western senatorial aristocracy, if increasingly differentiated in its composition and orientation, nevertheless reemerged in the fourth century as a political as well as social force of real consequence. The prestige of this order continued in spite of the political weakness of the senate as an institution and in spite of the many changes in its composition, now legally redefined. To understand why this was so, we must look more closely at the status culture of the senatorial aristocracy.

The Status Culture of the Senatorial Aristocracy

Senatorial aristocrats from all parts of the empire, distinguished from one another in many respects, nonetheless shared a deep concern for their honor. This concern infused their value systems, shaped their institutions, and expressed itself in everyday life in ways minute and large. Imperial grants of honor and office could bestow senatorial rank but did not necessarily confer the confirmation that peer acceptance and support did. Since aristocrats relied so heavily on one another for recognition, they held the keys to each other's identities, conferring and withdrawing approval in relation to a highly detailed but unwritten code of honorable activity in the circles in which they moved. Thus the status culture of the senatorial aristocracy was a significant unifying system, weaker or stronger depending upon the individual's inclination and position in it.

It is possible to see the influence of status concerns in all areas of senatorial aristocratic life. In this section I will examine the play of status in three major spheres: leisure, work, and home. Much of the evidence comes from texts and from the *Letters* and *Orations* of one aristocrat in particular, Symmachus. Although he lived at the center of high society in Rome and although his works reflect the views of his circle, much of what Symmachus tells us about an aristocrat's daily life, about the ways in which family and friends were valued, and about the importance of public office and leisure activities reflects the sentiments of the senatorial aristocracy at large and not just the core pagan elite of Rome.

Aristocrats at Leisure

In the society of late antiquity, leisure pursuits were in many ways at the center of a senatorial aristocrat's life and the primary means to express his fidelity to the pursuit of honor among his peers. Since most public offices were annual appointments, many aristocrats had considerable time for leisure. No wonder, then, that the high-minded, conservative Symmachus adopted Cato's notion that leisure *(otium)* should not be time passed in idle pleasures but should be used as a sort of investment to prepare oneself for work *(negotium)*.[141] Not all aristocrats were as calculating as Symmachus; Ammianus Marcellinus' brutally sarcastic vision of the late Roman aristocracy depicts a world devoted almost entirely to pleasure. Even Symmachus evidences a wide range of typical aristocratic pleasures, telling not only of cultural pursuits—such as writing poetry, letters, and orations—but also about hunting, dining, socializing, sailing, traveling, arranging marriages, and attending horse races and circus games. In Symmachus' *Letters,* as in other texts and in archaeological remains, we find the outlines of aristocratic leisure activities that expressed the status concerns of this class.

Hunting was an energetically pursued pleasure of many a Mediterranean aristocrat. Regarded as a test of one's manliness and virtue in conquering hostile forces, hunting was also traditionally seen as good training for warfare.[142] Some remnants of the ideal remain when, for example, Symmachus commends the noble youths Olybrius and Probinus for their progress in this sport.[143] For some, danger made hunting and riding pleasurable as well as manly. Myths of hunters killed by wild animals, such as the myth of Adonis, entertained aristocrats and underscored the dangers of the chase.[144]

Yet hunting had changed greatly by the late fourth century. Ammianus

Marcellinus mocked the practices of some aristocrats of his day: "Some of them . . . if they hunt by the labours of others, think that they have equalled the marches of Alexander the Great or of Caesar."[145] These nobles made their minions do the real work of riding and killing. One suspects that the situation described by Ammianus was more typical than not; the fourth-century aristocrat often hunted in large parties where the many slaves, attendants, and underlings could protect the lord from any real danger.[146] Indeed, many aristocrats gained pleasure primarily from being seen in control of such an expedition, dressed in expensive clothing and possessing fine equipment. One such aristocrat, Paulinus of Pella, tells us that this was the case for him. As a young man he devoted his time to hunting, riding, and playing ball. His pride and self-esteem, his sense of worth, as he recalls it, resided in the finery of his and his horses' attire, his excellent groom, his hunting hawk, and dog.[147]

Reflecting this aristocratic pleasure, countless mosaics depicting realistic scenes of hunting were commissioned for the homes of aristocrats. Not surprisingly, then, many a late Roman mosaicist, at the request of their patrons, inscribed the names of the master's favorite horse or hunting dog into the hunting scenes executed for the floors adorning their homes.[148] The mosaic of the "Small Hunt" from Villa Casale at Piazza Armerina, Sicily, shows hunters in action, then enjoying the rewards of their pursuit as they recline, richly attired beneath overhanging trees, to share a picnic dinner prepared by servants hovering nearby.[149] These hunting scenes uniformly depict the superiority of the master and his companions: often only they are on horseback; only they face the animal head on (servants merely help); only they wear the gaudy clothing that manifested prestige. Not even the bloody work of hunting disturbed the attire "which reveals each man's rank."[150]

The desire to manifest status is evident too in mosaics that depict exotic and wild animals being rounded up or hunted in the amphitheater.[151] These scenes visually state the wealth and prestige of the aristocrat who paid for such displays. Some mosaics represent hunters setting out from the villa of a *dominus,* indicating that the *dominus* was responsible for the funding and supply of animals for the hunts that were staged in the amphitheaters. Hence the hunt is a visual statement of the high status of the mosaic's owner, directed at those who enter his home.[152]

Most often, it would appear, aristocrats visited the homes of other aristocrats for the occasion of a dinner party. Eating together was a central feature of life, punctuating the aristocrat's day and ideally offering pleasurable interaction with family and friends. Shared meals and conversation spread feelings of belonging to a community. Symmachus and Ausonius cemented their initial friendship over dinner, a point recalled fondly in their letters.[153] In addition, dinner parties gave aristocrats countless ways to impress their friends, clients, and family members. Every aspect of the aristocratic Roman dining experience—from the mosaic work for the floor of the dining room, to the room itself, to the seating, to the theatrical display of the courses— were areas that the *dominus* controlled and could use, like hunting, to demonstrate his social status.

Some aristocrats went to extraordinary lengths in their concerns to impress their guests with the food served at their dinners.[154] Such habits lent themselves easily to satire. Ammianus, for example, lampoons the Roman noble, so eager to impress his guests that he brought scales to the table to weigh the fish, birds, and dormice that were served; the noble then repeated the weights many times over dinner.[155]

As befits the social importance of dining, the dining rooms in the homes of late Roman aristocrats were designed to display the status of its owner in an ostentatious manner. Size and decoration were visual indicators of status. The dining rooms could be vast.[156] The mosaic decoration of a floor could, as in the House of Venus at Mactar, contain a virtual catalog of edible marine life, with over two hundred items; fish, as Ammianus noted, were a delicacy, and scenes such as these would recall the largesse of the host.[157]

Dining as a social occasion may have increased in importance over the course of the fourth century. The substitution of semicircular couches for rectangular ones allowed a larger number of guests and gave the room the shape of a triconch. This change, attested in several western provinces from the early fourth century onwards, has been interpreted as a direct reflection of the increased patronage power of aristocrats who may have copied this shape from imperial palaces and churches.[158]

Since the good opinion of other aristocrats was a key to status, aristocrats spent much time visiting the houses and estates of their peers. Symmachus writes countless letters of invitation to one or another of his friends. His note to Attalus is hard to resist; in it he spells out what a visit to his coastal villa at Formia will be like. Symmachus promises excellent hunting on well-traveled estate roads and, if the game is not plentiful, good conversation and literary exchanges that far surpass the pleasures of a Sicilian or Tarentine retreat.[159] In a letter to Marinianus, similarly intended to entice, Symmachus describes himself enjoying life as a gentleman farmer. As he looks after the

storage of the new wine and the crushing of the olives, he hears the hunts-
men in the distance and sees the farmers at work in the fields.[160]

The image of a close-knit, status-conscious society is reflected in Symmachus' letters about his travels, primarily up and down the coast of Italy.
At times, weariness with urban problems brought Symmachus to seek a retreat in a suburban villa where the visits of friends revive him and he can
live without being surrounded by retainers and clients.[161] At other times,
Symmachus travels to a villa on the coast of Campania where the healthy
climate and warm waters bring a welcome change from the heat of Rome.[162]
Mutual visits were frequent since aristocrats built their villas close to one an-
other. The families of the persons mentioned by Symmachus—the Anicii,
Aradii, Valerii, Maecii Gracchi, Probi—had neighboring villas in the
Campanian fields, not far from Rome.[163]

Even on vacation, aristocrats took great pains with their dress because
aristocrats identified themselves to their contemporaries by their attire.[164]
Intricately woven brocades and cloth were signs of status. Ammianus notes
"fringes and tunics embroidered with party-coloured threads in multiform
figures of animals" and light cloth as preferred styles.[165] The aristocrat's concern for his dress sparked Ammianus' satirical remark that certain such
men, resplendent in their garments, looked as if they were being laid out for
their funerals.[166]

Jewelry was another component of status, since many an aristocratic family invested in their gems.[167] Some aristocrats wore jewelry even to the
baths. By ever so carefully removing rings and depositing them with slaves,
one such aristocrat, mocked by Ammianus, sought to make his wealth as
conspicuous as possible; his slaves ostentatiously dried him with the finest
linen and then dressed him in expensive clothing to reinforce the point.[168]

To Symmachus, leisure was best spent in cultural pursuits, literary or
philosophical, enjoyed in a rural or urban villa in the company of friends.
He felt he was not alone in this view. In a playful letter, Symmachus ex-
poses Praetextatus' claim to *otium* spent hunting as no more than a pretense
to read and compose poems on rustic pursuits.[169] Symmachus jests about
Praetextatus' literary leanings, but he knew that Praetextatus was proud of
his reputation as a philosopher and man of letters. Praetextatus' epitaph
proudly proclaimed that he had corrected an Aristotelian manuscript (either
in Greek or Latin) and translated Themistius' *Commentary on Aristotle*.[170]

Praetextatus was not the only late Roman aristocrat to undertake literary
or philosophical studies and to publicize these studies as a sign of status.

Nicomachus Flavianus the Elder, for one, transcribed Philostratus' *Life of Apollonius* from the Greek.[171] Members of the Nicomachi and of the Symmachi read and emended sections of the first decade of Livy's *History*.[172] Other aristocrats turned their hand to poetry, some of it humorous, as did Anicius Probinus.[173]

Many of the aristocrats who wrote, circulated, and discussed their works no doubt found real personal pleasure and satisfaction in such activities. Some were quite good at it. And many built friendships through literary or philosophical circles.[174] At the same time, these shared literary activities provided a common language and value system that distinguished aristocrats from those below them in society. It also gave aristocrats an important way to make connections with one another, uniting smaller groups of elites.

Literary achievements were a long-standing source of pride in aristocratic circles. In the early empire there were lists, such as we find in the works of Pliny the Elder, of aristocrats admired for their poetry.[175] The uniformity in educational curricula and training across the empire spread this appreciation of cultural and literary achievement throughout the aristocracy.[176] Literary accomplishment was so deeply associated with high status that in late second-century Gaul a schoolmaster could successfully pretend to be a senator, and even emperors, like Constantius II, felt the need to demonstrate cultural abilities by composing poetry, if not rhetoric.[177] This symbiosis of power and knowledge was assumed to lead to high office.[178] The pagan aristocrats of Rome in the 380s and 390s, it has been argued, used their literary accomplishments to claim a certain superiority over their Christian peers.[179]

The high value placed on cultural pursuits explains the force of Ammianus' critique of aristocratic society in Rome where "in place of the philosopher the singer is called in, and in place of the orator the teacher of stagecraft, and . . . the libraries are shut up forever like tombs."[180] Many aristocrats were probably more interested in their race horses and prostitutes than in reading the classics, whether they admitted it or not. Nor did lack of cultural accomplishments necessarily prevent an aristocrat from attaining honor or from making ties with other aristocrats. However, the expectation persisted that aristocrats should be as distinctive in their cultivation of high culture as in their dress and lifestyle. Failure to pursue or at least appreciate high culture could be used against an aristocrat; Ammianus, for example, finds fault with Orfitus for being "less equipped with the adornment of the liberal arts than became a man of noble rank."[181] A good deal of peer pressure must have been exerted on aristocrats to claim at least an appreciation for cultural pursuits. Some scholars have seen evidence for this in the marked increase in the fourth century in the production of handbooks of Roman history and literature, works commissioned for new men eager to acquire cultural knowledge quickly.[182]

Aristocrats at Work: Public Office, Private Business

Although Ammianus' satiric view of the late Roman aristocrat as idly devoted to a life of pleasure has some validity, it does not convey the whole truth about this class. Most aristocrats were actively engaged in work, be it public office or private matters. The separation between the two was in fact hard to make.

Aristocrats generally regarded high public office as their distinctive sphere of work, especially after Constantine's reforms had enhanced such service. The powerful aristocrat Sextus Petronius Probus is described as a "fish out of water" when not holding office.[183] An aristocrat who did not hold public office went against widespread expectations; inscriptions show how many aristocrats lived up to this ideal. Although it was fashionable for an aristocrat to profess that public office was "an encumbrance, accepted with reluctance and laid down with relief,"[184] aristocrats who did not undertake public service, preferring to devote themselves to their estates, opened themselves up to the sort of criticism that Sidonius Apollinaris leveled against his young friend Syagrius. Syagrius' devotion to his private business concerns was a "slur on the nobility."[185] In reality, many an aristocrat lived as did Syagrius, both in Rome and in the provinces. Yet this private lifestyle was still perceived by many aristocrats, such as Sidonius, as an ignoble failure to meet the expectations of one's peers.

The nature of public office in the fourth century reveals much about the status-oriented institutions and lifestyle of the aristocracy. The tenure for each office varied, but generally appointments lasted only for a year or two. How often an aristocrat held office also varied. We know that some aristocrats were in office virtually without a break, like Q. Flavius Maesius Egnatius Lollianus signo Mavortius; for many others, the intervals between office may be the result of lacunae in our sources rather than indicators of the typical pattern.[186] Yet there must have been some period of time out of office, especially as aristocrats climbed into higher offices where the appointments were scarcer and the competition greater.

Some offices were largely honorific, requiring ceremonial obligations rather than administrative expertise. The lower offices of quaestor and praetor fit this category, for by the fourth century they had no duties other than the celebration of public games and entertainments at Rome. Similarly, the suffect consulship, by the early decades of the fourth century, entailed only ceremonial responsibilities, primarily the giving of games.[187] Yet these offices were valued for they gave young aristocrats and their families the opportunity to advertise themselves against the appropriate, traditional backdrop of Rome—they provided entrées for young aristocrats embarked on public careers.

The higher the office, the greater the prestige and administrative responsibilities involved. Governors and vicars of provinces, for instance, made financial as well as judicial decisions about civil matters. Failure to administer or mediate disputes effectively could ruin one's career and fortunes; Orfitus fell under charges of embezzlement and Lampadius confronted an angry crowd rioting over food shortages.[188] Aristocrats felt pride in having met the challenges of office well; Symmachus, for example, proudly advertised his success as proconsul in Africa.[189]

The highest offices, urban prefecture, praetorian prefecture, and ordinary consulate, bestowed the highest rank, *illustris*. It was a signal honor to have attained all three, as did Lollianus signo Mavortius.[190] These positions were also the most demanding. In Rome the urban prefect stood in for the emperor at ceremonial moments and held supreme judicial and administrative authority. In addition, he was in charge of maintaining public monuments and provisioning the people.[191] With the honor of office came responsibility; when the winds delayed the grain shipments, an angry, worried crowd held the urban prefect Tertullus (359–361) responsible.[192] The praetorian prefect of a region faced even greater challenges; he was responsible for the provincial governors in his area as well as for financing the army, the post, and the public works. In addition, he was, after the emperor, the final judge of appeal and at times participated in the imperial consistory. Other prefects in the fourth century were attached to the emperor or his family and were members of the imperial consistory, acting as imperial deputies.[193]

Some military leaders (who had attained sufficiently high positions) were included within the senatorial aristocracy. They were actively engaged in military life, in deploying troops and developing strategies, on the front or at court. This segment, legally a part of the clarissimate since the reign of Constantine, remained somewhat distinct from their civilian peers, although many moved in the same social and court circles. Most senatorial aristocrats were not in the military; as noted earlier, the majority, holding

civic and imperial offices, did not have military responsibilities in this period. (Even the praetorian prefect was an administrative position.) Although
some aristocrats did combine military experience with civic office, men like
Locrius Verinus, who fought in war and then held civic senatorial appointments, culminating with his urban prefectureship under Constantine, were
rare.[194]

The duties, ceremonial and real, of high office required a man who possessed not only administrative expertise but also high status. Indeed, it was
widely believed that the man made the office, not the other way around;
Symmachus simply expressed this view when he stated that honor opened
the way to the highest offices.[195] In this world, office was a reflection of personal prestige. The aristocrat's innate worth contributed to the honor of the
office, and this conjunction gave the aristocratic office holder the ability to
settle disputes among men of lesser social prestige. The prestige of the senatorial aristocrat was one reason why Diocletian and Constantine were eager
to make ties to such men and to incorporate them into the service of the
state.

At the same time, office-holding allowed aristocrats to augment their
standing in the eyes of their peers, since "every political position, from that
of the emperor down to the petty official of a provincial town, every civic
pagan priesthood, . . . rejoiced in a certain traditional degree of honour, honour made patent to the world by special attire, seats at public events, and by
the accompaniment of appropriate retainers."[196] The degree of honor attached to each office was very precisely calculated so that it could be visible
to all. Offices that were not sufficiently honorable did not attract aristocratic
occupants.[197]

The honor of public office derived from numerous sources beyond the office itself. First, public office was generally obtained as a favor. To be appointed by the emperor or some great man indicated the esteem in which an
aristocrat was held by some powerful people. This process involved a series of exchanges between higher and lower officials. Higher officials appointed lower ones. In turn, the holders of these lower positions publicized
the favor of the great aristocrat who had appointed them. The status-conferring mechanism of the process also worked in a second way. It was commonly thought that offices went to those with the highest prestige; simply
attaining an office, then, was seen as winning a contest for social honor.
Men could thereby "prove to the world" that they had honor greater than
those they had defeated and as great as their colleagues in office.[198]

Once in office, the senatorial aristocrat was in public view and was expected to demonstrate the virtues of his order—wisdom, justice, self-control, courage.[199] A good reputation in public life might also lead to participation in the imperial court or to an imperial commission, another means of demonstrating and augmenting honor. The emperor, for his part, sought to appoint aristocrats with high social standing to increase his prestige and that of his government.

Although public office brought the highest honor, a senatorial aristocrat needed to find time to attend to private concerns as well. Since it was considered beneath the dignity of Roman aristocrats to be too directly involved in commercial matters, they turned to managers for a wide variety of tasks having to do with their property and estate management. Most important, managers leased and collected the rents from properties, especially those far removed from an aristocrat's principal residences.[200] Given the system of absentee ownership, there were numerous areas for misunderstanding and misuse of funds. Thus the *dominus* could not neglect to occupy himself with the income from his possessions, even if he was not directly involved in the decisions about agricultural production on each estate.[201]

A wealthy aristocrat generally visited some estates regularly. For nobles of Rome like Symmachus, these estates clustered in central Italy, Campania, and Sicily. When in residence, an aristocrat could be seen taking pride in his involvement with his property. Symmachus, for example, finds time and a certain pleasure in supervising projects, seeing to the repair and construction of new buildings on his father's estates in Campania or enthusiastically writing for information about a new type of mosaic work that he coveted for some baths in one of his other villas.[202] As master of the household, the aristocrat in residence was responsible for all that concerned it, allocating duties to stewards, slaves, and wife as he saw fit.[203]

Some aristocrats were less interested in the details of estate life than Symmachus, but insufficient attention could lead to serious loss that could, in turn, affect the economic resources that allowed the aristocrat to live as he should. The numerous references to property disputes and financial dealings in the letters of Symmachus and Ambrose suggest that aristocrats were quite aware of the importance of such matters; Ambrose relates a telling narrative about his brother, Satyrus, who traveled to Africa to see for himself why rents were not being collected from his lands.[204]

In addition to attending to his own financial concerns, an aristocrat expended much time and energy making arrangements to benefit friends, clients, and family. Letter writing—recommendations, requests for favors, simply keeping up contacts—was a constant obligation of an aristocrat's life. If the published correspondence of Symmachus is at all typical, such matters took up a considerable part of one's day; more than a quarter of his 902 extant letters were recommendations.[205] The wealthier and more powerful the man, the greater the number of arrangements and favors he had to find the time to give, receive, or deny. Throughout his life, whether in letters or in social interaction, the aristocrat was expected to wield his influence on behalf of his dependants and peers. In so doing, he demonstrated his power to help those whom he wished and reinforced his standing in aristocratic society.

Aristocrats at Home: Friends and Family

The relationship between the Roman aristocrat Symmachus and the Gallic poet Ausonius provides vivid insights into the importance of friendship. Ausonius had risen to prominence, largely on the basis of his cultural accomplishments, and attained imperial appointments, first as royal tutor for Gratian and then quaestor and consul. Ensconced at court, Ausonius did what any aristocrat would do—he cultivated ties with other aristocrats. The young but politically astute Symmachus initiated their relationship when he wrote to Ausonius, thirty years his senior. At the court in Trier the two became good friends, sharing common interests in literature and current affairs at many a pleasant dinner. After Symmachus left the court, the two continued their friendship through letters from 369 to 380.[206]

The correspondence of these two men is in many respects typical of the social intercourse that Symmachus—like other senatorial aristocrats—utilized to cultivate friends; an exquisitely polite respect for "the rules of courtesy and a careful observation of all due social rankings" is joined to "an attitude of earnest devotion, *religio amicitiae*."[207] Observing these conventions with a carefully studied style, Symmachus and Ausonius continued to share their appreciation of high culture; literary allusions pepper their letters as they exchange compositions and mutual praise.[208] Their extreme politeness to one another reaches almost ludicrous heights at times. In one letter Ausonius claims that Symmachus "approaches the charm of Aesop, the arguments of Demosthenes, the richness of Cicero, and the felicity of Vergil."[209]

On his side, Symmachus enthusiastically included Ausonius within his aristocratic community, addressing letters to him as "father and friend." Their age difference facilitated the parental metaphor, but it is emblematic of the importance of the friendship tie; when these letters were published, probably by Symmachus himself, his correspondence with Ausonius was prominently placed in Book 1 alongside letters to his father and brother.[210] Such positioning emphasizes the weight of the attachment as it blurs the boundaries between his "spiritual family"—his "father" Ausonius—and his natural family. Symmachus, like other aristocrats, used familial language to address friends as brothers or to address as sons certain younger men whom they had helped.[211] The language reflects the ways in which friendship constructed the aristocrat's sense of community; it was a bond as fundamental as that of family.

But more than mere affection prompted Symmachus to publicize and cultivate his friendship with Ausonius. P. Bruggisser noted a marked increase in their surviving letters after Ausonius' elevation to the office of quaestor; Ausonius now had more influence to wield on behalf of his friend. All the datable letters of recommendation occur after this point.[212] Yet it would be wrong to judge Symmachus a shallow opportunist on this basis. Symmachus was acting in accord with the aristocratic norms of his day; friendship—*amicitia*—was intended to be a free interchange that furthered mutual interests.[213] Letters of recommendation were a well-established means of doing this and hence of securing friendship. Symmachus refers to the letters themselves as the *fructus, cultus,* or *exemplum amicitiae*—proof of friendship.[214] Gaining favors for friends and for clients through letters augmented the prestige of the giver and secured his place in the aristocratic community.[215]

When called upon, the aristocrat who returned a friend's favor demonstrated that he too was a good and sincere friend (*fides*), attributes highly esteemed by aristocrats like Symmachus who, for example, writes of the *fiducia amicitiae* that he shares with Protadius.[216] Reciprocity was proof of loyalty and reliability. Such characteristics were valued for, among other things, they showed that a man had the ability to be a good friend. And only the "good people"—other aristocrats who demonstrated these characteristics—were really worth having as friends.[217]

Every aristocrat, pagan and Christian alike, was expected to follow these norms of friendship, for it was the social glue that united the aristocracy as a group; the pagan Symmachus and the Christian Ausonius thus came to be good friends. Aristocratic friends conferred acceptance and recognition; one would interact with such friends on a daily basis and cement ties by, among other things, granting and requesting favors. To an aristocrat, intent upon peer acceptance, it was the friendship, not the favor, that mattered most.[218]

Family was even more fundamental to an aristocrat's sense of identity than friends. It was on the basis of one's family that one claimed aristocratic status; *clarissimus* was an inherited title. Nobility depended on coming from a family that had achieved sufficiently high honors. The aristocrat grew up conscious of the traditions of his kin, alive or dead. Many an epitaph proclaims that the aristocrat has added to or been worthy of his family. So, for example, Alfenius C(a)eionius Iulianus signo Kamenius' epitaph begins: "In the presence of your ancestors and your sanctified parent, you have brilliantly displayed the merits of your virtues and your honors."[219] An old family name and good family connections could take one far in life and help substantially in the competition for status. Family was, in a very concrete way, a social resource. Clients were often passed down through families, as in the case of Alfenius' son who acquired patronage of Bulla Regia from his family, or, more grandly, as in the case of the patron of Naples, Nicomachus Flavianus the Younger.[220]

Yet aristocrats did not view their families in so functional a fashion. Although true affection and deep attachments certainly existed, at the same time it mattered most, in certain ways, to demonstrate status before one's family. Dinner was often the setting for status performances. Roman women and children had long dined with their male relatives and guests. Well-prepared feasts, lively conversation, and elegant settings were admired. At dinner, as in the household in general, the aristocratic *dominus* was in charge and could use the occasion to express his social standing to his family as well as to his friends and clients. The traditional patriarchal family structure, which persisted throughout the fourth century, reinforced the prestige of the male aristocrat at home as in public.

Since family was so important, aristocrats expended much energy in arranging marriages and weddings. The matches themselves were one important way to secure a family's standing, and the engagement as well as wedding arrangements were serious enough to be considered business, *negotium*.[221] Symmachus was probably typical in the attention he spent on betrothal and wedding arrangements not only for his own family but also for the families of his friends and clients. Aside from cementing the ties between his family and the Nicomachi, he served as a go-between in the marriage of the young, modestly wealthy Fulvius to the daughter of the well-connected Pompeianus.[222]

Once the engagement was settled, the wedding itself offered ample opportunity to demonstrate social standing through ostentatious display; the foods served, the attire, the gifts to guests, the guest list itself were standard ways to impress peers with wealth and prestige. Such ostentatious behavior was notorious; Ammianus caustically describes one wedding guest who, although sick, traveled from Rome to Spoleto to receive the gold wedding gifts from his host.[223] Being invited showed acceptance by the aristocratic community, and turning down an invitation could bring social disgrace; even leaving a wedding early was cause for profound apologies of the sort that Symmachus was forced to make.[224] As significant moments for social interaction among the elite, weddings reinforced family ties as they simultaneously demonstrated status.

The discussion thus far has focused on aristocratic men, but aristocratic women were as deeply embedded in the status culture as the men. As members of aristocratic families, women were part of an aristocratic man's social identity; they were ennobled with their husbands, a clear indication of how intimately associated female status was to that of their men.[225] An aristocratic woman's conduct (like that of her children) reflected upon the honor and prestige of her blood relatives and husband, as did theirs on hers. The dedication of an inscription to Anicia Faltonia Proba underscores this conjunction: Proba is called "the adornment of the Amnii, Pincii and Anicii."[226] Conduct and reputation mattered to women as much as they did to men.

Aristocratic women—like their male counterparts—dressed lavishly to show off their wealth and standing. Like men, they wore opulent jewelry and rich fabrics and had their hair carefully done as a sign of their prestige. Makeup, too, was associated with a female aristocrat's lifestyle.[227] Like men, women were concerned to travel in style; they went about Rome in covered litters.[228] Aristocratic women were eager to claim the honor and prestige that participation in religious and civic life granted to their male relatives. Some could attain such eminence through their activities as priestesses or patrons of cults or other associations. But even in these positions a woman's honor was often tied to that of her spouse or family. The title of high priestess, it is generally agreed, was held by women who were wives of high priests, and not by women in their own right. A woman like the aristocratic Paulina would even participate in mystery cults alongside her husband.[229]

Although intimately associated with their male relatives and spouses, the lives of Roman aristocratic women were more circumscribed than those of men. Certain activities that led to social status for men—like holding public office or hunting wild animals—were simply not open to women. Cultural activities were limited as well; educated women were appreciated, but expectations about a wife's education fell far below that of a husband.[230] Women were also constrained in the pursuit of friendships. Whenever an aristocratic woman was in public, she was supposed to be accompanied by other women or by attendants, maids, or slaves. In certain public places, like the circus games, women were probably segregated from men.[231] Perhaps the most fundamental limitation was the widespread assumption that women were simply inferior to men. This notion persisted, even though Roman law gave women economic protections and control over their own property, especially once freed from their father's *potestas*. Even so, women probably faced more financial constraints than men; an aristocratic woman's economic standing was tied to her inheritance and/or dotal gift, all of which derived from fathers, brothers, or husbands, who could, at times, limit a woman's access to her property.[232]

Perhaps because they had limited avenues to honor, marriage and child-bearing were central components of the social prestige of aristocratic women. Families were concerned that a young girl marry well to ensure not only the woman's standing but that of the family. They could have little regard for the girl's wishes.[233] The wedding itself, like the marriage, was primarily intended to promote the family's reputation, not the girl's desires. Once married, an aristocratic woman's standing increased as she bore children.

While this view of marriage and children may appear rather calculating, it did not preclude deep affection between husband and wife. Although aristocratic marriage was not supposed to be based on anything like the modern notion of romantic love, a union demonstrating respect, companionship, and affection was seen as desirable and added to the honor of the woman and man involved. Indeed, marital concord was a quality highly valued by aristocratic families who would publicize the harmony of the couple to proclaim the strength of the alliance between the families.[234]

Like their male counterparts, aristocratic women disdained physical labor. The mistress did not even dress herself or wash her own feet. Nor did aristocratic women do the physical work of running the household; slaves did that. Traditionally it was the responsibility of the *paterfamilias* to oversee the slaves and the steward of the household, whose job Ammianus likens to a general in charge of his troops.[235] Indeed, one of the most frequently cited reasons for a woman desiring marriage or remarriage is to attain a husband who can discipline disrespectful slaves and keep the steward in line.[236]

It seems unlikely that all aristocratic households were run in so patriarchal a fashion. Many a husband gave his wife charge of managing the household or parts of it.[237] What this might entail is outlined by Chrysostom, who describes the harried wife in charge of cooks, seamstresses, and the rest of the staff.[238] While the household responsibilities of aristocratic women must have varied considerably, fulfilling such duties did not, by and large, give them high social prestige, even if husbands appreciated such efforts or a wife's frugality.[239] Still, it was the husband who was considered head of the household financially, legally, and symbolically. And while the husband's control of the household may be idealized, it was an ideal that still existed.

Motherhood occupied considerable time, but here too aristocratic women were removed from physical labor. Babies and young children of the aristocracy were given generally to nurses and childminders. Beginning around age seven, the children were taught academic subjects and social manners by a *paedagogus* or governess who lived with the family. A mother might teach the rudiments of reading to her children, but tutors often did this, especially for boys and for children pursuing more advanced studies.[240] Given the Roman attitude toward physical labor, it is not surprising that elite women gained little prestige from the actual work of childrearing. Nonetheless, this situation did not prevent many aristocratic women from having close affective ties with their children.[241] Clearly, aristocratic mothers interacted with their children and modeled behavior for them.

The position of an aristocratic woman did change if her husband died. And given the marriage patterns of the aristocracy and life expectancies, women were more likely to outlive their spouses. Although women did not have legal control *(potestas)* over their children, we hear of widows left in charge of small children. Under a law of Theodosius I, a widow who vowed that she would not remarry could gain legal guardianship over her minor children. Whether this law represents an innovation or a restriction of a preexisting law is disputed.[242] How much control a widow exercised must have varied, although some widows did make decisions for their minor children and did control significant resources at least until the children reached majority. But while aristocratic women might be praised for being good mothers, how they played this role was not the key to their social status.

Values

The values that Roman senatorial aristocrats claimed to hold provided legitimating explanations for their lifestyle and institutions. To my mind, a succinct and vivid summary is provided by the epigrams that Symmachus' father, Avianius, composed about certain male aristocrats of the generation of Constantine. These men were linked to the great families of Rome and were set forth as models. The epigrams are not great poetry; they are filled with commonplaces, more like the conventional verses inscribed on modern greeting cards. For that very reason, however, they reflect values typical of senatorial aristocrats in general, and not just those from Rome. They thus provide a place to begin.

Avianius' epigram to Amnius Anicius Iulianus, urban prefect in 326–329 and consul in 322, summarizes the salient features of the ideal aristocrat—a man so illustrious that none would fail to yield to him on the grounds of wealth *(opes)* or nobility *(nobilitas)* or power *(potestas)*.[243] These virtues led him to surpass his peers. The element of service in acquiring honor is also clear. Iulianus' virtues made him "dear to all, prepared to contribute to help all."[244] His accomplishments conferred upon him the greatest prestige, but "he was greater *(grandior)* than these [i.e., wealth and honor], filling Rome with his eternal name."[245] This last line underscores the desired goal of an aristocrat's life—public recognition, especially by peers and family, who would read about him in verse and in laudatory inscriptions. Iulianus' success came in no small part from his family ties, for his was one of the wealthiest and most influential families of Rome, and one of the most well connected; his son married into another powerful Roman family, probably the Nicomachi.[246]

Perhaps no Roman aristocrat could claim a loftier descent than Valerius Proculus, whom Avianius eulogized in another epigram as one whose life and bearing were worthy of his lineage; his family, like others at Rome, claimed to have descended from the aristocratic Publicolae of the republic.[247] The historical accuracy of this claim is unlikely, yet the value placed on an old family tree is striking.[248] Proculus' brand of religiosity was similarly valued; a pagan, with numerous priesthoods to his credit, Proculus earned praise for his active and sincere participation in the state cult.[249]

Other sources about aristocratic values similarly reveal that lineage, wealth, service in office, superior morality, cultural activities, and good friends were frequent features of a fourth-century senatorial aristocratic ideal. They were the aspects of life that mattered.[250] The beginning of the epitaph of the renowned Sextus Petronius Probus is typical: "Rich in wealth, of noble family, exalted in office and distinguished in your consulship, worthy of your consular grandfather."[251] The emphasis on public office in the funerary inscriptions of aristocrats is striking. Its value, as expressed, resided not in its material rewards or patronage possibilities; on the contrary, these are rarely mentioned as incentives. Rather, it is the honor that one accrues that is consistently emphasized. So Sidonius warmly says to a friend on his appointment as urban prefect: "congratulations to you, for, although with your glorious prefectorian ancestry you had so far owed your reputation to your illustrious lineage, yet for yourself you did not shirk the most strenuous exertion to ensure that your descendants should gain enhanced glory from yourself."[252]

Next to public office, cultural achievements were frequently praised. Sextus Petronius Probus' tenants from Istria address him as "chief of the nobility, light of letters and eloquence, model of authority, master of foresight and management, fountain of philanthropy, advocate of moderation."[253] The association of these areas of cultural life is fulsome and formulaic but typical.

Finally, aristocrats express a high regard for friendship. True friends, in classical thought, shared not only letters and favors but feelings and activities. It was a commonplace to state that friends should "feel, blame, and praise the same thing."[254] Such a shared outlook was the ideal friendship to which many aristocrats aspired, and it justified the aristocratic quest for peer acceptance.

The most succinct and public statements of the values attributed to aristocratic women are found on funerary monuments. Paulina, the wife of the learned Praetextatus, belonged to the most elite circles of aristocratic society at Rome. Her funerary epitaph echoes the traditional female virtues—chastity, modesty, faithfulness, obedience to husband and parents. Paulina is praised for manifesting "the devotion of a mother, the gratitude of a wife, the bond of a sister, the modesty of a daughter."[255] The virtues attributed to Paulina are echoed frequently enough to have become the values by which many aristocratic women were expected to regulate their lives. At the end of the sixth century we find them still in the epitaph of a certain Philomathia: "wise, chaste, gracious, upright and kind . . . [who] by your sweet reasonableness combined things that are wont to be counted opposed, for a serious frankness and a merry modesty were the constant attendants of your virtuous life."[256]

These virtues were esteemed in all women, regardless of class. But aristocratic women, like their male counterparts, also valued and were valued for their lineage and wealth; they likewise gained honor from the accomplishments of their families.[257] A woman's luxurious dress and sumptuous life-style stated publicly her position in aristocratic society. Women desired and valued recognition of their status. Although John Chrysostom was openly critical of women who wanted to marry influential men to share in their husband's honor, many aristocratic women did just that precisely because they valued their standing in society.[258]

Religion

Religion, too, was part of this senatorial aristocratic status culture. At the beginning of the fourth century, aristocrats devoted their religious energies to the pagan gods. At home the male aristocrat was in charge of the family ancestral cult and was responsible for the correct performance of its rituals. In public male aristocrats were expected to participate in the ceremonial celebrations of the state cults as priests, magistrates, or family representatives. Female aristocrats had designated rituals to perform in public and private as well. The degree of participation of any individual varied considerably, as did the degree of sincerity. But even if an aristocrat did not hold a priesthood, he or she would nevertheless be considered a supporter of the state cults; there were few atheists in the Roman empire, even among aristocrats. Aristocratic involvement in the pagan cults was simply part of the way life was organized, and therefore part of how aristocrats expressed who they were in society.

Paganism

The same aristocrats who regarded the highest public offices as their prerogative and duty viewed the state cult and its priesthoods as their particular responsibility and honor. For centuries aristocrats, as magistrates and priests, had performed pagan rites aimed at securing the welfare of the state, both in Rome and in the provinces.[259]

The incentives for aristocrats to hold public priesthoods were similar to those for holding high office; both sorts of positions allowed aristocrats to play an important role in the state and thereby to gain the public approval they coveted. What motivated them "was the deference secured forever from one's fellow citizens through one's being, for only a day, or for only a few days in a year, at the head of the parade, or in front of crowds, and thereafter known by a new title and memorialized in stone in the forum."[260]

On statues in honor of aristocrats like Proculus, pagan priesthoods were cited along with public offices. Such honors demonstrated that Proculus had the requisite *gloria* to live up to his family name.[261]

While Proculus, like many other aristocrats, enhanced his prestige through his priesthoods, it is misleading to surmise that he did so solely to gain honor. Rather, to many aristocrats holding a public priesthood served a civic function; the games, festivals, and building projects that inspired *philotimia* among the elite were for the good of the state's gods, and hence for the good of the state. This association was reiterated often. Maximus, the noted pagan grammarian of Madauros, wrote to Augustine (ca. 388): "We see and approve of the forum of our city filled with many salutary gods."[262] Symmachus makes this same point in his request for the return of the altar of Victory to the senate house in 384: "We seek to have restored therefore the religious institutions that have served the state well for so long."[263]

Since election to a public priesthood was by cooption, the successful candidate had first to win peer approval. Therefore, being a priest proved that one had the good opinion of fellow aristocrats. The duties of a priesthood added to an aristocrat's social prestige and made him a symbolic focus for the community. One virtually compulsory requirement for a priest was to provide a sumptuous banquet for colleagues and dependents in conjunction with public holidays.[264] Priests organized and participated in ceremonies and sacrifices, usually in public view, in front of the temple of the divinity honored in conjunction with the public holidays and games.

The aristocrat intent upon winning greater prestige customarily augmented the funds for the public games from his own monies. The munificence of the individual varied, depending upon his finances and the norms of the city. As A. H. M. Jones remarked, "At Rome, members of great families, who had a tradition of munificence and ample fortunes to indulge their tastes, sometimes squandered fabulous sums on them [the games]. Symmachus is said to have spent 2000 lb. of gold on his son's praetorian games, and Petronius Maximus, one of the richest men in the empire, double that sum on his own."[265] Such games honoring the pagan gods led many an aristocrat to overspend in order to make his mark on society. Although emperors tried to restrict these expenditures, they did not oppose a system that encouraged aristocrats to underwrite public entertainment.[266]

Polytheism offered numerous opportunities for aristocrats to gain prestige as priests and magistrates. As priests, aristocrats took part in the dedication of temples and served as advisers to the senate or the local town council on cult matters. On such occasions the priest demonstrated his special role by wearing distinctive clothing like the *toga praetexta* with its purple border. At the theater pagan priests sat in the orchestra, the most conspicuous area, along with magistrates. In the provinces they sat with the town councilors. Such privileges, along with the much sought-after exemption from public *munera,* demonstrated the status of the aristocratic priest to the community at large.[267]

Aristocrats also gained honor by patronizing specific cults. While the building and major repairs of temples came to be seen as the responsibility of the state in late antiquity, such work was frequently supervised or augmented by aristocratic office holders. So the urban prefect, Memmius Vitrasius Orfitus, conspicuously dedicated a temple to Apollo in Rome in the years 356–359.[268] The choice of deity may have been predicated upon his family's association with Apollo/Sol. If so, the temple dedication shows the continuity of traditions that could tie an aristocrat and his family to a particular cult over generations.[269]

As patron of a cult, an aristocrat could contribute monies for building or restoring temples, as did Flavianus the Younger.[270] More frequently, in the fourth century individuals contributed to extraordinary cult expenses, giving monies for a particularly fine banquet, incense, or statuary. Aristocrats could also leave money in their wills for a favored cult. A family or person of high rank might be made personally liable for maintenance of a temple.[271] Such expenditures in Rome as in the provinces enabled aristocrats to demonstrate the "social inequality which enabled them to give so generously and forced the recipients gratefully to receive."[272]

Private pagan cults also offered aristocrats avenues for augmenting social honor. They allowed aristocrats to prominently assert individual and/or family identity within an intimate, elite context. Just as families and individuals choose to join a specific church or synagogue as a means of showing who they are, so too, in antiquity, aristocrats had the freedom to choose to support any one of a number of deities as a means of expressing identity and social standing. The wealthy aristocrat could even introduce a new cult; few cities would deny such a request if a respectable and influential person were to propose the introduction of a new cult to a popular god and had the financial resources to endow it.[273]

Certain private cults were favored by aristocrats at certain times and places. In Rome, for example, the private rites of the Magna Mater and Attis, with their *taurobolium* ritual promising "rebirth" of a sort, were popular among the aristocracy in the fourth century. The cost attached to the ritual of bull sacrifice may have been part of its attraction, since such expenditure signaled wealth and status as it limited participation.[274] Perhaps, too, this cult rite grew popular among the Roman elite who wanted to counter Christian notions of sacrifice.[275] Sharing such a ritualized moment in the presence of other aristocrats reinforced ties even as it allowed individuals to show that they belonged to the right elite circle. Perhaps for similar reasons, this cult was also popular in Carthage.[276]

Families could patronize a particular cult as a means of reinforcing bonds with one another while asserting their prestige; so, for example, the cult of Mithras was warmly embraced by the aristocratic father, Aurelius Victor Augentius, and his sons, one of whom also proudly proclaimed that he had built a cave for and funded the cult of the god.[277] Similarly, a husband and wife could reinforce their ties by participating together in private cult rituals and then enhance their standing by proclaiming such actions in inscriptions set up in public.[278]

THE PRESTIGE OF PAGAN PRIESTHOODS.   Some scholars have argued that by the third and fourth centuries priesthoods had sunk considerably in social esteem either as a result of the rise of mystery cults or due to the failure of the civic model.[279] But the evidence in the western empire does not entirely support this view. Into the late third century patrician aristocratic families continued to hold and even monopolize certain priesthoods.[280] When Aurelian instituted his new cult of Sol in 274, he chose as *pontifices Solis* senatorial aristocrats, and they continued in this role into the late fourth century. Indeed, holding a priesthood of Sol appears to have been associated with certain families who saw it as a point of family honor.[281]

In the early fourth-century West, literary sources suggest that the social prestige of the public priesthoods remained high. So, for example, in the *Mathesis* of Firmicus Maternus, begun in 334 and dedicated to a Roman aristocrat, the author of this work, himself a Roman senator and aristocrat, advises the would-be astrologer to try, in his training and principles, to outdo those of good pagan priests.[282] One sees this positive assessment of pagan priests again in Maternus' predictions; those who are lucky become "sacerdotes divinos, haruspices, augures," in contrast with those who are "inreligiosos, sacrilegos, spoliatores templorum, damnatos, damnabiles."[283] In the province of Africa pagan priests are listed alongside the holders of civic honors in a document dated no later than 367–368, indicating that the privileged legal position of priests had remained intact there, as was presumably the case in other localities.[284]

Aristocrats continued to proclaim with pride their pagan priesthoods alongside their public offices in inscriptions into the second half of the fourth century. It was a rare aristocrat who could claim, as did Praetextatus, to be augur, priest of Vesta, priest of the Sun, *quindecemvir,* and curial of Hercules, as well as being consecrated to Liber, a participant in the Eleusian mysteries, high priest and temple overseer *(neocorus),* an initiate of the *taurobolium,* and a priest of Mithras. In this period aristocrats did frequently hold more than one cult office.[285] Even in the early fifth century the office of *pontifex* was desirable, or so it was to the consul Tertullus who addressed the senate as consul and would-be *pontifex,* claiming that these were "offices of which I hold the first and hope to obtain the second."[286]

But by the last decades of the fourth century there are signs that not all aristocrats were eager to hold priesthoods in the state cults; the cumulation of religious offices by Praetextatus could suggest a dearth of candidates, although it could also be evidence of his religiosity and prestige. Symmachus, however, attributed an aristocrat's unwillingness to hold pagan priesthoods to a desire for advancement.[287] The traditional honor that once came with holding a pagan priesthood was under attack, even as some of the most prestigious senators, like Symmachus himself, were still eager to lend their personal honor to cult office and to see the holding of a priesthood as a sign of elite status.[288]

SENATE OF ROME.   The senate at Rome also played a key role in public cult into the late fourth century. Traditionally, the senators attended the games and festivals of the gods as well as the ceremonies of the imperial cult.[289] At such communal moments they prominently manifested their standing by their actions, attire, and special seating. The senate also had important duties to perform. Although since the tetrarchic period the senate no longer decided upon the *consecratio* of the dead emperor, it did ratify imperial deification.[290] It selected the Vestal Virgins and undertook special consultations of the gods or of the Sibylline books in times of public emergency.[291] Such duties contributed to the prestige of the senate. The controversy over the removal of the altar of Victory from the Roman senate house shows, in part, the strength of the tie between the senate and public cult even into the last decades of the fourth century.

The senate at Rome set the model for town councils throughout the western empire. As in Rome, the local town council was responsible for selecting, organizing, and financing the state cults. It was the town council that oversaw the religious activities of the local magistrates and priests. Although the town councils were composed of local elites and not *clarissimi*, increasingly senatorial aristocrats who resided in the provinces played a role in the council's decisions, religious and otherwise, as they did, for example, in a city like Carthage or Timgad.[292] By tradition, these town councils had gained prestige through their association with pagan cult, and resident senatorial aristocrats could gain honor by supporting local pagan cults.[293]

Christianization

If we see how status in the Weberian sense worked to create a particular senatorial aristocratic lifestyle, value system, and set of institutions, we can better understand Christianization. To the late Roman aristocrat, religious affiliation was meant to secure and augment status. Those senatorial aristocrats who were deeply invested in paganism as a source of honor would likely be most resistant to change. As I shall show, those in Rome, in Italy, from older aristocratic families, were in precisely this position. Conversely, a religious affiliation that did not confer prestige was at the least problematic, if not unappealing.

Scholarly approaches that attempt to explain religious change by emphasizing the psychological or theological/ideological factors that led late Roman aristocrats to gravitate toward a new religious message fail to take into account how aristocrats traditionally viewed religious activity. Religious affiliation was not, conventionally, the locus of strongly held beliefs or emotions. And yet theorists tell us that religions succeed most easily when they do not present radically new ideas or behaviors but can instead be interpreted in ways that people already understand.[294] Only when Christianity, through a combination of social, cultural, and political change, was able to address the status concerns that animated so much of late Roman aristocratic life and its institutions would it make significant progress in converting this order.

Some of the success of Christianity in converting the senatorial aristocracy was due to its acquisition of status within Roman society. With imperial support Christianity acquired a prominence and prestige that made it appealing to aristocrats. However, the centrality of the established senatorial aristocratic status culture limited the political influence of the emperor in converting the aristocracy because, among other things, the emperor was not the sole source of honor. The acceptance of friends and family was key in establishing aristocratic honor. The considerable resources of the aristocracy and their cultural traditions (which to some degree included independence from imperial authority) gave them alternative avenues for status confirmation aside from imperial appointments. Thus aristocratic institutions, lifestyle, and values acted as a cushion between aristocrats and imperial or ecclesiastic influences. In this system family, friends, clients, and patrons were also important.

In the fourth century Christian leaders were eager to address the status concerns of senatorial aristocrats. They encouraged aristocrats to take on prestigious roles in Christian institutions as patrons and ultimately as bishops. Moreover, these roles brought with them the honor that an aristocrat coveted. The willingness to incorporate aristocrats as donors to church building is one way in which Christian leaders addressed the values and behavior patterns of this class. Christian leaders were attentive to how they spoke to issues at the heart of aristocratic concerns. As they discussed wealth, "nobility," office, friends—deeply held ideologies—they were attentive to the ways in which they could appeal to aristocrats anxious about their social standing, as we shall see in Chapter 7. Christian leaders also devalued the honors that came traditionally from pagan cult, such as priesthoods and sacrifice.

In sum, any attempt to understand the conversion of the senatorial aristocracy must look at the question from the viewpoint of the aristocrats to whom status was central. Their concern would be what role the aristocracy would play in the new, state-supported religion, and how Christianity would affect their honor. Of course, not every aristocrat would see this new religious option in the same light. As the aristocracy had grown and changed in composition over the course of the fourth and fifth centuries, differences in position and perspective were sharpened. Even the elite nobility of Rome had changed, although it still claimed to be at the pinnacle of western Roman society and many aristocrats still defined themselves in terms of this circle so ideally portrayed by Symmachus. Other circles, in the provinces, and at the imperial courts, and in the military, developed and supported new aristocratic communities equally concerned with status affirmation but more closely tied to the emperor and to the new state religion.

I have highlighted the central role of the senatorial aristocratic status culture in explaining Christianization, but I believe it is also necessary to consider differences within the aristocracy. Understanding the making of a Christian senatorial aristocracy requires that we take into account the way that changes in the social and political environment and composition of the order affected the lives of aristocratic men and women located in different regions, social networks, and careers. That is the goal of the next three chapters.

CHAPTER 3

Aristocratic Men: Social Origins

When once upon a time Rome was the abode of all the virtues,
many of the nobles detained here foreigners of free birth by various
kindly attentions, as the Lotuseaters of Homer did by the sweetness
of their fruits. But now the vain arrogance of some men regards everything born outside the *pomerium* of our city as worthless.

—Ammianus Marcellinus, *Res Gestae* (trans. John C. Rolfe)

Senatorial aristocrats were united by a status culture that separated them from other classes, but the qualities that defined aristocrats simultaneously situated them in very different worlds. Senatorial aristocrats
came from Rome, Italy, or the provinces, from old or new families, from
families with great or only moderate economic resources, from imperial bureaucratic, military, or civic careers. Such differences mattered to aristocrats
all the more as the aristocracy grew in an unprecedentedly rapid fashion and
as the tight social bonds and ideals that once united the aristocracy strained
under this expansion.

In this world family and geographic origin were emphasized greatly; they
were basic means of distinction among senatorial aristocrats, valued not
only for material advantage but for social prestige. Aristocrats from Rome
claimed the honor of birth with great arrogance, as Ammianus remarked
with chagrin in the epigraph to this chapter. Family pedigree formed one basis for senatorial status, since the rank of *clarissimus* was hereditary. Birth
also gave the aristocrat wealth in the form of inherited land, familial and
friendship connections, and influence. Even clients could be inherited. A
man born with a lofty lineage also gained the distinction of *nobilitas;* certain
of the most ancient senatorial families who had held high office in previous
generations still formed a self-designated elite group within the aristocracy
that enjoyed a marked predominance over newcomers.[1] Many of these
nobles maintained attachments to Rome, as Ammianus noted above. In

69

contrast, men whose fathers had not held the lowest senatorial rank of *clarissimus* were considered "new men."[2] To avoid this label, some men lied; the production of false pedigrees from the third to the fifth centuries is a telling indicator of the weight attached to a venerable family tree.[3]

Important differences also grew out of the various opportunities open to aristocrats to exercise influence and to advance themselves. In the fourth and fifth centuries, aristocrats could pursue a number of distinct career paths or none at all. The emergence of a formalized system of rank in the second half of the fourth century, based largely on office, crystallized these differences. The most powerful, active, and influential office-holding aristocrats claimed the distinctive title of *illustris* and received fiscal and judicial privileges that distinguished these men from those below them, the *spectabiles* and *clarissimi*.[4] Thus differences in rank and in career path, together with differences in family and geographic origin, allowed aristocrats to define themselves against other aristocrats.

The importance of those social distinctions within the senatorial aristocracy has too often been ignored by historians who see the spread of Christianity in this group as essentially a response to imperial influence. For historians like T. D. Barnes and R. MacMullen, once the emperor converted, the days of the pagan aristocracy were numbered.[5] These historians see the emperor as the key and view senatorial aristocrats as dependent on imperial patronage, subject to imperial incentives and pro-Christian regulations. This model, emphasizing imperial influence, remains the prevailing one among scholars of late antiquity. The logic of such a view can seem inescapable. Emperors, after all, made the laws, controlled appointments, conferred honors, and set the tone of social and cultural life. For such historians Roman aristocratic society was vast and complex, but it had an obvious imperial center.

Such a view, however, is at odds in important ways with the evidence that I have gathered. Differences within the senatorial aristocracy did matter for religious change. The picture that emerges is of a resistant pagan core of established senatorial families located in Rome and Italy, pursuing traditional career paths although responsive to provincial and new aristocratic families. The persistence of pagan aristocrats within certain spheres of influence, in Rome and Italy and among older families, shows the limits of imperial power. These differences in family and regional origin affected both the rate and level of conversion of aristocrats. Among senatorial aristocrats from provincial families, I find Christians in larger proportions than among aristocrats whose families originate in Rome and Italy. And among aristocrats from families newly advanced into the aristocracy, I find indications also of a greater propensity to adopt Christianity.

In time the senatorial aristocracy did convert. Even the pagan aristocratic core in Rome and Italy was open to change; certain of its families turned to Christianity as early as the reign of Constantine. These Christian aristocrats from Rome, as we shall see, were often men whose families had connections to the imperial bureaucracy. And older, established families, faced with the growing strength of the new religion, also shifted allegiance by the end of the fourth and beginning of the fifth centuries. But the reality of a divided senatorial aristocracy and a resistant core forces us to put aside a top-down model to explain the spread of Christianity and to adopt a more complex analysis based on spheres of influence and a slower than imagined triumph of the new ways.

Core and Periphery: Geographic Origins

Place of birth was of key importance in the ancient world. Ancient rhetorical theory gave the glory of one's origins a prominent role; eulogies of great men began with them.[6] Ties to one's native city or home were often deeply felt: the Christian Flavius Mallius Theodorus claimed he preferred his Milanese hometown to Rome.[7] Maternus Cynegius, praetorian prefect of the Orient in 384–388 and consul in 388, died on his way home to Spain from Constantinople. His widow, Achantia, took his corpse back home for burial. She was presumably responding to his wishes, despite the fact that as a Christian the site of Cynegius' burial should have been irrelevant to her and to the dying man.[8]

For Cynegius, like most aristocrats, home was the center of his most important relationships with family, friends, and clients. In addition to affective ties, aristocrats had practical reasons to maintain their local connections. Usually, the late Roman aristocrat had property and other economic interests in his homeland, making him an influential figure in the area. Even aristocrats who pursued careers in Rome or at the imperial court attended closely to their local interests and connections. So, for example, Petronius Probianus, who flourished under Constantine and whose offspring married into prominent aristocratic families in Rome, maintained ties to his hometown of Verona. The family had a house and significant landholdings in the area, which explains why his son and grandson continued to pay attention to this region.[9]

Aristocrats reinforced ties to their home regions in a variety of ways. Many held high office there.[10] Many also performed acts of civic munificence—*philotimia*—for their home areas, which, while not reaching the levels of philanthropy manifested by their second-century predecessors, nonetheless demonstrate the persistence of aristocratic patronage in the form of statues, repairs of public buildings, and subsidized public games.

The pull of home upon aristocrats was strengthened by changes in residency requirements in the fourth century. These changes made it easier for aristocrats to obtain a leave of absence to remain on their provincial estates even as they met their obligations.[11] While senators were still legally required to maintain a residence in Rome, a growing number preferred to live in their home regions. By the reign of Theodosius II (426–442), this state of affairs was recognized by a law that released all but the *illustres* from even the formality of requesting a leave of absence.[12] This trend sharpened differences between aristocrats from the provinces and those from Rome, as it simultaneously encouraged provincials to focus on their home areas.[13]

Aristocrats' strongly felt ties to home were often associated with their religious affiliation, be they pagan or Christian. Paganism was predicated upon place; individuals and communities claimed special relationships to a local version of a deity that merged with its more universal aspects. So, for example, Jupiter Optimus Maximus was identified with Jupiter Dolichenus in the West, especially in the Danubian provinces.[14] Rituals, too, developed as a reflection of local cults. Similarly, in fourth- and fifth-century Christianity each city developed its distinctive list of martyrs, defining itself by its choice, and each followed local traditions in liturgy.[15] Augustine's mother, Monica, for example, followed African country custom by bringing certain cheesecakes, bread, and wine into the oratories in Milan until told otherwise by the urbane bishop Ambrose.[16]

Aristocrats from Rome and Italy felt the weight of local traditions very strongly. The *Codex-Calendar of 354* attested the vitality of polytheism practiced in Rome. Depictions of cult rituals signal the popularity of local practices for deities like the Magna Mater and Isis. Notations like that for the *Natalis Annonae,* the day to celebrate the distribution of grain in the city, mark the commemoration of local events. One hundred and seventy-seven days devoted to games and circuses to honor the gods and imperial cult reveal the popularity of pagan holidays in this city, funded by aristocratic and imperial monies.[17]

The gods of Rome and Italy occupied a specially privileged position.

Rome, a sovereign and independent city, enjoyed a unique role as the symbolic center of empire. Aristocrats and nonaristocrats alike saw Rome's gods as central to the state. That is one reason why the head of the cults at Rome, the *pontifex maximus,* was the emperor; his title was another sign of the centrality of the city and its cults to the empire. Since he was rarely present in the fourth-century city, the senate and the urban aristocracy directed the city and its cults. But the unique position of Rome justified special privileges for the priests and Vestal Virgins there, privileges that remained intact until the time of Gratian.[18] Even as late as 386, Libanius claimed sacrifice was tolerated in Rome and not elsewhere.[19]

Given the importance of place in shaping ritual and cult in antiquity, it is understandable why an aristocrat's religious affiliation was affected by his place of origin. Whether he came from Rome or Carthage made a difference in the gods that he worshipped. A pagan aristocrat from Carthage, for example, would most likely have included Caelestis in his pantheon. Traveling to Rome, he might take a statuette of this deity and continue to honor her when abroad. For a Carthaginian, conversion to Christianity entailed turning away from deities, practices, and institutional structures that were different from those of an aristocrat from Gaul or one from Rome.

Since geographic origin comprised much of an aristocrat's religious and social experience, it also influenced conversion. Provenance provided the aristocrat an initial network of people with whom he interacted in religious as well as nonreligious settings throughout his lifetime. If an aristocrat converted, he changed not only his own religious behaviors but also influenced others around him. Moreover, the upwardly mobile provincial landowner, eager to attain clarissimate status, depended on his local network of friends, family, and clients as he moved into imperial or Roman senatorial circles. Thus even "new men," whose identity and resources were not as tightly tied to home and venerable family lines, were nonetheless influenced by their origins and by their associations with the gods, rituals, and people of their place of birth. No wonder, then, that provenance played a role in conversion.

Rome and Italy

Many scholars have viewed the population of Rome and Italy as predominantly pagan well into the late fourth and early fifth centuries. They consider the leading senatorial aristocratic families as the most pagan of all the elites in the western empire.[20] Most scholars simply assert this as a fact, but there are good reasons, historical and institutional, to take this view.

THE PERSISTENCE OF PAGANISM.   A series of public political conflicts revolving around religion gives the impression that the aristocrats of Rome were committed to persisting in their paganism in the face of increasingly aggressive imperial attacks. In 382 the emperor Gratian, whether influenced by Christian careerists or by Bishop Ambrose of Milan, confiscated monies for the public sacrifices and removed the privileged exemption of pagan priests from compulsory public service. He also ordered the removal of the altar of Victory from the Roman senate, although he allowed the statue of Victory to remain.[21] These actions led to a protest by prominent pagan senators. In his *Third State Paper*, Symmachus, urban prefect in 384, at the insistence of his fellow senators urged the emperor to return the altar to the senate house.[22] Symmachus had the support of pagans like Praetextatus, whose strong attachment to paganism is well attested.

The pagans' requests provoked a response by Ambrose. He successfully dissuaded Gratian and his successor, Valentianian II, from returning the altar. Both Symmachus' and Ambrose's writings survive, as well as Prudentius' poems devoted to the controversy.[23] This rich documentation has been the focus of scholars, for, as J. Matthews noted, it provides one of the few "lucid episodes in the untidy and unplanned process by which the Roman governing classes . . . [converted]."[24] Thus the altar controversy has taken on a scholarly significance that goes beyond its immediate political impact.

Another episode often noted as evidence of the vitality of paganism among the aristocrats of Rome and Italy occurred after the stringent antipagan legislation of Theodosius. The usurpation by the mildly Christian Eugenius and the pagan Arbogastes that led to the battle of Frigidus (392–394) appears in many modern histories as the "last stand of the last pagans of Rome," even though J. J. O'Donnell, among others, has argued that this battle was motivated by dynastic and not religious concerns.[25]

Eugenius did, however, try to use religion to win the support of pagan senators for his usurpation by returning the altar of Victory and providing monies to finance pagan ceremonies.[26] But the extent of pagan involvement in this uprising has been disputed, as has the polemical intent of the one piece of evidence for widespread pagan support of the revolt, the restoration of the temple of Hercules at Ostia.[27] With the defeat of Eugenius, only one pagan is known to have committed suicide, Nicomachus Flavianus. The other pagans, whoever they were and however many, were pardoned and went home. Thus, while Christian writers interpreted the conflict as one that revolved around religion, that does not seem likely. Even so, the willingness of some pagans to publicly register anger over antipagan policy does indicate the persistence of paganism among the aristocrats of Rome and Italy.

Many of the pagan aristocrats active in Rome in the last decades of the fourth century are known from the sources. Some appear prominently in the *Saturnalia* of Macrobius, a work set on the eve of Praetextatus' death in 384. These, the last pagans of Rome, the *"saeculum Praetextati,"* represent the kinds of men whom scholars like E. Türk and P. V. Davies once saw as typical of the ardent pagans from Rome and Italy, "leaders of the 'anti-Christian Fronde.'"[28] Even if, as now appears likely, the *Saturnalia* is a product of the 420s or 430s, the glorification of the pagans in it still seems to reflect the paganism of late Roman aristocrats in the last decades of the fourth century.[29] This view has received more general support from prosopographic studies.[30]

Institutional reasons reinforce the impression left by the political episodes and literary sources that the aristocracy of Rome and Italy persisted in its paganism into the 390s. In arguing for the return of the altar of Victory, Symmachus focused on the ways in which paganism had long supported the state and the senate: if not at the altar, "Where are we [the senators] to swear loyalty to your laws and decrees? . . . That altar binds the friendship of all, that altar guarantees the faith of individuals and nothing gives greater authority to our decisions than the fact that our order passes all its decrees as if acting under oath. Shall our seat of government, no longer holy, be exposed to perjurers?"[31] Imperial legislation aimed at dissolving this tie had prompted the pagans to take a public stand.

Symmachus saw the breaking of long-standing ties between the state and paganism as undermining the status of his class. It was, after all, the urban senatorial aristocracy who played the prominent role in the maintenance, dedication, and celebration of pagan anniversaries and festivals in the city, as articulated by the *Codex-Calendar of 354.*[32] This link, as Symmachus saw it in the 380s, was vital. Like his friend Praetextatus, Symmachus emerges from this controversy as a man "emotionally committed to a self-identity that included continued attachment to pagan cult."[33]

The aristocrats of Rome and Italy had the resources, material as well as social, to resist pressure from pro-Christian emperors. The senate's distance from the court favored autonomy, and the senate at Rome prided itself on its independence from imperial influence. It exercised its voice when, for example, a senatorial delegation protested the punishment of senators or when it chose to banish rather than execute a man, against the wishes of the then-emperor Valentinian.[34] Fourth-century emperors tended to accept senatorial autonomy for, among other things, they relied upon the senate for maintaining control of the urban plebs.[35] Its independence was easy to tolerate for another reason; the senate had little real power over economic or military decisions outside of Rome and Campania.

The wealthy aristocrats of Rome and Italy, removed as many were from the imperial court, could act with greater independence than those who personally served the emperor or were involved in the high levels of the imperial bureaucracy. Moreover, they were praised by fellow aristocrats, like Symmachus, for exercising such autonomy; when Symmachus likened the Roman pagan aristocrat Proculus to the republican Publicola, he also praised the independence of Proculus exercised in the face of the Constantinian dynasty.[36] Such autonomy signaled an aristocrat of high status. Moreover, many of the aristocrats from Rome and Italy possessed such ample economic resources that they were assured of continued influence in civic and social life on a local level, a confidence that contributed to independent action. With such resources, and possessed of a wide-ranging network of family and friends, Roman aristocrats had many avenues to demonstrate and accrue social prestige without having to curry imperial favor.

The pagan cults gave Roman aristocrats the opportunity to demonstrate and augment status in areas increasingly removed from imperial circles. For some aristocratic families, status-laden ties to a particular cult, like their patronage of certain cities, were hereditary. So, for example, the *gens C(a)eionia* supported not only the state cult but the cult of the Magna Mater in Rome. C. C(a)eionius Rufius Volusianus, urban prefect from 313 to 315, was a *quindecimvir sacris faciundis,* as was his grandson, Lampadius, who, in addition, was a *pontifex maior.* Lampadius, his son C(a)eionius Rufius Volusianus, his daughter Rufia Volusiana, and his daughter's husband, Petronius Apollodorus, were all *tauroboliati,* initiates in the cult of the Magna Mater in Rome.[37] Inscriptions commemorating these activities indicate how the prestige of this family was proudly asserted through its association with this cult. Thus paganism offered an alternative source of status from that which derived from emperor-supported Christianity. This difference, as well as its traditionalism, contributed to the value of paganism within certain aristocratic families that valued autonomy more than engagement with imperial circles. Such aristocrats declined high office and simply enjoyed the status and aristocratic lifestyle, acquired with birth, that was intimately tied to paganism.

QUANTITATIVE EVIDENCE.   The evidence in my population study suggests that aristocrats from Rome and Italy were predominantly pagan well into the last decades of the fourth century.[38] Throughout the period aristocratic families from Italy (including Rome) have a greater proportion of pagans (60%, 47 out of 79) as compared to Christians (35%, 24 out of 68) (see Table 3.1). Paganism was particularly strong among aristocrats whose families were from Rome: 53% (42 out of 79) of the pagan aristocrats are from Rome whereas only 28% (19 out of 68) of the Christian aristocrats are from Rome. In addition, almost two-thirds (5 out of 9) of the pagan converts to Christianity come from Rome. The raw numbers are small, but the pattern supports the impression that the aristocrats from Rome and Italy were predominantly pagan over the time period of this study.

The large number of pagans who held property and office in Italy in this study (see Tables 3.2 and 3.3) reinforces the impression that pagans were predominant there. For centuries, aristocrats had acquired property and held office in specific areas where they wanted to strengthen their local ties. Scholars have tended to view the land and estates in Italy as owned mostly by the older and more established aristocratic families, who had acquired them through inheritance, marriage, and purchase.[39] Among these families, paganism was predominant.[40] This was certainly the case among the aristocrats from Rome and Italy in this study. The majority—58% (43 out of 74)—of landowners in Rome and Italy were pagan; 35% (26 out of 74) were Christian (see Table 3.2).

Aristocrats reinforced their ties to their land by holding local offices. In this regard too, pagans were a strong majority in Italy. Of all men who held offices in Italy, 68% (52 out of 76) were pagan or converts to paganism as compared with 32% (24 out of 76) who were Christian or converts to Christianity (see Table 3.3).

Office often combined with patronage, passed down from generation to generation, to reinforce these local ties. The pagan, Nicomachus Flavianus the Younger, for one, was *patronus originalis* of Naples, an honor that implied his family was the city's traditional patron; although the title did not necessarily mean that the aristocratic patron came from this area, it did indicate that he was regarded as an "honorary citizen" to commemorate and encour-

age long-standing family ties to a place.[41] Nicomachus Flavianus the Younger, like many others, strengthened his associations by accepting an appointment as consular of Campania.[42] Christian aristocrats maintained a similar
nexus of property, office, and patronage. The Christian Anicius Auchenius
Bassus, urban prefect in 382–383, was lauded as a *patronus originalis* of
Beneventum and Naples. Like Nicomachus Flavianus the Younger, he too
held an office in this region, proconsul of Campania.[43] Positions, like the title
of *patronus,* could be virtually hereditary; the pagan Vettius Agorius Praetextatus and his father were both governors of Etruria, where, it seems, they
also owned property.[44]

Thus the evidence from my study concerning patterns of family origin,
property-holding, and location of office reinforces the impression from
other literary and historical sources that the majority of aristocrats in Rome
and Italy remained pagan into the last two decades of the fourth century.
Hereditary patronage lent further support to this predominantly pagan aristocracy.

DATING THE CONVERSION.   But the aristocracy from Rome and Italy
did eventually convert. When can we see a decisive change? Some aristocrats converted as early as the reign of Constantine (306–337). Two of the
Christian high office holders under Constantine in my study came from old
Roman aristocratic families.[45] Such bits of evidence have led some scholars,
like T. D. Barnes, to see the conversion of aristocratic high office holders as
well under way by this time.[46]

Conversions continued among the core aristocrats of Rome in the years
when Constantine's sons ruled the West. Hence some scholars, like Peter
Brown, date the beginnings of a widespread, respectable aristocratic Christianity in Rome to the 340s and 350s, a time when we hear of some aristocrats turning to Christianity.[47] The 350s are also the time when, as sole
emperor in the West, Constantius II appointed four Christian high office
holders from among Roman and Italian aristocratic families.[48] From this period as well, we find evidence for the beginnings of aristocratic Christianity
in artifacts such as the *Codex-Calendar of 354.* Yet this date is seen as problematic by other scholars; K. Rosen, for one, has argued that the aristocracy
in Rome, the landowning *nobiles,* were almost entirely pagan in the 350s.
As evidence he cites Augustine's account of the conversion of Marius
Victorinus, a teacher of rhetoric at Rome who feared to openly profess his
Christianity lest he alienate the pagan aristocratic parents of his students.[49]

Most scholars have dated the conversion of the aristocracy of Rome and Italy later in the century. R. von Haehling emphasized the period under Gratian and Valentinian I (367–383) as the turning point for the conversion of high office holders. J. Matthews reached the same conclusion. He was persuaded by Symmachus' failure to refute Ambrose's claim that Christians were in the majority in the senate.[50] Scholars have been much influenced by the growing number of Christian ascetics, men and women like Jerome who claimed predominance. In 379 he wrote: "In our day Rome possesses what the world of days gone by knew not of. Then few of the wise or mighty or noble were Christians; now many wise, powerful and noble are not Christians only but even monks."[51] Certainly, the 380s saw rapid growth in the ascetic movement in Italy and in Rome among the aristocracy.[52]

The growth of asceticism, however, is not tantamount to the conversion of the pagan aristocracy in Rome and Italy. Moreover, relying on the triumphalist statements of Christians to date the turning point of the aristocracy in Rome is problematic; as G. Clemente has trenchantly observed, Christians who claimed that "everyone was now Christian" were engaged in rhetorical debate, not objective reporting.[53] Consequently, some scholars have considered Rome as more pagan than Christian until the 390s, and have thought that the "non-Christians . . . outweighed the Christians in wealth and position."[54] The stringent antipagan laws of Theodosius and imperial policies in the decade after the defeat of Eugenius (394) were critical in the conversion of Roman Italy and its aristocracy.[55] Indeed, if the aristocrats of Rome and Italy were "the most pagan" of all, then a date in the 390s for their conversion makes some sense. Following along these lines, some historians dated the turning point for aristocratic conversion even later, to 404–415, based on political developments and textual evidence.[56]

Unfortunately, a compelling resolution to the dating of the conversion of the aristocracy in Rome and in Italy on quantitative grounds still eludes us. Dating aristocrats from Italian families reduces the sheer number of men whose religious affiliation we can observe; the patterns of religious choice in this population study do, however, elucidate the general scholarly view. In this population aristocrats remained pagan into the 380s and 390s, and only after Gratian and Valentinian I, especially after 367, did Christianity make significant advances. Of the pagans from Italy (including Rome), 58% (19 out of 33) had their highest office before the reign of Gratian, that is before 367. Only a small proportion (15%, 3 out of 20) of the Christians from Italy (including Rome) are attested with highest office in this early period (see Table 3.4). But Christians begin to become more numerous in the study population in the years beginning with Gratian and continuing down through 423 (the last year of this study). Indeed, the Christian families are heavily concentrated in this later period (85%, 17 out of 20) while the pagan families are not (42%, 14 out of 33). Aristocrats from pagan families of Italy (including Rome) continue to make a strong showing in the 380s in this study; in the total study population from Italy for the years 383–392, 12% (4 out of 33) of the pagans as compared to 5% (1 out of 20) of the Christians held their highest office. After 392, however, aristocrats from Christian families from Italy are in the majority; 18% (6 out of 33) of the pagans had their highest office during these later years as compared to 35% (7 out of 20) of the Christians.

While the quantitative evidence for the turning point in the conversion of aristocrats from Rome and Italy is not conclusive, the people in this study lend substance to the statements of contemporaries who see a powerful core of pagan aristocrats in Rome in the 380s and 390s alongside a significant Christian presence there, beginning with Gratian's rule and becoming increasingly visible in the 380s. The presence of so many Christians in Rome explains why Symmachus and his peers felt their identity was threatened by the removal of the altar of Victory. This dating, emphasizing the reign of Gratian for male aristocrats from Rome and Italy, coincides with that proposed by R. von Haehling in his study of male high office holders from the East and West.[57] I depart from von Haehling's dating in seeing this period as one of change for the aristocracy of Rome and Italy as a whole, not just for the male high office holders.

Christianity succeeded among aristocrats from Rome in the post-Gratianic period in part because it had acquired status and respectability within the seventy years since Constantine had shown that it was his favored religion. At the same time, paganism remained vibrant among aristocrats in Rome into the early fifth century. The complexities of this process of social and religious change is suggested by the fate of an aristocratic family like the Turcii.

THE CONVERSION OF A TYPICAL ARISTOCRATIC FAMILY FROM ROME: THE TURCII.   We can trace the Turcii to an L. Turcius Secundus, suffect consul ca. 300. His son, L. Turcius Apronianus, attained the prefectureship of Rome in 339. In the next generation two sons, L. Turcius Apronianus signo Asterius and L. Turcius Secundus signo Asterius, lived up to traditional aristocratic ideals and followed in their father's pagan ways.

The brothers held high civic office and priesthoods in public pagan cults. Both were active in the state cult, holding the position of *quindecimvir sacris faciundis*.[58] Their civic offices were those most sought after by Roman senators; L. Turcius Apronianus signo Asterius attained the urban prefectureship of Rome, the office held previously by his father, in 362–364 as a reward from the emperor Julian.[59] His brother attained a governorship *(corrector)* of Flaminia-Picenum in 340/350, a position often held by Roman aristocrats.[60]

But in the second half of the fourth century some members of this family converted. A Turcius Secundus married a Christian bride, Proiecta; her bridal chest, found in the silver treasure from the Esquiline Hill in Rome where the family had one of its houses, bears the Christian formula, "*Vivatis in Christo.*"[61] Such a dedication indicates that the husband as well as the bride was a Christian or a catechumen. This Turcius Secundus, tied to the family of the Turcii at Rome, may have been the first of his family to convert. His wife, Proiecta, is most likely the same girl who, commemorated by Pope Damasus, died at age sixteen by the year 385.[62] This identification placed a Christian Turcius in Rome in the 380s, a decade of religious change among the aristocrats of Rome.

Yet paganism persisted in parts of this family beyond the 380s. One of its members, Turcius Apronianus, was a prominent pagan in the senate at Rome in the last decades of the fourth century.[63] The family's traditions of service to the state and to pagan cult endured until the early fifth century regardless of the marriages that some of its male members made with prominent Christian aristocratic women. Only gradually did this old pagan aristocratic family turn to Christianity. Although a pagan, Turcius Apronianus married a well-placed Christian woman, Avita, and was converted to Christianity by his wife's aunt, Melania the Elder, probably around the year 400.[64] As a Christian family, the Turcii continued to flourish in Rome. The last recorded member, Fl. Turcius Rufius Apronianus Asterius, was urban prefect and consul in 494.[65] Like the aristocrats in my study, the Turcii reveal that as some of the core members of the aristocracy of Rome embraced Christianity, others persisted in their paganism into the late fourth and early fifth centuries.

NORTHERN ITALY.   There are two contrary views of the spread of Christianity among the aristocracy in northern Italy. According to J. Matthews, the conversion of the aristocracy in northern Italy, in comparison to the situation in Rome and central Italy, was faster and easier. In the fourth century,

Matthews observed, "the increasing importance of north Italy as an administrative and military center had been accompanied . . . by a transformation of the social and economic life of that region."[66] The presence of a Christian court in Milan and the leadership of the forceful Bishop Ambrose contributed to the Christianization of the aristocracy there. That, too, is what the Christian Jerome asserted, claiming that with the elevation of Ambrose all of Italy converted to "the right belief."[67] The episodes of pagan resistance, revolving around the altar of Victory and the defeat of Maximus and Nicomachus Flavianus, are taken to support this view; these events brought to the forefront tensions between the predominantly pagan aristocracy of Rome and the Christian court elite in Milan. In this view the failure of the pagan cause only hastened the conversion of the aristocracy in the North.

A very different image is depicted by other scholars. Most notably, R. Lizzi, in a study of the sermons of Ambrose and his contemporary bishops, saw a slower time frame for the conversion of the aristocracy in northern Italy, more in keeping with the elite in other parts of the peninsula. Lizzi's view rested, in part, on the rhetorical strategies adopted by Christians. Bishops like Zeno, for example, made a "contrast between the illicit *mores* of those still adhering to ancient cults and the sanctity of small groups of neophytes."[68] Such remarks suggest that bishops addressed towns only partially Christian. The attempts of bishops to convert aristocrats and to redirect their wealth to the churches in their towns were of only limited success in the fourth century. The archaeological record reveals that most of the church building in northern Italy was modest; the richly endowed churches in Aquileia and Milan are the exception. Moreover, there are indications that paganism remained strong in northern Italy, as in Rome. In the Val de Non in 397 a pagan population resisted evangelizing Christian priests. In Turin the Bishop Maximus preached against paganism as rustic ignorance and gave the task of converting rural tenants to the *domini* (landowners) because, as Lizzi noted, many landowners secretly preserved pagan temples on their estates. Their resistance signals that "the faith of the *domini* was often a facade."[69]

The contrasting images of the conversion of the aristocracy from northern Italy underscore important differences within the aristocracy. R. Lizzi saw a landowning aristocracy resistant to Christianity; J. Matthews saw an urban and court elite much influenced by imperial religious example. These two elite segments were present in northern Italy, and my study reflects them both. What is, however, of greater note and what lies at the heart of such competing views is the reality that differences in lifestyle and career path, two basic components of an aristocrat's identity, were associated with different religious choices among the elite of northern Italy.

The Western Provinces

For this study the western provinces include modern France, comprising late Roman Galliae and Septem Provinciae (or Viennensis); modern Spain, comprising Roman Hispaniae; modern England or ancient Brittaniae; and modern North Africa, comprising Roman Africa, provinces shown by the fourth-century *Notitia Dignitatum*.[70] In these provinces, as in Italy, an aristocrat's identity revolved around a status culture that incorporated religion. Like Roman aristocrats in their roles as priests, magistrates, and senators, the elite in their town councils made decisions about cult issues in their respective cities and gained social honor from these leadership positions. Provincials who held priesthoods in the state cults acquired prestige and privilege; pagan priests in the West for most of the fourth century were automatically freed from curial duties and often, as in Africa, were incorporated under the *honorati* of the town council.[71]

Some provincial elites, who gained prestige and privilege from their role in the public state cult as priests and magistrates and from their identification with the pagan aristocrats from Rome, were, plausibly, resistant to religious change. This was the case especially for ambitious provincials who sought advancement through the support of powerful, old pagan aristocratic families. That this did occur with some frequency is suggested by Symmachus' correspondence and several of his *Orations* in which he is shown using his influence to advance provincials and new men into the clarissimate.[72] A provincial needed the approval of powerful aristocrats, as well as money and the affirmation of the emperor, to attain the lowest senatorial offices (quaestor and praetor) that made a man eligible for clarissimate status.[73]

Other provincials sought status and social advancement in other ways. Many ambitious provincials, eager to attain clarissimate rank, tried to obtain imperial favor as a more direct avenue toward that end.[74] Curials in the fourth century had an added incentive to seek the clarissimate since this rank released them from certain of their obligations to their local town councils.[75] The relaxation of rules requiring domicile in Rome noted earlier facilitated the advancement of provincials in particular. The emperor had much discretion in these matters. He granted offices and honorific titles such as consular or *praeses* that conferred clarissimate status automatically. He even adlected palatine civil servants to the clarissimate rank if he saw fit.[76] Provincial advancement was at times explicit imperial policy, or so it was praised as such by the Gallic orator Nazarius in his *Panegyric of 321* on Constantine.[77] If an ambitious provincial saw Christianity as a way to curry imperial favor and advance his promotion, he possibly had reason enough to change his religious affiliation. Christian leaders complained that the desire for secular advancement motivated many a convert.[78]

The receptivity of any particular provincial depended, in part, on his reference group. If an ambitious provincial desired acceptance by the core of Rome's traditionally pagan aristocrats, then conversion to Christianity might be viewed negatively. This concern was expressed by the African rhetor Marius Victorinus, who feared to publicize his conversion to Christianity lest he alienate the pagan aristocratic parents of his students in Rome.[79] If a provincial aristocrat valued imperial approval, he may have been more open to Christianity. So, for example, Apollinaris, the first convert in Sidonius Apollinaris' family, was apparently influenced in part by his association with the Christian usurper Constantine III.[80]

Western provincial aristocrats in general stood in a different relationship to the state and its gods than did their counterparts in Rome and Italy. Provincials had to contend with levels of power and prestige above theirs, with higher imperial officials and institutions.[81] To incorporate a new cult, to build a new temple or new aqueduct, required the approval of imperial authorities as well as local town councils. Nor did these provincial authorities enjoy the same legal and religious privileges as did their peers in Rome and Italy. Provincial elites in their town councils were less autonomous and more restricted in their religious, as well as in their political and social, decisions as compared to their Rome-based peers.

In addition to these structural differences, the aristocrats in the western provinces, as compared to those in Italy, were generally more closely tied to the emperor and the imperial cult and were more dependent on paths of advancement controlled by the emperor and his resident court. The presence of the imperial court and the imperial bureaucracy reinforced the emperor's influence in these areas and the importance of the imperial cult. Indeed, all provincial aristocrats were united in their veneration of the emperor in the imperial cult. Although some variations emerge from province to province, the imperial cult in the West formed a uniform and coherent system, "with an organization, worship and ritual that can be seen as broadly similar throughout most of the Latin West."[82] The imperial cult, which had revived under Diocletian and Constantine, was a center of public, communal attention. Its focus on the living emperor and his family lent it a vital, contemporary significance that drew the support of the provincial elites. Imperial cult celebrations, supported largely by imperial monies on the municipal and provincial levels, continued to grow in number and importance.[83]

These structural differences, and the closer connections—cultural as well as structural—to the emperor, made the western provincials more open to Christianity than their Italian counterparts. Culturally, provincials, who identified closely with the emperor as a symbol of *Romanitas*, were probably much influenced by his conversion to Christianity, and more so than their Rome-based peers who had different traditions tied to the cults of Rome and who had a different relationship to the imperial cult. It was on the emperor that the provincial elites focused primarily as a symbol of unity.[84]

Identification with the emperor was presumably strengthened if a man was in imperial service or advanced through imperial favor. Provincials who had acquired their positions through their association with the emperor were probably more open to imperial example. Nor was a Christian provincial prevented from holding a prestigious position in the provincial and municipal imperial cult because of his religion; Constantine's willingness to support the imperial cult in Umbria as long as rites offensive to Christians (notably animal sacrifice) were omitted provided a model for subsequent Christian emperors.[85]

The historical and literary evidence provides reasons to suspect that the western provinces were relatively hospitable grounds for Christianity. The imperial cult was a focus of unifying symbolism; the emperors with their resident courts were more directly pertinent to the status aspirations of local elites; and the imperial bureaucracy offered a direct means for provincials to advance. Structurally, too, provincial elites were in charge of local cults but their leadership was mediated through imperial administrators who were themselves much influenced by the Christian emperors and their courts.

The quantitative evidence supports the view I have presented here of the western provinces as relatively receptive to Christianity as compared to Rome and Italy. In my study 47% (36 out of 77) of the Christians (including converts to Christianity) had families from the western provinces as compared to 26% (21 out of 80) of the pagans (including converts to paganism) (see Table 3.1). The difference is substantial without being overwhelming.

Clearly, the provinces, while hospitable to Christianity, were areas of mixed religion. Depending on the play of interest, tradition, and association, men could and did make different choices. To better understand these patterns, we need to examine the elites of different regions separately because they show substantive differences in their approach to Christianity.

GAUL. The Gallic empire in the mid-third century had enabled many Gauls to enter the senatorial aristocracy after a relatively low level of representation in the preceding two centuries.[86] The imperial presence in Gaul in the fourth century also fueled the growth of an aristocracy.[87] With the Diocletianic division of the empire, Trier became an important imperial capital, a center for political, social, and cultural life. The emperor was an almost continual presence from 367–392. It has been suggested that the presence of an imperial court and the growing bureaucracy in Gaul "facilitated and refueled the readiness of Gauls to serve the emperors and the rulers' willingness to employ members of the local aristocracy" in the fourth century.[88] The presence of a large army in the Rhineland is likely also to have fueled the growth of this class since it, too, offered avenues of social mobility for Gallic provincials. The flourishing of schools of rhetoric in southern Gaul gave men the training to take advantage of opportunities in the military or imperial service. As Gaul flourished in the fourth century, its inhabitants made use of the opportunities offered and gathered the resources necessary to advance upward into the clarissimate.[89]

Some successful Gallic aristocrats were pagan. Saturninius Secundus Salutius, for one, enjoyed a long career in imperial service, beginning under Constans, then serving Julian as praetorian prefect of the Orient in 361, before retiring in old age in 367 after serving Valens.[90] Several pagan Franks, like Flavius Bauto and Flavius Richomeres, rose to high military office that carried with it aristocratic standing.[91]

In my study population, however, most of the aristocrats whose families came from Gaul were Christian. Of the 31 Gauls (including Franks), 65% (20 out of 31) were Christian, 7% (2 out of 31) were converts to Christianity, and only 29% (9 out of 31) were pagan (see Table 3.1).[92] The clear predominance of Christians among this group is striking. It is supported as well by von Haehling's study of the high office holders of Gallic provenance.[93]

An examination of the lives and careers of the Christian Gallic aristocrats in this study population reinforces the view that the presence of an imperial court and the possibilities inherent in state service greatly favored the spread of Christianity in the Gallic aristocracy. Although all Gauls benefited from these institutions, Christians benefited most, especially when strong pro-Christian emperors were in residence. That was clearly the case under Valentinian's son, Gratian (367–383), who favored Gallic Christians in particular in his appointments to high office.[94] We can see Gratian's influence most strikingly in the careers of the Christian Ausonius and Ausonius' family and friends. But this one emperor's support does not fully explain the strong Christian predominance in the Gallic aristocrats in this study; before and after Gratian, Gallic Christians were able to succeed.[95] The imperial service is key to understanding this trend.

The Christian Gaul Claudius Postumus Dardanus is exemplary of the ways imperial service facilitated the advancement of Gallic provincials. Dardanus came from a wealthy, but probably not aristocratic, family. He had large landholdings at Sisteron, in Narbonensis Secunda, where he, his brother, and his wife established a Christian community called Theopolis. Dardanus advanced through imperial service. He had the right skills, namely legal and rhetorical training, to hold two palatine posts and two praetorian prefectures between 401 and 413.[96] Even old aristocratic families boasted of their attainments in the traditionally high-status elite activities of law and rhetoric, as did Apollinaris, grandfather of Sidonius Apollinaris.[97] Dardanus, like other ambitious provincials, parlayed these skills into high office.[98]

An upwardly mobile Gaul like Dardanus would know that Christianity had been the religion of the Gallic court ever since Constantine had summoned Lactantius to Trier in 316/317 to tutor his son Crispus.[99] When there as caesar, Julian attended church services, hiding his paganism.[100] Being a Christian allowed a man to fit more easily into imperial court circles and state service. Ausonius, for one, saw it as beneficial to write a string of Easter verses (his *Versus Paschales*) after coming to court at Trier. Ausonius was not the only ambitious provincial to see the advantages of being a Christian. Since the study population reflects the evidentiary biases in favor of the most active, most visible, and most successful aristocrats, the predominance of Gallic Christians in it underscores the high level of attainment that this segment actually enjoyed, primarily through imperial service.

Areas in southern Gaul (primarily Aquitanica I and II, Narbonensis I and II, and Viennensis), the areas most Romanized, produced most of the Christian aristocrats in this study population.[101] Social proximity and shared friendships facilitated to some degree the spread of Christianity in these regions in Gaul. A consideration of the social ties of Ausonius illustrates the kinds of networks through which Christianity spread. From his estate near Bourdeaux, inherited from his father and presumably passed on to his son, Ausonius lived in the midst of the cultured society of other Aquitanian nobles.[102] He fostered these ties as professor of rhetoric in Bordeaux and accepted the son of a fellow Aquitanian, Paulinus, as a student. Later, Ausonius helped his former student attain his first office, consular of Campania. Paulinus then returned home to Bordeaux and resumed his life within a community of like-minded Christian aristocrats.[103] Paulinus married Therasia, a wealthy Spaniard, and spent his time overseeing their estates in Spain, Gaul, and Italy as he kept up friendships with other Christians from southern Gaul, such as Aper and Amanda.[104]

The vitality of the southern Gallic aristocratic community, reinforced by the Christian imperial court in Trier, explains why some historians viewed the conversion of the Gallic aristocracy as, in K. Stroheker's view, "smoother and less passionate than in Rome."[105] Pagan aristocrats in Gaul did not publicly protest the disestablishment of pagan cult at the end of the fourth century, as did their Roman and African peers. But it would have been surprising if they had; the imperial presence was a strong deterrent. Moreover, the numerous status-laden priesthoods that aristocrats in Rome held in the public cults did not exist in the same way in Gaul. But the lack of a public protest does not mean that all Gallic aristocrats converted quietly with the dismantling of public cult under Gratian and Theodosius. Pagan aristocrats persisted and are attested in this study well into the early fifth century. Some Gallic aristocrats felt strongly about the gods, and especially their native Gallic ones. Others identified with the pagan core group at Rome. Protadius, a probable pagan, is one such Gallic aristocrat who enjoyed a successful career, attained the urban prefecture of Rome in 400, and maintained friendship ties with Rome-based aristocrats like Symmachus.[106]

In a study of the Gallic aristocracy, K. Stroheker outlined what has become the most widespread view of the dating of their conversion to Christianity: after the defeat of Julian, the evangelical work of Martin of Tours (361–397) was decisive; Gratian's pro-Christian policies favored conversion, but it was not until the year 400 that the Gallic aristocracy was predominantly Christian.[107] Other historians have focused on the fifth century as the time of real Christianization; the demise of imperial authority, amid the barbarian invasions and civil wars, diminished opportunities for local elites to acquire prestige through state service and led aristocrats to high ecclesiastical offices. Thus, to historians like R. Van Dam and R. Mathisen, it was in the fifth century that the aristocracy of Gaul reoriented their traditional *cursus honorum* and fully embraced Christianity, transforming Christianity to conform to existing "aristocratic ideologies of prestige."[108] Such a reorientation suggests that the Christianization of Gaul's aristocracy was essentially a fifth-century phenomenon.

Against this latter view, I conclude that the Gallic aristocracy came to be Christian in large numbers in the last quarter of the fourth century. Among the Christian Gallic aristocrats in this study, the period beginning with Gratian and Valentinian I (367–383) sees the first real surge in Christian aristocrats, a trend that emerges more distinctly by the late fourth century and that continues until the study ends in 423.[109] While locating the Gallic aristocrats in narrower time periods reduces the number of men in each period, this more refined categorization highlights the importance of the years 367–383 for the spread of Christianity. Moreover, the story of the numbers accords with what we know from other sources. Changes in the religious affiliation of Gallic aristocrats begin to take shape in the texts about this time, a period that coincides with the beginning of St. Martin's episcopate (ca. 371–397).[110] I would not attribute this change to Martin only or primarily; a letter of Paulinus of Nola to Vitricius lets slip that "such things are happening throughout Gaul."[111] Sulpicius Severus misrepresents Martin's influence by omitting references to the evangelizing work of other bishops at this time.[112] Nor would I attribute this change to Gratian alone; although Gratian's policies were significant, aristocrats in imperial service had, for more than fifty years now, been subject to imperial influences that favored conversion.[113] By the early 400s, I would suggest, the Gallic aristocracy was securely Christian, even if some pagans persisted, as they did, into the fifth century.

The evidence raised here supports the notion that Christianity made deeper inroads in Gaul than in Italy. However, the turning point in the conversion of aristocrats from Gaul and Italy appears to occur about the same time, beginning with Gratian's reign (367–383). The numbers from Gaul are, admittedly, weaker than those for Italy, and neither is entirely conclusive as to dating. However, the quantitative evidence, when viewed in conjunction with the other evidence, does suggest that Christianity spread more completely among Gallic aristocrats in the later fourth century than among Italian ones. In Gaul, Christian aristocrats were dominant in the time period of Gratian's reign and appear even more decisively so in the last decade of the fourth century and continuing until the end of the study in 423. In Italy, by contrast, Christians and pagans reached equal proportions only in the last decade of the fourth century and the early fifth century, one indication that pagans remained a significant presence there (see Table 3.4).

The conversion of the aristocracy in Gaul did not, however, happen at once nor was it uniform across the province. Gregory notes that in Tours a senator's home had to be used as a church until 397, largely because private Christian aristocratic donors were not available.[114] In contrast, Arles had a basilica on a prime urban site from the early or mid-fourth century, probably because of wealthy Christian aristocratic patrons and imperial support.[115] Not only cities but regions as well varied as to when their elites embraced Christianity. Southern Gaul, as noted, had a strong Christian aristocratic presence and is well attested as such even by the 370s. Regions with many urban centers tended to adopt Christianity sooner than regions with large rural areas.[116] The educated and the elite of Gaul, attached to urban centers, apparently converted to the new faith sooner than did the populace, which adhered "with great tenacity to their old gods and inherited customs."[117]

It may be useful here to draw on W. Klingshirn's distinction between conversion and Christianization in his study of Arles. Conversion, the removal of pagan monuments and degradation of pagan sites initiated with the legal closure of temples, is differentiated from Christianization, the building of an alternative Christian landscape.[118] In Klingshirn's terms, Gallic aristocrats appear in my study to have converted to Christianity in greater proportions in the 370s to 400, continuing to do so into the early fifth century. But their construction of an alternate model of service was largely a fifth-century phenomenon. It is likely that their dependence upon imperial service and the influence of a resident court made them more resistant to changing their *cursus honorum* at the same time that it made them more willing to convert to the religion of the emperor.

SPAIN.   Many historians believe that since the aristocracy of Spain was intimately tied to that of southern Gaul, this group underwent a similar conversion trajectory.[119] Unfortunately, prosopographic studies of Spanish aristocrats do not allow us to see this process with the same clarity that is possible for the Gallic aristocracy.[120] Even if certainty is not possible, the demonstrable ties between Spanish and southern Gallic aristocracies do make it seem likely that the process of Christianization was similar in both areas.

As in Gaul, archaeological remains indicate that there were Christians in Spain by the early fourth century, and literary evidence supports the presence of Christian institutional structures there as well; there were Christian bishops at the Council of Elvira (ca. 309) and at the court of Constantine.[121]

But, as in Gaul, few Spanish *clarissimi* are attested in the first half of the century; the consul Acilius Severus, who corresponded with Lactantius and served under Constantine, and the poet Iuvencus stand out in my study because of their early fourth-century dating.[122] As in Gaul, most of the Spanish aristocrats appeared in the last quarter of the fourth century, with the 380s and 390s being especially important as Theodosius advanced compatriots. Thus, if the similarities hold, by the early 400s Christians probably dominated the Spanish aristocracy as they did the Gallic one.

In this study population the number of known Spanish aristocrats with attested religiosity is far smaller than the number of Gallic aristocrats. The group included only eight Christian and one pagan Spanish aristocrat. Christian aristocrats are better attested as wealthy landowners in Spain than pagans, but the numbers are again small (see Tables 3.1 and 3.2).

As in Gaul, in Spain men advanced into and up the ranks of the senatorial aristocracy primarily through imperial service. Again, much would depend on the circles in which a man moved. Marinianus, from western Hispania, and probably a pagan, is known to us in large part because of his correspondence with the Roman pagan aristocrat Symmachus.[123] But most of the Spanish aristocrats in this study, like their Gallic peers, found Christianity, indeed orthodox Christianity, compatible with achieving and reinforcing aristocratic status as they advanced through imperial service. These Spanish aristocrats, like their Gallic peers, appear more open to Christianity than aristocrats from Rome and Italy.

The career of Nummius Aemilianus Dexter provides an instructive example of a Spanish provincial who benefited from imperial favor; the son of a bishop of Barcelona and a new man, Dexter was a zealous Christian who supported Theodosius and advanced through imperial service to the proconsulship of Asia before attaining the praetorian prefecture of Italy in the early 390s.[124] Like Dexter, the Spaniard Maternus Cynegius rose through imperial service to attain high office, attaining the consulship in 388; Cynegius is perhaps most known for a rabid religiosity that led him to destroy a pagan temple in the East without the emperor's permission.[125] Ironically, this same man is the alleged owner of a luxurious villa in Carranque, north of Toledo, whose dining room is decorated with scenes from the pagan myths.[126] The Spanish poet Prudentius also rose due to imperial favor; Prudentius probably held a provincial governorship before a court position under Theodosius or his sons allowed him to compose verse acceptable to an orthodox court.[127]

My analysis of the Gallic aristocracy based on prosopographic evidence indicated that the more Romanized area of this province produced the most Christian aristocrats. In Spain, too, P. de Palol found a link between Christianity and the most Romanized areas, namely the eastern part of the Tarraconensis up to the Ebro River, and the regions along the borders of Carthaginiensis, Baetica, and Lusitania. Although de Palol acknowledged that his survey, dependent on the survival of evidence, might simply indicate that Christianity was simply better attested where there are Roman remains, my analysis of Gallic aristocrats supports the notion that Romanization and Christianity can also be linked in Spain.[128]

To supplement our meager evidence from Spain, scholars have looked at the expansion of the Priscillianist movement as an important indicator of the spread of Christianity among the aristocracy there.[129] Priscillian, an educated layman but not of aristocratic status, advocated an extreme asceticism that was tied to Manichaeism by his critics. He was eventually charged with sorcery and immorality, such as praying naked in private with women.[130] Since Priscillian's writings do not support these allegations, some historians have argued that Priscillian's real heresy lay in overstepping his authority within the Christian community by giving too much prominence and influence to laymen and widows.[131] Priscillian's supporters in the 370s and 380s, as far as we can trace them, were wealthy, often educated laymen, like Tiberianus, or local notables and wealthy single women, like Euchrotia and Procula, the widow and daughter of the successful pagan professor of Bordeaux, Attius Tiro Delphidius.[132] Some local officials, like Volventius, the governor of Lusitania, protected Priscillian, but none of these men are known as Priscillianists themselves.[133]

What is striking is the limited extent of Priscillianism; educated and wealthy laymen were involved, but they were not of clarissimate standing. There are only two attested Priscillianists of the clarissimate rank in this study population, Severus and Severa, the relatives of the Spanish count Asterius (not a Priscillianist himself), and both dated to the first quarter of the fifth century.[134] They stand in contrast to the majority of Spanish aristocrats in this study who were "Catholic" Christians, ascribing to the orthodoxy of the emperor Theodosius.

The small number of Priscillianists of clarissimate rank forces a reevaluation of the value of this heresy for understanding the conversion of the aristocracy. This heresy in the 370s and 380s tells us something about the spread of Christianity among the educated and wealthy local elites of southern Gaul and Spain; some upwardly mobile, educated Christian provincials evidently found no avenue for their abilities within the ecclesiastical structure, and were either unsuccessful or uninterested in pursuing clarissimate standing, a path that was made more difficult by Theodosius' 386 confirmation of laws requiring provincial elites who did advance to the clarissimate to fulfill all local duties.[135] Priscillianism offered provincial elites an alternative way to claim authority and social prestige. Moreover, if it is true that only after a movement has acquired a critical mass does it spawn splinter groups, then the growth of Priscillianism in the 380s also suggests a quickened pace for the conversion of the provincial elite in Spain and to some degree in southern Gaul.

The Priscillianist heresy cannot, however, tell us much about the conversion of the clarissimate per se. The Spanish Christian aristocrats who were of clarissimate status followed mostly the religion of the emperor, the Catholic Theodosius. These men were, by and large, also successful in imperial service or high civic office. Their orthodoxy admittedly enabled them more readily to acquire status and move within the highest elite and imperial circles, but the Priscillianist movement tells us little about such men and their families.[136]

Roman Africa

Although most historians have opined that Christianity spread rapidly in Roman Africa in the second half of the third century, a few have seen aristocratic conversion as a much later phenomenon.[137] In the words of J. Geffcken, Carthage high society acted as the "custodian of the old religion." Geffcken pointed to the continuity of pagan rites at public expense into the fourth century and to the fact that the important African deity Dea Caelestis lost her temple only in 399.[138] G. Charles-Picard also focused on the end of the fourth century as the time of conversion of the great aristocratic landowners.[139]

In a sermon delivered in 430 Augustine noted that "not one of us does not have one or more pagans among our grandparents"; this comment well applies to the men in my study population.[140] Eleven of the African aristocrats with attested family origins were pagan; six were Christian (see Table 3.1). The pattern stands in sharp contrast to the predominance of Christians from Spain and Gaul, and calls for some explanation.

One important key, in my view, is the strong set of connections linking Roman and African aristocrats. Many African aristocrats had close personal and financial ties to Rome-based aristocrats.[141] Many aristocrats (Roman and African) held land in Italy and Africa; overlapping economic interest brought with it social as well as financial associations that further strengthened the bonds between the two groups. Marriages between Roman and African elites were signs of such ties. Among Rome-based aristocrats, however, status was strongly associated with paganism. The African landowners, who had strong ties to their Roman pagan peers, would plausibly be more likely to resist religious change. While these ties cannot be demonstrated in all cases, in this study African landowning aristocrats were indeed more often pagan than Christian (see Table 3.2).

Pagan aristocrats from Rome, for their part, often had strong ties to Africa as well. And these also tended to favor the persistence of paganism. We can turn, for example, to the Roman aristocrat M. C(a)eionius Iulianus signo Kamenius, urban prefect of 333/334, and a probable pagan, of old consular family. He had strong ties to Africa, where he was honored as patron of Madaura and Bulla Regia, the latter an inherited honor. His family fostered this connection; one of his relations, the Roman pagan aristocrat Alfenius C(a)eionius Iulianus signo Kamenius, became consular of Numidia and later vicar of Africa.[142] The presence of such families in Africa offered a pagan alternative to provincials who sought advancement through their support.

The epigraphic evidence reinforces the impression that paganism remained a vital force among the African aristocracy throughout the fourth century. In his study of the inscriptions pertaining to municipal life in Roman African cities, C. Lepelley noted that no text mentioned the intervention of municipal authorities in the inauguration of Christian monuments. On the other hand, Lepelley observed, private donors, aristocrats included, did build some Christian monuments in Roman North Africa in the fourth century. Although such patronage provides some evidence for the conversion of the aristocracy, these private Christian donors stand side by side with aristocrats who held priesthoods and privately supported pagan temples in the cities and on their rural estates.[143] Moreover, the pagan population flourished in North Africa, in Carthage and elsewhere, throughout the fourth century. Pagans were involved in violent outbursts against Christians at Calama and Madauros, both in the Bagradas valley, and at Sufes and Carthage.[144] Public outbursts, at times with the support of African aristocrats, show the vitality of paganism in this region and in this class.

One African family, the Aradii, exemplifies the patterns for conversion proposed here. This family survived the third-century upheavals to become one of the most influential in fourth-century aristocratic circles in Africa and Rome.[145] Aradius Rufinus, a pagan, had the status, wealth, and influence to become urban prefect of Rome three times, including once under Maxentius and once again (a sign of his personal *dignitas*) under the new emperor, Constantine. His standing and acumen earned the praise of the Roman Avianius Symmachus.[146] When he married, Aradius probably chose as a bride a member of the eminent Roman family, the Valerii; the names of his two sons preserve the connection, being identified, most probably, with L. Aradius Valerius Proculus signo Populonius and Q. Aradius Rufinus Valerius Proculus signo Populonius.[147] The two sons of Aradius, as *quindecimviri*, made a dedication "To Mercury the companion and custodian of the Lares Penates" in Rome; this inscription, probably from the *lararium* of their home, highlights both their paganism and their residence in Rome.[148] In this, the Aradii followed the tradition of many older aristocratic families who, whatever their origin, preferred to live in Rome. Moreover, residency in Rome facilitated the careers of the father and his son L. Aradius Valerius Proculus, both of whom attained urban prefectureships of the city.[149] Yet the Aradii also carefully cultivated their influence in Africa and held offices there.[150]

The Aradii remained staunchly pagan through most of the fourth century, a religious choice that well suited the old Roman noble circles in which they moved. Not only the antiquity of this family but "sincere worship of the gods" distinguished one of its sons, L. Aradius Valerius Proculus signo Populonius.[151] If another Aradius Rufinus who was urban prefect in 376 is the son of L. Aradius Valerius Proculus, as many scholars have conjectured, he was even born in Rome. Indeed, Rufinus' life marks a turning point in the religiosity of this family. He was an aristocrat who felt the currents of change: Christianity, by the late 370s, had become more compatible with aristocratic status in Rome. A pagan in his early life, this Rufinus advanced to *comes* of the Orient under the pagan Julian, and later returned to Rome, where, by the time of his urban prefecture in 376, he appears to have become a Christian.[152]

The conversion of the aristocrats in this study, like that of the Aradii, is a phenomenon not noted until the second half of the fourth century, especially in the 380s and 390s. All of the African pagan aristocrats held their highest offices (see Table 3.4) in the first half of the fourth century; African Christian aristocrats are not attested in my study population until the second half of the fourth century and continue into the early fifth century.[153] This dating may explain why, even as late as 440, Salvian complained about the superficial conversion of the African nobility.[154]

In addition to the influence of Rome-based aristocrats, the rivalry of Christian sects, so fiercely fought there, retarded the conversion of the African aristocracy. Augustine, writing in the late fourth and early fifth centuries, attests that the conversion of aristocrats from Donatism to orthodoxy was as much a concern for him as the conversion of pagans.[155] In part to repress the strong Donatist presence, the emperor tried to exert a strong influence on the African elites in favor of "Catholic Christianity." Since most of the great landowners in Africa converted after Constantine had made clear his support for "Catholic Christianity," most were Catholic Christians, not Donatists.[156]

Summary

Provenance affected the rate and nature of the conversion of the aristocracy in the western Roman empire. Senatorial aristocrats from Gaul and Spain in this study were more open to Christianity than were those from Italy and Roman Africa. Receptivity was influenced by the aristocratic circles to which a man belonged and through which he gained prestige. If, as in Gaul and Spain, imperial service was key to a man's status, he was more open to Christianity, the religious uniform of the resident imperial court. In Roman Africa, as in Rome and Italy, there were, however, good alternatives to imperial service for ambitious provincials. Key was the influence of the old aristocratic families of Rome, Italy, and Africa. In these, polytheism survived, incorporated into a traditional aristocratic lifestyle and a set of institutions that supported it. For men who identified themselves with such aristocrats, many of whom were removed from direct imperial involvement, paganism remained a status-affirming option, retarding the forces in favor of conversion.

Although the empirical evidence supports the notion that Christianity made greater inroads in the western provinces than in Italy, the turning point in the conversion of senatorial aristocrats from Gaul and Italy appears to have occurred at about the same time, beginning with the rule of Gratian with Valentinian I (367–383). If this dating stands, the evidence nevertheless suggests that Christianity spread more extensively in Gaul than in Italy in this period. The influence of a resident Christian imperial court and bureaucracy for some fifty years prior to Gratian is one explanation for this difference. Relevant, too, is the evidence from the late third century for the spread of Christianity in the curial class, the provincial seedbed for the clarissimate. Christian clergy were recruited from these local elites, and wealthy curial Christians are attested in a variety of third-century sources.[157] This trend stands out against the handful of attested Christian senatorial aristocrats before the rule of Constantine.[158] If Christianity had spread among the curial class in Gaul and nearby Spain in the late third century, some upwardly mobile provincial aristocrats may have been Christian before their advancement.

Old Families and New Men: Social Origins

An old family tree, filled with high office holders, was not a requirement for admission into the fourth-century aristocracy, but it still mattered greatly. High birth brought material advantages and conferred social honor. When St. Jerome traced Julius Festus Hymetius and his brother Toxotius to Julius Caesar, his family genealogy was specious, but his compliments were genuine; if these families were considered old, they were especially prestigious by fourth-century standards.[159]

The greatest honor belonged to the nobility, certainly to the most ancient senatorial families who still formed a special group within the aristocracy and enjoyed a marked predominance over newcomers.[160] With their inherited networks of clients and friends as well as landholdings extended over generations, the old families were economically and socially entrenched in a way that was hard for non-nobles to match. The nobility still remained at the core of the aristocracy in Rome and Italy.

Elitist sentiments about family background reinforced the widespread perception that a new man began with a handicap as he competed with the members of older aristocratic families for offices, clients, favors, and other signs of honor. At the end of the fourth century, Symmachus claimed: "The offspring of a family, by whatever extent they are distant from new men, by the same extent they proceed toward the heights of nobility."[161] Such notions did not, however, prevent the assimilation of new families into the nobility over a generation or two, nor did they limit friendship ties between nobles and non-nobles.[162] But they do reflect a meaningful social division.

As the aristocracy grew over the course of the fourth and fifth centuries, social divisions were accentuated. Divisions based on family lineage were articulated forcefully to differentiate between aristocrats. Older families felt the tension because there was an increasing number of new men and options for them to ascend into the aristocracy.

In their quest for aristocratic status, some new men found certain emperors very favorably disposed to helping them advance. This was not a novel development; since the early empire, emperors had advanced men who came from nonsenatorial backgrounds, either equestrians, members of the local elite in the provinces, or men from military backgrounds. Emperors had many reasons for turning to new men: they needed capable, experienced men to serve in the bureaucracy or in the military; they were suspicious of older, more entrenched aristocratic families whose traditions of independence might go against imperial wishes; and they desired to build loyalty and dependence among members of an elite, men who would likely be grateful for the opportunities they received. Such considerations entered into imperial policy at various points throughout the fourth century, an age characterized by its social mobility and rapidly increasing bureaucracy. The late fourth-century emperors, Valentinian and Valens, known for their hostility to older aristocrats, went so far as to consider men who often were from low social origins, but serving as palatine civil servants, counts, and tribunes, as worthy of advancement into the senatorial order; such men were regularly adlected so that they would not have to pay for the games associated with entrance into the clarissimate.[163]

There are reasons to believe that an ambitious man from a nonaristocratic family would be more likely to become Christian than one from an old aristocratic family. Such a man, who did not have strong family or traditional ties to paganism, had fewer encumbrances should he follow the emperor's religion. In this, he would be following a standard pattern of behavior since the religious inclinations of the emperor had for centuries been proclaimed as the model for all to follow, especially the elite.[164]

Moreover, after Constantine's accession, it was increasingly apparent that Christianity was in a favored position. Under certain of Constantine's successors in the West, notably Constantius II, Gratian, and Theodosius, imperial favor was said to flow more freely for Christians. Even nobles and older established aristocrats were susceptible to such influence.[165] But new men may have been more susceptible to this perception and its influence insofar as they were more dependent on imperial favor.

A number of historians, including A. H. M. Jones and A. Chastagnol, have noted the advancement of new men in the fourth century, and some have associated this advance with the spread of Christianity.[166] But as yet there has been no systematic, detailed study of this assumed tendency of new men to adopt Christianity earlier and more fully than men from older established aristocratic families. Since new men did not generally broadcast their humble origins, it is often difficult to identify these individuals with certainty. And since I sought men whose origins could be known, the number of new men in my study population is low.[167] Nevertheless, I did find some evidence for the connection between Christianity and new men as early as the reign of Constantine. Imperial efforts varied, but the determined efforts of certain pro-Christian emperors appear to have had some influence, judging from certain trends among the new men in this study population.

New Men and Constantine

The preference for new men varied according to emperor, but it was perceived as particularly strong under Constantine. According to Eusebius, Constantine was extremely generous in granting senatorial rank.[168] The statements of Zosimus and Eutropius alleging Constantinian liberality provide additional evidence for the widespread perception about this emperor's willingness to advance his favorites, many of whom were new to the aristocracy.[169] Ammianus' allegation that Constantine admitted barbarians to the consulship suggests one source of new men.[170] But new men traditionally came from equestrian or provincial backgrounds. The equestrian origin is seen, for example, in the four men adlected into the aristocracy by Constantine.[171] Constantine's willingness to turn to new men is also indicated by his military appointments. We know of eight generals who rose to high military positions under Constantine, none of whom belong to the imperial family; none are related to more established officer families and four are from low-status families, while the remaining four are of unknown descent.[172]

Such patterns of appointment of new men may suggest why some contemporaries viewed Constantine as overly concerned to favor Christians in his appointments and as recipients of gifts.[173] This perception led even a supporter, such as Eusebius, to decry the "scandalous hypocrisy of men who crept into the Church, and assumed the name and character of Christians" solely to win imperial favor. At other times Eusebius, as well as the later Christian writers Theodoret and Sozomen, noted imperial favors to Christians with approval.[174] Ammianus' criticism of Constantine's military appointments, noted above, may have been a veiled complaint about this emperor's advancement of Christians.[175] There was a noticeable increase in Christian high office holders under Constantine compared to the tetrarchic period, although Christian writers who claim a predominance of Christians in high office in the West under Constantine were certainly exaggerating.[176]

Texts alone cannot tell us if the perception that Constantine favored Christian new men was borne out in reality. This study does, however, provide some evidence to support this view. In this study population we know most about Constantine's appointees to high office in the West. We have certain evidence of religious affiliation for seven Christians and twelve pagans among those who were appointed to the offices of praetorian prefect of Italy or Gaul, urban prefect, and proconsul of Africa beginning in 313 and continuing through 337.[177] Of the seven Christians in this study, one, Flavius Ablabius, was certainly of nonclarissimate background: he served Constantine, became a senator in the East, and went on to become praetorian prefect, active in the East and West.[178] Four Christian appointees had fathers whose aristocratic status is not known, an omission that *may* suggest they were new men since new men did not advertise their origins.[179] Moreover, three of Constantine's Christian appointees to high office, Optatianus, Acilius Severus, and Flavius Ablabius, were from provincial backgrounds, Africa, Spain, and Crete, respectively; two, Flavius Ianuarinus and Gregorius, were of unattested provenance as well as unattested parental status, while only two, Sextus Anicius Paulinus and Ovinius Gallicanus, were Roman and senatorial in origin.[180]

The pagan high office holders under Constantine included in this study look somewhat different from their Christian counterparts, and this reinforces my view of an association between Christianity and new men at this time. Of the twelve attested pagan high office holders in the West under Constantine, nine were from aristocratic families; only three were unknown.[181] Their provenance followed similar patterns; seven of the nine men from aristocratic families came from Rome; the three men who were of unknown family origin were of unknown provenance; one man, M. C(a)eionius Iulianus signo Kamenius, of consular family, is of unattested provenance, although his name suggests an Italian background.[182] Despite the real limitations of the historical evidence, these appointments indicate the significance of the older, Rome-based aristocracy under Constantine. These families outnumber the unknown appointees, three to one, reversing the trend noted among the Christian officials.[183]

One other indication of the suggested link between new men and Christianity under Constantine appears if we look at the Christians who held their first office under this emperor. These men owed their advancement largely to imperial favor. Among the eight Christians who had their first office under Constantine, we find men like Flavius Ablabius, the anomalous easterner of nonsenatorial background, and Acilius Severus, a Spaniard from an unknown family.[184]

The connection between new men and Christianity under Constantine did not, however, prevent the emperor from actively seeking men from old well-established aristocratic families for his appointments. This was true both before and after the civil war with Licinius. Most of Constantine's pagan appointees in the West were from old Roman families. Constantine needed administrators, and men from old pagan aristocratic families had the requisite honor to govern. Moreover, Constantine recognized that such aristocrats were most effective if appointed to areas in which they and their families owned land and had client ties. In taking such factors into account, Constantine demonstrated that religious affiliation was not the sole consideration in choosing appointees.[185]

Emperors and New Men after Constantine

The connection between Christianity and new men that appears in outline under Constantine comes into sharper focus intermittently in the West in the decades after his death. Some emperors were particularly active in advancing new men, and Christians in particular. Two of these emperors are worthy of special note.

CONSTANTIUS II.   The court of Constantius II (337–361), established in the East, won a reputation for its circle of Christian courtiers, "a profane crew" in the eyes of a pagan like Libanius.[186] A number of these Christian courtiers were from humble origins. Among such easterners a man like Datianus, a Christian, allegedly the son of a bath attendant, is exemplary; his lowly family origins did not stop him from serving the emperor and advancing to senatorial status, and even a consulship in 358.[187] He, like several others, served in the corps of notaries, a bureau that underwent rapid expansion under Constantius II. Senior notaries carried out confidential missions, often becoming personally involved with the emperor and obtaining rapid promotion to the clarissimate.[188]

Some of these upwardly mobile Christian easterners came west and were included in this study. The Christian Flavius Taurus, for one, came from a modest family, became a notary, and then served Constantius in the West as prefect of Italy and later, in 361, as consul.[189] This man had good relations with the senate, who replaced his statue in the Forum of Trajan.[190] Like other eastern Christians of nonsenatorial origins, Taurus held offices traditionally granted to western aristocrats, and some westerners no doubt resented this change.

Constantius' appointments to high office in the West in the decade when he acquired sole control, from 350 to 361, show his willingness to advance Christians, and a certain number of these Christians were new men; of ten Christians included in this study, two were easterners of nonsenatorial backgrounds, three were of unknown parentage (a possible indicator of new aristocratic status), and five came from aristocratic families.[191] This high proportion of men of uncertain origins may show the incursion of new men into Constantius' government in the West.

Christianity was making its way into old Roman families in this decade, attracting nobles like Sextus Claudius Petronius Probus and Q. Clodius Hermogenianus Olybrius. Of the five men from Christian aristocratic families in this study who were appointed under Constantius to high office in the decade when he was in sole control in the West, four were from Rome. These men made close ties to the emperor and flourished. N(a)eratius Cerealis, for one, proclaimed his support for Constantius publicly by putting up an equestrian statue of Constantius in the Roman Forum in 353.[192] By appointing such men, Constantius, like his father, showed his desire to win the support of the old Roman aristocracy. His pagan appointees to high office show this as well; four of his six pagan appointees included in this study are from old aristocratic families from Rome. Of the two pagans from uncertain parentage, the Gaul, Saturninius Secundus Salutius, may have been a new man.[193]

GRATIAN. Constantius' successor in the West, Valentinian I, eagerly promoted his Pannonian friends, many of whom were new men but experienced administrators. Some of these new men were also Christian, but that association does not appear consistently. Only after 375, when Gratian came into sole control of the western empire, does this connection emerge clearly. Making a clean sweep of Valentinian's Pannonian appointments (who had incurred the hostility of western senatorial aristocrats), Gratian drew heavily upon Gallic provincials for his administrators. These men were often Christian, and some were new.[194]

If we look at the family origins of the men in this study who were appointed to the highest offices (praetorian prefect, urban prefect of Rome, and proconsul of Africa) in Gratian's years as sole ruler in the West (375–383), the social mobility of Christians and new men is marked (see Appendix 4). Of fourteen Christians (including converts), three were from nonsenatorial families, one was the son of a new man, and three others were from families whose senatorial status is not known. Three of these nonsenatorial men are also of provincial origin; Ausonius and Arborius are from Gaul, and Flavius Mallius Theodorus is from a nonsenatorial family of northern Italy.[195]

The emergence of Gallic aristocratic families under Gratian is intriguing, for we cannot be certain in many instances if the family under discussion was already in the clarissimate but only now assumed high office, or if these were new families, from nonsenatorial origins, who were upwardly mobile. Only a handful of Gauls are known to have entered the senatorial aristocracy before Julian.[196]

What is clear is that Gratian was open to advancing new men, all three of whom in this study were Christian. He favored Gauls, who resided near his court. Yet he, like his predecessors, was keenly aware of the desirability of maintaining ties to the old aristocracy in Rome. Seven of the fourteen Christians appointed to the highest offices in this study were men from senatorial families, and another was the son of a new man, but the six remaining Christians were from Rome.[197]

CHRISTIAN NEW MEN AFTER 375: PERCEPTION AND REALITY.   After Gratian's death in 375, we still hear the grumblings of clergy denouncing the conversions of ambitious new men who see advantages from being or becoming Christian. A prominent case involved a Carthaginian by the name of Faustinus who, in 401, was accused of wanting to be baptised to further his municipal career. Rather than turn him away, Augustine urged his flock to accept Faustinus' conversion even though he was himself doubtful about the man's motives.[198] Such complaints, expressed too by the pagan Symmachus, show the continued perception that Christianity facilitated upward social mobility.

New men, often of provincial origin like Faustinus, were the most likely targets for such suspicions since they were typically seen as eager for advancement to the clarissimate in order to escape from their obligations to their town councils. The emperors were so concerned with such upward movement that they legislated repeated restrictions against it.[199] As a new man moved upward into the aristocracy, he would naturally feel the need to be accepted by his peers. If his peers were Christian courtiers or bureaucrats who emulated a Christian emperor, it is understandable, in human terms, why such a new man would be viewed as receptive to Christianity.

While some contemporaries were quick to ascribe the religious allegiance of ambitious men to hypocrisy, such an answer is too simple and too cynical. The Christian Flavius Mallius Theodorus may exemplify some of the complex influences on new men. Claudian's fulsome praise of Theodorus' merits and his total silence about his ancestors implicitly signal the consul's humble origins.[200] Theodorus was an able administrator, who had worked his way up from an advocate in the court of the praetorian prefect to become the praetorian prefect under Gratian. Theodorus left imperial service after Gratian's demise and became active in the literate circles around the court of Theodosius at Milan. Here, near the center of imperial life, Theodorus wrote on Christian themes within a Neoplatonic context.[201] Although Theodorus, like many new men, may have been Christian before his promotion, his involvement with Gratian and the court of Theodosius had reinforced his religious choice.

As I have noted, some evidence suggests that in some regions, notably Gaul and Spain, Christianity had spread among the decurion classes in the third century. This would help to explain the connections between some new men of provincial origin and Christianity. One such man, the Spaniard Nummius Aemilianus Dexter, discussed earlier, was perhaps from a decurion family; his father was a cleric. Dexter advanced through imperial service to the emperor Theodosius.[202] No doubt, Dexter's Christianity helped him feel comfortable at court under the emperor to whom he owed his position.

A new man, perhaps more so than his well-entrenched aristocratic peers, might be especially sensitive to the religious predispositions of the group into which he was moving. This could be as true for pagans as for Christians, if they were moving into pagan-dominated spheres. Exemplary of one such pagan, albeit earlier in the fourth century, was the new man C. Iulius Rufinianus Ablabius Tatianus. His father was an orator but not aristocratic. Adlected among the consulars by Constantine for his service in the state bureaucracy, he was consular, first of Aemilia and Liguria, and later of Campania. Tatianus' sphere of action, attested by an inscription that honors him as patron of Abellinum (Campania), places him easily within the pagan aristocratic society that flourished in Rome and Campania, so well described in

Symmachus' correspondence at the end of the century. Although a new man, Tatianus sought to fit in with these elite pagan circles. So in an inscription he proudly proclaimed his pagan priesthoods, pontifex of Vesta and priest of Hercules, alongside his offices.[203]

THE EVIDENCE FROM RANK.   Since a man born into the aristocracy had only the lowest rank, *clarissimus*, any man who moved up to a higher rank did so as the result of his own efforts. My study population shows a higher proportion of Christians of the rank of *illustris* than pagans. This, too, lends credence to the perception of the extraordinary social mobility of Christians and Christian new men in particular: 49% (66 out of 134) of the Christians and 40% (58 out of 145) of the pagans were *illustres* (see Table 3.5). Although the large number of Christian and pagan *illustres* in this study results, in part, from the nature of a historical record that preserves information about the most successful members of a group, the strong representation of Christian *illustres* in the study is nonetheless striking.[204]

If, as seems likely, more Christians started from nonclarissimate or newly clarissimate backgrounds than did pagans, they were still able to advance to the highest rank in greater proportions than pagans. Christian mobility in this study is even more marked if we take into account the observation that fewer Christian aristocrats than pagans had parents of aristocratic status before the age of Constantine (see Table 3.6). Yet, over the time period of this study, the Christians came to achieve parity with their pagan peers in terms of the highest rank. In my view, imperial preference for Christians and the rising status of their religion contributed to reduce the natural advantages that pagans had at the beginning of the century even as such incentives fueled the willingness of ambitious men to convert.

Summary

The evidence for new men in my study population is not as strong as the evidence for distinct geographic spheres of Christian and pagan influence. The evidence suggests a modest connection between Christianity and new men as seen in the favoritism for Christians, who were also often from families new to the aristocracy, in the appointments of the strongly proactive Christian emperors Constantine, Constantius II, and Gratian. This connection supports the perception of imperial favoritism found in anecdotal sources. But these actively Christianizing emperors, like their less active peers, were constrained in the appointments they could make. Emperors had to consider factors other than religion, such as proven abilities, prestige among the local population, and favors owed to important families. No emperor could be blind to these considerations nor to the high status of the powerful old aristocratic families, many of whom persisted in their paganism into the early fifth century. Not surprisingly, then, the connection between new men and Christianity in the quantitative evidence was modest.

CHAPTER 4

Aristocratic Men: Career Paths

> You have appointed, and will appoint others also as consuls, most
> kindly Gratian, but never on similar grounds. Men of military re-
> nown . . . men of ancient and famous lineage . . . men distinguished
> for their trustworthiness and tested by official duties; . . . and so far
> as the path to honors is concerned, I differ in my qualifications.
>
> —Ausonius, *Gratiarum Actio* 4 (trans. H. G. Evelyn White)

In a hierarchical society like that in the western Roman empire, geographic origin and family lineage were fundamental components of
an aristocrat's identity. But this was a world in which there was also tremendous social mobility. Men could and did change their positions in society.
They advanced in large measure through their career paths and through the
associations that they forged as they pursued their careers. A large part of
who a man was, in late Roman society, depended on what office he held.

In the fourth and early fifth centuries, many aristocrats lived up to conventional expectations as to how to acquire honor by pursuing a senatorial
civic *cursus honorum* (path of honors).[1] In this age of ambition, other career
paths were open to senatorial aristocrats *(clarissimi)* or would-be aristocrats,
and these alternatives were widely known, as is clear from the speech delivered by Ausonius in appreciation of his consulship of 379, quoted in the epigraph to this chapter. Ausonius' rhetoric works because it assumes commonplaces. Some men, he notes, attain high office by virtue of their military
glory, others due to their descent from old noble families, others because of
their loyalty and offices held in imperial service. Ausonius asserts that he
himself arose via a different route. He was summoned to court to be
Gratian's tutor, then was named *comes* and quaestor, then praetorian prefect,
and finally consul. While Ausonius would like to see himself as unique in
his mobility, many men did, like him, gain distinction first as teachers, poets,
or lawyers before moving into more established career paths.

Ausonius emphasized the role of the emperor Gratian in his own advancement. This is rhetorically effective within a set speech of thanks to an emperor. Clearly, perceptions about imperial preference did play some role in the appointment process. The notion that being a member of one or other religious group could help an appointment may have influenced the religious choices of some men. Indeed, during the reign of Gratian, Symmachus noted that some thought it advantageous to their careers to stay away from pagan altars.[2] But it is misleading to see the emperor as the sole source of honor and means of social mobility. A man advancing upward or into the senatorial aristocracy faced different groups of evaluators, and these evaluators limited the role of the emperor. A man needed powerful aristocratic patrons at each level and in each career path. Depending upon his trajectory, a man came into contact with distinct groups of aristocrats and nonaristocrats, traveled to different places, encountered new ideas and peoples, and found varied opportunities to augment his network of friends and family in his pursuit of status.

Differences in career paths, like differences in family and geographic origin, led to differences in associations and thus the social influences to which a man was exposed. Anecdotal evidence, such as Augustine's account of the fourth-century African Ponticianus, elucidates how this could be the case. One day when Ponticianus was at court in Trier, he and three other comrades, all imperial bureaucrats, were at leisure to wander the town since the emperor was busy watching the afternoon circus games. The men broke into two groups of two. One pair (identified as "public agents," *agentes in rebus*) happened upon a house filled with ascetic Christians and the writings of the desert father, Antony. This chance encounter filled one of the public agents with doubts about the value of pursuing his worldly career. Turning to his friend, he said, "as for you, if it troubles you to imitate me, do not stand in my way." The account continues: "the other answered that he would closely stick to him, as his partner in so ample a reward, and his fellow in so great a service."[3] Both men then abandoned their secular careers. But the second pair of imperial bureaucrats returned to court.[4]

This vignette is crafted by Augustine to inspire his audience of Christian believers to devote themselves to a higher calling. But I want to underscore something else in the story, namely the effects of association with others in a similar career path. The men in Augustine's account obviously spent much time together, sharing work as well as leisure. Their attachment to one another was so strong that it led one of the men to follow his friend's example and to adopt asceticism too. As they shared careers in life, so they shared in their religious choices.

Associative ties connected with career paths could also work to favor paganism. If a man was involved in pagan aristocratic circles in Rome, and actively engaged in a senatorial civic career, the social influences on his conduct differed and would usually support a willingness to pursue pagan traditions. Aurelius Celsinus, a man most likely tied to the family of the Symmachi, lived up to the expectations of his pagan contemporaries when he, as proconsul of Africa in 338–339, restored a precinct of Mercury.[5]

The importance of preexisting networks in spreading new social and religious movements has long been recognized by social scientists.[6] Career paths affected these networks and thus are important for understanding religious change. However, few historians have considered career and its importance for Christianization.[7] Among those who have, there has been an overemphasis on the role of the emperor and insufficient attention paid to aristocratic spheres of influence.

Perhaps the most significant statement of the impact of careers on Christianity remains that of A. H. M. Jones. For Jones, the "formation of the new imperial nobility of service" by Diocletian was "of crucial importance for the future of Christianity . . . And since [the] members [of this nobility] were dependent on imperial patronage for their advancement, it was inevitably subservient to the emperor's will . . . Constantine and his Christian successors were thus able to build up an aristocracy in sympathy with their religious policy."[8] Jones focused on the emperor as he contrasted this new nobility sympathetic to Christianity to the "great old aristocratic families" in the West who "remained on the whole faithful to their traditional religion . . . from a sense of *noblesse oblige.*"[9] Although Jones did sketch some of the broad social divisions relevant to Christianization, he conflated geographic and family origin with career paths. Moreover, Jones did not examine his observations in relation to detailed prosopographical evidence.

In discussing the new service aristocracy, historians following Jones have focused on the importance of emperors who showed direct favor to Christians through their appointments to high office. They have been led to this emphasis in part by the statements of late Roman authors, Christian and pagan, who, from Constantine on, assert that emperors preferred Christians.[10] Historians have tried to ascertain the reality behind this perception of imperial favoritism. R. von Haehling's 1978 study of imperial appointments to high office has been the most authoritative work in this vein.[11] A careful prosopographic analysis led von Haehling to conclude that regardless of perceptions, imperial appointments to high office did not simply favor Christians in an upwardly spiraling movement beginning with Constantine. Although some emperors did appoint Christians and even preferred them, thereby letting their religious preferences be known, a range of considerations—political, religious, and social—contributed to imperial decisions on appointments to high office. In some areas and under some emperors, pagans were regularly appointed to high offices and in higher proportions than Christians.[12]

The focus on imperial appointments to high office has overemphasized the role of the emperor at the expense of the senatorial aristocracy itself. It is as if seeing the tip of an iceberg, a person purported to understand how the iceberg had formed. The highest offices were one point, albeit the most prestigious one, in a man's life. But the highest offices were the result of years spent in certain career paths, and these careers developed in a social context. It is therefore necessary to examine the career paths, and not simply the highest offices, for their connection to the process of Christianization.

Career Paths Defined

Before presenting my analysis, I want to clarify the terminology I will be using in describing men's careers. What I have deemed a "career path" differs somewhat from modern notions. It would have been difficult for a late Roman senatorial aristocrat to distinguish who he was from what he did, nor would he have drawn a sharp line between his public and his private persona. Symmachus' judgment on Magnillus as vicar in Africa was based on his actions "in public and in private according to the testimony of all."[13] Indeed, it was Magnillus' aristocratic standing and influence, his honor and glory, that opened the way to high office in the first place.[14] Consequently, Magnillus was expected to display proper aristocratic conduct in all areas of his life; only then could he acquire higher positions and greater prestige.

The late Roman senatorial aristocrat thought it inappropriate to profess eagerness for a "career." Especially among the core aristocrats of Rome, it was conventional to show a certain disdainful hesitancy about *negotium* and public office in particular. Symmachus' letter to Sextus Petronius Probus echoes the commonly heard preference for leisure over public office as he commiserates with Probus' appointment as praetorian prefect in 383: "Be calm and patient under the imposition of this burden . . . put aside your nostalgic thoughts of leisure . . . be tolerant, as you are, of all duties, and perform this obligation which you owe to the emperors; for in exacting it, they have considered more your abilities than your desires."[15]

Symmachus' encouragement to an allegedly reluctant Probus, pining for the delights of private life, rings hollow; this is the same man whom Ammianus described as a "fish out of water" when not in office.[16] Not all aristocrats were as avid for office as Probus, and some did lead lives devoted to private matters. But these men were the exception; they did not live up to the expectation that honor is pursued through public service.[17] Like Probus and Symmachus himself, most aristocrats felt that the rewards and prestige of a career warranted their best efforts. However fleeting many such rewards may seem—the pleasure of sitting in specially designated seats in the amphitheater, the admiration of the crowd, the pleasure of wearing the distinctive toga of an official—they distinguished men in late Roman society and were gained only through successful pursuit of a career in public life.

The Four Main Career Paths

I have classified men in my study population into four career paths. These paths are attested in the source material and fit the major patterns in the study population. They are the military career, the senatorial civic career, the imperial bureaucratic career, and the religious career.[18] Since women in this period could not be said to have had public career paths in the same ways as men, I discuss their lives and options separately in Chapter 5.

Aristocratic male careers took distinct shapes that were typical enough to allow me to determine when a man was mainly involved in one or other path. These paths did change somewhat over the century, so that some paths came to include different offices or the sequence in which an aristocrat held certain positions changed. And some men followed careers that were more mixed than others; these more mixed paths were more common in the early fifth century.[19] However, the outlines of the different career paths were so well established that it was generally possible to categorize the career paths even of men who held only one office, if that office was sufficiently distinctive for the path. For example, a man attested as quaestor or praetor is located in the senatorial civic *cursus*. By combining men who followed a purely senatorial civic career path with those who followed a mainly senatorial civic career path, I hope to have minimized the necessity of changing my analysis should new information come to light on any one individual.

In the end, there were thirteen men for whom I could not determine where they spent the bulk of their careers (see Table 4.1). I classified these men as "mixed/indeterminate," a category that reflects the vagaries that bring evidence to light. While we are better informed about the careers of men from Rome, Italy, and Africa than those from Spain and Gaul because of the survival of *cursus* inscriptions there,[20] gaps in our knowledge remain. A man attested only with two offices from two different career paths belongs in the "mixed/indeterminate" category since it is impossible to determine which office better reflects where he devoted his energies. (Ae)milius Florus Paternus, for example, held an office in the imperial administrative career path (*comes sacrarum largitionum,* 396–398) after holding one in the senatorial civic career path (proconsul of Africa, 393).[21] A man known only as praetorian prefect also belongs in the "mixed/indeterminate" category because this office, found in both the senatorial civic and imperial bureaucratic paths, is not distinctive enough to allow for a more precise classification.

Each career path included different offices. The senatorial civic career path, as it developed over the course of the fourth century, included the traditional republican magistracies, quaestor and/or praetor or suffect consul, and then a provincial governorship *(consularis, corrector)* or a civic office once associated with the diocesan administration *(vicarius, comes,* or at times *praefectus Augustalis)* or proconsul. Some aristocrats rose to the highest offices that bore the rank of *illustris:* the urban prefect, praetorian prefect, or, rarely, ordinary consul. The praetorian prefecture had been outside the career of the senatorial aristocrat in the early empire, but the development of regional prefectures in the fourth century and the changing nature of the duties of the prefects, now divorced entirely from military concerns, made this an influential civic office filled by aristocrats in the fourth century as part of a senatorial civic *cursus honorum.*[22]

The aristocrat involved in this career path at the level of provincial governor or higher gained social prestige, but he also confronted problems that called for administrative skills. Symmachus' *Relationes* to the emperor reveal that his year as urban prefect in 384 was taken up with a series of crises— corn shortages, riots, public disturbances, and bureaucratic dilemmas.[23] Because of the duties and expertise required, the higher the senatorial civic office, the longer was its tenure.[24] In pursuing a senatorial civic career, an aristocrat might also be called upon to act as a judge on a special commission, or he might be sent on a special embassy to court where he made contacts with imperial bureaucrats and/or the emperor. Clodius Octavianus, sent by the senate to Julian, earned the emperor's respect and favor: Octavianus was honored with the title of *comes primi ordinis* and appointed proconsul of Africa.[25]

Proximity to the emperor and his court offered possibilities for upward mobility especially for those pursuing an imperial bureaucratic career. If a man became the head of one of the imperial offices (*magister epistularum, libellorum*, etc.), he received *clarissimus* status or, after Gratian, *spectabilis* status. If he was designated one of the major palatine ministers (*quaestor sacri palatii, comes sacrarum largitionum, comes rei privatae, magister officiorum*) that entailed membership in the imperial consistory, he was granted senatorial aristocratic status and the rank of *spectabilis* or, after Gratian, that of *illustris*.[26] Imperial administrators could also attain the praetorian prefectureship or ordinary consulship, which conferred the rank of *illustris*. Both the imperial bureaucratic and the senatorial career path included the office of praetorian prefect since more men were needed in this office in this period. Indeed, until the 360s this office included both regional prefects as well as the old-style praetorian prefects who were attached to an emperor and acted as his deputy.[27]

The four major palatine ministers had close contact with the emperor, for they were included in the imperial consistory. These were influential positions since, among their duties, the major palatine ministers recommended appointments to numerous positions. Indeed, in a world where patronage counted, connection with the imperial consistory was an honor that a man wanted to publicize; men who had received the honorific title of count (*comes primi ordinis*, a title introduced by Constantine) would specify that they held this honor within the consistory (*intra consistorium*) to distinguish themselves from men who were honored as counts at court or in imperial service.[28]

The offices that were part of the imperial bureaucratic career path were increasingly formalized and tied to senatorial rank over the course of the century. In the 340s Constantius II raised the prestige of many imperial bureaucratic posts initiated by Constantine.[29] As I noted in Chapter 2, this trend continued, leading to the codification of this career path by Valentinian in 372, with some additional alterations under Gratian in 380 and 381.[30] The high status of these offices appears toward the end of the century, where we find Messianus holding high senatorial civic office (proconsul of Africa, 385) before advancing into a high court office (*comes rei privatae*, 389); twenty-five years earlier, Publius Ampelius held one of the four high court offices (*magister officiorum*, possibly in 358) prior to a string of senatorial civic offices (culminating with the proconsulship of Africa in 364 and urban prefecture in 371–372).[31]

It was also possible to enter the aristocracy by holding a high office in the military. The highest ranking generals with the office of *magister militum* or *magister equitum et peditum* had *illustris* status; a *comes rei militaris* had *spectabilis* or *clarissimus* standing; and even a *dux*, a lower-level command position, was granted the clarissimate after the reign of Valentinian I and Valens.[32]

Religion is a career in the modern sense only for Christians (i.e., bishops, priests, or monks), since pagan priesthoods did not require full-time activity in the same way that Christian office did.[33] Pagan aristocrats generally held priesthoods alongside senatorial, civic, or imperial administrative office. Claudius Hermogenianus Caesarius is typical in this regard; he held several senatorial civic offices, including proconsul of Africa (before 379) and urban prefect in 374, along with a prestigious priesthood, the *quindecimvir sacris faciundis*.[34] However, since some aristocrats (seventeen in all) are known to us only as the holders of pagan priesthoods, I recorded these men in this category.

The Process of Appointment

Appointment to the highest offices in the senatorial civic, imperial bureaucratic, and military career paths required the approval of the emperor. Although this system allowed emperors to appoint coreligionists if they chose to do so, a consideration of the appointment process indicates that imperial choices were constrained by a number of considerations. Most notable among these was the incentive to maintain legitimacy in the eyes of other aristocrats.

In making appointments, emperors relied greatly upon recommendations, verbal as well as written. The opinions of courtiers had an impact but so too did the reputation of the person giving the recommendation. Indeed, the good emperor Severus Alexander is described as recording, along with an appointment, the name of the man on whose recommendation a promotion was made.[35] Since appointment to office depended on the recommendation of a powerful person, many an aristocrat spent his time writing letters or speeches in support of one or another protégé. This process was so well known that it had its own vocabulary: the system of recommendations, or favors, was called *suffragium;* the person who recommended a candidate was called the *suffragator.*[36]

Recommendations were also of considerable weight in gaining even a low-level appointment in which the emperor's involvement was only indirect or formal. This was true of the designation of the lower magistracies of praetor and quaestor, which by 356 were primarily the responsibility of the senate.[37] The emperor generally signed off on the list of suggested candidates presented to him. But even these entry-level positions required the support of powerful aristocratic patrons. The speeches and letters of Symmachus exemplify the way the system worked; Symmachus used his influence and prestige to help friends, family, and dependents. In so doing, Symmachus increased his own status.[38]

The system worked toward making the recommender all the more influential because, unlike modern bureaucracies, the Roman appointment process was not based on the technical qualifications of the candidate. Merit, in the modern sense of being the "most able" and "best trained" for the job, was not considered in any objective way. Moreover, high officials, such as the urban prefect, did not even determine which men could best serve him. Rather, as we hear from the bitter complaints of the urban prefect Symmachus, men of poor experience or character were sent to him by the imperial government.[39] Only a handful of high officials, like the praetorian prefects, had a say in choosing who would serve them. Even this was rare and when it did occur, the choices were similarly based on the recommendations of powerful people.

Since recommendations were based on friendship and family ties, not qualifications, the system of *suffragium* highlights the important role that elite networks played in advancing a man's career. Consequently, the appointment process diffused the influence of any emperor or religious group. Even pro-Christian emperors could not use appointments as a simple weapon to advance Christianity; ties of patronage and favors exchanged lie behind decisions about appointments to high and low office. In addition, emperors had to take into account a range of other factors concerning the candidate, not all of which were religious—previous offices and performance of the candidate, his social origin, his loyalty, his lifestyle and cultural attainments, and the needs of the job.

Such considerations affected appointments even to those few positions that required technical expertise; the office of *quaestor sacri palatii*, for example, whose main function was to draft imperial constitutions, was usually filled by a lawyer or rhetorician. Yet in choosing a man for this powerful position, the emperor continued to follow the outlines of a system based on recommendations. In the military career path, training and leadership were critical for survival, and religious conformity may not have been a relevant factor at all. In the appointment process religious affiliation may have been one of many criteria taken into account, but the process itself diffused its importance and made it more or less relevant to advancement, depending upon circumstances and the career path followed.

Correlation of Career Paths with Religious Identification

In my study population pagans were more in evidence in the senatorial civic career path than in other career paths. Christians, on the other hand, were predominant in the imperial bureaucratic track. I shall discuss the reasons for these patterns at length below; here, I want to emphasize that the differences in the career paths of pagan and Christian aristocrats is one of the most significant results of the growth and differentiation that occurred within the aristocracy in the fourth and early fifth centuries. For aristocrats in military careers, however, there is evidence of only a weak association with Christianity. Finally, by the end of the fourth century, a new career option began to emerge for Christian aristocrats—that of church office. While the proportion of Christian *clarissimi* attracted to this new career was small, the aristocrats who followed this path are the first signs of important changes to come in the fifth century.

Senatorial Civic Career Path

The senatorial civic career path had long been the normative one, and it traditionally conferred the status and prestige so desired by late Roman aristocrats. Diocletian, Constantine, and their successors renewed the honors attached to the offices in this path and used them to attract senatorial aristocrats to state service and to support their rule.[40] Among senatorial aristocrats the ideal resurfaced that the senate was still, in the words of an early fourth-century panegyrist, "the flower of the world."[41] Later in the century Symmachus' father echoed conventional ideology in describing senatorial civic office as proof of aristocratic virtue and the inherited duty of this order.[42] In the late fifth century the Gallic aristocrat Sidonius Apollinaris can still proudly assert the honor inherited from his ancestor's senatorial civic office and praise a friend's appointment as urban prefect as simply living up to an illustrious heritage.[43]

In my study population pagans dominate the offices in this traditional senatorial aristocratic career path and were more likely than Christians to follow it: 69% (86 out of 125) of all pagans were in the senatorial civic career path as compared to 52% (49 out of 95) of all Christians (see Table 4.1).[44] Moreover, this career path attracted a disproportionate share of men from Rome and Italy, the core of the old senatorial aristocracy. Eighty-six percent of all Italians (55 out of 64) in my study followed a senatorial civic career path (see Table 4.2). These men, endowed with the requisite financial, social, and political resources, were best positioned to benefit from and successfully administer civic offices. Many belonged to established aristocratic families from Roman nobility, the sorts of men who proudly traced their heritage through a long series of consuls and praetorian prefects to the great families of the Republic. Among them are men like C. C(a)eionius Rufius Volusianus signo Lampadius, urban prefect of 365, son of C(a)eionius Rufius Albinus and grandson of C. C(a)eionius Rufius Volusianus; Ammianus described Lampadius as so proud of his lineage that "he felt even his spittle deserved praise."[45]

However, as the aspirations of the Gallic Apollinares indicate, the senatorial civic career path attracted provincial aristocrats as well. In this study population these men came primarily from Gaul and Africa; 26% of all Gauls (6 out of 23) and 86% of all Africans (12 out of 14) had senatorial civic careers (see Table 4.2). Provincials in this career path sometimes followed a somewhat different sequence of offices. Men from old Roman families were typically quaestors, praetors, provincial governors, and suffect consuls early on before gaining the highest offices in this path, whereas frequently men of provincial origin or of low status entered this career path by way of the law, by adlection, or by holding an imperial bureaucratic post.[46]

The senatorial civic career path, as with other career paths, included men of different abilities and social origins. We can be certain of nonaristocratic family origin for a few men in this career path, such as the pagan C. Iulius Rufinianus Ablabius Tatianus and the Christian Nummius Aemilianus Dexter, both of whom pursued mixed but mainly senatorial civic career paths.[47] As a group, the men in this path were less homogenous than had been the case in the early empire. However, the core of this group consisted of Roman and Italian aristocrats, many of whom traced their families back for centuries.

PAGANISM AND SENATORIAL CIVIC CAREERS. In my study population the association between paganism and the senatorial civic career path continued throughout most of the fourth century. Pagans predominated over Christians in senatorial civic careers until the time of Gratian, who ruled first with Valentinian I and later with Valentinian II (367–383). At this time, the tide shifted noticeably; 63% (12 out of 19) of the aristocrats in the senatorial civic career path were Christian as opposed to the 37% (7 out of 19) who were pagan (see Table 4.3).[48] After Valentinian II (i.e., after 392), the predominance of Christians in the senatorial civic career path is firm (see Table 4.3).

To men like Symmachus and the pagan aristocrats in his circle, it was the duty of the *boni* to take care of state affairs, and this entailed not only senatorial civic office but also public state cult positions. The conjunction of these two responsibilities comes out most forcefully in Symmachus' *Third State Paper*. In this document Symmachus, as urban prefect and as the envoy of the senate and the people, argues that the senate and the people want to ensure the continuity of the public cults that had for so long benefited the state.[49]

The association of polytheism with the well-being of the state justified holding both civic and priestly office, a pattern that informed the lives of other late Roman aristocrats as well. Aco Catullinus signo Philomathius, for example, united paganism with a senatorial civic career, following in the footsteps of his father, Aco Catullinus, proconsul of Africa in 317–318. (As far as we can determine, the senior Catullinus was the first clarissimate *praeses* of Byzacena in 313–314.) The son, Catullinus signo Philomathius, successfully held a string of senatorial civic offices—suffect consul, *praeses,* and vicar of Africa—in the same area as his father before attaining the prestigious praetorian prefectureship in 341 (probably in Italy), urban prefectureship in 342–344, and, unusually, consulship in 349.[50] Catullinus signo Philomathius' paganism made him a good candidate for praetorian prefect of Italy, an office that pagans filled for most of the century (see Appendix 4). One testament to his attachment to paganism is the younger Catullinus' dedication to Jupiter Optimus Maximus. This same man was apparently also responsible for the law that preserved the temples in Rome from imperial prohibition of sacrifice (*C.Th.* 16.10.3). His daughter, Fabia Aconia Paulina, inherited her father's religiosity; she wed the eminent pagan Praetextatus and actively participated in cults alongside her husband.[51]

Symmachus' own career is emblematic. The son of a pagan *illustris*, Symmachus was quaestor, then praetor, before becoming a provincial governor, *corrector Lucaniae et Brittiorum,* in 365, and then *proconsul Africae* in 373. He attained the office of urban prefect in 384–385 and consul in 391.[52] The public prestige attached to such offices inspired Symmachus to pursue this path and to spend lavishly on the games that were the requisite components of office. Alongside his civic offices, Symmachus also held the pagan priesthood, *pontifex maior*, as early as 365. In this honor, too, he followed the example set by his much-admired father, Avianius.

Symmachus' circle of friends reveals as well the characteristic conjunction of senatorial civic office and paganism that survived into the late fourth century. His brother, Celsinus Titianus, was *vicarius* of Africa, presumably after his quaestorship and praetorship, and probably also *pontifex Vestae et Solis*.[53] This same conjunction marks the careers of Praetextatus and Nicomachus Flavianus, two of the most prominent pagans in Symmachus' world. Although these men may have been unusual in their conscious defense of the value of paganism to the state, they could claim, nonetheless, that their own pursuit of a senatorial civic career in conjunction with support for the pagan state cult followed the pattern of generations of Roman aristocrats before them.

The association between paganism and senatorial civic office extended even to specific offices. Praetorian prefects in Italy were almost entirely pagan until 368, and then pagans and Christians are both attested until 395, after which point only Christians are attested (see Appendix 4). The office of provincial governor of Campania, one attractive to Roman nobles at the commencement of their career, was similarly held predominantly by pagans.[54]

Some explanation for this strong, ongoing association of paganism with the traditional senatorial civic career path, so deeply ingrained in senatorial aristocrats from Rome and Italy in particular, is called for. This group, the core of the established senatorial aristocracy, were wealthy landowners with the social and economic resources necessary to pursue a civic *cursus;* heavy expenditures on the games were required for the entry-level offices to this career path.[55] For centuries these families had held civic office as a sign of status and honor. This group had also sought public recognition by holding pagan priesthoods and by funding temples and buildings in Rome and Italy. Such associations were deeply engrained; Praetextatus proudly associated himself with the rebuilding of the Portico of the Consenting Gods in Rome.[56]

For centuries pagan religious responsibilities were part of the traditional duties of Roman magistrates. In the third century Tertullian felt such religious duties made it impossible for a Christian to be a magistrate, for as such he would be forced to sacrifice, to let contracts for the provisioning of sacrificial victims, to assign to others the maintenance of pagan temples, and to present pagan spectacles.[57] Constantine faced a similar problem when he, in Rome as *triumphator,* was expected to sacrifice to Jupiter Optimus Maximus; it took an emperor to break with such engrained traditions.[58] But it was not until a 341 law outlawing all *superstitiones,* including arguably pagan sacrifice in the West, that sacrifice would have been removed from the list of duties of magistrates.[59]

The games and circuses, however, remained the primary responsibility of the senatorial civic magistrates, with imperial approval. Deeply rooted in late Roman civic life, they served important political and social functions. A string of fourth-century Christian emperors attempted to redefine the paganism in these events as secular, neutral entertainments *(voluptates),* devoid of any pagan significance.[60] But emperors could not so suddenly change the meaning of the games, and pagans and Christians alike continued to view them otherwise. Even imperial laws against pagan sacrifice, a far easier ban to enforce, went unheeded in places, and especially in Rome if Libanius can be believed.[61] Imperial attempts to neutralize the games may have provoked unintended reactions; as P. Sabbatini Tumolesi notes, the increased emphasis on gladiatorial games in fourth-century Rome is most likely a response to Christian attempts to neutralize these spectacles.[62]

Even Christian emperors saw that it was advantageous for pagans to rule pagans. As noted above, the praetorian prefects of Italy were pagan until 368, and were a strong presence until the end of the century. In Africa the proconsul was almost always pagan until 374, and pagans continued to be appointed thereafter (see Appendix 4).[63] Christian emperors may have slowed down the entry of Christians into the civic career path by appointing pagans in areas where there were religious controversies. So, for example, the pagan Praetextatus was made urban prefect in Rome to reassert order after the riots between the supporters of Damasus against those of Ursinus for the Roman bishopric.[64] Even if inadvertent, imperial appointments reinforced the association between paganism and the senatorial civic career path.

The aristocratic networks of family and friends that made it possible to advance in this career path also reinforced the ties between a senatorial civic career and paganism, even as these limited the influence of the emperor. The pagan aristocrats in Rome were in a particularly strong position to advance their friends and family to the offices of quaestor and praetor, the launching platform for a civic career. Reforms in the adlection process had strengthened their influence. By the later years of Constantine's rule, the senate in Rome had acquired direct control over the lower offices of prefect and quaestor, the gateposts for a senatorial civic *cursus*.[65] To win nomination by one's peers in Rome entailed winning the support of a group that remained largely pagan into the last quarter of the fourth century. The extant *Orations* of Symmachus reveal the ways in which aristocrats helped one another advance in this path, as when Symmachus supported the son of Trygetius for the praetorship or used his influence to gain senatorial rank for Severus. At other times, Symmachus sought to relieve certain senators of the costly expenditures for the games attached to the praetorship, as in his speech on behalf of Valerius Fortunatus.[66]

Pagans did not only support pagans; aristocratic friendships did not divide simply along religious lines. Symmachus was typical in embracing within his orbit men of both religious affiliations. However, the mere fact that pagan aristocrats could and did advance the interests of their friends and family reinforced the impression that these offices were tied to pagans.

The perception of the association between a senatorial civic career and paganism would almost certainly have influenced men aspiring to such a career. We see this, for example, in a letter dated around 398 from the Christian Paulinus of Nola to Licentius, a youthful poet and pupil of Augustine seeking clarissimate status. Paulinus tried to undermine the attractions of a senatorial civic career in part because of its pagan elements, and so advised Licentius as follows:

> Avoid the slippery dangers of exacting state service. Position has an inviting title, but it brings evil slavery and a wretched end . . . Those who voluntarily but wretchedly put up with Rome know how great a price is paid in sweat and loss of honour for the distinction of a palace cloak or a Roman office . . . Good grief! Is it for such men, Licentius, that you linger in Rome? Do you repeatedly address as lords and greet with bowed head men whom you see as slaves of wood and stone? They worship gold and silver under the name of gods; their religion is what diseased greed loves.[67]

The strength of Paulinus' venom shows the powerful hold that Christians perceived pagans to have on these offices.

Indeed, the perception that pagans controlled the senatorial civic career path appears widespread. In the late fourth-century anonymous *Poem against the Pagans*, a virulent attack on an unnamed pagan official includes the accusation that the pagan in question used his office to support paganism:

> Thus in his madness he wanted to damn many worshippers of Christ were they willing to die outside the Law, and would give honors to those he would ensnare, through demonic artifice, forgetful of their true selves, seeking to influence the minds of certain people by gifts and to make others profane with a small bribe . . . He who wanted pious agreements to replace the laws had Leucadius put in charge of the African farms, to corrupt Marcianus so that he might be his proconsul.[68]

The accusation that this "demonic" pagan consul used his civic office to "damn" lower officials by leading them away from true faith is evidence of Christian fears. This attitude may lie, too, behind a 391 law that targets provincial governors who "either on tour or in the city" exploited their official position to enter temples and hold formal pagan ceremonies.[69] Both show the perception that pagan aristocrats as holders of senatorial civic offices were able, even during a time of religious change, to use their positions to influence others to follow their pagan ways. That pagan office holders did use their offices in this way is a very real possibility.

CHRISTIANITY AND SENATORIAL CIVIC CAREERS. The conservative, pagan appearance of the senate and of those in the senatorial civic career path gradually changed. By the end of the fourth century, it had become easier for Christians to perform the tasks that were required of officials in a senatorial civic career path. By 365, for example, we find a law stipulating that Christians should not be appointed custodians of temples.[70] And prohibitions on pagan sacrifice, reiterated most forcefully at the end of the century, would have eased the tensions felt by Christian magistrates about this part of their public duties.[71] Ambrose claimed there was a significant number, indeed a majority, of Christians in the Roman senate in the 380s.[72]

Although Ambrose's statement may or may not have been true in the 380s, Christians did gradually succeed in senatorial civic careers. In this study, pagans and Christians become equally prevalent in senatorial civic offices during the years 367–383 (see Table 4.3), and there was a sizable representation of Christians in these positions even earlier in the century. Under the sons of Constantine (337–361), 32% (7 out of 22) of the men who had senatorial civic careers were Christian; 68% (15 out of 22) were pagan. This representation demonstrates that as early as mid-century Christians were far from rare in traditional offices of a senatorial civic career.

Christians were eager to pursue status and prestige via a traditional senatorial civic career. Nearly two out of three of the Christians in the period under Gratian, who ruled with Valentinian I and later with Valentinian II (367–383), were found in this career path (see Table 4.3). The young Licentius, the addressee of Paulinus' letter, and Paulinus himself had embarked on such careers; Paulinus had become a suffect consul in 378 and consular (or proconsul) of Campania in 381 before turning away from a secular career to pursue an ascetic lifestyle. His decision was seen as extraordinary; Ambrose describes the shock felt by his contemporaries at Paulinus' renunciation of secular ambitions: "What will our leading citizens say? It is unthinkable that a man of such family, such background, such genius, fitted with such eloquence should retire from the Senate and that the succession of so noble a family should be broken."[73]

Christian senatorial aristocrats, like Paulinus, who hailed from old families were expected and pressured as much as pagans to follow conventional expectations into a senatorial civic career. Paulinus' turning away from worldly concerns was associated primarily with ascetic Christians in the late fourth century. Only ascetics, like Melania the Elder, mourned the worldly ambitions of their offspring if they died still eager for "senatorial dignity."[74] Most fourth-century Christian senatorial aristocrats appear to have been as interested as their pagan peers in gaining status and honor by holding senatorial civic office. By the 370s and 380s, Christian aristocrats were increasingly pursuing these honors alongside their pagan peers.

Anicius Paulinus, a Christian from one of the most well-established old Roman families, lived up to the traditional ideals of the aristocrat and sought to distinguish himself by his senatorial civic career. A proconsul of Campania, he was prefect of Rome in 380 and honored by Capua as *patronus originalis.*[75] Like his eminent contemporary, Sextus Petronius Probus, Anicius saw no conflict between his Christianity and the accretion of secular honors in this, the most traditionally pagan of the paths open to senatorial aristocrats.[76]

Imperial Bureaucratic Career Path

Influenced by the work of A. Chastagnol, several historians have asserted that the imperial bureaucratic career path attracted provincial elites and offered them senatorial aristocratic standing.[77] Since these men were dependent on imperial favor to pursue their careers, historians tend to assume that they were also so influenced by the emperor that they became Christian.[78] Only some of these assumptions can be supported. Careers in the imperial bureaucracy did offer provincials a well-trodden road to the clarissimate, and here the influence of pro-Christian emperors is marked. Nevertheless, imperial influence has been over emphasized. Other forces were at work as well. The social and cultural networks within which aristocrats advanced in this career path, the system of recommendations and patronage, were also significant factors in making this the most Christian of all career paths.

WHAT SORTS OF MEN WENT INTO THE IMPERIAL BUREAUCRACY? Certain offices within the imperial bureaucracy required specialized knowledge and abilities that ambitious provincials could acquire. For example, one of the four great palatine ministries, the *quaestor sacri palatii,* had as his main function the drafting of imperial constitutions for the emperor and consistory. As a member of the consistory, some late fourth-century holders of this office acted as legal advisers to the emperor, although the primary focus of the quaestor seems to have been on the style of imperial law.[79] Since this office required rhetorical training and some legal knowledge, often a rhetorician, like Ausonius, or a barrister, like the Gallic Claudius Postumus Dardanus, held it. Teachers of rhetoric and law trained ambitious provincials who sought these skills to advance themselves.[80]

A number of men in the imperial bureaucratic career path began life as notaries or shorthand scribes. Their duties brought them into intimate contact with powerful people. A prestigious corps of such notaries, established by Constantine to take down the minutes of the imperial consistory, attracted so many applicants that the eastern orator, Libanius, complained that the parents of his students were far more intent upon their learning shorthand than rhetoric and philosophy. In the East, especially under Constantius II, notaries undertook important missions, to the disgust of more established aristocrats.[81] Similarly, in the West some notaries held imperial bureaucratic office before becoming members of the imperial consistory.[82] One such figure, Felix, a notary of unknown origin, was appointed by Constantius in 360 to be Julian's *magister officiorum,* head of the other chief palatine offices. Sent to Gaul, Felix did his job so well that Julian subsequently made him *comes sacrarum largitionum,* responsible for the public monies (the gold mines and mints, taxes, payment of monies to the army and civil service).[83] Another notary, the pagan Decentius, later became *magister officiorum* in the East in 364–365.[84] Both men had demonstrated skill in administration and gained the support of prestigious men, including the emperor.

As these instances show, provincials were attracted to imperial bureaucratic careers in part because they could advance more easily here. The key to advancement lay, in large measure, with the support of a powerful figure, either within or without the imperial bureaucracy. The most obvious potential recommenders were powerful people within the same career track, especially those who held prestigious imperial bureaucratic posts at court. One such man was the Christian Flavius Eugenius who spent his entire life in offices in the imperial bureaucracy. Designated as a *comes primi ordinis* at court, and then *magister officiorum* in the West under Constans, he used his positions to support Athanasius, among others.[85] Ausonius, himself a provincial, showed great interest in advancing the interests of other imperial bureaucrats; among his other efforts, he supported a law that equated the rank of imperial secretaries *(notarii)* with that of the provincial governors *(consulares),* thereby enabling the former to claim clarissimate status.[86]

Provincials in the imperial bureaucratic career path could find and more easily make associations with men like themselves, from the provinces and often of nonclarissimate origin. Although they may have lacked the social networks and economic resources necessary to pursue a senatorial civic career, provincials of ambition and talent found opportunities for advancement within the imperial bureaucracy. And they could use their proximity to the court and its powerful figures, including even the emperor himself, to advance, as did the Spaniard Maternus Cynegius under his fellow countryman, Theodosius.[87] This study population supports the view that imperial court careers attracted provincials; nearly all of the men in this path are either of provincial (42%, 11 out of 26) or unattested (54%, 14 out of 26) provenance (see Tables 4.1 and 4.2).

CHRISTIANITY AND IMPERIAL BUREAUCRATIC CAREERS. My study indicates a link not only between provincial origin and imperial bureaucratic careers but a further association of this career path with Christianity. In my study population 19% of the Christians (18 out of 95) followed this career path as compared with 6% (8 out of 125) of the pagans (see Table 4.1). In other words, Christians were more likely than pagans to have made their careers in the imperial bureaucracy. When these men are grouped according to time period, this association begins to emerge in the reign of Constantine's sons, beginning in the 340s with Constans, Constantine II, and Constantius II (see Table 4.3). But thereafter the association between Christianity and the imperial bureaucracy continues throughout the fourth century, with the only reversal noted during the reigns of the pagan emperor Julian and Valentinian I as sole ruler (see Table 4.3).

Why were Christians more likely than pagans to find a home in the imperial bureaucracy? In part, the provincial origins of the men in this career path may help to explain the predominance of Christians here. As observed in Chapter 3, Christianity seems to have spread more rapidly among the aristocrats from the provinces in the West. Some of these provincials may well have brought their Christianity with them as they moved up into the imperial bureaucracy.

The social mobility that many of these provincial aristocrats experienced may also have made them more open to Christianity. Many had moved, geographically, as part of their training or career. Such movement exposed these men to new relationships, enabling them to build bonds with men who were, like themselves, seeking a future via their careers. At the same time, their careers fractured the ties to place and family that were the cornerstones of traditional paganism. Under such circumstances the bonds that were formed with co-careerists could replace the old ties to provenance. The vignette described by Ponticianus in Augustine's *Confessions* noted earlier in this chapter captures well the strength of the bond that a man could develop with fellow bureaucrats. In the absence of tradition tied to family and place, religion could enable men to share areas of their lives. Christianity was especially well suited to this role.

The networks that favored the dissemination of Christianity among imperial bureaucrats came not only from colleagues but also from the emperor. If the emperor was an ardent Christian who wanted to be surrounded by coreligionists, his known preferences for Christians may well have influenced those who wanted to advance through an imperial bureaucratic career. Since the four palatine offices represented the pinnacle of this career track and each entailed membership in the imperial consistory, an ambitious bureaucrat easily perceived the advantages to sharing an emperor's religious leanings.

Some emperors openly expressed their desire to be surrounded by coreligionists at court. According to Eusebius, Constantine "was attended only by a few whose faith and pious devotion he esteemed."[88] Although Constantine had pagans at his court as well as Christians, in time it nonetheless became known that being a Christian was a desirable trait there. Christian writers promulgated this perception; Sozomen, for one, reiterates this point, noting that "the emperor did not require military aid; for Christian men *belonging to the palace* went from city to city bearing imperial letters" that ordered the destruction of pagan idols.[89] Libanius noted too that the imperial consistory under Constantius was hostile to paganism.[90] Such perceptions existed in the West as well as the East. Ausonius' *Paschal Verses* make clear that the court participated in Easter celebrations, and such communal activities reinforced the view that it was desirable under a Christian emperor that imperial bureaucrats at the highest levels be Christian.

The preponderance of Christians in the imperial court career path reflects, in part, the influence of Christian emperors, notably Constantine, Constantius II, Gratian, and Theodosius, all of whom expressed their strong religious preferences openly and often. That emperors could influence men in the imperial bureaucracy is suggested, too, by the conversions of two court bureaucrats, Felix and Helpidius, from Christianity to paganism under the pagan emperor Julian.[91] By 408 the desire of the emperor to be surrounded by coreligionists is enshrined in law: "We prohibit those persons who are hostile to the Catholic sect to perform imperial service within the palace, so that no person who disagrees with us in faith and in religion should be associated with Us in any way."[92] Although directed primarily at heretics, this law was also used against pagans.

Although the influence of the emperor was strong in the making and breaking of careers in imperial service, it would be a mistake to ignore the importance of elite networks in advancing new men and in spreading Christianity. Direct imperial involvement was often only a formality, especially in decisions concerning men in the lower bureaucratic offices. So, for example, the pagan Sextilius Agesilaus Aedesius, who began as a barrister, held several lower offices in the imperial bureaucracy, interrupting his bureaucratic career to hold a provincial governorship in Spain. He was not known to have had ties to the court but evidently advanced because of the recommendations of powerful friends. He owed his success to the system of *suffragium*.[93] Similarly, the Christian Ausonius was able to advance family and friends into prestigious positions, both inside and outside the imperial bureaucracy, but many of his protégés did not themselves have direct ties to the emperor.

The forces that tended to work toward the spread of Christianity in imperial bureaucratic circles, in and out of court, were often viewed as opportunism in the rhetorical tracts of Christians. The bishop Ambrose, for example, writing some twenty years after Julian, criticized a man for expecting that his recent conversion would facilitate attaining a high administrative position.[94] In 401 Augustine observed that many believed it was his desire to facilitate his municipal career as an *exactor* that led a certain Faustinus to convert; his paganism was said to have so upset the populace in a Carthage church that they cried out: "Let the more powerful men not be pagans, so that the pagans might not rule over Christians."[95] The perception that the imperial bureaucrat could succeed far better as a Christian was in itself a factor that favored the spread of Christianity among men pursuing careers in the imperial bureaucracy.

But opportunism alone does not explain the spread of Christianity among aristocrats in this career path.[96] Rather, Christianity spread through the associations, the shared experiences, and the ties that developed between like-minded, and similarly status-conscious, men involved in a common world of administration and law. Christianity soon became part of their common culture.

Military Career Path

The men who held clarissimate rank by virtue of their military office were technically members of the senatorial aristocracy. These were the men who held the highest military offices; only with Valentinian I were commanders at the level of *dux* rewarded clarissimate standing. I argued in Chapter 2 that these men should be considered part of the senatorial aristocracy not only for legal reasons. It is clear that they coveted status and were eager for the acceptance of fellow aristocrats. Although they were themselves often removed from the literary interests prized by other aristocrats, many were eager for their children to share in the aristocratic status culture, to be raised with the manners, behaviors, and, to a certain extent, values of the established group of large landowning senatorial families of Rome and Italy. At the same time, as I noted in Chapter 2, the degree to which these men ascribed to the aristocratic status culture varied, and the evidence suggests that in certain respects the military aristocracy constituted a quite distinct group within the clarissimate.

Their expertise, training, experiences, and, to some degree, provenance made the military aristocracy different from other segments of the aristocracy. High military officers were involved in warfare or in setting military strategy either on campaigns or at court. Their talents were required for preparing and leading troops to victory; the general Generidus, for one, is specifically praised for his efficiency in training troops.[97] But successful generals also had to have considerable administrative skills to organize a campaign and lead a force. They had to demonstrate the qualities of leadership that would earn them the respect and loyalty of their troops.[98]

Unlike aristocrats in other career paths, a growing number of high military officers came not only from the provinces but from non-Roman or barbarian origin, being of Frankish, Germanic, Sarmatian, Vandal, or Gothic provenance, or from areas in the eastern empire. Some were the products of mixed marriages between Romans and non-Romans, as was the marriage of the general Gaudentius, a Scythian, to a noble Roman lady.[99] These men were recognizably different to their contemporaries: their blond hair showed northern provenance; their beards, too, were associated with barbarian origin; and their accents distinguished them. Some military men were denigrated for their "barbarian" provenance, especially in times of political crisis. Thus the defeated general Fravitta was accused of failing to pursue Gainas because both were barbarians.[100] Aurelius Victor, for one, complained that the senators, by their retreat from military service, left the armed forces to soldiers and barbarians.[101] Such hostility contributed to the alienation of the military aristocracy from other segments of the aristocracy and civil society.

Emperors reinforced the distance between the military and other elites in a variety of ways. The attire of the military aristocracy was, by law, different from that of the senatorial aristocrat in state service; generals wore the *cingulum* of the solider as a sign of status. And, most significant, emperors allowed little movement between the military and civilian career paths.[102] When an emperor wanted to reward a successful military man, he named him as consul, an honorific title with no civic duties.

At the same time, emperors were intent on forging strong ties with the military aristocracy since their survival depended on them. In fact, all of the fourth-century imperial dynasties emerged from military circles. These military emperors turned to their fellow provincial officers to ensure that those who served them would be loyal. Valentinian advanced Pannonians; Theodosius advanced Spaniards. Some emperors tried to ensure loyalty by making their military officers dependent only on them; thus they appointed new men and barbarians (i.e., non-Romans) who were more easily isolated from other groups within society, as did the emperor Constantine.[103] Barbarians had the requisite military expertise to succeed, and it was their military expertise, not their culture, that the emperors valued. Moreover, the troops, who were also often barbarian in origin, at times preferred to follow leaders more like themselves, with professional military skills, and they were sometimes openly hostile to imperial bureaucrats.[104]

To further ensure the loyalty of the military aristocracy, emperors entered into ties of friendship and marriage with this aristocratic group. So, for example, Eusebia, the daughter of the eastern *magister militum*, Flavius Eusebius, probably married the emperor Constantius II.[105] The daughter of the Frankish general Bauto later wed the emperor Arcadius, and the powerful general Stilicho married the emperor Theodosius' niece and adopted daughter, Serena. Stilicho's daughters, Maria and Thermantia, were united to the emperor Honorius.[106]

The military aristocracy was not, however, thoroughly separated from other senatorial aristocrats. As members of imperial circles, high army officers worked and socialized with others in imperial service, with men in the imperial bureaucratic career path, courtiers, and with those in the imperial consistory most of all. Not surprisingly, we find them involved in political intrigues with such men, sharing similar aims and perspectives; some barbarians did undertake friendship ties with Roman aristocrats, as Bauto and Richomeres did with Symmachus.[107] And some military aristocrats did wed aristocrats from families outside their sphere, although marriages to nonmilitary aristocrats were rare in the late fourth and early fifth centuries.[108] But in many respects military aristocrats were separated from other aristocrats, and that distance reinforced the links that men in this career path forged with one another and with the emperor.

Since most military aristocrats were tied to the fourth-century emperors for advancement, it would seem likely that this group, like the imperial bureaucratic elite, would be more open to Christianity. There is some evidence in R. von Haehling's study of high office holders that this was the case. Von Haehling found a slightly higher proportion of Christians than pagans holding the prestigious post of *magister militum* in the West. He noted that this predominance sharpened greatly after 423.[109]

Most historians, however, do not see a strong link between the military aristocracy and Christianity. They argue that the religious affiliations of military men were largely irrelevant to advancement at the uppermost levels.[110] Skill in command, a vital trait in an empire more or less continually at war, would be much more important than religious practice in the advancement of military men. What emperor would care about a military man's religion if he showed the ability to lead and defeat the enemy in battle? Moreover, the army was largely recruited from pagan areas. These recruitment patterns brought in a constant flow of pagans into an organization that long had a tradition of tolerance of religious diversity.[111] Military men had little incentive to change their traditional religious preferences even if they advanced into aristocratic society. For these reasons, many historians think it likely that the military and its leadership remained predominantly pagan, at least until 360 and for a good time after that.[112]

In my study population, which included all clarissimate military men and hence was somewhat broader than that defined by R. von Haehling, military aristocrats were only slightly more likely to be Christian than pagan, especially in the last decades of the fourth century (see Tables 4.1, 4.3).[113] The close ties between emperors and high army officers may have had at least a minor influence on the religious preferences of the military elite. Certain emperors appear deeply engaged in efforts to influence the religiosity of the military elites who served them: Constantine gave sermons to his courtly entourage; Constantius and subsequent emperors held Christian services at court, which generals as well as imperial bureaucrats attended.[114]

At the same time, no emperor could afford to overvalue the importance of religion in selecting military leaders.[115] Even the most Christian emperors prized military victory over religious conformity. The devout Gratian turned to the pagan Frank, Flavius Bauto, as his *magister equitum* from 380–383, and the Christian emperor Honorius appointed the pagan Generidus as *magister militum* in 408–409, even though doing so forced him to withdraw his directive that civil and military officials must be Catholic Christians.[116] In these key appointments a host of considerations having to do with command priorities outweighed religious ones. Reasons like these explain why the military aristocracy was not overwhelmingly Christian.

Moreover, military aristocrats were very dependent on one another; they, too, sought honor from their immediate circles and pursued wealth to sustain their position. Victory and booty enabled the generals to reward and patronize dependents and to live in accord with peer expectations. They tended to intermarry within other military elites to build friendship ties and accrue honor. And, like other aristocrats, they sought to advance family and friends, although their ambitions tended to focus on high military positions; Cretio, *comes* of Africa, placed his son in military service and helped him to become *protector domesticus* under Valentinian I.[117] The strong ties of the military elite to one another limited the influence of the emperor over this group and their religious orientation.

Religious Career Path

CHURCH OFFICES.   In a detail preserved by Jerome, the pagan senatorial aristocrat Praetextatus said mockingly to Damasus, the pope of Rome, "Make me the Bishop of Rome and I will immediately be a Christian."[118] This quip suggests that to Praetextatus' mind, there was only one church office that was in any way comparable with his status as senatorial aristocrat. Not even the bishopric of Rome, the most powerful Christian office available in the West, would necessarily attract a Roman aristocrat. Status and prestige, friendships and family ties led the late Roman aristocrat to the traditional aristocratic career paths. The large proportion of Christians in the senatorial civic career path suggests that most Christian aristocrats chose not to devote their energies to pursuing church office.

Only a small proportion of Christian aristocrats devoted themselves to a career in the church as priest, bishop, or monastic leader. A mere 12% (11 out of 95) of the Christians were found in mainly religious careers. Of these, four had first entered into a senatorial civic career path before turning to a religious one (see Table 4.1).[119] By the end of the fourth century the prestige of the church and a bishopric had risen considerably, but, even so, only a few aristocrats in the West chose this new career option. Church office lacked the status and advantages associated with other aristocratic career paths.

The expectation that a Christian aristocrat would pursue a secular career is underscored by the shocked response to Paulinus of Nola's decision to devote himself to the church. Ambrose describes the reaction of leading citizens, who find it "unthinkable that a man of such family, such background, such genius" would make this choice.[120] Paulinus' decision in 394 to become a priest at Barcelona and later bishop in Nola may have dismayed contemporaries, but, as R. Van Dam observed, there is some irony in the fact that Paulinus' religious career ultimately served well the interests of his family and friends; as bishop of Nola, Paulinus attained the resources that enabled him to protect their worldly assets.[121]

Aristocratic discomfort with Paulinus' career choice fits well with the disdain ascribed to other fourth-century aristocrats for careers in the church. Valerius Pinianus, for example, had devoted himself to asceticism, but he refused to accept a priesthood insistently offered him at Hippo.[122] Paulinus of

Pella, too, was hesitant. He had been appointed *comes privatarum largitionum* by Attalus around 414–415 but had not been successful in his secular career. Subsequently, he had a religious experience that, along with his worldly troubles, made him seriously consider becoming a monk, but he ultimately decided to perform penance instead. After his financial position improved, he remained a layman until his death.[123]

Ambrose was among the first aristocrats in the West to hold a bishopric. The son of a former praetorian prefect of Gaul, Ambrose had pursued a senatorial civic career first as advocate, then assessor, and, later, consular of Aemilia and Liguria. His early training in law and his desire to advance by this roundabout sequence of offices have suggested to his most recent biographer that he was on the margins of the Roman elite.[124] In 374 he was sent to Milan to restore peace and order in a city torn apart by rival Arian and orthodox claimants to the episcopate. His senatorial civic career ended with his acceptance of the bishopric. Ambrose's standing as an aristocrat gave him a distinct advantage in establishing his objectives as bishop of Milan from 374 to 397. In a manual devoted to the duties of priests, Ambrose underscores the novelty of his decision, observing that each one is wont to follow his parent's choice of lifestyle. A father in military service predisposes his son to follow his lead, but, he claims, that is not the case for those who choose to follow a career as a Christian priest.[125]

Two other aristocratic Christians, Marcellus and C. Vettius Aquilinus Iuvencus, were called *sacerdotes*, which may indicate either presbyter or bishop; both are dated to the fourth century.[126] Not all aristocrats following religious careers in this study were bishops.[127] Venantius was noted as an ascetic and a priest.[128] Arsenius' career, in the late fourth and early fifth centuries, indicates a changing attitude toward church office. Born to a Roman senatorial family, he served as deacon in Rome before being summoned to Constantinople to act as a tutor to Theodosius' young sons. Arsenius was an active figure in the imperial court until, around the age of forty, he devoted himself to the life of a desert ascetic.[129]

The aristocratic reluctance to enter church office changed markedly in the first half of the fifth century. Political upheavals and the growing prestige of the church made an episcopate increasingly desirable. By 400 Sulpicius Severus in Gaul complained about the seeking of church office for "depraved ambitions."[130] In Gaul especially, in the second quarter of the fifth century and after, striking examples of aristocratic families turning from senatorial civic careers to religious ones exist, giving rise to the growth of an "ecclesiastical aristocracy".[131] After 423—the end of this study—several aristocrats held bishoprics or became monks, including Hilarius, bishop of Arles from ca. 428, and Petronius, a monk in his youth and bishop of Bologna ca. 425–450. The invasions and sack of Rome in 410 called into question the viability of a senatorial civic career. Men were seeking church office, and were accused of ambition for doing so by Pope Zosimus in Rome in 418.[132] In Rome, too, in the middle of the fifth century, there arose "a double oligarchy of senators and clergymen now closely interrelated."[133]

PAGAN PRIESTHOODS.   The men attested only as the holders of pagan priesthoods or initiates did not pursue career paths in the same way as did Christian senatorial aristocrats. Typically, a man held a pagan priesthood or office in a cult in the context of a secular career. Forty-seven percent (15 out of 32, including here two converts to paganism) of the pagans in this study population were involved in this way in the state cult while also holding secular office.

For seventeen pagan priests or initiates in this study population, there is no surviving evidence to indicate whether they held a secular office.[134] This group is interesting. For one, the dating of the men attested only as pagan priests suggests the declining status attached to the pagan priesthoods by the late fourth century (see Table 4.1). Although 14% (17 out of 125) of the pagans were known solely as priests or public cult officers, all but one of them were active in the late third century or in the fourth century into the 370s. The one pagan who is attested as an active priest after this point was Lucius Ragonius Venustus, a public augur in the 390s.[135] This does not mean that pagans held no priesthoods after the 370s. Nevertheless, the clustering of the dating for pagans evidenced only with cult office through the 370s and the dearth of later attestations lend some support to Symmachus' remark about ambitious men staying away from pagan altars in the 380s.

This same pattern of change appears if we look at the careers of men who held office in the public state cult. Although 37% (32 out of 86) of all pagans involved in the public state cults were attested as office holders in this study, pagan state cult office holders were best represented in the late third century and continuing through the first quarter of the fourth century (see Table 4.4). The population shows a gradual decline in the second half of the century, with a strong falling off after 392 following the reign of Valentinian II.

Thus by the end of the fourth century the position of a pagan state cult office holder or of a priest was no longer a prestigious component of an aristocrat's identity. The diminished attraction of these positions is even more marked if we take into account that not one of the eight pagans who pursued careers in the imperial bureaucracy nor any of the seven pagans who were in the military in this study population held offices or priesthoods in the state cult at any point in the fourth century.

Summary

Pagans in this study population were the dominant group in the traditional senatorial civic career path until the reign of Gratian with Valentinian I, and later with Valentinian II, when Christians then gained some parity and, in the 390s, a majority. Yet pagans were perceived as in control of this career path well into the 390s. Indeed, their presence was significant here in advancing other pagans. Christians, and Christian provincials in particular, were clearly dominant in the imperial bureaucratic career path in this study population. When we turn to the military elites, we found a noticeable presence of "barbarians" and only a slightly higher proportion of Christians in this path.

The quantitative patterns suggest the important role of the emperor in helping spread Christianity among men in the imperial bureaucratic path and, to a lesser degree, among those in the military path. The emperor's role in religious change was, however, constrained by the influence of aristocrats. The persistence of pagans in the senatorial civic career shows this clearly. But in all three areas, aristocrats influenced one another through their networks of shared friends, family ties, and experiences. These networks exercised a strong counterweight to the imperial court and its emperor.

Although by the end of the fourth century it was possible for senatorial aristocrats to pursue a career within the church, few did. The viability of church office for aristocrats emerged as a primarily fifth-century phenomenon, after 423 and thus after the end of this study. By that time, church office was a status-laden option for aristocrats in their ongoing pursuit of honor.

Conclusions: The Two-Step Process of Christianization

My analysis of the social and geographic origins of senatorial aristocratic men in Chapter 3 in conjunction with my study of their careers leads me to propose a different model of religious change from those found in the scholarly literature. Until recently, historians have tended to argue that the Christianization of the Roman senatorial aristocracy in the years after Constantine went hand and hand with an increasing defensiveness among die-hard traditionalists, conservative defenders of the old religion and the aristocratic way of life, especially in the last two decades of the fourth century. These historians point to the militancy of a Nicomachus Flavianus the Elder and the stubborn conservatism of a Symmachus to support their views. For revisionists the conflictual nature of relations between pagans and Christians has been overstated. In their view neither the defiant Flavianus nor the dogmatic Symmachus is typical. Revisionists describe this period as one of fluid and relatively amicable coexistence between pagans and Christians.[136]

As an alternative to both these views, I would suggest a two-step process of assimilation. The first step was a gradual turning away by pagans from pagan institutions. One can see this process beginning in the middle of the fourth century in the dates of the pagan state cult officials noted above (see Table 4.4). The second step was the gradual convergence of Christian and pagan career paths. Pagan control of the senatorial civic *cursus* began to slip as early as the rule of Constantius II. From this point on and continuing under Christian emperors through the 380s, pagans continued to make up a greater proportion of aristocrats in the senatorial civic career path but not to the same extent as earlier in the century (see Table 4.3). Christians became acceptable in the careers most closely associated with the core of aristocratic paganism.[137]

A similar tendency toward breaking down the boundaries between paganism and Christianity can be seen also in the sumptuous artifacts from the fourth century. The depiction of the pagan Venus along with a Christian cross on the silver casket of the Christian bride Proiecta is emblematic of the ease with which pagan and Christian imagery could be united in an elite work of art. Even the Virgilianizing verses on Christ written by the Christian aristocratic poetess Proba show the merging of once distinct pagan and Christian worlds. So, too, does the pagan *Codex-Calendar of 354*, designed for a Christian recipient and including lists of popes and bishops.[138]

This two-step process—a moving away by pagans from traditionally pagan religious structures and a breaking down of once significant differences between pagan and Christian aristocrats—occurred in episodic fashion. The rising prestige of the church as an institution in secular society, as evidenced by its legal privileges and economic expansion, was clearly a key factor. In addition, the intervention of determined Christian emperors, like Constantine, Constantius II, Gratian, and Theodosius, made Christianity a viable, prestige-laden option for the elite. These changes are reflected by the growth of a respectable aristocratic Christianity, seen too in luxurious Christian artifacts. As eminent aristocrats like Sextus Petronius Probus turned to Christianity, it seemed to many aristocrats that the Christians in elite society were not all that different from their pagan peers. Aristocratic networks of friends and family included both Christians and pagans, and men of both religious affiliations actively pursued honors in secular careers. Appointment recommendations were made, in most cases, without regard for religious conformity, and similar career paths led pagans and Christians to live very similar lives. At some point in the later fourth century a critical mass of aristocratic Christians existed. From that point on, Christianity could be considered a prestigious, status-laden option. The number of aristocratic Christians in secular society contributed toward making religious change more viable for the remaining pagan families.

CHAPTER 5

Aristocratic Women

A wife ought not to make friends of her own, but to enjoy her husband's friends in common with him. The gods are the first and most important friends. Wherefore it is becoming for a wife to worship and to know only the gods that her husband believes in, and to shut the front door tight upon all queer rituals and outlandish superstitions. For with no god do stealthy and secret rites performed by a woman find any favor.

—Plutarch, *Moralia* 140D (trans. Frank Cole Babbitt)

Urge with friendly kindness, all those of your household, whom you have in Sinis or in Hippo, to join in communion with the Catholic Church.

—Augustine to Donatus (African magistrate), *Epistle* 112 (trans. Wilfrid Parsons)

The Christianization of aristocratic women in the fourth century requires consideration of a different set of social and religious influences than those most relevant for aristocratic men. Careers in public, in the military or government, were not options for women; legal restraints ruled this out in the late empire as they had in the early empire. Just as the public lives of women and men differed, so too did their private lives. If we are to believe the accounts of Ammianus and Jerome, wealthy aristocratic women lived in a world apart from men, peopled by children, servants, slaves, and sycophants. At Rome, at any rate, aristocratic women evolved their own "competitive salon culture" and vied for social prestige within these private spheres as did their male counterparts within broader public ones.[1]

In this closed woman's world, family was central; it was the basis for social prestige, rank, and wealth. A woman's future was largely determined by her family. Family arranged marriages, bestowed dowries, and left inheritances. It was also the dominant force in socializing women for their future roles in

the world. Given their very different positions within Roman society, aristocratic women would look at Christianity differently than aristocratic men.

This difference in perception was recognized by Adolf Harnack in his
monumental work, *Die Mission und Ausbreitung des Christentums in den Ersten
Drei Jahrhunderten,* first published in German in 1902, in which Harnack
claimed that Christianity was laid hold of by women in particular, and that
the percentage of Christian women, especially among the upper classes, was
larger than that of Christian men.[2] Virtually all social histories of early Christianity since the turn of the century have been profoundly influenced by
Harnack's views on the affinity between women—especially aristocratic
women—and Christianity.[3] Feminist historians, in particular, have followed
up on Harnack's work.[4] Using the textual evidence, some feminist scholars
explain this affinity between women and Christianity by pointing to the
greater opportunities for influence and equality women enjoyed in the
church as compared to the pagan cults.[5] Other feminist historians emphasize
the liberation from restrictive social conditions or from conflicting expectations for Roman matrons that Christianity—and especially ascetic Christianity—offered women.[6] Still others focus on the support—social as well as
spiritual and psychological—that Christianity offered women.[7]

Not only have most historians accepted the view that Christianity was
particularly attractive to women in the first three centuries and continuing
into the fourth, they have also tended to see women as a critical, active force
in conversion. In an important article published in 1961, Peter Brown attributed the gradual process of accommodation of the Roman aristocracy to
Christianity and the resulting syncretistic religious milieu to the role of aristocratic women in the socialization process within Roman households: as
wives and mothers, these women gradually influenced their relatives and
children to bring about a respectable aristocratic Christianity.[8] Brown saw
this process beginning as early as the reign of Constantius II (337–361).

Brown's view of the role of aristocratic women in this process has been accepted by a number of historians.[9] So has the assumption shared by Brown
and others of the continuing special affinity between Christianity and aristocratic women in the fourth century. Many who ascribe to these views have
done a careful reading of the literary evidence. Treatises exhorting women
to asceticism, and especially the letters of Jerome written in the 380s to his
aristocratic female friends, gave prominence to certain ascetic women in this
period. But does that prominence indicate that aristocratic women were actually drawn more strongly to Christianity at the time than aristocratic

men? Does it mean that they were unusually active in converting other
women and men? Can we read the literary texts that suggest womanly attraction to Christianity as proof for what women did?

I think not. As I noted in Chapter 1, the extant texts can be wrong; and
even if not demonstrably inaccurate, they can be quite biased. Texts must be
read within the context of what we know about the institutions and realities
of late Roman society. The letters of Jerome are a good example, for they are
often colored by his personal animosities and theological rancor. A case in
point is Jerome's criticism and subsequent silence about the prominent role
of Melania the Elder in church affairs at Rome and in the ascetic movement
in the East.[10] Were it not for other texts to counterbalance Jerome's, we
could not assess just how historically inaccurate this portrait was. And what
is true about his shaping of the portrait of Melania is true of his letters to
women on a wide range of topics.[11]

My suspicions about the by now conventional view among historians of
the critical role of women in the religious transformation of the Roman aristocracy in the years after Constantine were raised by analysis of my study
population of 414 aristocrats. The patterns observed in this group suggest
that the role of aristocratic women in the Christianization of the Roman aristocracy after Constantine has been overemphasized. Study of the historical
and social evidence pertaining to the late Roman family also leads me to argue against the notion that women were the dominant figures in the spread
of Christianity.

Aristocratic women did, over the time period of this study, turn to Christianity. But the key to understanding this change, I believe, is the influence
of the family and aristocratic men on late Roman aristocratic women. Economically, socially, and legally, aristocratic women were still very much tied
to and constrained by their families. Moreover, families were decidedly patriarchal in structure; women were subordinate to men.[12] In my view, the
historical evidence indicates that Christianity did not alter the fundamental
dynamics of aristocratic families and the role of aristocratic women in them.
Thus, through the institutions, values, and networks of aristocratic status
culture, the family and aristocratic men were the instruments for spreading
Christianity among aristocratic women.

Furthermore, the evidence does not support the conventional scholarly
view that women were critical, active converters: various factors—the nature of the Roman family as an institution and the patterns of religious life in
them; the position of women in late antiquity in general; and the public
stand of the church on women as teachers and proselytizers in public and

private—lead me to argue against this view of women as active converters in the fourth century. The status-laden structures of aristocratic society prevented most aristocratic women from taking on the role of converter.

Christianity did offer new roles to some aristocratic women who chose to remain celibate, but most aristocratic women did not follow that path to Christianity. Most conformed to traditional social and legal patterns of behavior. Consequently, most followed the religious lead of the men in their lives, their husbands, fathers, and brothers. That, too, is what Augustine and Plutarch, quoted in the epigraph of this chapter, urged women to do.

While emphasizing the overarching influence of the family and men in aristocratic society, I do not wish to paint an image of aristocratic women as totally dependent beings. Indeed, the constant reiteration that women be subordinate to men suggests that reality did not so perfectly adhere to this "ideal." There was, indeed, tremendous variation in the levels of conformity to the normative ideal, depending upon the personalities and resources of the people involved.

Nevertheless, there is enough evidence to indicate that the ideal of the subordinate wife was very much alive and that it did indeed inform relationships in aristocratic families and in society at large. It is a telling indication of that general state of affairs that most of the conflict within families that we hear about in our fourth-century sources does not center on women turning to Christianity. Rather, conflict emerges only when aristocratic women turned to ascetic or celibate lifestyles *against* the wishes of their families who felt that such a choice threatened family continuity or financial stability.

Were Aristocratic Women Active Converters to Christianity?

The assumption that women were more attracted than men to Christianity has led to the widely held view that women were also responsible for the conversion of their families and husbands. However, the quantitative evidence from my study population and the historical evidence relating to the institutions, ideals, and roles of women within late Roman families do not support this interpretation.[13]

Quantitative Evidence

The numbers in my study population initially seem to suggest that Christianity did appeal particularly to aristocratic women. Among the 315 men, comprising 76% of the total population, there were roughly equal proportions of pagans (48%, 152 out of 315) and Christians (46%, 146 out of 315), with a small percentage of converts to Christianity (4%, 13 out of 315) and converts to paganism (1%, 4 out of 315). Among the 99 women, comprising 24% of the total population, 14% (14 out of 99) were pagan while 85% (84 out of 99) were Christian, with 1% (1 out of 99) converting to Christianity (see Table 5.1).

The predominance of Christian women as compared to pagan women in my study population is the result, in large part, of the nature of the surviving evidence; among the pagan women, 10 of the 14 are attested by inscriptions whereas only 4 are known solely from literary sources. In contrast, more than half of the Christian women—44 out of 84—are noted by only literary sources, with the remaining 40 (plus one convert to Christianity) attested by inscriptions.

Leaving aside the question of literary attestation, it is also important to note that a much smaller number of pagan women (10) are attested epigraphically as compared to Christian women (40). These meager remains for pagan women are probably due to the fact that pagan aristocratic women far less frequently than men put their names and vows on stone.[14] This anepigraphic habit combined with the silence of the literary sources also accounts for the far smaller proportion of pagan women to pagan men as compared to the proportion of Christian women to Christian men that occurs in the sample.

There are several reasons for these differences in the epigraphic attestations for women, none of which lead to the conclusion that there were, in fact, fewer pagan than Christian women during the period. For women of the aristocracy, social expectations and customs seem to have been the factors determining the different patterns of epigraphic usage between pagans and Christians. Among pagans, the dedication of religious inscriptions and funerary monuments was the prerogative, predominantly, of the male population.[15] Indeed, participation by women in all cults, especially traditional Greco-Roman state cults, was circumscribed. Moreover, in the early and late empire the assertion of family ties in inscriptions of the aristocratic class was relatively low as compared to the population at large;[16] hence the number of inscriptions that preserve the names of aristocratic women is proportionally smaller.

In addition to male control over inscriptions among pagans, particular aspects of Christianity ensure a large number of surviving inscriptions for

Christian women. First, many of the Christian women are attested because of funeral inscriptions that have come to light from the excavations of catacombs or churches. Thus their statistical prominence for this period as compared with pagan women may also be affected by our knowing more about Christian burial grounds than pagan ones. Second, Christians of the late empire tended to note religious preferences, not secular personal relations, on their tombstones. Many Christian inscriptions for men and women indicate only a name and a Christian message, whereas their pagan counterparts note personal ties or civic honors, not religious affiliations.[17]

Although we cannot assume that the differences in the absolute numbers of surviving inscriptions for pagan and Christian women represent the actual population, we can nevertheless examine certain social characteristics of the women in this sample. Most often we know whom they married, when they lived, who their children were, and whether their children followed their parents' religious choice. As I will show, this evidence can yield revealing patterns.

COMPARING CONVERSION DATES FOR ARISTOCRATIC WOMEN
WITH ARISTOCRATIC MEN.   Christian women in my study population who reached age 20 before the year 367 did not appear to convert earlier than men. Christians do not appear in large numbers in this study until the reign of Gratian with Valentinian I (i.e., after 367). Approximately 76% (35 out of 46) of the Christian women and 74% (26 out of 35) of the Christian men were dated between 367–423 (see Table 5.2).[18] If women had played the leading role in conversion—as they are so often assumed to have played—it seems reasonable to expect that a majority of Christian women in this study population would have come from earlier periods (i.e., before 367). But, in fact, the proportion of Christian women to Christian men in the first half of the fourth century is roughly similar.

Later in the century, in the period beginning with Gratian and Valentinian I and continuing through the sole rulership of Valentinian II (367–392), Christian women are somewhat better represented than Christian men; 41% (19 out of 46) of the Christian women as compared to 31% (11 out of 35) of the Christian men fell in this period. Although the higher proportion of women in these years might suggest that women were taking the lead— and this is certainly the time when asceticism is growing within the western Roman aristocracy—the nature of the surviving sources on asceticism provides a more likely explanation for this predominance. Fourteen of the nineteen women from this time period are known because they are cited in ascetic texts, mostly in the letters of Jerome. In no other instance in this study is the evidence as skewed by a single recognizable factor of survival.

Thus in the first half of the fourth century, down until the reign of Gratian with Valentinian I, there is little difference in the rates of conversion of aristocratic women and aristocratic men in my study population. A Melania the Elder or a Marcella, early fourth-century female aristocratic Christians, appears to be an individual case, representative of the beginnings of a movement toward Christianity but not the predominant trend in the Roman aristocracy at large. For both men and women, it is the years 367–392, beginning with Gratian's rule with Valentinian I, that evidence a significant increase in this study population. In this period, ascetic Christian women are better represented than men in large part, one suspects, due to the survival of texts about asceticism. After Valentinian II (392–423), the presence of both Christian men and women is high, with men (43%, 15 out of 35 of the men) taking only a small lead over the women (35%, 16 out of 46 of the women).

INTERMARRIAGE.   Some scholars have emphasized intermarriage as a significant means of Christianizing the Roman aristocracy. Statements of Christians like Jerome who advocated marriage only insofar as it provided recruits for Christianity, or better yet, ascetic Christianity, would seem to support this view, and Jerome's hopes that Laeta would eventually convert her pagan father appear plausible.[19]

But the historical evidence and the evidence of this study population provide little support for this view. The hopes of Jerome were not realized; of the fifteen Christian aristocratic women attested by name in the letters of Jerome, conversion of a spouse is certain in only one case: Toxotius, a pagan, was converted by his Christian wife Laeta.[20]

Historians also point to the well-known edict of Pope Callistus in the early third century (ca. 214–218) as evidence of an excess of prominent women in the Christian church that led to a high rate of intermarriage and hence conversion. The edict allowed senatorial women to wed men of any rank, even freedmen or slaves, without losing "their nobility."[21] However, marriages between women of high status and prominent slaves and freedmen were not unique to the Christian community. The emperor Augustus strongly stated the penalties for marrying below one's senatorial class, and subsequent emperors reiterated these strictures.[22] In the late second and early third centuries, however, we find imperial women and even some senatorial ladies who kept their rank although married to nonsenators. Julia Soaemias, the niece of Julia Domna and mother of the emperor Elagabalus, married an equestrian but retained her rank; the emperor Caracalla even advanced her husband into the senatorial order.[23] The problem of an adequate supply of senatorial men for senatorial women to wed extended well beyond the Christian community to the class as a whole.[24]

A similarly weak argument for Christian intermarriage as a means of conversion is the Christian tolerance for mixed marriages, observed in the writings of Augustine and in the canons of some church councils. Such unions did not necessarily bring about the conversion of the spouse.[25] Consider, for example, the second- and third-century *Apocryphal Acts of the Apostles,* which do not relate actual conversion experiences of historical women or men but may nevertheless reflect Christian beliefs concerning such experiences; even in these accounts the husbands rarely convert.[26]

In my study population intermarriage between pagans and Christians was infrequent. Pagans marry pagans and Christians marry Christians. Evidence of the religion of spouses exists for 90 people in this study population: 82 of these people were married to coreligionists. Only eight are attested as having mixed marriages. The predominant pattern of endogamy argues against the view that intermarriage was the major or even a highly significant means of Christianizing the Roman aristocracy.[27]

Even in the very few certain cases of attested intermarriage in this study, there is little evidence for the role of aristocratic wives as critical in the process of Christianization. Within this population the most common pattern of intermarriage is for male pagans to marry female Christians; all mixed marriages fit this pattern.[28] It should be noted, however, that this pattern may also reflect the bias in our sources; as noted previously, we know far more about Christian women than about pagan women in this sample. Moreover, when intermarriage did occur, the role of the wife as a proselytizer appears limited. Of the certain cases of intermarriage between pagans and Christians, the pagan converted after marriage, suggesting a spouse's influence, in but one instance.[29] Turcius Apronianus, wed to the Christian Avita, became a Christian; however, if we can trust the evidence, it was his wife's aunt, the powerful Melania the Elder, who pressured him into converting.[30] The remaining cases of intermarriage did not yield any religious change on the part of the spouses; Publilius C(a)eionius Caecina Albinus and C(a)eionius Rufius Albinus remained pagan, although wed to Christian wives.[31] In these cases of intermarriage, religious differences within the family were either tolerated or ignored. Plutarch's often-quoted advice (see the epigraph to this chapter) that husbands should make their wives conform to their choice of gods as of friends may have been the ideal, but it was apparently not always followed by the male aristocrats in this study.

Contrary to scholarly opinion, the example of Augustine, inspired to true belief by the guiding faith of his mother Monica, was not typical. Nor was the case of Constantine, who, according to one tradition, was led to the faith by his Christian mother Helena.[32] The women in this study who intermarried appeared to exercise only a limited influence on religious choice through their role as mothers. The assumption that the mother had the greatest influence over the religious training of the Roman child in late antiquity has a plausible modern air about it. That, however, was not always the case. In two mixed marriages in this study, the sons followed the religion of their fathers. The son of the pagan Publilius C(a)eionius Caecina Albinus remained pagan, and the son of C(a)eionius Rufius Albinus, Rufius Antonius Agrypnius Volusianus, remained pagan until his niece Melania induced him to accept baptism upon his deathbed in 437.[33] In this case the vitality of male hereditary lines was allied to ancestral paganism.[34] Since the most frequent pattern for intermarriage was that of pagan male to Christian female, it would appear that the impact of intermarriage on Christianization in the Roman aristocracy is limited. Only when the father in a mixed marriage converted to Christianity did the son follow his lead.[35] However, the daughters of these mixed marriages tended to follow their mothers and adopt Christianity.[36]

CHILDREN IN THIS STUDY POPULATION.   Based on this study population, it would appear that religion in late Roman society was transmitted across generations. The majority of cases show sons and daughters following the religion of the parent. Obedience in religion, as in so many areas of social life, is the norm among the aristocracy. In this study parents of boys, pagan and Christian, were more likely to have their sons follow them than their daughters. Christian mothers could be somewhat more confident that their daughters would follow their religion as compared to their sons. Among parents with children, boys follow their parents' religion in higher proportions (55%, or 48 out of 87) than do girls (34%, or 30 out of 87). The evidence, although far from authoritative, suggests that religious conformity between Christian mothers and daughters might have been slightly greater than between Christian mothers and sons. Female children of Christian mothers follow them (50%, or 14 out of 28) in roughly the same proportion as do male children (43%, or 12 out of 28), and only boys are attested as not following their Christian mothers; 2 out of 28 do not follow their Christian mothers (see Table 5.3).

When children do not follow the religion of their parents, boys seem to have a slightly greater tendency to change than girls. Eight percent of the parents (7 out of 87) have sons who do not follow their religion, while only 2% of the parents (2 out of 87) have daughters who do not follow their religious choice. Again, these numbers are too small to generate confident assessments of change. But it is reasonable to suggest that boys were more independent given the requirements of public action for males and their leading role within the family.

These patterns suggest that when parents and children were of the same sex, religion was passed on as an aspect of one's gendered social identity. The case of Constantine himself is interesting in this regard; according to his biographer, Eusebius, Constantine followed in the footsteps of his father, who was a Christian, and actually converted his mother Helena to Christianity.[37] The evidence for religious education in late antiquity, discussed below, would also support this variant version.

The results of the present study indicate that ties within the family between husband and wife were not the most significant means of Christianization: intermarriage between pagans and Christians was infrequent, and in the years after Constantine, aristocratic women did not convert to Christianity substantially earlier than men. A predominance of women in the period from Gratian with Valentinian I and later with Valentinian II may indicate an influx of ascetic women among the aristocracy in the 370s and 380s, or it may be a result of the survival of sources. In the last decade of the fourth century and into the first quarter of the fifth, Christian men and women appear in large numbers. Although these patterns are based on a limited number of cases, they do suggest that if the progress of Christianity had been left to private family affairs, it would have taken centuries longer to win the West.

The Nature of the Late Roman Family

Given the institutions, values, and role of women within the late Roman family and family cult, it would be surprising to find women taking on the pivotal role of active converters to Christianity. Yet that is what many scholars have argued. It seems far more likely that in most cases men were key to the conversion of aristocratic women and not the other way around.

In the traditional Roman family, as in society at large, women were expected to be subordinate to men. As Augustine put it: "It is the natural order of things for mankind that women should serve men, and children their parents, because this is justice itself, that the weaker reason [*ratio*] should serve the stronger."[38] In Augustine's eyes, the marriage contract made wives subservient to their husbands, a condition women should accept because "if the wife was subdued to his [the husband's] *dominium*, there reigned a *pax recta* in the household; if not and the wife dominated, a *pax perversa*."[39] Deep affection, mutual respect, and companionship could and did exist in marriage, and they were valued. But these sentiments did not entail equality between spouses, nor did they change the deference expected of a wife or, in certain cases, her fear of reprisal. One cannot dismiss Augustine's master-slave view of marriage as idiosyncratic, since his view is validated by reports of actual behavior as well as by the statements of contemporaries.[40]

The fourth-century Latin church fathers generally counseled women to be obedient in marriage as in society. The church fathers often claimed that their teachings in these matters had been universally accepted by all men, and they cited scripture to support womanly obedience.[41] So in the late fourth century Ambrosiaster used examples from the Old and New Testaments to demonstrate that women should be submissive to men: Sarah called her husband master; Adam's creation before Eve showed his superiority and dominance over his wife.[42] The assertive woman was deemed arrogant and risked compromising the reputation of her husband.[43]

Not all women lived by these expectations. Families, then as now, varied, as men and women negotiated their lives together. Some women took the leading role in the household and family for a variety of reasons. Some men may have been too busy or disinterested to take on this role. In some marriages a woman with greater wealth than her husband could dominate her spouse and the household. In addition, since women tended to marry at a younger age than men, more women were probably widowed than men. The position of widow allowed wealthy aristocratic women greater influence over household and economic resources. Although women did not possess legal control *(potestas)* over their offspring, a widow in the late fourth century who renounced remarriage and was of age could gain legal guardianship over her children until they reached majority.[44] As a widow, a wealthy aristocratic woman could take a dominant role in family and household life; for example, she could choose a son-in-law for her daughter.

Certainly, women differed in the degree to which they followed the normative ideas of subordination. Some, like Melania the Elder, lived their lives with a striking disregard for conventional expectations. Widowed at a young age, Melania left her teenage son under the tutelage of a guardian and sailed to Alexandria to visit the desert fathers before settling in Palestine.[45] Another woman, Ecdicia, gave away her inheritance to the church, acting as she most likely had a legal right to do. Yet Augustine criticized Ecdicia because she acted "without the knowledge" of either her husband or her son, her prospective heir.[46] While these women exhibited a high degree of independence that no doubt inspired some women, neither they nor other such nonconforming women destroyed the influence of the patriarchal ideal on the late Roman family.

Sozomen regarded the conversion of his grandfather, a pagan in Palestine, with that of his whole family in the time of Julian as miraculous, yet for us the story is paradigmatic of the dynamics of the religious life of a late Roman patriarchal household. When a monk expelled a devil from Sozomen's grandfather by simply calling on the name of Christ, he and his entire family immediately converted.[47] In this family, as within aristocratic families in general, the father was charged with the responsibility for the household's religious life. Church fathers presumed the responsibility of the *dominus* not only for his family and household but also for all who resided on his lands.[48] That is the point, too, of the remarks of Augustine, quoted in the epigraph to this chapter. The assumption of paternal responsibility for family and household lies behind even an anonymous fourth-century *Homily on Virginity,* addressed to fathers, that urges them to keep their daughters safe from the dangers of vigils, assemblies, and funerals.[49] While most texts on asceticism are addressed to women, the assumption that fathers take over these duties to preserve their daughters' chastity fits with the pattern of paternal control over the religious life of the family.

When an aristocratic family wanted to date its conversion, including that of its women, it did so by mentioning the first male convert in the family: so Sidonius Apollinaris dated the conversion of his family to the baptism of his grandfather.[50] The same was true for the poet Prudentius who claimed the conversion of Rome by recording the names of prominent male members of the noble Roman families: "The quick faith of a Paulinus and a Bassus did not hesitate to surrender to Christ and to lift up the proud stock of a patrician clan to meet the age that was to come."[51]

RELIGIOUS HARMONY OF HUSBANDS AND WIVES.   The submission of women to family interests extended to their religious activities as well. In the epigraph to this chapter, the second-century Plutarch expressed a common sentiment when he advised young husbands to make their wives conform to their choice of gods. This ideal is reflected in the numerous sarcophagi of the second and third centuries from Italy and Asia Minor in which "the wife was shown standing attentively, or sitting, in front of her husband, as he raised his right hand to make a point, while in his left hand he displayed the scroll which represented the superior literary culture on which he based his claim to outright dominance, in society at large as in his marriage."[52] These husband-wife sarcophagi also show the ideal of religious harmony within the couple, since the couple is depicted as sharing the same deities. Religious concordance was a positive attribute in a wife, as the fourth-century pagan Praetextatus noted of his virtuous wife:

> And so as friends we have been joined in trust,
> By long acquaintance, by shared initiations of the gods,
> All in one bond of faith, one single heart, united in one mind.[53]

The ideal notion of deference leading to harmony in the religious affiliation of a couple was shared by Christians as well. Ambrose tells the husband to "direct his wife, as if a ruler [*gubernator*], to honor her as a partner of his life."[54] The good husband, according to Ambrose, is responsible for his wife's religious activities and does not "allow his wife to be deprived of religious activities, nor does he avariciously usurp all of them for himself . . . What pertains to piety should be something common to both."[55] Thus the good Christian husband is charged with sharing the duties pertaining to salvation.

Religious concordance—pagans marrying pagans and Christians marrying Christians—was the norm. This helps to explain why the evidence from this study population showed a similar trajectory in the conversion of aristocratic men and women. Behind this pattern lies the ideal of husband and wife having the same religious affiliation, an ideal common to pagans and Christians alike. The epitaph of the pagan Praetextatus cited above praised the bond with his wife of "shared initiations of the gods." In pagan cult, when women appear as high priestesses they do so largely because of their role as wives or daughters of high priests; even the majority of imperial priesthoods were husband- and-wife teams.[56] Among Christians we find couples like Aper and Amanda praised. Aper, a successful lawyer and provincial governor, withdrew from the world with the support of his wife, Amanda. Since the couple had sons and considerable wealth, Amanda devoted herself to managing the couple's secular affairs to release her husband to pursue higher spiritual goals. Even though "she, too, prefers to despise the world and not enjoy it," Paulinus of Nola praised Amanda "for she put your [Aper's] spiritual welfare first, preferring you before herself."[57]

The good wife not only shared the religious life of her husband, she subordinated her religious goals to his or to that of her family.[58] To Paulinus, this was the ideal family: "I am sure He [Christ] is lodging in the very midst of your house where parents and children form a single group of many souls."[59] This was the expectation, even among the most zealous of Christians.[60] According to her biographer, the fourteen-year-old Melania the Younger did not want to marry her eighteen-year-old husband, Pinianus, but did so because of family pressure. Once wed, she wanted to live in chastity with her husband, but he was unwilling to do so until they had produced the requisite heirs. Again, she subordinated her religious desires, this time to that of her husband. Only after Melania gave birth to two children, both of whom died in infancy, did she, gravely ill, persuade her husband to acquiesce to her desires to live chastely.[61] A woman who failed to subordinate her desires to that of her husband received the disapproval of church leaders like Augustine:

> Although you were refraining by mutual consent from carnal intercourse, as his wife you should have been subject to your husband in other things according to the marriage bond, especially as you are both members of the Body of Christ. And indeed, if you, a believer, had had an unbelieving husband, you ought to have conducted yourself with a submissive demeanor that you might win him for the Lord, as the Apostles advise. I say nothing of the fact that I know you undertook this state of continence, contrary to sound doctrine, before he gave consent.[62]

FAMILIES IN CONFLICT. The tremendous influence of husbands and families on the religious choices of their wives and daughters comes to the forefront in our sources in moments of conflict. Most often these conflicts erupt over aristocratic women whose desire to devote themselves to asceticism or celibacy threatens the economic or social interests of their family. By going *against* the wishes of her family, a woman also incurred the condemnation of fellow aristocrats and, often, church fathers. The pious and independent widow Marcella wanted to give her jewels and her property to the poor, but she was constrained by her mother, Albina, to give them to her family instead. Albina, although herself living an ascetic life at Rome, was nevertheless "devoted to her kinsfolk, and wished to leave all her property to her brother's children, being without sons and grandsons."[63]

A renowned instance of the kinds of family pressures exerted upon women to conform to aristocratic social expectations and fulfil family obligations is recorded in the *Vita Sanctae Melaniae*. As noted above, Melania the Younger was pressured into marrying because her parents, "illustrious members of the Roman senate . . . expected that through her they would have a succession of the family line."[64] Melania had to wait for years for her father, on his deathbed, to finally consent, allegedly, to her request that she be allowed to give away her inheritance.[65] When she and her husband had given away much of their money to the poor and made public their plan to sell their property and slaves in Rome, Melania's relatives as well as her husband's brother, Severus, protested, even going to the civil authorities. Feelings ran so high that only external intervention could end the family feud, although the hostility of the senators and their wives toward the couple remained so fierce that the elder Melania's biographer, Palladius, likened them to "beasts."[66]

Accounts of women's conflicts with their families exemplify the expectation *among the aristocracy* that women would serve the interests of their families, even if that went against a woman's religious preferences. Excessive charity and the refusal of women to continue family lineage and capital to the next generation were viewed as harmful to the aristocracy as a whole, not just to one family; these families were, after all, intimately interrelated. Nor was the aristocracy alone in this view of women's role; they could turn to the more moderate church fathers for support. Paulinus and Augustine, in the cases noted above, praised women who chose to support their husbands rather than follow their own religious inclinations. There were proponents of asceticism who took a more radical stance, opposing the subordination of women to family interests, but these voices went against widespread norms of behavior and the views of most Christians, both leaders and laypeople. Ambrose, one such advocate, noted how prevalent was this perspective when he noted an unnamed "noble" girl whose family and friends opposed her choice of asceticism on the grounds that her deceased father had not given his approval. Ambrose did not support the family's and friends' intervention, but here he underscores that, in general, the choice of asceticism required paternal consent.[67]

The ideal of religious harmony presented a problem for Christian women married to pagan husbands. This helps to explain why some, if not most, late fourth-century church fathers and councils opposed contracting mixed marriages.[68] Their teachings seem to have had some impact, at least among the aristocracy; I found only eight people attested as having mixed marriages in my study population. Yet a certain number of mixed marriages did take place, and by the late fourth century, Augustine claims, marriages between pagans and Christians were no longer considered sinful.[69]

To a spouse in a mixed marriage, such as Monica, Augustine's mother, toleration was advised, at least by some church fathers. Since Paul had said that it was better that a Christian married to a non-Christian remain married, the Christian spouse might separate only if the unbelieving spouse wished it. By remaining married, Paul said, "the unbelieving spouse is made holy through his wife, and the unbelieving wife is made holy through her husband"; and in any case, their children would be "holy" (*1 Cor.* 7.10–16). Paul claimed that spouses and children would somehow be saved though their familial relationship, but he did not specify how this salvation would occur nor did he counsel actively converting one's spouse to achieve it. Although some fervent Christian women no doubt attempted active conversion, Monica's quiet prayers for and patient acceptance of her pagan husband and wayward son are, in Augustine's eyes, the ideal way to influence the conversion of a spouse or child.[70]

Given the dynamics of late Roman family life, a woman who took an overtly active or aggressive role as a teacher or converter of her husband would be viewed as overstepping her bounds.[71] The words of Paul could again be used to buttress fourth-century expectations for women concerning their role as teachers: "let a woman learn in silence with all submissiveness. I permit no woman to teach or to have authority over men; she is to keep silent" (*1 Tim.* 2.11–12). In explaining this passage, Chrysostom, taking into account the *Corinthians* passage cited above, explains that public teaching is outlawed to women, although private discourse is not; the husband, if he is able, should instruct the wife. Where the woman is wiser, explains Chrysostom, she may instruct her husband but only when no qualified male is available. The case of Priscilla teaching her husband Apollos is an extraordinary exception in the days of Paul, says Chrysostom, and one that "puts men to shame."[72]

In John's view, wives instructing husbands, like public teaching, is a "shameful" anachronism. The *Commentaries* of Pelagius on this same passage present a more balanced view, one perhaps closer to reality. Pelagius also opposes women teaching in public but allows women to teach a son or brother in private or to prophesy to other women at home.[73] Pelagius' testimony suggests that some women did instruct others at home, despite the opposition of the Fathers and of traditional aristocratic society. Yet to do so raised concerns. Jerome sarcastically castigates the husband who did not teach his wife about religion and views his student role as unmanly: "Therefore . . . imitate her whom you ought yourself to have taught. For shame! The weaker sex overcomes the world, and the stronger is overcome by it!"[74]

The pressures on a Christian wife not to incur her husband's displeasure were strong. A Christian wife would not want to divorce or make her husband divorce her, since the church, following Paul, frowned on it. The state, from the time of Constantine, sometimes tightened, sometimes loosened restrictions on divorce, but it, too, took a more negative view of divorce in the fourth century, either in response to Christian attitudes or to changing social morality.[75] Although more economically independent than their lower-class sisters, aristocratic women might still be hesitant to divorce or separate because of secular disadvantages. If divorced, the husband retained legal control of the children, and although the wife could legally have her dowry returned in a divorce that she had not provoked, the property was not always there to reclaim; as John Chrysostom pointed out, a powerful husband could simply constrain his wife.[76] The woman who tried to convert or instruct a disapproving husband could provoke a divorce, which could deprive her of her dowry or her husband's dotal gift.

Some women were nonetheless willing to put their faith above their obedience to husband or family, and especially in the early church, certain Christian thinkers deemed it right to do so.[77] After the acceptance of Christianity by Constantine, however, the church fathers did not generally advocate that its adherents turn away from their families. Most western Christian fathers of the fourth century advised women to submit to their husbands, fathers, and bishops. Women who acted independently and without the consent of their husbands, even for good religious reasons such as charity, were disapproved of by several church fathers; so, for example, Pelagius criticized Celantia as Augustine did Ecdicia for choosing continence without the permission of their husbands.[78]

If a Christian woman gave up on converting her pagan spouse, she might yet try to raise his children as Christians. Here, as in modern mixed marriages, the attitude of the father might be more or less tolerant. But if a pagan father felt strongly, the Christian mother who went against her husband's wishes as regards the religious upbringing of their children put herself at risk, opposing convention and the law; where there were disagreements between parents concerning a child's welfare, the father's wishes, not the mother's, carried legal weight.[79] This meant that the mother's influence on the child was to a large degree determined by her relations with her husband; or, as an old Roman maxim put it, the *materfamilias* commanded second through her obedience to her husband.[80] After social and legal prestige mounted in favor of Christianity in the last decades of the fourth century, pagan husbands may have accepted in increasing numbers the views of their Christian wives as regards their children and themselves.

But it should be emphasized that it was the father who had direct control over the sons and daughters in a Roman family. Even if, as A. Arjava has recently argued, *patria potestas* in the late antique world generally lasted only as long as the children were underage, legally the father still had the ultimate right of decision on their education, marriage, and domicile until the time he chose to forgo it or died.[81] Symmachus' reiterations to his *domina filia* to act as "*priscae feminae*" and work wool fulfilled his parental role.[82] The dominant role of the father in the life of the family extended as well to the religious activities of the children. Thus it would be through the father—and not the mother—that one would expect religious change to occur among the aristocracy.

GENDERED ROLES IN TRADITIONAL PAGANISM: THE SECONDARY ROLE OF THE MATRONA. A brief consideration of the religious activities of a late Roman pagan family supports the impression that the father bore the primary responsibility for maintaining not only the family but its religious life, and for passing on these traditions to the children. The mother certainly had a role, but hers was secondary to his.

The *paterfamilias* was in charge of carrying out the private family rites. He sacrificed regularly to the resident household gods, the Lares, Penates and the Genius, on behalf of the entire family; the *paterfamilias* was so closely associated with the Genius that the birthday of the former was the great feast day of the latter.[83] In his poem attacking paganism, Prudentius recreates the circumstances under which a young heir, following the "fathers' pagan rites," learns to "shudder" before the rites of his "hoary ancestors" and to worship whatever they—the *atavi*—have designated; even as infants they "taste the sacrificial meal" and "see the Lares dripping with unguent."[84] The good mother contributes to the young heir's paganism by worshipping Fortuna.[85] That is all she could do because "women were deemed unfit to take part in the most important elements of religious ritual: the slaughter, butchering, and distribution of the meat of the sacrificial victim" were roles reserved for men.[86]

Ideally, children followed the directions of the *paterfamilias* at home. According to Servius' late fourth-century commentary, children played a role in the household cult on a daily basis; they announced that the household gods were propitious when the *paterfamilias* offered sacrifice in the course of a meal.[87] Adult sons and unmarried daughters under their father's *potestas* continued to take part in their father's family cult as Marcus Aurelius did for his father, Antoninus Pius.[88]

In addition to such daily rituals, the *paterfamilias* was expected to maintain worship of his ancestral gods and ensure that his offspring would do the same at important ceremonial moments. At the annual rites to the dead ancestors in February (the *Parentalia*), the father led the family in maintaining the memory of deceased relatives at their tombs, pouring libations of wine, milk, and blood.[89] The father was in charge of the funeral rites for the dead; as Augustine describes the funeral of one fourth-century pagan *paterfamilias*, he notes the tradition of the sons and grandsons accompanying the body of the old grandfather to the tomb.[90] Men delivered eulogies and celebrated the prescribed sacrifices in private and in public cult.[91] At the great public ceremonies, festivals, and banquets attended by fathers and sons, the latter would observe and be trained to imitate the dominant role and sacerdotal responsibilities of their fathers.

In these ways we see the *paterfamilias* setting the patterns that his sons and daughters were expected to follow. Indeed, it was the traditional Roman attitude to view the father as "the ideal teacher" in matters that affected his household, including the divine.[92] Fathers wrote and dedicated didactic treatises about religion to their children: Macrobius wrote his *Saturnalia* for his son; Martianus Capella addressed his *De Nuptiis Philologiae et Mercurii* to his son, Martianus.[93] And if a child needed specialized religious training, it was the father who would be called upon to finance it and find the appropriate priest or teacher. So, for example, the father might have to engage a priest so that his pagan children, like their Christian counterparts, might learn to read or recite classical texts or hymns. A priest might train them to learn sacred hymns to sing in a choir, and choirs of children from aristocratic

Roman households are attested in the third century.[94] Similarly, if a young man wanted to enter a mystery cult or if an older son was elected to a college of priests, he, being financially and legally dependent, would turn to his father for the economic and social resources to support these activities.

The primary role of the father in maintaining the ancestral cult and in family religious activities reinforced the secondary position of the wife in her husband's household. Although married, a woman legally remained under the protection of her father; she was not seen as creating a new family with her spouse but of entering into an already existing one. The wife owed obedience to the husband, but law and convention still linked her to her natal family.[95] This situation meant, technically, that a woman belonged to her father's family cult, even if, as in the poem of Prudentius, she is present at her husband's ancestral cult ceremonies.[96]

Although secondary, the Roman *matrona* did play a role in the religious life of the household and, consequently, in that of her children. Like their husbands, Roman *matronae* were religious role models for their children, especially for their daughters. They assisted their men, and so were appropriately portrayed on so-called marriage sarcophagi as handing boxes of incense to their husbands who perform the sacrificial rite.[97] In certain cults women did perform religious rites; in the private household cult of Vesta, for example, women hung garlands over the hearth and prayed to the household gods on certain days. Some of Vesta's holidays required the participation only of women; the holiday designated as *Vesta aperit[ur]* in the *Codex-Calendar of 354* indicated that on that day the inner sanctum of the temple of Vesta was open only to women. A period of activity, including the *Vestalia*, would conclude with *Vesta cluditur*, the ritual cleansing by women of the temple of Vesta.[98] In some goddess cults, such as the *Bona Dea*, women could even perform sacrifices.[99]

In these rites we see an important role for women, even if "they could not perform important rites in the Forum or the family atrium . . . and in normal times and regular places of worship they were not permitted to officiate at sacrifices."[100] Yet children were socialized into seeing women as secondary in the religious life of the family. The influence of the maternal model seems strongest on daughters, or so it would appear from my study population; there was a slightly higher affinity between mothers and daughters in terms of religion, as compared to mothers and sons. Similarly, sons in my study modeled themselves more often on their fathers. These gendered patterns reinforce the view of religion as part of social identity, and they suggest, too, that the father played a primary role in the religious lives of late Roman pagan families.

Gendered Roles in Christianity: Who Will Teach the Children?

The father's assumption of paternal responsibility for the religious activities of his family appears in Christian aristocratic families as well as pagan ones. This is not surprising since Christians lived in the same world as their pagan peers; Christians, too, were socialized into the male-dominated social structures that inhibited women from taking on the role of converters. We also see the emphasis on the father in the role given to them in the religious education of Christian children and in the views of Christian leaders on women as teachers.

Although both parents were involved in the upbringing of children, the father, as head of the household, had primary responsibility, even for the education of children and especially for the education of older children. So when Jerome tries to encourage Furia to remain a widow, he satirizes the reasons that young widows want to remarry: "the helpless widow cries out—Who will educate my little children and bring up my house-slaves?"[101] Typically, the father would choose a tutor, as was the case of Paulinus whose education, around the age of seven, was entrusted to his father's friend, Ausonius, presumably by his father.[102]

The dominant role of the Christian father extended to religious education. When John Chrysostom admonished his upper-class audience in Constantinople on the right way to raise children, he presented an idealized account that no doubt appealed to male vanity. He addressed the fathers as the ones who will be in charge: the father will tell the son his bible stories; the mother is pictured as sitting by so that "she too may take part" and repeat the story when necessary.[103] The father is pictured as taking his son to church.[104] The bridegroom must learn about religion so that he may "train his own sons in this way, and they theirs in turn, and the result will be a golden cord."[105] Criticized are those fathers who are concerned about giving their boys worldly possessions but care nothing about their souls.[106] In homilies delivered at Antioch, John again focused on the father: fathers who bring up their children in the proper way "are builders of temples in which Christ dwells and the guardians of heavenly athletes."[107] In John's view, the role of the woman in educating the young is secondary, especially when it comes to

sons; as to training daughters, restraint from luxury and drunkenness is prescribed.[108]

Although Chrysostom is describing the ideal way of bringing up children
as he addresses his well-to-do audience in Constantinople, his assumption
that the father had primary responsibility for the religious education of his
Christian children would ring a familiar note, since it is in accord with the
traditional legal and social expectations of the *paterfamilias*.[109] Christians
could buttress this view with passages from the New Testament; in *Ephesians*
and *Colossians* fathers were told to raise their children "in the discipline and
instruction of the Lord" (*Eph.* 6.4; *Col.* 3.20). Thus the evidence, albeit limited, shows Christian fathers being urged to take the leading role in the religious education of their children, especially when sons are concerned. Not
every father took as active a role as did the well-off father of Origen who exercised his son at length in scripture as well as in the usual liberal education.[110] But the assumption that the father was responsible for the religious
choices of his son was so conventional that it could appear in a martyr's account of a proconsul questioning a Donatist family.[111]

Christian fathers, like their pagan peers, turned to specialists to ensure
proper religious training for their children. Since it was the father who was
typically responsible for choosing tutors, he was also the natural one to find
religious instruction for Christian children; Eusebius praises Constantine for
his careful choice of religious tutors for his sons.[112] Constantius, in his turn,
took care that his nephews Julian and Gallus were well instructed in religion
by none other than the Christian bishop George.[113] Theodosius summoned
Arsenius, then a deacon, to Constantinople to be a tutor for Arcadius and
Honorius.[114]

Christian fathers were important, too, in training daughters. When the
Roman father Gaudentius wrote to Jerome for advice about how to raise
his daughter, Pacatula, a dedicated virgin, Jerome replied with instructions
on the choice of a governess: pick one who is "not given to much wine, one
who, as the apostle says, is not idle or a tattler."[115] Since governesses were
the norm among the aristocracy, Jerome sets the virgin Paula apart from
other girls by urging her parents to find a distinguished male tutor.[116] Although Jerome assigned responsibilities to both parents in raising Paula, he
nevertheless indicated how central was the role of the father by making the
father's salvation rest upon it: "A man will lose God's favor because of his
child's faults as did the Priest Eli. A man cannot be made a bishop who has

profligate and disorderly sons."[117] In this same passage Jerome observes that the mother is to be a role model for the girl. "It is written of the woman: she will be saved in childbearing, if she continue in faith and charity and holiness with chastity."[118]

Christian mothers, like their pagan counterparts, were also involved in educating their children, especially in the early years but, again, theirs was a secondary role. The aristocratic mother could teach the children to read, and she could read scriptures with them.[119] But among aristocratic families most girls and boys probably learned the basics of reading from tutors, nurses, or governesses; Proba's *Cento* may have been composed for governesses of the children of the elite rather than for their mothers.[120] The well-educated Christian mother might teach her daughter to read more advanced works since aristocratic girls, unlike their brothers, did not generally go to school or leave home to pursue advanced studies. Claudian paints a rosy image of the young bride-to-be, Maria, reading Latin and Greek classics with her mother, benefiting from her mother's teaching and *mores*.[121] But most Christian aristocratic girls, in contrast to their brothers, did not study the classics or the scriptures in depth. For the aristocratic girls whom we know about, reading and memorizing passages from the scriptures or psalms appear the desired educational goal, along with spinning.[122] Some aristocratic Christian women pursued advanced study of scripture, as did Paula and her daughters under Jerome's tutelage; these women sought to deepen their own spiritual lives, but they did so generally as individuals, not as mothers.[123]

Given these gendered educational expectations, it would be more likely for aristocratic women to influence their daughters than their sons, and there were some indications of this pattern in my study population. Very young boys might read at home with their mothers, but early on they were given over to tutors chosen by the father and later sent to school. Thus boys would be open to very different religious and intellectual influences than girls. For advanced religious education—for daughters as well as sons—children were often turned over to a male religionist, generally from outside the family; hence Paula and her daughters took lessons from Jerome.

Of course, there were ways other than by reading that Christian mothers might influence the religious lives of their children, and it would be misleading to suggest that reading the scriptures was the only way Christianity spread; for most Christians, the message was transmitted orally.[124] A Christian aristocratic mother who attended church regularly and celebrated

Christian holidays would be setting patterns that her children might follow. A mother could be a spiritual role model, as Jerome posits Laeta should be for Paula. But this sort of activity on the part of aristocratic mothers does not mean that women were active converters of their families. Paula and Albina were conspicuous for their personal devotion yet both produced pagan sons.[125]

Nor were Christian aristocratic women considered appropriate figures for taking an active public role in conversion or instruction outside the family. It was a man's task to go out and preach because "women have less resolution in proclaiming the word and are weaker in following it."[126] As A. Arjava observed: "Both pagans and Christians were convinced that the best place for a woman was in her own house where she could take care of her children and exert control over the family slaves so that the husband was free to attend to the public life."[127] Taking care of children did not necessarily entail religious instruction; on the contrary, the church had careful prescriptions that any woman teaching in private should regard the proprieties and be deferential to men.[128] When the learned Marcella answered questions on exegesis, she gave the credit to her teacher Jerome or to some other man "so that she might not seem to do a wrong to the male sex, and sometimes even to priests."[129] When Melania the Younger spoke in public in Constantinople, she is said to have exhorted noble women to constancy. But even this remarkable woman was described not as preaching but as simply engaging in a private discussion.[130] When women were prominent in theological issues, the groups with which they were involved were often branded as heretical, and the dominant role of women in them was frequently used as a criticism since it was widely believed that "women are naturally more credulous than men, and that it is quite improper for them to be in authority."[131]

How Did Christianity Spread among Aristocratic Women?

The same family and social structures that constrained women and made them unlikely converters were also key to the spread of Christianity among aristocratic women in the fourth and early fifth centuries. In this section I will examine not whether women were instigators of conversion, but how Christianity spread among aristocratic women. In my view, women converted due to the influence of fathers, husbands, and sons who, as those primarily responsible for the religious activities of the family, also orchestrated women's religious choices. Although fourth-century Christianity did offer certain women new social roles—namely, as ascetics or celibates or, to a lesser degree, as patrons and holders of church office—these new "careers" cannot explain how and why Christianity spread among most aristocratic women. The family remained the central institution in the lives of most aristocratic women, and it was the primary means of spreading Christianity among them in the fourth century.

The Influence of the Family

Some proponents of asceticism voiced opposition to the conventional subordination of women to family control and influence. Jerome counseled the noble lady Furia to "honour your father, but only if he does not separate you from your true Father."[132] In this advice he followed a strand of Christian thinking that emphasized the conflict between Christianity and family, found in texts such as the third-century *Passion of Perpetua*.

After Constantine, however, the nature of the conflict between family and religion had changed. As J. Goody observed, Christianity by then had turned from being a sect to a church that "welcome[d] doctrinal continuity in the family, ensured by the endogamy of the faithful . . . [The church became concerned with] ensuring that [it] hold on to the faith of those who had acquired their religion in the bosom of their families, and struggled against heresy and apostasy."[133] Thus, as the church became institutionalized in post-Constantinian elite society, it insisted more and more on patriarchal authority, in the family and in the state. While no church father would argue that family ties stood above religion, a moderate position emerges from figures such as Augustine, who counseled women to obey husbands and fathers at home and patriarchal authority in church. Jerome's support for radical asceticism at the expense of family interests and church authority ultimately isolated him from the majority opinion of the aristocracy and of the Roman clergy, an isolation that ultimately led to his flight from Rome.[134]

The authoritarian trend in the fourth-century church coincided with the spread of Christianity to the upper classes, where the patriarchal family model was long established. The two models reinforced one another. Simultaneously, a respectable, aristocratic Christianity was growing that enabled women, like men, to turn to Christianity without losing the social prestige that came from family. Thus when most aristocratic women did convert, they could do so within the context of their patriarchal families and households.

A TYPICAL CHRISTIAN WOMAN. I want to dwell briefly on a text actually written by an aristocratic woman, Proba, that suggests what was, in many ways, the typical woman's response to Christianity in the fourth century. Married to Clodius Celsinus signo Adelphius, Proba had impeccable aristocratic ties. She was also well educated, having composed a now lost epic poem on the civil war between Magnentius and Constantius II before writing her *Cento*, a patchwork poem drawn from the lines of Virgil in praise of Christ. In retelling the life of Christ, Proba combined traditional womanly aristocratic values—namely, filial devotion, domestic harmony, and family reputation—with the message of Christianity.[135]

Unlike Christians who propounded celibacy and asceticism over family, "nowhere does Proba present either Jesus or Mary as a model for the Christian celibate; rather, it is Mary's maternity that is stressed."[136] The message of Jesus is similarly reinterpreted by Proba to fit comfortably with traditional aristocratic womanly values. Christ's teaching, according to Proba, stressed devotion to family and sharing with kin. For Proba's Christ, to strike a parent leads to eternal punishment.[137] Her Jesus counsels a rich youth not to forsake his brother.[138] Such injunctions support the family as aristocrats valued it. Even wealth and honor are justified: Proba "distort[s] the words of Jesus to the rich young man so that he is no longer commanded to sell his goods and give the proceeds to the poor" but is urged instead to simply "learn contempt for wealth."[139]

Perhaps most striking, given its loaded symbolism in contemporary ascetic tracts, is Proba's depiction of the "marriage" of Adam and Eve in terms of a Roman wedding and the blissful, positive image of their sexuality and married life before their fall. Even Eve's sin is portrayed as listening to bad advice, and she tempts her husband by pleading with him, "moving his mind with unexpected charm," not through sexual favors.[140] Marital devotion is a recurrent theme. In tracing the borrowings from the Virgilian matrons Creusa, Dido, and Andromache, the editors of the text, E. Clark and D. Hatch, note as "most significant, [that] Creusa's salutation to Aeneas, 'Sweet husband,' is borrowed by Proba to address her own spouse, Adelphius, in the closing lines of the *Cento*."[141]

Proba's poem represents an articulate, mid-fourth-century woman's solution to the merging of traditional aristocratic values with Christianity. In my view, hers is the more typical response by aristocratic women who turned to Christianity. Perhaps a convert herself, Proba wanted to hold on to her aristocratic family values and structures as she embraced Christianity. And if this *Cento* was used for didactic purposes, Proba's ideals may well have had a wide audience.

INDIVIDUAL SALVATION VERSUS FAMILY TIES.   In emphasizing the role of family in spreading Christianity among aristocratic women I would not deny that Christianity's emphasis on the individual and his or her salvation might have appealed to women. Christianity gave a woman a claim to a spiritual state "of her own." This idea may well have helped in the spread of Christianity, but the appeal of this message does not contradict the social significance of the family for the conversion of most fourth-century aristocratic women; most had to reach individual salvation within the context of a family household. Even women who chose an ascetic lifestyle did so, by and large, within their own home or in a house shared with other women. Until the very end of the fourth century there were no convents or monasteries in the western empire.[142]

Not all women were equally committed to Christianity; for many, questions of individual salvation paled before questions of status and family. Aristocratic women could, and did, wield significant social influence and prestige, which they gained through their family. Some were quite wealthy. But to relinquish one's social position by going against the wishes of their family would be difficult for most. When it became possible to adopt Christianity within the bosom of the family and to retain social standing, Christianity attracted more aristocratic men and their women.

DID CHANGES IN THE LAW UNDERMINE THE LATE ROMAN FAMILY? In viewing the family and male influence as key to the spread of Christianity among aristocratic women, I am also aware that the late Roman family did not remain a static feature in the changing landscape of the fourth century. The major changes are legal, however, not social. In the eyes of certain scholars, changes in the civic laws pertaining to marriage and inheritance, especially under Constantine, altered or undermined the late Roman family.[143] If these changes had this sort of direct impact, then we might be led to reconsider the role of the family in the conversion of aristocratic women. It does not, however, seem likely that these legal changes had such a destructive or sudden impact.

Constantine repealed the Augustan law that made celibate men and women inferior and removed the penalties for childlessness.[144] But to see this change as a "great infringement upon traditional family life and especially on the rights and powers of the *paterfamilias* . . . [that also] created a serious conflict between the church and the men of the Roman families" is to misrepresent the impact of the change.[145] The law that Constantine repealed concerning celibacy was hardly oppressive; unmarried persons were forbidden to inherit except from kin within the sixth degree, which includes a very wide circle of kinship. Nor did this law radically change the status of widows. Roman women had always exercised a certain autonomy about remarriage. Although women had to give legal consent to marry, it was far easier to pressure a young girl into her first marriage than to compel a widow to remarry.[146] Since Roman women became legally independent upon the death of their father (a situation that the demographics and marriage patterns suggest was faced often by adult children), many widows were already exercising considerable independence in decisions about second marriages.[147] If a woman wanted to remain a widow, to be distinguished with the title of *univira,* she could find ways to do so, although most women before the rise of Christianity did not normally choose widowhood.[148]

The repeal on penalties for celibacy was quite welcome to many aristocratic families, for it made the transfer of property within families easier.[149] And some families also saw celibacy as a useful tool: "Given the Roman legal expectation of equal partibility of estates among surviving children, the devotion of surplus sons and especially daughters to celibacy allowed families to preserve the size and unity of family inheritances, and to avoid the expense of a dowry, however slight that may be."[150] Women and young girls especially could be pressured into celibacy, as into marriage; both Jerome and Basil had encountered families who had dedicated a daughter to virginity to save on her dowry.[151] Girls given to the church in this way could be withdrawn by their families, in a high-handed fashion, when a better use could be made of them. In one case, a widow, who had dedicated her virgin daughter to Christ when the girl was ill, decided to marry off the now healthy girl after her son died and to offer instead to remain a widow.[152]

Changes in the law on celibacy made it easier for a woman to remain celibate, but it did not mean that celibate women destroyed the ties of the Roman family or male patriarchal authority over women. Constantine did not change the restrictions on inheritance between spouses, a practice that gave relatives by blood priority over spouses in inheritance claims.[153] Moreover, unmarried widows and virgins still had to obey traditional and Christian male ideals of feminine comportment—subservience to men and modesty—and were still to "tailor their asceticism to the wishes of fathers and husbands."[154] When Melania the Elder left Rome in 374 for the East, she did so only after taking care that her son was left well off and well connected, a care she had exercised for the past twelve years of her widowhood.[155] Not surprisingly, we hear very little opposition to celibacy on the part of the western aristocracy until the 380s, and then mostly against its radical proponents who advocated celibacy against the wishes of the family involved.[156]

New Roles: Religious "Career Paths" for Aristocratic Women?

In concluding her study on women in late antiquity, G. Clark astutely remarked:

> the texture [of late Roman society] over all is that of inherited assumptions . . . that women are domestic . . . that they are expected to manifest the traditional virtues of modesty, chastity and piety towards gods and family . . . But Christianity did enlarge the possibilities for women. The really important shift of belief here is that commitment to God may require, in both men and women, abandonment of duties to family and State. For the first time, women (some women) could reject marriage and child-bearing, and live at home with their mothers, or in solitude, or in a community of women.[157]

The balanced antithesis in Clark's conclusion is important to keep in mind; the basic assumptions about the traditional role of women remained intact, even though Christianity offered new options to some women.

Some aristocratic women did pursue these new options and some were influential as they did so, but their importance in spreading Christianity has been overemphasized by scholars who have, in my view, been too swayed by the surviving texts that reiterate the *topos* of womanly piety and highlight women's new roles as virgins or widows. The *topos* of woman's influence in these new religious roles, often associated with celibacy in this period, is better explained as a strategy adopted by Christian men to assert their dominance in a competition for honor and authority within the Christian community rather than as evidence of what women actually did.[158]

I would argue that these new options—in particular asceticism, celibacy, and holding office within the church—were of limited importance in spreading Christianity among aristocratic women for the following reasons. First, the number of women who followed these new options remained relatively small. Second, the proscriptions on women teaching and evangelizing restricted the influence of women in these new roles. In turn, these limitations reduced the importance of these new roles in spreading Christianity. Third, the new options created a negative reaction that reduced their attraction for many women and undermined the influence of the women who did take them up.[159]

ASCETICISM AND CELIBACY. Discussions of the appeal of celibate and ascetic lifestyles for late antique aristocratic women have been informed by modern feminist and antifeminist positions. Consequently, some scholars have celebrated celibacy and asceticism as womanly liberation and have emphasized the texts that discuss the distastefulness of married life, the demands of sexuality and childbearing, and the subordination of women to their fathers, husbands, and families.[160] But in my view, as in that of other scholars, the new role that a celibate woman could play was not so "free"; husbands, fathers, and families still exerted control over celibate women. Most ascetic women in the West in the fourth and early fifth centuries still lived at home or in a home with other women where "they were still expected to follow patterns of modest domesticity."[161]

While it may be impossible to come to a general statement about women's motives for choosing celibacy and asceticism, I would argue that these roles were not key in the spread of Christianity among aristocratic women. The impact of aristocratic women in the ascetic movement in Italy in the 380s and 390s—coming as it did after the turning point in the conversion of that class—was chronologically later and hence of lesser significance in converting and spreading Christianity among men and women of the aristocracy than previously argued.

THE EVIDENCE FROM ROME. What we would like to know is when many of these aristocratic ascetic women or their families first turned from paganism to Christianity and if they took up ascetic roles upon conversion. The evidence from Rome does not suggest that asceticism was the initial attraction for most aristocratic women. In Rome we find the beginnings of the ascetic movement among aristocratic women in the 350s and 360s. Marcella, whom Jerome proclaimed the "first" among ascetic women, refused a second marriage, probably after 358, in keeping with Christian notions, but

only in the third quarter of the fourth century do we find Marcella practic-
ing "house asceticism" in her palace on the Aventine.[162] Other indications of
ascetic women in the 350s suggest only a small number of aristocratic
women were involved in the movement at that time.[163]

In the 350s, however, we do hear of the flourishing of a respectable "normal" aristocratic lifestyle adopted by Christian women. The aristocratic poetess Proba, perhaps just recently converted to Christianity after 353, is one
example.[164] A delegation of married aristocratic women who implored
Constantius in 357 to return the bishop Liberius to the city was not composed of ascetics; their husbands, hesitant to approach the emperor, suggested that the women approach him "in all their customary splendour of
array, that so the sovereign, judging their rank from their dress, might count
them worthy of being treated with courtesy and kindness."[165] These instances suggest that although some advocated asceticism as "the favored
mode of life for Christians," not many aristocratic women embraced it in
Rome in the 350s.[166]

In addition to these chronological considerations, it does not seem likely
that most aristocratic women turned to ascetic Christianity directly from paganism. Most of the consecrated virgins were daughters of widows, already
raised as Christians.[167] Rather, asceticism appears most often as a "second
stage" Christian choice. Marcella, who, because she was a Christian, had refused a second marriage and then became increasingly interested in asceticism, appears to represent the typical pattern.[168] Similarly, Asella, possibly
Marcella's sister and thus probably an aristocrat, was dedicated to virginity
by her Christian parents.[169] This pattern suggests the limited importance of
the ascetic role model in converting aristocratic women from paganism to
Christianity.

What we can gather from the sources also indicates that the ascetic circles
around these aristocratic women remained small, albeit influential. When
Jerome came to Rome in 382, he found that Marcella, with her mother, had
gathered around her a few Christian women interested in living according
to ascetic ideals.[170] But hers was just one of many such "salons" at Rome devoted to a wide range of issues. We hear of senatorial women, as well as
men, being implicated in a range of activities that, under Valentinian, were
condemned as tied to magic and adultery.[171] Manichaeism also contended
with ascetic Christianity from the second half of the fourth century on. Yet
these aristocratic groups remained a minority in the aristocracy in the West.

Although the majority of the treatises on virginity are addressed to
women, this does not indicate that virginity enjoyed a widespread appeal.

Such treatises "may suggest that women had greater religious commitment, or were more eager than men to avoid marriage, but perhaps the reverse is true: women needed more convincing. A woman who did not marry renounced her only social role and might come under great family pressure. A man could opt to renounce marriage without renouncing a career: he could make compromises and had more freedom of choice."[172] In this we hear again echoes of issues of late twentieth-century feminism reverberating in the fourth century; why should women have to give up family for profession of faith and a "career in religion"?[173]

Moreover, by turning away from this world and denying the importance of creating or maintaining family ties, celibate and ascetic women apparently minimized their impact on the conversion of their families. Some aristocrats, pagan and Christian alike, accounted the ascetic lifestyle of a Lea "madness."[174] But the reaction could be more hostile still; the condemnation of Melania the Younger by "all of Roman society" may be exaggerated, but many aristocrats—pagan and Christian—disapproved of her actions for threatening the security of her family.[175] The radical asceticism of a Jerome ran counter to the ethos and desires of most aristocrats—men and women. The force of the hostile reaction by ascetics like Jerome to Jovinian, a proponent of marriage over celibacy, suggests how much support there was for these moderate views within the Christian community in Rome.[176] Hostility toward aristocratic ascetic women could erupt at any time, as it did in the Priscillianist controversy.[177]

THE TOPOS OF WOMANLY INFLUENCE. If my view of the conversion of female aristocrats is right, why do so many of the texts from late antiquity dwell on the influence of women and ascetic women in particular? This question was the subject of noteworthy studies published by K. Cooper.[178] To my mind, Cooper's studies provide compelling reasons for the apparent disjuncture between my analysis and the dominant scholarly *opinio communis*.

Cooper's premise is that "Roman male discourse about female power served more often than not as a rhetorical strategy within competition for power among males themselves." She observes that texts "which ascribe social or religious innovation to the influence of women on their male sexual partners cannot be read at face value. Rather, these ascriptions must be seen as attempts to assign value, whether positive or negative, to the decisions of men."[179] By focusing on womanly influence, bishops "could find in the rhetoric of sexual moderation a tool for undermining the authority of men who had not professed celibacy."[180] In essence, the *topos* of womanly influence was a response to a conflict for power among Roman men, between "married men in positions of civic or cultural importance (some married to baptized women, some themselves baptized, others strictly polytheist) and celibate men, usually of lesser rank, who wished to advise the married."[181] In this confrontation celibacy took on a growing importance in the Christian idea of authority, although the other side, advocating an honored role for the *matrona,* survives in certain fifth- and sixth-century texts.[182]

Thus the prominence of women in so many fourth-century ascetic texts should not be read as indicative of how women actually lived, nor do these ascetic texts prove that a great number of women were attracted to ascetic Christianity.[183] The rhetorical ends of the authors of these texts, and the elaborate rhetorical stylization of gender in them, must be taken into account. We should note, as Averil Cameron did, "the number of women who took Jerome's ascetic strictures seriously were only a small minority."[184] My population study of aristocrats and research into the historical evidence also suggest how limited was the importance of this new "career" for the spread of Christianity among aristocratic women.

CHURCH OFFICES.   Among the various social factors seen as attracting women especially to Christianity is the possibility of attaining an honored position in the church hierarchy. Women had held pagan priesthoods (e.g., *sacerdos publica, flaminica*), but these were essentially social honors, granted in recognition of a social position that a woman had by virtue of her family and marriage connections, not "careers" in the modern sense of a full-time occupation. In the church women were given offices as deaconess, widow, and virgin.[185] Were the offices that the fourth-century church in the Latin West offered aristocratic women significant influences in favor of their conversion? And did aristocratic women use these offices to actively convert other aristocratic women? A brief overview of these offices and their functions indicates their limited importance.

Women are attested as deaconesses in the Greek East, fulfilling a role that existed in many ways because "there were some cultic functions men could not perform with respect to women without raising the specter of impropriety."[186] The fourth-century eastern *Apostolic Constitutions* stipulated that bishops choose deaconesses from widows and virgins to serve women, to visit them when they are sick, and to assist in the baptism of women.

Their presence was also required, for matters of decency, when a woman visited a deacon or bishop. They welcomed women to religious services and, along with male deacons, kept the congregation quiet. But their role was proscribed in terms of liturgy; they could not make benedictions or perform services.[187] Regardless of such limitations, this office could be very influential in spreading Christianity. So, for instance, as deaconesses performed their duty of visiting sick women, pagan as well as Christian, they could bring their spiritual message along with physical aid.

Although the office of deaconess is well attested in the eastern empire among aristocrats, it does not appear as a popular option for aristocratic women in the western empire.[188] There is not a single case that I have found of an aristocratic woman in the Latin West attested as a deaconess during the time period of this study. Indeed, of the estimated 5,000 Christian inscriptions from Rome, not one deaconess is mentioned.[189] And texts from the western empire record the opposition of church fathers to this office. The earliest church council from the West citing "women in the ministry" is from Nîmes in 396. It does not indicate where these women are located but does describe them as at odds with Christian traditions. Some scholars interpret this text as referring to deaconesses, even though the term is not used in the text and the reference to "women in the ministry" is unspecific.[190]

The absence of the office of deaconess in the West in the fourth century may reflect regional differences in the role and status of women; in the East, where Romans claimed occasionally that women were more segregated, where women went veiled in public in certain areas, the necessity of deaconesses to attend to women in private is understandable.[191] In the West, however, and especially among the aristocracy, women were not so removed from the society of men, and this may help to explain why this office was not important there.

Unlike the order of deaconesses, those of widows and virgins received official church support and are attested in the western empire. Widows and virgins derived their claim to authority from their pursuit of celibacy. But, as I have already argued, celibacy and asceticism appealed to only a small minority among the elite. Similarly, the offices of widow and virgin had only limited appeal for aristocratic women, and hence were of far less significance in spreading Christianity than in honoring women already Christian. The duties ascribed to each reinforce this impression.

Chaste widows, a distinct order within the church in the West, formally vowed to renounce remarriage and to devote themselves to God.[192] In his treatise *On Widows,* Ambrose notes their foremost duty is to pray and fast, like the sacred Anna; then to practice hospitality and humble service; to serve the ministry of mercy and liberality; and, lastly, to perform "every good work."[193] In Ambrosiaster's view, these duties make widows worthy of special honor and material support from the church. For example, if their families are not treating them with respect, they are to be taken in by the church.[194]

The honors given to consecrated widows varied regionally, but their public recognition and communal support were clearly key to their role within the Christian community. Widows were visually set apart in church by their special seating, either with the clergy, as the African Tertullian suggests, or in the front, as the *Apostolic Constitutions* suggest.[195] And their dress, shabby and dark, would also have distinguished them in public.[196] In some places they even had their names inscribed on church monuments.[197] At the same time, consecrated aristocratic widows, living at home, could satisfy family expectations; they had provided heirs. In certain Christian circles, having a prominent consecrated widow in the family could be prestigious. There were secular advantages for widowhood as well, as Jerome and Ambrose both emphasized; by the late fourth century, a dedicated widow could, for one, remain in control of her children's property.[198] Thus the office of widow could be attractive to devout aristocratic women and their families.

The impact of the office of widow, I suspect, was greatest upon other Christians. The duties of widows noted by fourth-century Latin writers—prayers, asceticism, liberality, good works—were aimed at benefiting mostly other believers.[199] The charitable works of aristocratic widows could extend to the pagan poor, but Christian leaders, like Jerome, consistently advised women to give "especially unto them that are of the household of faith."[200] Charity was to start at home. Widows served as role models but primarily for other Christians, even if some pagans might have been impressed by their honors and actions.

It should be emphasized, however, that in the fourth century the church limited the teaching and evangelizing influence of the order of widows. Their spiritual devotion and exemplary moral life should, by their very virtue, teach, but widows were told not to speak in public, or evangelize, or even teach catechumens, as they may well have done earlier in the East.[201] Ambrose, Jerome, and Ambrosiaster, in discussing widows, explicitly prohibit these activities. Rather, the elder woman should teach young women "good things," including obedience to their husbands.[202] Since the formal duties and public role of the widow were restricted by the church fathers, the office of widow, insofar as it influenced others, impressed mostly other Christians.

Similarly, the office of virgin had only a limited role in spreading Christianity. Although over the course of the fourth century virginity came to be seen as superior to widowhood in merit and precedence within the church, the duties of virgins were even more circumscribed than those of widows. Jerome, in describing the obligations of virgins—study, prayer, fasting, obedience, liberality for Christ, and constant industry—consistently emphasizes the importance of giving; the upper-class virgin was expected to be "powerful in revenue, a mother to the poor."[203] Neither here, nor in his earlier letter to Eustochium on virgins, does Jerome indicate an evangelizing or teaching role for virgins. On the contrary, the ideal virgin was not to visit any women who had not taken vows of chastity and was to be restricted to her chamber to serve Christ better.[204] Thus, "by remaining enclosed in her house, [a virgin] was living the metaphor of her closed body."[205] Although not all may have lived up to such lofty ideals, most aristocratic virgins that we hear of in the fourth-century West did live restricted lives at home or in a household with other ascetic women.[206]

The office of virgin attracted certain aristocratic women. To some, it offered prestige: the public ceremony that marked the virgin's commitment reinforced the honor of this office within the Christian community.[207] Then, too, to some families the office was economically advantageous: "Men who pride themselves on their religion give to their virgin daughters sums scarcely sufficient for their maintenance, and bestow the bulk of their property upon sons and daughters living in the world."[208]

Yet, regardless of the office's appeal, the duties of virgins reveal how limited a role such a life had in spreading Christianity. Virgins had no evangelical or teaching responsibilities. They were separated from mainstream society and isolated within their family. Their influence was spiritual, but it was greatest on fellow Christians who would be most aware of their presence within the community. Most Christian aristocratic young women did not enter this order. Thus, I would suggest, the office of virgin was of limited influence in spreading Christianity, however prestigious some of its advocates—male and female—were individually.

WOMEN AS PATRONS.   Liberality directed primarily at Christians and the church was one of the duties of the office of widows and virgins in the fourth century. But an aristocratic woman need not be celibate to be a patron of Christ and to thereby gain honor. This was a church that was in need of benefactors. "Few provincial churches possessed extensive estates of their own: they depended on intermittent gifts of ready money and of valuables such as pious noblewomen could provide." Thus, in Peter Brown's view, "the influence of aristocratic female patrons on the Church was far out of proportion to their numbers."[209]

The impact of one very wealthy ascetic woman could be widespread, judging from the patronage activities of the very rich and very generous Melania the Younger. She was so wealthy that when she sold her properties, she was able to distribute funds to "Mesopotamia, Syria, all of Palestine, and Egypt," in short, to "all the West and the East"; she gave whole islands to the church to be used for monasteries for monks and virgins, furnishing each with enough money for maintenance as well as for altars, silk cloth, and costly furnishings.[210] At one point Melania is said to have given 45,000 pieces of gold to the poor and to the saints.[211] The building of monasteries by Melania the Elder and Paula in Jerusalem and their distribution of wealth made possible the monastic and scholarly undertakings of Rufinus and Jerome.[212] Such a wealthy patron as Melania the Younger could influence not only Christian leaders but the religious choices of those below her in society. In North Africa, Melania allegedly used her money to persuade young men and women to lead chaste Christian lives: "Only the Lord knows how many Samaritans, pagans and heretics she persuaded through money and exhortations to come back to God."[213]

But Melania's role as patron would not have had such a direct influence over those in her own class with whom she was not involved in a patron-client relationship. Rather, she would be seen as a peer, a potential and powerful friend who chose to advocate Christianity. So, for example, at Constantinople she "greatly benefitted even the Christ-loving imperial women" through her conversations, not her patronage.[214] Her role as patron was of limited influence over other aristocrats as compared to her impact on those below her in society. And even though Melania was a good deal richer than many other aristocrats, she still had to interact with them in such a way as to win their approval if she were to be accepted within Christian elite circles.[215]

Even on a smaller scale women patrons could influence their local communities as donors and founders of buildings. Fabiola, in penance for a divorce following remarriage, founded the first hospital in Rome and a hostelry for travelers *(xenodochium)* at Porto Romano. Her generosity to clerics,

monks, and virgins extended throughout Italy.[216] Other Christian aristocratic women could gain prestige through their patronage of Christian writers and thinkers, as their pagan peers had supported pagan literati. This sort
of patronage gave some women an influence on the intellectual life in the
Greek East that Peter Brown called "unparalleled."[217]

But was their role as patron relevant for the spread of Christianity among
aristocratic women in the western empire? It does not seem likely that
Christian women were notably more active than pagan women in this regard. A few Christian women are known in the West as literary patrons; female supporters of Jerome, Rufinus, and Priscillian are well attested as
benefactors.[218] But propertied pagan women had for centuries played the
role of donor, founder, and patron of the arts and had thereby achieved
honor. Women in the third century had been patrons of "secular" as well as
religious cults in their communities.[219] The epigraphic evidence decreases after the mid-third century, but this does not mean that female patronage declined. An aristocratic pagan woman, like Fabia Aconia Paulina, could win
recognition by dedicating a statue to the Vestal Virgin or, as did a Turrania
Anicia Iuliana, by setting up a statue to Venus.[220] There is little reason to
think that pagan women did not also continue to act as patrons, nor does the
role of Christian patron appear markedly different from that offered to pagan women.[221]

The growth of Christianity in the post-Constantinian West opened up
many possibilities for female aristocratic benefactors, as it did for their male
peers. The activities of wealthy women on behalf of the church may have
contributed to the scholarly impression that the role of patron was uniquely
important to Christian women. Indeed, as the pace of conversion increased,
there was a growing number of positive social and political advantages to
women and their families who decided to act as patrons in support of the
preferred religion of the emperor. But there is little reason to suggest that
these considerations influenced aristocratic women more than men. Thus I
would suggest that the role of women as patrons cannot be separated from
these other social and religious changes, and was in itself of limited import
in converting or spreading Christianity among other aristocratic women.

Conclusions

I realize that my analysis of the role of family in the Christianization of
women is at odds with the views of many scholars, both those who have

seen women as the primary converters to the faith and those who have considered the new options that Christianity offered women—the possibility of denying marriage and living in ascetic communities or at home—as key to the conversion of aristocratic women. Treatises exhorting virginity or widowhood addressed to women are used to support these views. However, the textual evidence gives prominence to an area of Christianity that, although important within Christianity and within certain well-documented aristocratic circles, was not key to the conversion of aristocratic women in the fourth century in general. The texts that support these views need to be handled with a greater awareness of the rhetorical ends of their male authors. These texts can tell us a good deal about the attitudes of some people, but they must be read against what we know about late Roman institutions and the patterns of behavior of people at the time.

Based on my study population, I see three reasons to question the emphasis on aristocratic women in the process of conversion. First, women in this study did not convert any earlier than men in the years after Constantine, which they should have done if they were a key factor in Christianization. Second, the study population also shows little evidence of intermarriage, indicating an adequately large population of pagan aristocratic women available at all times for pagan aristocratic men to marry. And, third, given the predominance of same-religion marriages, there is little evidence to suggest that Christian women were influencing the religious affiliation of children; the majority of children conform to the religious identities of their parents. Moreover, the patterns in this study population are consistent with the historical evidence concerning the patriarchal nature of the Roman family as an institution and the position of women in late antiquity. The church, too, publicly opposed women as teachers and proselytizers in public and private. The evidence thus leads me to view women as unlikely "converters" to Christianity.

Christianity did not alter the fundamental dynamics of aristocratic families and the role of women in them; economically, socially, and legally, aristocratic women were constrained by a patriarchal family and social structure that the church, as it gained in secular prestige after Constantine, reinforced. As Christianity spread, the family still remained at the center of most aristocratic women's lives, in their religious choices as in all else.

There was, to be sure, individual variation, and some women did not conform to these restrictive conventions. There are spectacular instances of aristocratic women who were attracted to celibacy. But, even if some women did choose to take up new roles, most aristocratic women did not. Analysis of new options for women as ascetics, celibates, church officers, or patrons indicates the limited impact of these new roles in the Christianization of the women of the Roman aristocracy. For most aristocratic women, it was still the family and "male" influence that were the key factors in their adopting Christianity. This does not mean that women lacked agency. As Christianity spread among the aristocracy, women were participants in the same world that was shaping the choices and actions of their male peers. But, in my view, since men generally orchestrated the religious affiliation of the late Roman family, they were also the ones who were primarily responsible for spreading Christianity among women in the fourth and fifth centuries.

CHAPTER 6

The Emperor's Influence on Aristocratic Conversion

> Julian received them [two distinguished senators] with honour, and
> passing over the better man, . . . made Maximus prefect of the eter-
> nal city, to please Vulcacius Rufinus, whose nephew he knew him
> to be.
>
> —Ammianus Marcellinus, *Res Gestae* (trans. John C. Rolfe)

Whether one sees in Constantine's conversion to Christianity
in 312 a sincere religious experience, or the Machiavellian manipulations of
a savvy politician, or "an erratic block which has diverted the stream of history," the influence that this emperor—and a succession of Christian emperors—exercised in bringing about the Christianization of the aristocracy—is
of key historical importance for many scholars, ranging from Edward Gibbon to T. D. Barnes and R. MacMullen.[1] In essence, the top-down view of
Christianization concludes that once the emperors had adopted Christianity,
there were so many benefits and incentives in favor of adopting the religion
of the emperor that the conversion of the aristocracy, like that of the population at large, was more or less inevitable.

It is certainly true that the emperor had influence, but that is not the
whole story. Indeed, a top-down model expresses but one side of a vital relationship in which both emperors and aristocrats had power and resources
at their disposal. This view erroneously assumes that influence and honor
flowed only in one direction and ignores the need of emperors to be seen as
legitimate rulers. It is necessary to bring the aristocracy back in as active participants in a dynamic relationship. The epigraph to this chapter provides
one anecdotal indication of how influence flowed in two directions. Ammianus noted that Julian, in weighing the merits of two distinguished senators, passed over the better man (the elder Symmachus) and chose in his
place Maximus, the nephew of Vulcacius Rufinus, as prefect of Rome "to

178

please Vulcacius" *(ad Rufini Vulcatii gratiam)*. By making this appointment, which would bring honor to Vulcacius, Julian sought to reaffirm ties to this powerful Roman aristocrat and his family. Julian, as all Roman emperors, was influenced by a system of honor and patronage that was at the heart of the aristocratic status culture, a system in which he, as emperor, was also enmeshed.

Emperors were considered "the most aristocratic of all aristocrats," and that is why Symmachus could praise the emperor Valentinian I as a noble who had simply exchanged the garments of private life for the imperial purple.[2] In a law of 362 the emperor Julian expressly referred to himself as a member of the senatorial order.[3] But since the emperor was seen as a member of the aristocracy, he was expected to abide by the values and norms of aristocratic society. So, for example, Diocletian's attempt to establish an emperor-centered, military-style administrative hierarchy based on service and achievement failed because he did not follow established aristocratic notions of *honos* and status as the basis for service.[4] Similarly, if an emperor were to favor only Christians, to make appointments solely for religious reasons, he would deny the conventions and networks that validated imperial authority. No emperor would single-mindedly pursue such a course of action for, although the fourth-century emperors were recognized as supreme, they could not successfully rule as autocrats. They needed to gain the legitimating support of the aristocracy, a class in possession of significant resources and prestige as well as expertise of the sort needed to maintain the imperial bureaucracy. Indeed, it was precisely because the aristocracy was key to imperial rule and legitimacy that emperors from Diocletian on worked to incorporate them into the service of the state. Aristocrats, like the elder Symmachus, recognized it as part of their mission to help the "good" emperor.[5] But as participants in the aristocrats' status culture, emperors were limited in what they could and would do to influence the spread of Christianity.

Of course, the emperor was not a marginal actor in the conversion of the aristocracy. As I have shown, the environment favoring Christianity, including the emperor's contribution to that environment, was most influential in relation to new men and to those from the provinces pursuing imperial bureaucratic and military careers. The same resources the emperors had to build ties with and encourage the support of aristocrats could be used to influence their religious choices. In their appointments to office, in the laws they passed, in their patronage of the church, in their granting honors and rank, in their marriage alliances, in their promulgation of a model of behavior—in all these ways, emperors could influence aristocrats to adopt Christianity. Some emperors used these resources toward religious ends, but others seem not to have made conversion a priority during their reign.

Even the activist emperors, as I will show, did not advance only Christians. Rather, pagans continued to hold high office in large numbers throughout the century. Emperors confronted a complicated world in which political and social realities limited the degree to which they could or would encourage conversion. To confront a serious military threat, for example, the pious Honorius chose to annul a law rather than lose the support of Generidus, the pagan high commander stationed at Rome in 408.[6] Thus circumstances and nonreligious considerations, along with the structurally strong position of the late Roman aristocracy, made emperors more or less energetic in influencing aristocratic conversion whatever their personal preferences. Some emperors appear wholly unconcerned with conversion as a goal.

The aristocratic status culture clearly limited what emperors could do— or could even think of doing—to encourage religious change. In order to achieve their ends and to sustain legitimacy, emperors needed to appeal to the status culture of the aristocracy and to maintain ties with powerful aristocratic families in the military and civic spheres. Emperors adopted positions and acted in ways that would enhance their standing in the eyes of aristocrats. So the Christian Constantius II visited Rome to celebrate his triumphs; he addressed the nobility in the senate house; and he gave games where he accepted the crowd's heckling him with the license traditionally granted by emperors.[7] Constantius is but one example but there are many more. Thus it is necessary to consider not only the Christianization of the emperor's role but the ongoing influence of the aristocracy on the now Christian emperor.

The Varying Influence of Christian Emperors

More than the other emperors of the fourth and early fifth centuries, Constantine, Constantius II, Gratian, and Theodosius emerge as rulers who energetically used their resources to influence the religious affiliation of aristocrats. Constans, Jovian, Valentinian I, and Valentinian II appear much less intent upon conversion, while Julian consciously worked to bring Christians to paganism.[8]

The Active Emperors

Constantine had the most dramatic impact on late Roman society. As he ushered in legislation to make Christianity a licit religion and took on the role of patron of the church, he showed that Christianity was a viable, indeed imperially favored, option. Churches and clergy became the recipients of imperial patronage in the form of land, buildings, and funding.[9] The clergy received the sorts of privileges and exemptions reserved for the state priests, such as exemption from the curia to avoid performing compulsory public service *(nominationes)* and from serving as tax receivers *(susceptiones)* (*C.Th.* 16.2.1, 16.2.7). Clergy even received certain benefits that made clear their favored status. So, for instance, clergy and other Christians were granted the rather unusual right of freeing their slaves in church according to Roman law (*C.Th.* 4.7.1 [321]). This is one indication of this emperor's willingness to use law to support the institutional prestige of the church.

At the same time, Constantine reasserted the importance for the state of an expanded and honored aristocracy, and appointed to high office aristocrats, some old, some new, and some Christian. He made it increasingly known that Christian aristocrats would receive honors and privileges as great—in the eyes of some, even greater than—their pagan peers. By such actions, Constantine fostered the perception that being a Christian could place one in the favor of this emperor.

Above all, Constantine appreciated the symbolic force of his position as emperor. He used it to control internal dissensions within the Christian community, as, for example, taking a stand against the Donatists or advancing a version of the creed that all bishops would agree to at Nicaea.[10] When he claimed to be "bishop of those outside," he was articulating a leading religious role for himself and his successors both within the church and outside it. To this end, he wrote letters and delivered public discourses as well as listened to them at court and elsewhere.[11] One such oration, the *Oration to the Saints,* shows a ruler deeply committed to the belief that the promulgation of Christianity benefits the state as well as the emperor.[12]

Constantine's son, Constantius II, took certain of his father's religious policies even further. After a series of civil wars left him sole ruler of the empire by 350, Constantius II emerged as a zealous supporter of Christianizing efforts. With some fanfare, Constantius II supported two major missionary campaigns, one beyond the southern frontiers of the empire and one to the Goths on the Danube; although both missions served political and financial as well as religious ends, the implications of imperial involvement in such conversion efforts were not lost on contemporaries.[13]

Within the empire Constantius II concerned himself with internal dissensions in the church as well as with advancing Christianity through law and through personal patronage. The nuances of his involvement in Arianism and other doctrinal debates are too complicated to discuss at length here, but it is sufficient to say that, for better or worse, this ruler directed considerable energy toward religious ends.[14] His very zealousness prompted the complaint of the pagan historian Ammianus Marcellinus: "The plain [*absolutam*] and simple religion of the Christians he obscured by a dotard's superstition, and by subtle and involved discussions about dogma, rather than by seriously trying to make them agree, he aroused many controversies; and as these spread more and more, he fed them with contentious words."[15]

In one law concerning exemptions of clergy from public service, Constantius II professed as his motivation that "our state is sustained more by religion than by official duties and physical toil and sweat" (*C.Th.* 16.2.16).[16] The rhetoric is of note, for it shows how central was Christianity (or Constantius' version of it) to this emperor's stated views. Constantius II, like Constantine, was conspicuous in granting privileges and special honors to the church and its clergy. In addition to the exemptions noted above, bishops were prohibited from being accused in secular courts (*C.Th.* 16.2.12 [355]), and clergy were freed from any additional or extraordinary taxes (*C.Th.* 16.2.8 [343]). Constantius did not legislate directly against paganism per se, but he did restrict certain pagan cult practices, such as sacrifice (*C.Th.* 16.10.2 [341], 16.10.4 [356–361], 16.10.6 [356]), and decreed that the pagan temples be closed (*C.Th.* 16.10.4 [356–361]).[17]

Some twenty years after the death of Constantius II, the emperor Gratian's actions occasioned the first documented public protestation by pagan senators. In 382 Gratian confiscated monies intended for maintaining public sacrifices and ceremonies, confiscated property willed by aristocrats and Vestals for the upkeep of pagan ritual, and put an end to the exemption of pagan religious officials from compulsory public duties. He also ordered the removal of the altar, but not statue, of Victory from the Roman senate.

Soon after, Gratian publicly repudiated paganism by renouncing the title of *pontifex maximus*.[18] These actions led a number of prominent Roman pagan senators to request the return of the altar of Victory and a return to the imperial policy of tolerance. These requests were sent via the urban prefect Symmachus but were denied by Gratian and by his successor, Valentinian II.

The zealousness of Gratian to advance Christianity at the expense of senatorial traditions was matched by that of Theodosius I, whose methods were even more aggressive, especially after 390. As emperor in the East during the time of Gratian and later that of Valentinian II, Theodosius allied himself with men whose religious ideology matched his own. He advanced fellow Spanish aristocrats, family, and friends who shared his orthodox view of Christianity. Men like Maternus Cynegius and Nebridius, brother-in-law of the empress Flaccilla, typify the "zealous new western supporters" of Theodosius who, upon their arrival at court in Constantinople, facilitated the alliance between Theodosius and the "most militant wing of Christianity [an alliance] which had such ominous implications for the survival of paganism in the eastern provinces."[19] Theodosius' support also affected the western aristocracy, for he furthered the prestige of Christian aristocrats and institutions.

Theodosius I passed laws outlawing pagan rites, closing the temples, and removing privileges from pagan priests, even as he supported Christians embroiled in armed conflict.[20] According to the pagan historian Zosimus (discussed in Chapter 1), Theodosius tried to directly persuade senators to adopt Christianity; when he visited Rome in 394, Theodosius abolished the pagan sacrifices and dispensations, and then addressed the senate and tried to convince the senators to give up the "error" of their pagan ways. Even if the visit is disputed as fact, the antipagan policies of Theodosius are not.[21] The anecdote reveals the widespread perception that this emperor was directly concerned with the conversion of the aristocracy.

In his legislation Theodosius I indicated his willingness to use force to punish those who disobeyed his restrictions on pagan rites, such as sacrifice.[22] But even Theodosius did not attempt to force conversion. Rather, he used more subtle methods, persuasion and symbolic action, to gain his ends. Theodosius' refusal to return the altar of Victory to the Roman senate house had such symbolic resonance. And it may well have been to influence the Roman aristocracy through similar action that Theodosius chose as consuls for the year 395 (the year after Zosimus claimed he visited Rome) two members of the Anicii, an illustrious Roman family that had been Christian for a generation.[23]

The Less Active Emperors

Even the most zealous emperors of the fourth century did not marshal their resources in a single-minded way to support Christians nor were they always motivated by religious ends. The emperors' efforts to resolve conflicts within Christian communities should not be confused with policies aimed at promoting Christianization.[24] Indeed, certain emperors were far less active than the ones discussed above in promoting the conversion of the aristocracy.

After Constantine's death, his son, Constans, ruled alone in the western empire for a decade (340–350) in which there was little direct imperial action taken to convert the aristocracy. Constans, a pious Christian, followed the outlines of policy set by his father when he continued to express tolerance for pagan cult but legislated against pagan sacrifice.[25] Yet, like his father, he legislated to maintain pagan games with imperial monies and also to preserve pagan temples outside the city of Rome.[26] And, like his father, Constans devoted most of his religious energies to trying to resolve conflicts within the Christian community rather than taking new initiatives against paganism or pagan aristocrats, as was urged by his contemporaries like Firmicus Maternus.[27]

A decade later, the pagan Julian took the opposite stand on promoting Christianity. Although Julian initially proclaimed a policy of religious tolerance, his overt support for pagan cult and sacrifice, made real in law and by his own actions, was intended to stop the spread of Christianity.[28] He sought to undermine Christianity's appeal to the upwardly mobile local elites by removing tax exemptions from clerics.[29] Julian's brief reign grew increasingly intolerant of Christians and their institutions. He later prohibited Christians from teaching pagan literature, a law that was controversial in his lifetime, even for a pagan like Ammianus Marcellinus.[30] Julian's goal, to actively prevent conversion and foster paganism, ended with his death and the succession of the Christian Jovian (363–364), who proclaimed a broad policy of toleration, allowing "legal" (i.e., not magical) sacrifices.[31] Jovian's brief reign saw no large-scale Christianizing attempts; his efforts appear directed toward resolving disputes within the Christian community.[32]

The accession of the orthodox Valentinian I (364–375) in the West and

Valens (364–378) in the East led to a return to imperial policies that openly tolerated religious difference. Pagans noted this development with favor, for some evidently feared a backlash to Julian's anti-Christian policies.[33] Valentinian's reign shows not only tolerance but a lack of any real effort to convert the aristocracy. His appointments to high office favored Pannonians and men of military background but did not show any consistent concern to advance Christians over pagans (see Tables 6.1 and 6.2 and Chapter 4).

Nor do Valentinian's laws show him as actively working to advance Christianity among the aristocracy. As Ammianus remarked in praise, "he remained neutral on religious differences neither troubling anyone on that ground nor coercing him to reverence this or that. He did not bend the necks of his subjects to his own belief by threatening edicts, but left such matters undisturbed as he found them."[34] Both Valentinian I in the West and his brother Valens in the East allowed public cult of the gods, including the burning of incense, but not the animal sacrifices that were so offensive to Christians. The banning of nocturnal sacrifices by these emperors is consistent with their well-known concern to repress divinatory magic.[35]

Religious tolerance did not prevent Valentinian I from taking a stand on issues pertaining to the Christian community. He did, for instance, outlaw certain groups as heretical and penalized clerics who defrauded their flocks.[36] But these laws did not advance conversion directly. Rather, this emperor and his brother Valens appear far more engaged in pursuing military goals than advancing Christianity.[37]

Conversion Incentives: Imperial Appointment to High Office

One way in which historians have viewed emperors as influencing the conversion of aristocrats has been through their appointments to public office. I looked at appointments to high office within my study population from two different perspectives. First, I considered the highest office attained by each aristocrat in my study population and categorized him by the emperor under whom that individual served (see Table 6.1). This analysis indicates the peak of success for each man and under which emperor that highest office was reached. Second, I examined imperial appointments not of every man in this study but to the highest offices in the western empire. These included the offices of praetorian prefect of Italy, Gaul, and Africa; urban prefect of Rome; proconsul of Africa; consul in the western empire; military commander (*magister militum* or *equitum*); and high imperial bureaucratic offices *(comes rei privatae, comes sacrarum largitionum, quaestor sacri palatii,* and *magister officiorum).*[38] Since these were the appointments that the emperors were most concerned with, their influence would be paramount here, if anywhere. I then categorized these office holders chronologically by imperial reign (see Table 6.2). Both measures led to similar conclusions.

Based on the highest offices held by each aristocrat in my study population (see Table 6.1), I found that the pagans were predominant from 284 C.E. and continuing until the end of the reign of Valentinian I as sole ruler in 367. But under Constantine's sons, from 337–361, Christians (14%, or 13 out of 95) reached their highest offices in proportions that approached those of their pagan contemporaries (20%, or 19 out of 95). Under the emperors who followed Constantius (the pagan Julian, the Christian Jovian, and the early years of the Christian Valentinian I as sole ruler, from 361–367), pagans (19%, or 18 out of 95) again made up a larger proportion than Christians (1%, or 1 out of 95).[39]

But under the succeeding emperors, Gratian with Valentinian I and later with Valentinian II (367–383), Christians (22%, or 21 out of 95) were more in evidence than pagans (8%, or 8 out of 95). This was also the period in which three out of twenty-one converts to Christianity were located. It appears that the proportion of pagans and Christians was evened out in the course of the turbulent decade from 383–392 (10%, or 9 out of 95 pagans; 6%, or 6 out of 95 Christians). But it was only after Valentinian II, in the last decade of the fourth century and continuing into the first quarter of the fifth century, that Christians reaching their highest office (55%, or 52 out of 95) were again dominant as compared to pagans (22%, or 21 out of 95) (see Table 6.1).

My analysis of appointments to the highest offices in the western empire (see Table 6.2) reached essentially the same results. Pagans predominate in the period considered from 284 down through 367, but in the period from 337–361 (under the sons of Constantine) Christians appear (16%, or 12 out of 74) in equal proportions to pagans (17%, or 11 out of 65). Again, proportions of pagans to Christians reversed under Gratian with Valentinian I and Valentinian II (367–383); Christians (23%, or 17 out of 74) were more in evidence than pagans (5%, or 3 out of 65). The proportions of pagans (11%, or 7 out of 65) and Christians (7%, or 5 out of 74) even out in the decade 383–392 under Valentinian II as sole ruler, with a predominance of Christians (50%, or 37 out of 74) as compared to pagans (26%, or 17 out of 65) in the period after his rule, from 392–423.

These trends coincide with the known religious preferences of the emperors. Constantine and Constantius II were active, pro-Christian emperors; Julian was notoriously pro-pagan; and Valentinian I was reputed to be tolerant in religious matters. Gratian's rule, especially after the death of Valentinian I in 375, produced the highest proportion to this point of Christians achieving their highest office as compared to their pagan counterparts (see Table 6.1).[40]

After Gratian, under Valentinian II as sole ruler the Christian appointments ease (see Tables 6.1, 6.2).[41] Part of the reason for this change may lie in the politics of the day. Valentinian II wanted to signal a change from his predecessor's emphatically pro-Christian policies at the beginning of his sole rule.[42] A. Chastagnol, observing this same reversal in this emperor's appointments to urban prefect, suggested that Valentinian II was pursuing an intentional policy to win over the pagan aristocracy against the usurper Maximus, master of Gaul.[43] This interpretation is questionable, since Valentinian II refused to return the altar of Victory or to reestablish monetary support for the pagan cults. Politics offers another possible explanation for the high number of pagans under this emperor. Theodosius was at odds with Ambrose at this time, leading some scholars to conjecture that pagans were appointed to counter the bishop's influence, a policy (if it was one) that lasted until Theodosius reconciled with Ambrose by Christmas 390.[44]

Conversion Incentives: Imperial Appointment to Low Office

Although appointments to the highest offices are the clearest indicator of imperial policy, appointments to lower offices can also be revealing. I collected evidence for the lowest attested (often the first) appointments held by aristocrats in this study population, resulting in a group of 166 men.[45] The pattern observed here is somewhat different from that for appointments to highest office, perhaps indicating the greater ideological significance of appointments to high offices.

In the thirteen years of Constantine's sole rule, 324–337, my study population shows a parity of appointments to lowest offices; of twelve appointees in total, there was an even split between pagans and Christians. This parity did not persist under the sons of Constantine (337–361) where we find pagans (24%, or 19 out of 80) once again clearly predominant over Christians (14%, or 12 out of 86) (see Table 6.3). Like the highest appointments, the first clear reversal of the proportion of pagans to Christians occurs under Gratian with Valentinian I and with Valentinian II (367–383), when 8% (6 out of 80) of the pagan aristocrats were appointed to their lowest office as compared to 15% (13 out of 86) of the Christian aristocrats. Under Valentinian II as sole ruler and continuing thereafter, Christians continued to be appointed to their lowest offices in higher proportions than were pagan aristocrats.

Christians were not represented in proportions equal to those of pagans in the years of rule under Constantine's sons, as had been the case with their highest appointments. This pattern suggests that during the first seventy years of the fourth century, emperors were less concerned about religious affiliation in low than in high offices. Perhaps not until Gratian was there a concentrated effort to attain religious conformity in appointments to the lower offices.

Given the oft-expressed view that Christian emperors of the fourth century favored coreligionists, it is noteworthy that the office-holding patterns among Roman aristocrats in this study population show that Christians were not predominant from Constantine's time on. Nor do they show that Christianity spread in a smooth linear progression. Conversion was not the immediate reaction of most aristocrats to Constantine's or his successors' open support for Christianity. Rather, increases occur in an episodic fashion, reflecting only at times and imperfectly the preferences of the emperor under whom an aristocrat served.

Limits to Imperial Influence on Conversion

A variety of considerations limited the ability of even the most zealous emperors to use appointments to office to influence the religious choices of aristocrats. Specific political interests, as, for example, the desirability of a pagan governing a pagan province, could make a difference. But status concerns and patronage ties were even more important, in my view, in constraining emperors. As the epigraph to this chapter indicates, emperors were susceptible to the pressures that other aristocrats faced to do favors for and to maintain honor in the eyes of family and friends. Such interdependence in social and political life placed limits upon what emperors could do to influence the conversion of aristocrats. Imperial law was limited as well by this system.

The Emperor's Status Concerns

Honor was a primary concern to emperors. An emperor had to manifest and augment his honor as much as any aristocrat. This meant that the emperor had to act in such a way as to win the approval of other aristocrats. To do that, he had to live up to the same status culture ideals as they. As J. Lendon observed: "Emperors, in order to preserve their honour in aristocratic eyes, did indeed apply a great deal of attention to the norms that regulated aristocratic behaviour, while avoiding 'vices ill-bred and injurious to the soul which destroy the imperial prestige': for proof, consider the extraordinary consistency with which the emperors and members of the imperial family practised literature."[46]

In the fourth and fifth centuries, as in the third, the military was the key to an emperor's success. This could at times create a certain distance between emperors and those aristocrats from traditional, old Roman families, a distance that would seem to work against the need for the emperor to acquiesce in the traditional values and norms of the aristocracy. But no emperor escaped the need to conform to aristocratic expectations. Even the great military emperor, Valentinian I, took care that his son and designated heir, Gratian, receive a proper aristocratic education in rhetoric and literature.[47]

Active Christianizing emperors sought the support of the aristocracy in their quest for honor. Constantius II, for example, was eager to maintain good relations with the pagan Roman senatorial aristocracy; when he visited Rome in 357, he admired the pagan temples and filled the pagan priesthoods.[48] It was certainly best for the emperor to win honor from aristocrats without force; the use of violence to attain it rang false and was traditionally criticized.[49] To win honor voluntarily, emperors had to live by the norms of the aristocratic status culture. Theodosius I, for example, politely visited the homes of private senators at Rome, as if he too were one of their group.[50]

Other indicators also suggest the extent to which emperors remained identified with the values and practices of the aristocracy. The fourth-century emperors and their family members continued, for example, to hold the consulship, one obvious sign of their desire to acquire honor according to well-established elite norms. Emperors practiced literature and were praised for their abilities, as was Constantine by Aurelius Victor, or decried for lacking them, as was Valentinian I by Ammianus Marcellinus and Zosimus.[51] Indeed, lack of education was cited as cause for dismissing an eminent military man, Flavius Equitius, as a candidate for the throne.[52]

Emperors also fostered literary culture in their families and at their courts, thereby living up to another conventional expectation of the emperor as patron. Constantine patronized, among others, the Christian poet Publilius Optatianus signo Porphyrius.[53] Constantius II had the pagan rhetor Bemarchius give a recitation at the inauguration of a church he had built.[54] The imperial courts at Milan and Trier in the late fourth century were centers for pagan and Christian poets and philosophers, such as the poet Claudian, a probable pagan, and the Christian Neoplatonist Flavius Mallius Theodorus.[55]

Paganism had long been a component of elite culture and was intimately linked to notions of prestige. In dealing with those aristocrats whose pagan leanings remained strong, the late Roman emperor could not go beyond a certain range of actions without endangering both his honor and his relationships. At one extreme, he could not, for instance, torture aristocrats nor inflict punishments more severe than offences warranted. When Valentinian I was accused of such by a delegation of noble Romans led by the pagan Praetextatus, the emperor protested his innocence and took care to change the policy.[56] Similarly, emperors could not coerce conversion without going against the norms of religious freedom and autonomy that aristocrats traditionally enjoyed. To take an aggressive stand against pagan aristocrats could undermine the basis of imperial honor and unravel a network of relationships that worked to their mutual benefit. No wonder then that Constantius II, when in Rome, filled the pagan priesthoods rather than risk losing the support of a group whose approval he sought.

Political Interdependence

While the late Roman emperor had great wealth, power, and influence at his disposal, to rule successfully, to secure dynastic and personal ends, the emperor needed to build ties to members of the aristocracy, and to the military aristocracy in particular. Traditionally, emperors could build such ties in two ways, by making marriage alliances and by advancing friends and family to high office. In these personal interactions, the late Roman emperor acted much as any aristocrat would, building ties to other members of the elite to reinforce and augment his status in society. Nor were emperors likely to act without taking into account the views of aristocrats when they made appointments to office or propounded law.

MARRIAGE ALLIANCES AND PATRONAGE. For centuries, Roman aristocrats had contracted marriages to signal political concord. Given the central role of family in late Roman society, it was understandable that marriage continued to be viewed as a social and political act uniting not only a man and a woman but, more to the point, two aristocratic men and their families.[57] Thus Constantia, a sister of Constantine, was married to Licinius in Milan in 313 as a strong statement of the harmony between the two rulers, even though the marriage failed to prevent the civil war. Eutropia, another sister of Constantine, similarly made a strategic marriage when she wed the aristocrat Virius Nepotianus.[58]

In the fourth and fifth centuries the tendency for emperors to make marriage alliances with military aristocrats is one indicator of the central role of the army in imperial power. The two daughters of the great general Stilicho, a Christian, were wed, consecutively, to the emperor Theodosius' son, Honorius.[59] The pagan Frankish general, Bauto, had a daughter who lived in Constantinople and evidently converted prior to being wed to Arcadius, the son of Theodosius.[60] Such alliances worked to benefit both emperor and general, granting legitimacy and prestige to the former while reinforcing the loyalty and honor of the latter.

Emperors also fostered ties to aristocrats by arranging the marriages of distant relatives and by supporting the marriage requests of powerful men. So, in a famous case, the pagan Fravitta, leader of the Visigoths, sought the permission of the orthodox emperor Theodosius to wed a Roman girl of noble origin. This pious emperor granted his permission to secure the support of the general.[61] A woman named Constantia, associated in all likelihood with the Constantinian family, may have wed the eminent Roman aristocrat, Memmius Vitrasius Orfitus, in the 340s or early 350s; such a marriage would have indicated the ties between the Roman aristocracy and Constantius II and would explain why Orfitus was chosen as ambassador to the emperor during the conflict with Magnentius.[62] Here, too, such a marriage would have served the political goals of emperor and aristocrat.

Generosity—*liberalitas*—was also a conventional way for emperors to build ties to elites as well as being an integral part of the public expectation of the emperor.[63] This virtue is rather fulsomely articulated by the panegyrist Pacatus in his address to the emperor Theodosius: "By your deeds, and not merely by words you have affirmed that the feelings of a prince ought to be all the more benevolent toward his subjects the greater his fortune is, for you act with equal loyalty and generosity, and as emperor you extend to your friends what you had wished for them when a private citizen."[64]

Emperors, like other aristocrats, wanted to be honored as generous patrons. That meant not only doing favors for friends and family but, just as important, being seen as willing to listen to the recommendations of powerful supporters. What mattered most, as was so often stated, was that relationships be reaffirmed with other important aristocrats. In appointments to office, for instance, emperors were often more than willing to follow the recommendations of powerful men to appoint aristocrats they favored. By doing so, an emperor put that aristocrat in his debt. Moreover, both the emperor and the aristocrat accrued honor—the emperor by demonstrating his power, the aristocrat by obtaining the appointment that showed he enjoyed imperial favor. For an emperor to be unresponsive too often to the appeals of other aristocrats would be to show himself a "bad friend," thereby diminishing the esteem in which he was held by aristocrats.[65]

Insofar as there were powerful aristocratic supporters who continued to be pagan, emperors would appoint these men and listen to their recommendations. The emperor, as patron, was enmeshed in an interlocking network of relationships that reinforced his social prestige within elite society. Since that was true, there were limits on what emperors could do to influence the religious choice of any one individual. And that is why even the most ardently Christian emperors appointed pagans to high office.

PRAGMATIC CONCERNS.   Emperors also needed aristocrats as high office holders in their government for pragmatic reasons. Such men had the requisite prestige to rule effectively on behalf of the emperor. It was obvious to most emperors that pagan aristocrats were especially strongly ensconced in certain areas, notably in Rome and in Italy. And since these pagan aristocrats had both status and resources in these areas, to continue to be on good terms with the core of the aristocracy would facilitate the emperor's control there. Emperors desired the cooperation of aristocrats on a whole series of measures, from serving on commissions to acting as judges, as did the pagans M. Maecius Memmius Furius Baburius Caecilianus Placidus and Fabius Titianus.[66] Hence pragmatic considerations came into play and placed limits on what a Roman emperor would do to strain such relations and advance Christianity.

So too, by involving these men in office, the emperor ensured the continuation of the system of games and civic entertainments, funded in large part by aristocratic office holders. These games and entertainments, part of the duties of office, also augmented the honor of the aristocrats as well as maintained control over the urban plebs. In Rome that obligation fell increasingly into the hands of aristocrats whose activities in this regard came to be relied upon by emperors who no longer resided there.[67]

Perhaps most of all, emperors needed aristocrats as military commanders. Indeed, the centrality of the military elite to any emperor's rule is underlined by the simple fact that the imperial dynasties of the fourth century—those of Constantine, Valentinian I, and Theodosius I—all came from military backgrounds and acquired power through the support of the military. To survive, the emperor had to maintain the backing of the army and its generals. Even the most zealous of Christian emperors recognized this and appointed powerful pagan military leaders and ensured loyalty by making personal ties of marriage to families from the military aristocracy.

LIMITING FACTORS IN APPOINTMENTS TO OFFICE.   In theory, emperors had absolute control over appointments to office. If religious conversion was the sole concern, Christian emperors would have appointed only Christians. They did not; even by the end of the fourth century, when there was a larger pool of Christians to choose from, Christianizing emperors like Gratian and Theodosius continued to appoint pagan aristocrats to office (see Tables 6.1, 6.2). By and large, the Christian emperors did not want to alienate pagan aristocrats; rather, they desired to incorporate this prestigious segment of society in support of their rule.

In fact, for certain offices, and under certain conditions, it would have been advantageous to be a pagan. A whole string of fourth-century emperors in making appointments apparently considered the religion of the population that an official would govern; in Italy, for example, where the population was largely pagan and where the pagan aristocracy held great influence, emperors appointed pagan praetorian prefects who could use that very influence to govern most effectively. Emperors did so until the time of Gratian, and then intermittently until the very end of the fourth century.[68] In Gaul from 363 on, they favored Christian praetorian prefects.[69]

As I discussed in Chapter 4, several factors went into imperial decisions concerning appointments, including the status and position of the candidate; the prestige of the recommenders; the requirements of the office; the attitudes (including religion) of the population to be governed; the pool of available candidates; and the demonstrated loyalty of the appointee. These concerns affected the choices of Christians and pagans alike. In some cases religion may not have been a factor at all. But key to this system of appointment were the influence of recommendations and the network of elite patronage. This system constrained imperial choice and effectively diffused the influence of the emperor. These factors, and the systematic use of recommendations, limited the religious impact of imperial appointments.

Thus, from the perspective of the emperor, the religious affiliation of an appointee to office could count for or against the candidate, or not at all. Some emperors, by placing Christians in high office, were said to have signaled their willingness to advance coreligionists as they augmented the prestige of Christian aristocrats. Indeed, the literary record includes allegations about the opportunistic conversions of men eager to gain imperial favor; new men and those in imperial bureaucratic or military careers were particularly liable to this charge. However, imperial appointments of Christians seem unlikely to have had a strong causal effect on the conversion of the aristocracy for a number of reasons: appointments had to take into account a variety of factors, not just religion; the system of recommendations was based essentially on personal relationships in which religion figured only indirectly; and pagan aristocrats exercised considerable influence throughout the century via the system of recommendations for appointments. Thus imperial appointments appear to be rather a part of a changing aristocratic landscape that saw growing numbers of Christian aristocrats. These Christian aristocrats advanced through the same system of honor and prestige as did their pagan peers. Insofar as imperial appointments contributed to helping Christians advance, they contributed toward the making of a Christian aristocracy, but religious change did not occur as the direct result of appointments.

LIMITING FACTORS IN IMPERIAL LAW.   Study of the laws from the fourth and fifth centuries preserved in the Theodosian Code can provide insights into the policies emperors wanted to promulgate. Yet here too there were clearly limits to what laws emperors would pass to influence the religiosity of their subjects. Pagans were still a significant proportion of the population in 438; as late as 423 we find a law protecting pagans "who are living quietly and attempting nothing disorderly or contrary to law" as well as their property from overzealous Christians (*C.Th.* 16.10.24).[70] Even after a 380 law that effectively made orthodox Christianity the official religion of the Roman empire (*C.Th.* 16.1.2), no emperor legalized force to convert pagans until Justinian's edict in 529 (*C.J.* 1.11.10). And political considerations aside, enforced conversion raised theological problems that emperors, in search of harmony with and within the church, were apparently unwilling to provoke. This reticence to enforce conversion was even greater when dealing with aristocrats, whose prestige and support most emperors sought.

Through most of the fourth century, emperors approached Christianization through their laws only indirectly. They worked, first, toward granting the church privilege and prestige equal to that of the pagan cults. After Constantine, it was, for example, possible to bequeath monies to the church (*C.Th.* 16.2.4 [321]), and church lands were exempt from providing compulsory public service (*C.Th.* 16.2.15 [359–360]) or from extraordinary burdens (*C.Th.* 16.2.40 [411–412]). With these laws the emperors improved significantly the material well-being of the church and its clergy.

The emperors also made explicit the privileged position of the church within the state. Most important, in terms of influencing upwardly mobile local elites, were the codes granting exemptions to clergy from serving on local town councils and performing compulsory public service.[71] Pagan priests also enjoyed such exemptions.[72] But Constantine and his successors granted certain privileges to the church and its officials that went beyond those generally allowed to the pagan cults and their priests. So, for instance, bishops were prohibited from being accused in secular courts (*C.Th.* 16.2.12 [355]), and bishops were given judicial authority, deemed "sacred" and final (*C.Th.* 1.27.1 [318]).[73]

Thus through law the emperors gave prestige and honors to the church and its clergy, which in themselves made Christianity appealing to aristocrats imbued with the values of their status culture. Indeed, this was essentially the intent behind certain legal privileges. A code of 353 ascribed to Constantius II and Constans explicitly stated as much: "In order that organizations in the service of the churches may be filled with a great multitude of people, tax exemption shall be granted to clerics and their acolytes and they shall be protected from the exaction of compulsory public services of a menial nature."[74]

At the same time, the Theodosian Code records the mounting legal and economic hardships imposed on pagan cults. Most well-known are the laws against pagan sacrifice. Beginning with the extant law of 341 (*C.Th.* 16.10.2) and continuing until 435 (*C.Th.* 16.10.35), laws threatened increasingly harsh measures against sacrifice.[75] But it was not until 382 that state monies to support pagan cults were legally removed under Gratian.[76] Pagan temples were closed, beginning with a law of Constantius II (*C.Th.* 16.10.4; dated 346, 354, 356), but laws reiterating temple closings that continued until 399 (*C.Th.* 16.10.16) suggest that pagan temples, in fact, remained in use.

The privileges of pagan priests were preserved, however, until the 380s and 390s. Under Gratian in 384 certain pagan priests lost legal privileges (perhaps exemptions), and they and their cults lost the right to accept legacies.[77] But emperors did not deprive all pagan priests of all privileges until 396 (*C.Th.* 16.10.14). Here the influence of the aristocracy, the holders of most priesthoods, can be seen as the likely reason for the limited restrictions placed on these powerful figures. And the pagan games and festivals in which the pagan priests were involved continued, with imperial support, throughout the fourth century.[78]

Most imperial laws, and certainly the most restrictive ones that specify aristocrats, are dated late in the 390s, following the turning point in the conversion of the aristocracy. The first extant code to specify judges or governors of provinces as being bound by the law prohibiting "profane [i.e., pagan] rites and entering temples for the purpose of worship" is dated to 391 (*C.Th.* 16.10.10). The punishment for breaking this law is appropriate to men of high office and high status: "He [a judge] shall immediately be compelled to pay fifteen pounds of gold, and his office staff shall pay a like sum with similar haste . . . Governors with the rank of consular shall pay six pounds of gold each, their office staffs a like amount; those with the rank of corrector or of praeses shall pay four pounds each, and their apparitors, by equal lot, a like amount" (*C.Th.* 16.10.10). This law indicates that high officials were not following the general proscriptions against paganism.

The late date of laws against the apostasy of high officials underscores the imperial unwillingness to act against aristocratic office holders. Not until 391 do we find a code concerning apostasy that singles out high office holders, even though it may well have been a problem even earlier: "If any splendor of rank has been conferred upon or is inborn in those persons who have departed from the faith and are blinded in mind, who have deserted the cult and worship of the sacrosanct religion and have given themselves over to sacrifices, they shall forfeit such rank, so that, removed from their position and status, they shall be branded with perpetual infamy and shall not be numbered even among the lowest dregs of the ignoble crowd" (*C.Th.* 16.7.5).[79]

As I noted earlier, when Honorius passed a law in 408 prohibiting pagans from holding high office, the refusal of the high military official, Generidus, to perform his duties led the emperor to annul the law.[80] Here an emperor proved unwilling to provoke conflict with an aristocratic high office holder or to coerce religious change through law. Rather, he, as other emperors, seemed to legislate only after behaviors had already changed. So, for example, it was only in 416 that pagans were finally prohibited by law from being admitted into imperial service (*C.Th.* 16.10.21), a date long after the turning point in the conversion of this class.[81]

By the 390s emperors were using law to bring into play the final imperial resource, the threat of armed force. But there is little evidence that they actually used it. They clearly did not use armed force against the aristocracy. The publication of such a policy, forcefully stated, is a sign of the imperial desire to take a position on religious choice.[82] However, as my study population suggests, many aristocrats had already become Christian by this date. These laws were, therefore, not leading the way as much as reinforcing the influences in society that had by this date made Christianity a respectable option for western aristocrats, indeed an option that was increasing in prestige and honor. But here too, as in appointments and patronage, emperors could not do just as they pleased. They were constrained by political exigencies, social relations, and, above all, by the norms of aristocratic status culture.

The Emperor as the Ideal Christian Aristocrat: A New Symbolic Focus

The emperor was not only the head of the state; he was also the *pontifex maximus,* chief priest of the state religion until Gratian renounced this role ca. 382. As the symbolic head of the state and its religion, an emperor's religious preferences were publicized and determined which cults would be most lavishly funded and celebrated with public monies. But the participation of the now Christian emperors in traditionally pagan civic events posed something of a problem, as did their involvement in Christian rites and celebrations. Over the course of the fourth century the rituals and public ceremonies gradually evolved so as to incorporate the emperor's Christianity. So, for example, by the late fourth century important imperial cult rituals, such as victory celebrations, no longer focused on sacrifice to the pagan deities. Instead, they proclaimed imperial gratitude for victories owed to the Christian God; even the meaning of victory changed to include concern for the dead.[83] As the emperors took on new symbolic roles that incorporated their Christianity, they made themselves and their religious choice paradigmatic for aristocrats. In modeling such behavior, emperors influenced conversion, albeit indirectly.

Emperors also directed traditional modes of aristocratic patronage to support Christianity. The emperors gave monies and land to the church and its clergy, often for building projects, a conventional arena for elite patronage. Here, too, emperors varied. Constantine was extremely generous in his gifts to the church and its bishops; the *Liber Pontificalis* records the basilicas he funded over the western empire and the monies and lands that he bequeathed. Other emperors were not known for being as generous as Constantine, but most fourth-century emperors did support building projects or gave land to the church.[84] Such patronage made visible the new prestige of the church and its officials in society.

By supporting the church and its clergy in such conventionally aristocratic ways, the emperors established themselves as models of Christian patronage that other aristocrats could follow. By the end of the fourth century we find increasing numbers of wealthy aristocratic laypeople acting as patrons of the church, displaying their wealth as donors of the mosaic floors or of the liturgical vessels in the new basilicas that housed the Christian community. By the late fourth century aristocrats, as patrons, would "imitate the acts of the ruler" within a Christian context that conferred status and prestige.[85]

By incorporating Christian meanings within traditional imperial activities, and by patronizing the church and its officials, the emperor himself became a symbolic model of religious change. Some emperors, like Constantine, energetically embraced their symbolic roles. Thus Constantine proclaimed himself "bishop of those outside" the church.[86] He also tried to establish himself as a leader of his new religion, taking a dominant role in church councils, for instance, and establishing daily routines at court that included Christian rituals. What must a pagan aristocrat have thought and felt when he saw an emperor bent in prayer in the palace or reading holy scriptures to the assembled court?[87]

Emperors could show by their example not only their general support for Christianity, but how they, as any aristocrat, could embrace this new religion. Indeed, emperors may have hoped that their example would encourage others to take up Christianity. These actions are considered primary by Pacatus in the case of the emperor Theodosius I: "Nothing, I feel, has been more instrumental in the dispelling of vices and the adoption of virtue than the fact that you have always devoted yourself to the kind of men [i.e., aristocrats] whom the people ought to aspire to imitate; just as they were obedient and tractable pupils of yours, so they were excellent masters for the rest of mankind."[88]

By acting according to aristocratic norms—as patron, as leader, and as participant in an increasingly prestigious religious group—the emperors infused Christian practices and understandings into traditional areas of late Roman elite society. The emperors made themselves, in essence, exemplars of how to be aristocratic and Christian at the same time. Thus they became a symbolic focus, showing how it was possible to be Christian even as they remained prestigious members of the aristocracy.

CHAPTER 7

The Aristocrats' Influence on Christianity

Unless we ourselves take a hand now, they'll foist a republic on us. If we want things to stay as they are, things will have to change.

—Giuseppe Tomasi de Lampedusa, *The Leopard* (trans. A. Colquhoun)

In many ways Lampedusa's view of the late nineteenth-century Sicilian nobility expresses a truth about the interaction between the Roman aristocracy and the Christian leaders of the late fourth and early fifth centuries. By the 380s and 390s conversion may well have appeared to many late Roman aristocrats as the best way to preserve their world. Aristocrats did have to adapt in certain ways to become Christian, but what is often missed is that Christianity also adapted as it came into contact with the aristocracy. In the interaction between Christianity and the aristocracy, well advanced by the late fourth century, the message of Christianity changed in certain ways as church leaders assimilated key components of the aristocrats' worldview and status culture.

Church leaders who articulated the message of Christianity from their pulpits and in private discourse did so with a growing consciousness of the necessity of encouraging and facilitating the conversion of the aristocracy. It is understandable that they did, since the aristocracy was the predominant social class. Yet, in trying to appeal to aristocrats, Christian writers and thinkers had to address the values and attitudes of their audience and somehow adapt them to a Christian framework. Even the committed advocate of asceticism, Jerome, so obstinate in his negation of worldly concerns, reveals himself as attentive to aristocratic views.[1]

There were many versions of Christianity or, as so often stated, many Christianities.[2] This chapter attempts to analyze the main tendencies in Christianity in its interaction with the aristocracy in the late fourth and early fifth centuries in the western empire, not all the subtle variations in every

Christian thinker. In general, Christian leaders took aristocratic status culture into account in two ways. First, they communicated through the prevailing modes of discourse; they fashioned the rhetoric of Christianity to make it pleasing to educated elite listeners.[3] Second, Christian leaders shaped the message of Christianity in public and private so as to appeal to aristocrats, achieving a fit between Christian and aristocratic social concerns and values. As they spoke to issues at the heart of aristocratic status culture—honor, office, wealth, culture, friendship, *nobilitas*—they sought to change the aristocracy. Ironically, they also "aristocratized" Christianity's message, incorporating certain key elements of aristocratic status culture.

In emphasizing the influence of this status culture on Christianity, I am arguing against the views of scholars like P. Hadot and A. D. Nock, who explained conversion by focusing on changes within the *mentalité* of the aristocracy.[4] I am also arguing against those scholars who see in the aristocracy of the later Roman empire a growing need for salvation, a growing anxiety within its core that led this group to seek the assurances of the message of Christianity. These assurances have been found variously in such elements of Christian belief as monotheism, salvationism, and the fervent excoriation of sin, among others.[5] Such interpretations emphasize the psychological aspects of Christianity in an "age of anxiety." These views are not, however, sufficiently attuned to the social and political realities of the day.

Christian Adaptation of Aristocratic Status Culture

As Christian leaders addressed the concerns of their increasingly aristocratic audiences, they were forced to come to grips with certain fundamental values and aspects of elite status culture. For one, they had to acknowledge, in some sense, that this was a society in which the Weberian notion that the social estimation of honor attached to every typical component of life still held. Christian bishops in the late fourth and early fifth centuries were especially important in this process, for they often were entrusted with the task of converting the elite in their cities. In their evangelizing efforts many bishops tried to retain continuities with aristocrats' status culture by translating and assimilating as much of it as possible into a Christian framework. Even those leaders who claimed to deny the values of aristocratic society or tried to redefine its ideals pertaining to social honor often ended up validating and incorporating many of its fundamental tenets.

The efforts of Christian leaders to adapt aristocratic status culture into a

Christian framework were so successful that for the majority of fourth-century aristocrats, Christianity did not entail a radical reorientation—the classic notion of conversion—from their previous way of life.[6] Of course, this process of adapting Christianity to the aristocracy did provoke some dissent, and an ascetic wing emerged that strained against this adaptation. But the subversive implications of Christianity were, for many aristocrats, obscured by Christianity's adaptation of their status culture.

Honor and Office

Chief among the defining characteristics of the late Roman aristocracy was the value its members placed on acquiring honor by holding high office in the civic, imperial, or military spheres. Christian leaders, beginning with Constantine and continuing into the fifth century, acknowledged the honors attached to public office, thereby maintaining an important continuity with aristocratic status culture. Yet Christian leaders also tried to adapt the honor and dignity of office to a Christian framework.

Christian leaders, while acknowledging secular honors, nonetheless downplayed such honors as compared to those attained through Christianity. This attitude is perhaps best exemplified by the epitaph of the eminent Christian aristocrat Sextus Petronius Probus, which conceptualized his reward in heaven in ways familiar to any aristocrat:

> Rich in wealth, of noble family, exalted in office and distinguished in your Consulship . . . these worldly trappings, these noble titles you rose above when, in time, you were presented with the gift of Christ. This is your true office, this your nobility. Previously you rejoiced in the honour of the royal table, in the emperor's ear and the friendship of royalty. Now, closer to Christ after attaining the abode of the saints, you enjoy a new light . . . Now renewed, you have eternal rest and you wear gleaming white garments darkened by no stain, and are a new dweller in unaccustomed mansions . . . He [Probus] lives in the eternal abode of paradise in blessedness who, as he passed from view, put on the new garments of his heavenly duty.[7]

Probus has traded in his imperial honors for the more powerful king in Heaven; as he changed his purple lined consular toga for a purer whiter one, he merely augmented his honor. Church leaders apparently approved of such a notion, for the mausoleum that houses this epitaph is set on marble panels attached to columns behind the altar of St. Peter's, abutting the outside wall of the apse. This monument claimed the ongoing prestige not only of the man but of his family, as befit the conventions of aristocratic society. Probus' epitaph confidently states that his heavenly career will top even his earthly one, but the two were not at odds. Basically, Probus will enjoy honor in heaven much as he did on earth, but this honor will endure for eternity.

Some Christian leaders asserted that the greatest honor came not from secular offices but from ecclesiastical ones; that substitution was made more real when church office "used and redefined the distinctions of status previously acquired from holding civil offices."[8] The career of Paulinus of Nola shows some of the ways in which aristocrats' concern for honor and office were assimilated into Christian ecclesiastical office. An aristocrat from good Gallic stock, Paulinus was embarked on a civic career as suffect consul and then governor of Campania around 381 when he "converted" to asceticism and subsequently retired from the world.[9] His abandonment of his leisured aristocratic circle of moderate Christian friends in Gaul and his career change bewildered and angered other aristocrats.[10] Yet, as Paulinus devoted himself to his new patron, St. Felix, he felt, in the words of R. Van Dam, that "he had acquired a set of connections more important than the ones at the imperial court offered to him by Ausonius, for St. Felix had introduced him to the friends of the celestial Lord. As a result, in about 410 Paulinus became bishop of Nola, as well as, after the pope, the most prominent Christian leader in Italy."[11]

Paulinus' newfound prestige was not lost on him: "Did I have anything when I was called senator to match what I have here and now when I am called impoverished?"[12] In certain ways Paulinus saw his new life as a redefinition of traditional aristocratic notions, such as *otium*, now lived out in a Christian setting.[13] Nor did his choice bring ruin to himself and his family, as his friends had feared. Rather, Paulinus secured the continuing prosperity of his relations; his family continued to act as influential patrons, albeit of Christian shrines, still feuded with other aristocratic families, and still enjoyed their ancestral estates near Bordeaux into the fifth century.[14] Thus the family of Paulinus prospered in material terms (ecclesiastical office did not entail the loss of private income) and achieved social prestige—success in traditional aristocratic terms—but it did so by attaining ecclesiastical, not secular, office.

As Paulinus' career showed, church office could offer secure and satisfying opportunities for the acquisition and demonstration of honor. It was in many ways a better avenue to these rewards than civic office, which presented dangers of the sort noted by Paulinus in counseling one young man, Licentius, to choose the life of Christian ascetic over civic office: "Avoid the slippery dangers of exacting state service. Position is an inviting title, but it brings evil slavery and wretched end. He who now delights in desiring it, later repents of having desired it. It is pleasant to mount the summit, but fearsome to descend from it; if you stumble, your fall from the top of the citadel will be worse."[15]

We do not know what path Licentius chose, but we hear Jerome similarly emphasizing the limits of secular office in a letter of 397 to Pammachius, Roman senator and monk. Like Paulinus, Jerome argued in favor of asceticism, but his argument appealed to an aristocrat in terms of social prestige and competition for honor:

> Before he began to serve Christ with his whole heart, Pammachius was a well known person in the senate. Still there were many other senators who wore the badges of proconsular rank . . . Today all the churches of Christ are talking about Pammachius. The whole world admires as a poor man one whom heretofore it ignored as rich. Can anything be more splendid than the consulate? Yet the honor lasts only for a year and when another has succeeded to the post its former occupant gives way.[16]

The superiority of the ascetic's prestige is further reinforced because, claims Jerome, secular honor has decayed: now the consulate is "obtained by merely belonging to the army; and the shining robe of victory now envelops men who a little while ago were country bores."[17] While the notion of Christian ascetic as a way of life may be new, Jerome's language and logic belong to the traditional aristocratic status culture that valued social prestige, competition, and peer approval.

Although most Christians and their leaders through the fourth and early fifth centuries acknowledged the prestige of secular office, many ascetics and some bishops in the 380s and after made a concentrated effort to restrict those who held secular office from pursuing church office, at least if the applicant had been baptised.[18] In the 380s church leaders in Rome also tried to formulate a coherent ecclesiastical career path.[19] Both groups may well have been responding to the ethical dilemmas faced by Christian secular office holders; Paulinus, for one, emphasized the moral problems he confronted when, as magistrate, he was unwilling to condemn a man to death.[20] Increasingly, aristocrats chose to follow one track or another—secular or ecclesiastic—to acquire honor. By the mid-fifth century the bishops at Rome declared that the two paths were incompatible; no former magistrate could be ordained.[21]

As ecclesiastic careers crystallized, such offices increasingly offered opportunities for bishops to acquire prestige and influence in worldly terms.
Ambrose perhaps best represents the activist bishop who, as he condemned
the punishment meted out by the emperor Theodosius, intervened directly
in worldly affairs.[22] The growing prestige of the episcopate led the aristocratic Praetextatus to remark that he would convert immediately if Damasus
would make him bishop of Rome.[23]

The growing prestige of the church, along with political upheavals that
brought the collapse of imperial structures in certain parts of the empire,
contributed to making ecclesiastical office attractive to aristocrats. By the
470s in Gaul—an area that suffered from a series of crises earlier in the century—Sidonius Apollinaris could claim, "Beyond question, according to the
view of the best men, the humblest ecclesiastic ranks above the most exalted
secular dignity."[24] Yet the goal was familiar—honor through office.

Wealth and Patronage

Perhaps the most striking difficulty that Christianity presented to an aristocrat was that of his or her wealth. If "it was easier for a camel to pass through
the eye of a needle than for a rich man to get to heaven," how could rich
persons reconcile their wealth with Gospel injunctions to poverty? This was
a problem even for the first-century church; the Gospels of Matthew and
Luke and the Acts show a modification of the radical poverty advocated by
Christ in what may well have been an attempt to include the wealthy in the
first-century Christian community.[25]

This same approach appears in the influential second-century treatment
of the dilemma of wealth by Clement of Alexandria. Clement argued that
the rich should not be condemned out of hand simply because they happen
to possess much wealth; rather, Clement urged the wealthy to use their
riches for charitable purposes. Moreover, Clement did not command the renunciation of all one's goods for the sake of Christ.[26] Following Clement,
other second- and third-century Latin writers made similar suggestions
about the use of wealth; Cyprian of Carthage, for one, advocated giving alms
for the salvation of one's soul.[27] Thus, in the second and third centuries
when the illegal status of Christianity was an inhibiting factor for aristocrats,
Christians found a way to reconcile wealth with Christianity—by putting
one's wealth to good Christian use.

In the fourth and fifth centuries Christian leaders spent a good deal of time and energy explaining how wealthy aristocrats could be incorporated into the church. One such influential voice is that of Ambrose, whose aristocratic background is reflected in his position on wealth. There is no crime in being rich, Ambrose writes, only in not employing one's wealth in proper fashion.[28] His was a common position among church leaders. Augustine writes in a sermon: "Wealth is good, gold is good, silver is good, servants are good, possessions are good, all these things are good—but so that you might do good with them, not so that they might make you good."[29] The parable of the rich man and Lazarus in Luke 16.19–31 is often discussed in this period as a means of teaching the rich of the benefits of charity, not as a condemnation of riches per se.[30]

Almsgiving is the single most important justification for riches according to Ambrose: "You have money, redeem your sin. The Lord is not venal, but you are venal. You have been sold in sin; redeem yourself with your works, redeem yourself with your money. Money is base but mercy is precious."[31] The responsibility of almsgiving did not require a man to divest himself of wealth. Most church leaders urged moderation.[32] In a sermon Augustine reminded his audience that Paul told those who had money that they should share with those who were in need; but, as Augustine notes, Paul did not tell them to give away everything they owned.[33] Nor did almsgiving denote economic equality. As Augustine said in another sermon, "Use what is precious [for yourself] and give the poor the things that are inferior."[34]

Although many Christian bishops viewed asceticism and a life devoted to the church as a superior form of Christianity, they did not see it as necessary for all wealthy Christians. Ambrose noted, "The Lord does not want us to give away all our goods at once, but to impart them little by little; unless, indeed, our case is like that of Elisha . . . [who did so] that he might give up all things and devote himself to the prophetic teaching."[35] Instead, all aristocrats were encouraged to give alms with the proper humble attitude, a far more easily attainable goal. Indeed, it is with an aristocratic audience in mind that bishops so frequently state that true generosity means giving in a humble manner, not with pride nor out of self-pity, as pagans do.[36]

In discussing the recipients of aid, the bishops also reflect their awareness of their aristocratic audiences. Ambrose, Augustine, and Jerome note that there must be some discernment in almsgiving.[37] A person's first obligation was to his family, a sentiment in accord with the basic views of most aristocrats as well as the population at large.[38] Even those who took up asceticism and gave away all their wealth faced censure if they threatened the financial survival of their family; Augustine condemned Ecdicia for giving away her inheritance without consulting either her husband or her son, her prospective heir.[39] Significantly, Ambrose indicates as the most deserving those who were once rich and noble, but have suffered calamity.[40] In treatises by Ambrose and Augustine on the role of widows, neither author makes any reference to widows as recipients of charity, only as almsgivers.[41]

As Christian leaders justified wealth because it could be used for charity, they encouraged traditional patterns of expenditure on the part of aristocrats who, for centuries, had "done good for their cities" (*evergetai* in Greek) by contributing to public expenses. Now, these contributions—which scholars term "evergetism"—were being directed to a different use, namely the church, which was increasingly being seen as part of the public domain. Ambrose even urged the bishop-writers under his influence to consciously encourage such contributions. In a letter to Constantius, the bishop of Claterna, Ambrose advised: "Let them (your congregation) learn to search for the riches of good works and to be rich in character. The beauty of riches is not in the purses of the rich, but in their support for the poor."[42] Wealthy aristocrats could turn to Christianity secure in the knowledge that their traditional way of demonstrating social preeminence—evergetism—would continue to bring them prestige and the approval of a Christian community.

Simultaneously, Christian fathers tried to redefine the benefits of evergetism in spiritual, not secular, terms. They reiterated the notion that charity was the way to atone for sin. In particular, charity redeemed the sin of avarice, a vice that many bishops railed against in this period.[43] The bishop of Aquileia, Chromatius, expressed this position nicely in a sermon: "If anyone is burdened by the evil desire of avarice, which is more oppressive than any other disease of the soul (for the love of money is the root of all evils, as the Apostle says), the precept concerning good works is necessary for him, so that he might know that he cannot be healed unless from avariciousness he turn to mercy and from greediness to generosity."[44] Here Chromatius adapts the traditional Roman criticism of avarice as morally destructive into a Christian framework that justifies wealth.[45]

A few years after Ambrose's death, we find Maximus of Turin (ca. 390–408/423) still appealing to the aristocrat's concern with wealth and evergetism in ways that maintained essential continuities with elite attitudes and activities. Maximus worked out a contractual concept of almsgiving whereby "charitable deeds were calculated in terms of atonement and could redeem sin as a new baptism. Indeed, charity was more effective than baptism in that it could be repeated."[46] Maximus went so far as to suggest that charitable deeds be an alternative to levies.[47] Maximus' position represents the next stage, as it were, in moderating Christian attitudes toward wealth and almsgiving, suggesting ways that enabled aristocrats to convert without essentially changing their patterns of behavior and views concerning wealth. Maximus' message was well timed to facilitate the conversion of aristocrats, even as it reflected the increasing number of Christian aristocrats.

In their desire to incorporate wealthy aristocrats into the church, fourth- and fifth-century bishops adopted a rhetoric that reflected the aristocratic audiences they were trying to reach as they discussed almsgiving. Generosity to the poor was seen as a shrewd investment. In a sermon Augustine noted, "Give to the poor and you shall have treasure in heaven. You shall not be without treasure, but what you are worried about on earth you shall possess secure in heaven. Send it on ahead then."[48] Here Augustine adopts a striking image of the poor as servants of the rich, carrying their wealth into eternity. Elsewhere, he refers to the poor as *laturarii*, porters, who carry into the next life the benefits for the wealthy who give alms in this life.

Without a doubt, church leaders were advocating an important change in behavior concerning charity. It is one thing to give beneficently to friends, relations, clients, and fellow citizens, quite another to donate to the poor. Yet the blueprint for this action and a traditional motivation already existed. Paulinus of Nola described them in a sermon: "They [the poor] place you above their own children . . . In all the churches they pray for you, in all the public places they acclaim you."[49] Such rewards were what aristocrats traditionally understood as motivating charity, for in the classical world "charity had been a way of being rich—of exercising the privilege of one's status and wealth—and a way of carrying out the responsibilities of social relationships."[50] Thus, as the Christian fathers encouraged almsgiving, they were also building on and continuing aristocratic behavior patterns and attitudes about wealth and the acquisition of prestige.

As B. Ramsey recognized in his study of almsgiving in the Latin church in the fourth and fifth centuries, the impetus for charity remained fundamentally donor-centered. Although injunctions to give to the poor and to practice charity with humility were frequently repeated, and some Christian fathers criticized donors who practiced charity out of a desire for popular acclaim, the texts from this period do not demonstrate any real social concern. Rather, charity was valued as a spiritual exercise that brought benefits to the giver in the form of the remission of sin. The classical attitude persisted; the emphasis remained on the donor, not the poor, who are faceless in these texts.[51]

In fact, the texts from this period frequently state that the poor exist for the sake of the rich, to offer them opportunities for beneficence or to test them. Augustine succinctly noted that God makes "the rich to come to the aid of the poor, and the poor to test the rich."[52] Many bishops justified wealth, like poverty, as merely part of God's plan.[53] Since divine sanction lies behind the social order and justifies economic and social inequities in the world, aristocratic preeminence within a Christian society was justified.

The wealthy could also continue to demonstrate their affluence by donating funding for buildings and projects; the construction of huge public basilicas by Ambrose and his contemporary bishops in northern Italy indicated episcopal willingness to rely on traditional patterns of giving on the part of aristocratic landowners. This same acceptance of aristocratic patronage can be seen in the church's willingness to allow aristocrats to fund martyrs' shrines and monastic foundations.[54]

Although the arguments of church leaders appeal to self-interest, they were well attuned to the values of their audiences. The church did not require radical changes in aristocratic behavior and, in particular, evergetism. Instead, aristocrats could continue to exercise the privileges of their position and wealth while gaining spiritual rewards. Thus preexisting patterns of aristocratic gift-giving were encouraged, as was the possession of wealth itself, in ways that facilitated conversion without challenging the norms of aristocratic status culture.

Literary Culture

The literary culture that was at the heart of the aristocrat's claim to cultural preeminence went largely unchallenged by Christian leaders of the fourth and fifth centuries. Study of the Christian scriptures did not replace study of the classics, nor did Christian leaders advocate Christian schools to replace the traditional education in grammar and rhetoric that revolved around classical texts. Knowledge of scripture and theology was conveyed through preaching and letters. Some aristocrats did study these subjects, but they did so alongside study of the classical texts.[55]

Since the system remained in place, educated Christians had to develop a perspective on the study of classical texts. Jerome's famous dream that he would be accused of being a Ciceronian instead of a Christian articulates one end of a spectrum, ranging from outright rejection to acceptance and assimilation.[56] Some Christians, and ascetics like Jerome were perhaps the most vocal of all, struggled against the standard literary culture as they advocated change. But for the most part "peaceful coexistence" was the norm. A poet and teacher of rhetoric like Ausonius was able to easily bridge both worlds and counted Christians as well as pagans among his students. Some, like Paulinus of Nola and the Apollinares, tried to integrate the two literary cultures by dressing the scriptures in classical forms like epics or wedding hymns.[57]

While attitudes toward the pagan classics varied, Christian attitudes toward the value of literate culture per se appear more uniform. Christian leaders claimed that they were the heirs of a literature as ancient and as eminent as that of their pagan contemporaries. They prided themselves on possessing a religion of "the word"; their claim to "bookishness" would appeal to aristocrats for whom, it has been well observed, "literate culture conveyed power."[58] As Christian leaders enthusiastically established their claim to a different but equally prestigious literate culture, they continued long-held aristocratic notions of literary preeminence as a basis for claiming social status.

When appealing to aristocratic audiences, fourth- and fifth-century Christian leaders were attentive to the style of their message, expressed in sermons and letters. The efforts of the bishop Ambrose in northern Italy are exemplary of this concern. Ambrose urged the clerics and bishops under his influence to be attentive to the style and timing of their instruction: "Our discourse must not be too lengthy, nor too soon cut short, for fear the former should leave behind it a feeling of aversion, and the latter produce carelessness and neglect."[59] Even pronunciation was important: a bishop's speech should be "full of manly vigour. . . free from a rough and rustic twang," not "overly theatrical."[60] Ambrose emphasized that bishops adopt the appropriate style; by adopting a cultivated style when addressing educated audiences, a bishop could better lead his auditors to Christianity. He congratulated Felix, newly elected bishop of Comum, for his rhetorical skill in converting his flock.[61] Of course, Ambrose, like the most adept Christian writers, was able to adopt different styles to suit his audiences, reaching even the uneducated. To bishops evangelizing in the countryside, Ambrose urged a combination of a more direct style with one that could employ the tools and techniques of classical rhetoric.

A concern for the appropriate style also marked Christian letters, for these, like sermons, could be widely promulgated. When Marcellinus asked

Augustine to respond to the queries of the aristocrat Volusianus concerning Christian spirituality, Marcellinus urged the church father to respond in an appropriately polished and articulate fashion so that Marcellinus could share Augustine's response with others.[62] Christian concern to be seen as possessing the high style associated with a literate culture was also expressed in public inscriptions; Pope Damasus commemorated the tombs of martyrs in Rome with verses modeled after Virgil and inscribed in ornate lettering, a style that would appeal to cultured, literate aristocratic society.[63] In such texts bishops made Christianity consonant with and attractive to aristocrats brought up on classical literary culture.

Concern about style was valid. The young Augustine acknowledged in his *Confessions* the difficulties that he had in his spiritual progress because of deficiencies he saw in the style and stories in the New Testament.[64] Indeed, aristocratic Christians were well aware that some Christian leaders intentionally adopted a simple style in order to claim their liberation from classical literature, rhetoric, and aristocratic cultural distinctions. But church leaders instinctively grasped that most aristocrats would not warm to the message of Christianity unless it was presented in an appropriate style. Even those who claimed a simple style in rejecting classical literary culture reveal their willingness to use its rhetorical tools in order to reach audiences of aristocrats.[65]

Certainly, in addressing the relationship of literary culture to Christianity, Christian leaders of the fourth and fifth centuries were urging a change upon the elite. They were proposing that Christian scripture and a literature based on the Bible were a valid alternative. However, the willingness of many church figures to place these texts alongside classical literature and rhetoric, rather than as a replacement for it, supported the status quo and the prestige of traditional aristocratic literary culture. Admittedly, this compromise position faced some opposition, and pressures against it grew over time, but in the fourth and early fifth centuries, radical change was not called for by most Christians.

Friendship

Given the value placed on *amicitia* within aristocratic society, it is not surprising to find friendship so much discussed by the fourth- and fifth-century Christian bishops who addressed aristocrats and sought to convert them. In the fourth century, in the words of C. White, we find Christians considering friendship in "more serious and positive terms" than before.[66] Many Christian leaders and intelligentsia were addressing audiences composed of and involved in relationships with aristocrats. In these worlds friendship was a central fact of life. Some Christian bishops, monastics, and intellectuals were aristocrats themselves. As aristocrats converted in growing numbers, their concerns about friendship would naturally raise it as a topic for discussion by church leaders.

Friendship, like wealth, presented certain problems for Christians. The exclusivity of classical notions of friendship went against the universality of Christian salvation. Moreover, no Christian could claim that earthly ties competed with spiritual ties to God.[67] In addressing these tensions, church leaders, schooled in the academies of the empire, were understandably influenced by classical theories of friendship. Even those who were critical of their cultural heritage "recognized that certain characteristics of the ideal pagan friendship, such as spiritual unity and harmony of interest, reciprocity and sharing could accord with Christian ideals and even be developed further within a Christian context."[68] As C. White observed, rather than rejecting classical notions of friendship, church leaders seem either to have accepted aristocratic ideals of *amicitia* or to have modified them to conform to a Christian conception of a relationship that bound men to one another.

Some Christians considered both friendship and "Christian love" largely in classical philosophical terms. The writings of Ambrose are exemplary of this position. Ambrose's *De officiis ministrorum* imitates the form and accepts much of what Cicero and classical philosophers have to say about friendship. Indeed, Ambrose did not do much more than translate Cicero's views on friendship into a Christian tract.[69] Ambrose's text aimed at identifying biblical passages to illustrate Ciceronian ideas; so, for example, Ambrose cited the biblical examples of Jonathan and Ahimelech as men who rightly put friendship not before virtue, but before their own safety, an idea expressed in other words by Cicero.[70]

Alternatively, some Christians chose to transform preexisting notions of friendship to fit Christian ideals more directly. To Paulinus of Nola, for example, Christians could have true friendships only with other Christians; in a way, Paulinus was expanding the commonly held belief that friends shared all things, including religion.[71] But now, only by sharing in a spiritual communion with Christ could friendships remain intact. Paulinus was reworking classical notions of friendship by seeing it as a relationship that furthered one's spiritual progress.[72] And even friendship, in Paulinus' view, came from love of God; thus it too was cause to praise and thank God. As Paulinus stated in a letter to his friend and fellow aristocrat, Sulpicius Severus:

"through this [God's] grace He has united me to you not only as a most be-loved friend in our earlier life in the world, but also as an inseparable com-panion and partner in the spiritual brotherhood of His affairs."[73] Paulinus, like Augustine, preserved a role for individual friendships and for intimate ties to other Christians within the community of the faithful.[74]

Although Ambrose and Paulinus differed in their notions of Christian friendship, both men spent much time cultivating their relationships with other aristocrats. In their actions they show how strongly the behavior of devout Christians was shaped by the norms and values of the aristocratic status culture in which they had come of age and which they shared with their peers.[75] Paulinus, an aristocrat renowned for his ascetic renunciation of the secular world, nevertheless kept up varied and lively friendships with many contemporaries.[76] He did this, as aristocrats traditionally did, via let-ters and travel; he asked friends like Sulpicius Severus to visit or at least to write often.[77] Like their pagan contemporaries, Ambrose and Paulinus sprinkled their letters with literary references, though now the Bible pro-vided the primary source for their quotations. Like their pagan peers, they followed the conventional formalities of aristocratic correspondence. So, for example, Ambrose's letter to Alypius, urban prefect in 391, opens with the proper polite tone and acknowledgment of the status of his correspondent: "The honorable Antiochus delivered to me your Excellency's letter, and I have not been remiss in sending a reply." This and another letter to Antonius, consul of 382, end with the same conventional epistolary for-mula: "Farewell and love us, for we love you."[78]

Christian bishops recognized that *amicitia* was an important social institu-tion in aristocratic society in which they themselves participated. That rec-ognition helps to elucidate why their efforts to reconsider friendship as a concept were so strenuous in the fourth and early fifth centuries. As church leaders analyzed *amicitia,* they came to different visions of this ideal. But whatever the view that each finally reached, church leaders expanded Christian spirituality by making friendship a serious area of investigation and discussion for Christians. This trend represents something of a change in the message of Christianity and marks the influence of the aristocracy.

Nobilitas

Above all, late Roman senatorial aristocrats desired to possess *nobilitas.* This concept, originally derived from *noscere,* signified renown, distinction, or su-periority.[79] As applied to the Roman senators in the Republic, *nobilitas* referred to men who held the consulship or were of consular ancestry.[80] Hence it was a term used to recognize achievement and not only "notable" aristocratic birth. *Nobilitas* was closely connected with family pedigree.[81] Thus it was standard in aristocratic circles to associate *nobilitas* with high birth and outstanding achievement (most of all, with the attainment of consulship).[82] In addition, *nobilitas* and *nobilis* could also describe personal qualities thought to be characteristic of the well-born; these included superiority in or appreciation of cultural attainments, conspicuous civic commitment, a proud comportment, and outstanding virtue.[83]

The centrality of the concept of *nobilitas* to the late Roman aristocrat made it a key focus for the efforts of church leaders engaged in the conversion of this group. Typically, when Christian leaders spoke of *nobilitas,* they recognized the traditional criteria—family and office—but claimed such were of lesser worth in determining *nobilitas* than Christian piety. Christian leaders most often used as their examples of Christian "nobility" men and women who were already ennobled by traditional aristocratic standards. In these ways they essentially incorporated the traditional bases for *nobilitas* into their Christian version, even as they sought to place it at a lower level than Christian spirituality.

Such continuities show how deeply aristocratic status culture influenced Christian leaders. As J. Harries observed, this presents something of a paradox:

> The rejection of earthly nobility in order to achieve a parallel celestial status had by its very nature to be confined to those of noble birth in worldly terms. Jerome, Pelagius and Paulinus never seem to ennoble those not noble already. The formulation, therefore, of a new set of criteria of status, consisting of asceticism and renunciation did not actually lead to the formation of a new class encompassing a wider social range than the old one. The frontiers of nobility were not in real terms redefined.[84]

Yet the acceptance of cultural continuities between Christian leaders and their aristocratic audiences indicates, too, a certain change, for now a secular concept, *nobilitas,* is being adapted and incorporated into a Christian framework.[85]

A typical Christian construction of "nobility" can be found in the epitaph from the late 380s of the eminent aristocrat Sextus Petronius Probus, cited earlier. It claimed that Christian nobility is the true and final nobility, but it did not in any way deny the validity of the secular honors that Probus had achieved nor the value of his family. The competitive element in this epitaph and the need to demonstrate *nobilitas* before ancestors and peers show how little has changed. Moreover, as is frequently the case, this epitaph confers the highest nobility on one who is already noble on conventional grounds, and it does so on the basis of his adoption of Christianity.

In the writings of the late fourth-century Christian advocates of asceticism, we often find an ostensible negation of the traditional bases for *nobilitas*.[86] Perhaps most vocal on the subject of *nobilitas* was Jerome, who moved within senatorial circles in Rome and faced the "nobility" on a daily basis.[87] Jerome frequently makes the claim that the greatest nobility belongs to the ascetic Christian. Yet even he cannot resist dwelling on ascetics possessed of the traditional *nobilitas*. So Jerome describes Pammachius as "the glory of the Furian stock . . . whose grandfathers and great grandfathers have been consuls," and as "the most Christian of all nobles and the most noble of all Christians."[88] As in the epitaph of Sextus Petronius Probus, Jerome plays on the competitive element among aristocrats by contrasting the degree of *nobilitas* attained by ascetic Christians with just "average" Christians: "In our day Rome possesses what the world in days gone by knew not of. Then few of the wise or mighty or noble were Christians; now many wise, powerful, and noble are not Christians only but even monks. And among them is Pammachius, the wisest, the mightiest, the noblest; great among the great, a leader among leaders, he is the commander in chief of all monks."[89] This competitive element is reiterated in a letter of 406 to the aristocrat Julian: "You are of noble birth, so are they [i.e., Paulinus and Pammachius]: but in Christ they are made nobler still."[90] In both instances Jerome confers a higher *nobilitas* on those who already possess conventional aristocratic "nobility" of family and office.

We find this same hierarchical conjunction in the writings of Jerome's contemporaries, themselves advocates of asceticism who moved in senatorial circles.[91] Paulinus of Nola remarks about the senatorial monk, Pammachius, that his asceticism gives him the highest "nobility" yet he is "noble" by traditional critera.[92] Pammachius' feast for the poor at St. Peter's represents the channeling of a traditional act of patronage before a new audience, an act that will win him (in Paulinus' striking phrase) recognition among those who are truly "noble," the prophets, apostles, and martyrs who compose the "heavenly senate" *(caeli senatus)*.[93] Thus even ascetics—who most often opposed the process of its adaptation—reveal how influenced they are by the aristocratic status culture.

Most often in this period we find proponents of asceticism praising "noble" women who demonstrate their Christianity through private acts of piety, especially chastity and asceticism. So, for example, Jerome remarks of Paula that "noble in family, she was nobler still in holiness."[94] He introduces his praise of Demetrias by first extolling her family's ancestry.[95] Since, for Jerome, the highest form of Christian piety in women derived from asceticism, as demonstrated by a matron's chastity or by a young girl's virginity, this was the basis for ascribing the highest nobility to women. Yet time and again, he attributes this virtue to women already noble by traditional criteria (i.e., born in an old senatorial family that included consuls).[96] Jerome follows traditional attitudes toward aristocratic women when he claims that virginity brings "nobility" not only to the individual woman but to her family: "A virgin should make a noble house more noble still by her virginity."[97]

Ambrose often uses the noble virgin martyr to exemplify the highest Christian female nobility; the virgin martyr's claim to this distinction far surpasses that made on the basis of consulships and prefectureships.[98] Yet nobility was still being granted to aristocratic women for private virtue, such as chastity, rather than through wielding office and authority; the traditional basis for nobility was still reserved for their aristocratic brethren.[99] Augustine says much about normative expectations when, in a letter to two aristocratic women, he remarks that a "girl's chastity brings more nobility than being the foundress of an illustrious line through an earthly marriage."[100]

By the mid-fifth century the basis for *nobilitas* was effectively changed, for by then it was being conferred on men who held church, not secular, office. In the words of Avitus of Vienne, "true and unblemished nobility" lay in ecclesiastical office.[101] Those Christians who held an office in the church were "the most noble." In Italy, too, by the middle of the fifth century we find aristocrats accepting church office as a higher "nobility" than secular office.[102] In Gaul, by the fifth century it became a standard claim that a cleric was "noble by birth, more noble by religion."[103] But, paradoxically, as in the fourth century, men already ennobled by standard aristocratic notions of family attain a higher nobility through Christian office. The aristocratic notion of *nobilitas* was in place, now based on ecclesiastical, not secular, office.

A few Christian leaders articulated a more radical change in the conceptualization of *nobilitas*. Prudentius, a contemporary of Jerome's, may be moving toward a more universal definition of this idea when he has the martyr Romanus explain how pagan and Christian *nobilitas* differ: "Far be it from me that the blood of my parents or the law of the senate-chamber should make me noble; it is Christ's noble teaching that ennobles men [*viros*]."[104] Although Romanus is characterized as a noble of long descent, in this passage Romanus claims *nobilitas*—as a character trait—is open to men, presumably all men. If so, this passage suggests that *nobilitas* is a private, potentially universal virtue, apart from social class.[105] Such a view may reflect Prudentius' own position in the world; the poet came from Spanish provincial circles and returned there, removed from the senatorial aristocracy and its old consular families.

Some more determined Christian attacks on "nobility" appear in the fifth century. The *Sermo de Vita Sancti Honorati* by Hilarius of Gaul presents Honoratus as an aristocrat who had retained all his secular prestige, even after becoming a monk and later a bishop; his honor was so great that none of the other bishops (mostly nonaristocrats) considered themselves his equal.[106] However, Hilarius notes, Honoratus' nobility did not arise from his long family stemma nor his offices but, rather, from membership in the Christian brotherhood: "We are all one in Christ, and the height of nobility is to be reckoned among the sons of God. Our glory cannot be increased by the dignity of our earthly family except by renouncing it. No one in heaven is more glorious than he who has repudiated his family ancestry and chooses to be enrolled as only a descendant of Christ."[107]

Hilarius' willingness to view *nobilitas* as a personal characteristic is shared by Valerian, bishop of Cimiez in the mid-fifth century. Valerian, probably a noble himself, criticized certain elements of aristocratic society, and particularly singles out false pride in one's nobility: "Pride is the vice of lowliness [*vilitatis*] and an indication of ignobility [*ignobilitatis*]; nobility of mind [*nobilitas mentis*] does not know how to praise itself."[108] As Valerian proposes that the true noble is possessed of humility, he reverses the traditional notion of the noble whose status is manifested by proud comportment.

This more radical redefinition of *nobilitas* as a moral virtue and character trait independent of family status appears more as a fifth-century perspective. When the Latin Christian fathers of the fourth century spoke of *nobilitas,* they generally accepted much of the traditional class associations of the term, although they claimed that the traditional criteria—family and office—were of lesser worth in determining nobility than a strong Christian faith. That is why they so often used as examples of Christian nobility those men and women already ennobled by traditional aristocratic standards. This conception of *nobilitas* reveals how deeply Christian leaders were influenced by aristocrats' status culture. If it is true that changes in language occur when people's attitudes change, then the emphasis on *nobilitas* shows how little in elite society had changed as this key aristocratic value was incorporated into the message of Christianity.[109]

Although such a conservative approach facilitated conversion by making Christianity appear as less of a change to aristocrats, the redefinition of *nobilitas* was also an attempt to alter aristocratic attitudes by promulgating a new spiritual hierarchy of "nobility." Where "nobility" for the pagans had been a combination of social, attitudinal, and behavioral characteristics in no clearly defined order, it became, for the Christians, a hierarchical term with the social status of nobility clearly subordinated to attitudinal and behavioral ideals. Those "nobles" who rejected the traditional bases for their *nobilitas* in search of a higher, Christian one—often associated with asceticism and chastity in this period—were lauded as "the most noble" of all. The willingness of church leaders to adapt *nobilitas,* such a central component of aristocratic culture, reveals the extent of the aristocracy's influence on the developing outlook and message of Christianity.

Changing the Message of Christianity

To a degree, aristocrats, like their peers, saw in the message of Christianity something of what M. Mann has claimed lies behind the dominant religions today: Christianity, Hinduism, Buddhism, and Islam are alike in being "critically concerned with individual, universal *salvation*—the goal of relief from earthly sufferings through some kind of systematic moral life plan available to all, regardless of class or particularistic identity."[110] This was appealing; as Ambrose noted, even the rich die.[111] Late Roman aristocrats, however, rarely speak of universal salvation or egalitarian spirituality, two aspects of the message of Christianity that Mann and many others have seen as deriving from the Gospels in other times and places. Nor did fourth- and early fifth-century western bishops dwell on these aspects of Christianity in addressing their aristocratic audiences. This is but one instance of how preexisting aristocratic attitudes affected both what aristocrats heard of the Christian message and how Christianity was conveyed to them.

The message of Christianity was not transmitted to aristocrats in a vacuum. Rather, it was part of a world with its own horizons. The assumptions and practices of this world shaped how aristocrats heard the message of Christianity and influenced the ways in which Christian leaders communicated their message. The interaction between aristocrats' status culture and the message of Christianity helps us to understand how Christianity came to appeal to late Roman aristocrats and how, in its efforts to convert the aristocracy, Christianity was "aristocratized." Church leaders accepted as important certain central aristocratic ideals—such as *nobilitas, amicitia,* and *honos*—even as they attempted to redefine them to be consonant with a Christian message.

For the religious transformation of the class, however, certain elements of aristocratic identity and status culture were clearly more important than the message of Christianity per se. The expansion and advancement of many new men into the aristocracy by Constantine spread that status culture and augmented the influence of the class, even as differences among aristocrats emerged. This situation, full of the uncertainties of social mobility and the realities of patronage, made certain sorts of men more open to Christianity than others: provincials, men from newer families, and those in the imperial bureaucracy more readily approached Christianity. Those from more securely pagan spheres were more reluctant to listen to the message of Christianity. In this world women followed the religious predilections of their fathers and husbands more often than not.

In the end aristocrats came to adopt Christianity in the company of their family and friends. The aristocrats' status culture remained largely intact, albeit with certain modifications. What it meant to be an aristocrat changed. Humility and charity for the poor, for example, loomed larger. But what it could mean to be a Christian also changed, as concerns for *amicitia, honos,* culture, and *nobilitas* entered the discourse of the community of the faithful.

Tables

Table 3.1 Religious identification of men by region of origin, 284–423

Region	Pagan	Christian	Convert Pagan to Christian	Convert Christian to pagan
Italy	47 (61.1%)	24 (31.2%)	6 (7.8%)	0 (0.0%)
Gaul	9 (29.0%)	20 (64.5%)	2 (6.5%)	0 (0.0%)
Spain	1 (11.1%)	8 (88.9%)	0 (0.0%)	0 (0.0%)
Roman Africa	11 (64.7%)	6 (35.3%)	0 (0.0%)	0 (0.0%)
Asia, Egypt, et al.	11 (47.8%)	10 (43.5%)	1 (4.3%)	1 (4.3%)

Notes: Total N = 157. Missing observations = 158.
Due to rounding, the columns in this and following tables do not always add to 100%.

Table 3.2 Religious identification of men by region of main property holdings, 284–423

Region	Pagan	Christian	Convert Pagan to Christian	Convert Christian to pagan
Italy	43 (58.1%)	26 (35.1%)	5 (6.8%)	0 (0.0%)
Gaul, Britain	2 (11.8%)	14 (82.4%)	1 (5.9%)	0 (0.0%)
Spain	1 (16.7%)	5 (83.3%)	0 (0.0%)	0 (0.0%)
Roman Africa	12 (57.1%)	9 (42.9%)	0 (0.0%)	0 (0.0%)
Asia, Egypt, et al.	3 (30.0%)	6 (60.0%)	0 (0.0%)	1 (10.0%)

Notes: Total N = 128. Missing observations = 187.

Table 3.3 Religious identification of men by place of highest office, 284–423

Region	Pagan	Christian	Convert Pagan to Christian	Convert Christian to pagan
Italy	51 (67.1%)	23 (30.3%)	1 (1.3%)	1 (1.3%)
Gaul, Britain	2 (8.3%)	17 (70.8%)	4 (16.7%)	1 (4.2%)
Spain	5 (71.4%)	1 (14.3%)	1 (14.3%)	0 (0.0%)
Roman Africa	30 (47.6%)	29 (46.0%)	3 (4.8%)	1 (1.6%)
Asia, Egypt, et al.	30 (53.6%)	24 (42.9%)	1 (1.8%)	1 (1.8%)

Notes: Total N = 226. Missing observations = 89.

Table 3.4 Religious identification of men by region of origin and time period

Time period	Italy		Gaul		Spain		Roman Africa		Asia, Egypt, et al.		Total
	Pagan/ pagan convert	Christian/ Christian convert	Pagan/ pagan convert	Christian/ Christian convert	Pagan/ pagan convert	Christian/ Christian convert	Pagan/ pagan convert	Christian/ Christian convert	Pagan/ pagan convert	Christian/ Christian convert	
Pre-Constantine–Constantine (284–324)	4	1	0	0	0	1	5	0	1	0	12
Constans–Constantius II (337–361)[a]	9	2	0	0	0	0	3	0	2	4	20
Julian–Valentinian I (sole ruler) (361–367)	6	0	2	0	0	0	0	0	4	0	12
Gratian–Valentinian II (367–383)[b]	4	9	0	5	0	0	0	1	1	1	21
Valentinian II (sole ruler) (383–392)[c]	4	1	4	1	1	1	0	0	0	0	12
Post–Valentinian II (392–423)	6	7	3	7	0	3	0	4	3	6	39
Total	33	20	9	13	1	5	8	5	11	11	116

Notes: Missing observations = 199.

Time period is based on the western emperor at the time of each man's highest office.

No aristocrats in the sample for the years 324–337, Constantine as sole ruler.

a. This period includes the reigns of Constans, Constantine II, and Constantius II.

b. This period includes the reigns of Gratian with Valentinian I and later with Valentinian II.

c. This period includes the reign of the usurper Magnus Maximus, 383–388.

Table 3.5   Religious identification of men by highest senatorial rank

| | | | Convert | |
| | | | Pagan to | Christian |
Rank	Pagan	Christian	Christian	to pagan
Illustris	58 (40.0%)	66 (49.3%)	8 (66.7%)	4 (100.0%)
Spectabilis	23 (15.9%)	19 (14.2%)	0 (0.0%)	0 (0.0%)
Clarissimus	64 (44.1%)	49 (36.6%)	4 (33.3%)	0 (0.0%)

Notes: Total N = 295. Missing observations = 20.
The percentages reported are for columns.

Table 3.6   Religious identification of men by date of parent's senatorial status, 284–423

Parental status	Pagan/ pagan convert	Christian/ Christian convert
Senatorial before Constantine	16 (72.7%)	6 (27.3%)
Possibly senatorial before Constantine	5 (83.3%)	1 (16.7%)
Senatorial during or after Constantine	24 (45.8%)	29 (54.7%)
Possibly senatorial during or after Constantine	4 (44.4%)	5 (55.5%)

Notes: Total N = 90. Missing observations = 225.

Table 4.1   Religious identification of men by career path

Career path	Pagan/ pagan convert	Christian/ Christian convert
Senatorial civic	86 (68.8%)	49 (51.6%)
Military	7 (5.6%)	11 (11.6%)
Imperial bureaucratic	8 (6.4%)	18 (18.9%)
Religious	17 (13.6%)	11 (11.6%)
Mixed/indeterminate	7 (5.6%)	6 (6.3%)

Notes: Total N = 220. Missing observations = 95.
The percentages reported are for columns.
Each career path includes men who were entirely in the designated career path and those who were mainly in the career path.

Table 4.2 Career path of men by region of origin

Region	Senatorial civic	Military	Imperial bureaucratic	Religious	Mixed/ indeterminate
Italy	55 (85.9%)	0 (0.0%)	1 (1.6%)	6 (9.4%)	2 (3.1%)
Gaul	6 (26.1%)	4 (17.4%)	6 (26.1%)	5 (21.7%)	2 (8.7%)
Spain	2 (28.6%)	1 (14.3%)	1 (14.3%)	1 (14.3%)	2 (28.6%)
Roman Africa	12 (85.7%)	0 (0.0%)	0 (0.0%)	1 (7.1%)	1 (7.1%)
Asia, Egypt, et al.	9 (42.9%)	8 (38.1%)	4 (19.0%)	0 (0.0%)	0 (0.0%)

Notes: Total *N* = 129. Missing observations = 186.

Each career path includes men who were entirely in the designated career path and those who were mainly in the career path.

Table 4.3 Religious identification of men by career path and time period

Time period	Senatorial civic		Military		Imperial bureaucratic		Religious		Mixed/ indeterminate		Total
	Pagan/ pagan convert	Christian/ Christian convert	Pagan/ pagan convert	Christian/ Christian convert	Pagan/ pagan convert	Christian/ Christian convert	Pagan/ pagan convert	Christian/ Christian convert	Pagan/ pagan convert	Christian/ Christian convert	
Pre-Constantine– Constantine (284–324)	18	2	0	0	0	0	1	0	1	0	22
Constans–Constantius II (337–361)[a]	15	7	0	1	0	4	2	0	1	0	30
Julian–Valentinian I (sole ruler) (361–367)	11	0	2	1	4	0	1	0	0	0	19
Gratian–Valentinian II (367–383)[b]	7	12	0	1	1	3	0	2	0	1	27
Valentinian II (sole ruler) (383–392)[c]	4	1	3	0	0	3	1	0	1	2	15
Post-Valentinian II (392–423)	13	21	2	6	1	6	0	2	2	2	55
Total	68	43	7	9	6	16	5	4	5	5	168

Notes: Missing observations = 147.

No aristocrats appeared in the sample for the years 324–337, Constantine as sole ruler.

Each career path includes men who were entirely in the designated career path and those who were mainly in the career path.

Time period is based on the western emperor at the time of each man's highest office.

a. This period includes the reigns of Constans, Constantine II, and Constantius II.

b. This period includes the reigns of Gratian with Valentinian I and later with Valentinian II.

c. This period includes the reign of the usurper Magnus Maximus, 383–388.

Table 4.4 Office-holding by men in pagan state cults by time period, 284–423

Time period	Office holder in pagan state cult	Non–office holder in pagan state cult
Pre-Constantine–Constantine (284–324)	9 (45.0%)	11 (55.0%)
Constans–Constantius II (337–361)[a]	9 (50.0%)	9 (50.0%)
Julian–Valentinian I (sole ruler) (361–367)	6 (40.0%)	9 (60.0%)
Gratian–Valentinian II (367–383)[b]	4 (50.0%)	4 (50.0%)
Valentinian II (sole ruler) (383–392)[c]	3 (33.3%)	6 (66.7%)
Post–Valentinian II (392–423)	1 (6.3%)	15 (93.8%)

Notes: Total N = 86. Missing observations = 70.

No aristocrats in the sample for the years 324–337, Constantine as sole ruler.

Time period is based on the western emperor at the time of each man's highest office.

a. This period includes the reigns of Constans, Constantine II, and Constantius II.

b. This period includes the reigns of Gratian with Valentinian I and later with Valentinian II.

c. This period includes the reign of the usurper Magnus Maximus, 383–388.

Table 5.1 Religious identification by sex

			Convert	
Sex	Pagan	Christian	Pagan to Christian	Christian to pagan
Male	152 (48.3%)	146 (46.3%)	13 (4.1%)	4 (1.3%)
Female	14 (14.1%)	84 (84.8%)	1 (1.1%)	0 (0.0%)

Note: Total N = 414.

Table 5.2 Christian men reaching their first low office compared with Christian women at age 20 in four time periods

Time period	Male Christians and converts (pagan to Christian) reaching first low office	Female Christians at age 20
Pre-Constantine–Constantine (284–337)	3 (8.6%)	4 (8.7%)
Constans–Valentinian I (sole ruler) (337–367)[a]	6 (17.1%)	7 (15.2%)
Gratian–Valentinian II (sole ruler) (367–392)[b]	11 (31.4%)	19 (41.3%)
Post–Valentinian II (392–423)	15 (42.9%)	16 (34.8%)

Notes: Total $N = 81$. Missing observations $= 159$.

The percentages reported are for columns.

This table represents men and women for whom it was possible to estimate the date of their twentieth year. For women, this was based on birth, marriage, or death. (For the general age of marriage for late Roman aristocratic women, see B. Shaw, "The Age of Roman Girls at Marriage: Some Reconsiderations," *JRS* 77 (1987), pp. 30–46.) For men, these numbers were based on appointment to their first low office, held at approximately age 20. These offices included *praetor* (*praetor urbanus, tutelaris,* and *triumphalis*), *quaestor, consul suffectus, vicarius, consularis, praeses, comes* (*rei militaris* or *domesticorum*), *corrector, praefectus annonae, curator, notarius,* and *praepositus* or *tribunus* (regimental commander). These offices were the first stages in the career of a *clarissimus,* be it in the senatorial civic, imperial bureaucratic, or military career path. Quaestors, praetors, and suffect consuls were nominated as youths for offices held at a later date; for praetors there was a ten-year interval between nomination and office holding (*C.Th.* 6.4.22). Nominations for these offices were expected no later than age 16, and most receiving nomination were younger. See A. H. M. Jones (1964, 1986 reprint), p. 534; *C.Th.* 6.4.1; and A. Chastagnol, "Observations sur le consulat suffect et la préture du bas-empire," *Revue historique* 219 (1958), pp. 235–238. Chastagnol sees the suffect consulship as normally held around age 22, and praetorships held between ages 20–25.

a. This period includes the reigns of Constans, Constantine II, Constantius II, Julian, Jovian, and Valentinian I as sole ruler in the western empire.

b. This period includes the reigns of Gratian with Valentinian I and later with Valentinian II, and that of Valentinian II as sole ruler in the western empire.

Table 5.3   Religious affiliation of children

Child	Father		Mother		Total
	Pagan	Christian/ Christian convert	Pagan	Christian/ Christian convert	
Sons					
Follow parent	15	19	2	12	48
Do not follow parent	3	2	0	2	7
Daughters					
Follow parent	3	13	0	14	30
Do not follow parent	2	0	0	0	2
Total	23	34	2	28	87

Table 6.1   Religious identification of men by western emperor at time of highest office

Time period	Pagan/ pagan convert	Christian/ Christian convert
Pre-Constantine–Constantine (284–324)	20 (21.1%)	2 (2.1%)
Constans–Constantius II (337–361)[a]	19 (20.2%)	13 (13.7%)
Julian–Valentinian I (sole ruler) (361–367)	18 (18.9%)	1 (1.1%)
Gratian–Valentinian II (367–383)[b]	8 (8.4%)	21 (22.1%)
Valentinian II (sole ruler) (383–392)[c]	9 (9.5%)	6 (6.3%)
Post–Valentinian II (392–423)	21 (22.1%)	52 (54.7%)

Notes: Total $N = 190$. Missing observations $= 125$.

The percentages reported are for columns.

No aristocrats in the sample held their highest office in the years 324–337.

a. This period includes the reigns of Constans, Constantine II, and Constantius II.

b. This period includes the reigns of Gratian with Valentinian I and later with Valentinian II.

c. This period includes the reign of the usurper Magnus Maximus, 383–388.

Table 6.2   Religious identification of men by western emperor at time of
highest office (selected high offices only)

Time period	Pagan/ pagan convert	Christian/ Christian convert
Pre-Constantine–Constantine (284–324)	13 (20.0%)	2 (2.7%)
Constans–Constantius II (337–361)[a]	11 (16.9%)	12 (16.2%)
Julian–Valentinian I (sole ruler) (361–367)	14 (21.5%)	1 (1.4%)
Gratian–Valentinian II (367–383)[b]	3 (4.6%)	17 (23.0%)
Valentinian II (sole ruler) (383–392)[c]	7 (10.8%)	5 (6.8%)
Post–Valentinian II (392–423)	17 (26.2%)	37 (50.0%)

Notes: Total N = 139. Missing observations = 176.

The percentages reported are for columns.

Offices in table include only consul in the West; praetorian prefect of Italy, Gaul, or Africa; urban prefect of Rome; proconsul of Africa; *comes rei privatae; comes sacrarum largitionum; quaestor sacri palatii; magister officiorum;* and *magister militum* or *equitum.*

No aristocrats in the sample held their highest office in the years 324–337.

a. This period includes the reigns of Constans, Constantine II, and Constantius II.

b. This period includes the reigns of Gratian with Valentinian I and later with Valentinian II.

c. This period includes the reign of the usurper Magnus Maximus, 383–388.

Table 6.3 Religious identification of men by western emperor at time of
lowest office

Time period	Pagan/ pagan convert	Christian/ Christian convert
Pre-Constantine–Constantine (284–324)	23 (28.8%)	2 (2.3%)
Constantine (sole ruler) (324–337)	6 (7.5%)	6 (7.0%)
Constans–Constantius II (337–361)[a]	19 (23.8%)	12 (14.0%)
Julian–Valentinian I (sole ruler) (361–367)	11 (13.8%)	2 (2.3%)
Gratian–Valentinian II (367–383)[b]	6 (7.5%)	13 (15.1%)
Valentinian II (sole ruler) (383–392)[c]	4 (5.0%)	11 (12.8%)
Post–Valentinian II (392–423)	11 (13.8%)	40 (46.5%)

Notes: Total N = 166. Missing observations = 149.

The percentages reported are for columns.

a. This period includes the reigns of Constans, Constantine II, and Constantius II.

b. This period includes the reigns of Gratian with Valentinian I and later with Valentinian II.

c. This period includes the reign of the usurper Magnus Maximus, 383–388.

Appendix 1:
Sources, Criteria, and Variables
for the Database

A primary source for this database was *The Prosopography of the Later Roman Empire (PLRE)*, the first volume of which was published in 1971 and covers the period critical to this study, 260–395 C.E. The *PLRE*, drawn from both the literary and epigraphic evidence, is intended to include all "senators . . . equestrians . . . *comites* and holders of *honores* or *dignitates* down to provincial governors and tribunes, *praefecti* and *praepositi* of military units; also officials of the palatine ministries and of PPOs, PURs and MUMs, assessors of magistrates, lawyers, doctors, rhetors, grammarians and poets."[1] Altogether *PLRE* 1 includes 4,500 people.[2] With each entry the compilers attempted to cite all information concerning geographical origin, religion, wealth, and family relationships of the person named. In 1980 Volume 2 appeared, covering the years 395–527.

After the publication of *PLRE* 1, and again after the publication of *PLRE* 2, scholars contributed reviews that included addenda and corrigenda. As of "A Survey of the Significant Addenda to *PLRE*" published in 1987, over one thousand omissions have been cited by scholars.[3] In addition, several reviewers have offered lists of corrigenda to particular entries. I have used all of the published articles concerning corrigenda as well as addenda for the database. (See Appendix 3.)

One of the most problematic omissions from the *PLRE* for the purposes of this study is that of clergy, and especially those clergy who were senatorial aristocrats. The editors of the *PLRE* excluded clergy on the assumption that they would be included in the French-sponsored *Prosopographie chrétienne du Bas-Empire* (hereafter cited as *PC*). I consulted Part 1 of the *PC, Prosopographie de l'Afrique chrétienne (303–533)* (Paris, 1982), edited by A. Mandouze, which contains some 2,964 Christians and all pagans who had played a role in church history in Africa in the period 303–533. I also consulted C. Pietri,

231

"Appendice prosopographique à la *Roma christiana* (311–440)," in *Mélanges d'archéologie et d'histoire de l'école française de Rome: Antiquité* 88 (1977), pp. 371–415, which is incorporated into *Prosopographie chrétienne du Bas-Empire 2, Prosopographie de l'Italie chrétienne,* edited by C. Pietri and L. Pietri (Rome, 1999–2000).[4]

Interestingly, in this database pagan males were especially well attested through epigraphic sources (116 cases); only 36 pagan men in this database were not so found. For Christian males, epigraphic attestation was used in half of the cases: 73 Christian men were attested epigraphically; 73 Christian men were not. In contrast, converts of all sorts are best known from literary sources. Eleven male converts to Christianity were known from literary sources; only two were known from epigraphic sources. All four of the male converts to paganism were known only from literary sources.

Women are not so well attested epigraphically. Among the pagan women, 10 of 14 were attested by inscriptions whereas only 4 were known solely from literary sources. Christian women were better attested by literary rather than epigraphic remains, as were Christian males. But the proportion of women attested only by literary remains was slightly higher than that for Christian men; more than half of the Christian women—44 out of 84—were known from only literary sources, with the remainder (40) plus one convert to Christianity attested by inscriptions.

Biases and Limitations in the Sources

Analysis of Volume 1 of the *PC* added only a small number of names to the database. This was so, in part, because the criteria for inclusion in the *PC* meant that all officials were cited, and hence there was much overlap with the *PLRE*. But, additionally, the *PC* contains individuals who were often of doubtful historical existence, and of uncertain aristocratic standing and religious affiliation, because it included people drawn from, among other sources, hagiographical texts. How to assess the individuals in hagiographical sources had been a problem for the compilers of the *PLRE* as well. As T. D. Barnes succinctly argued, "no useful purpose is served by cataloguing holders of invented offices in hagiographical fiction."[5] Nevertheless, some real people may be included in hagiographical works.

Barnes' application of criteria for hagiographical texts like the *Acta Martyrum* provided a useful model in assessing the credibility of such works and the information in them; his study yielded some additional entries for this database.[6] But, when either the hagiographical source or the evidence left doubt as to the historical veracity of the person involved, the individual was omitted. I stress that I have adopted a conservative approach to such texts as the *Miracles of St. Stephen* and the *Passio of Maximian and Isaac* by Macrobius Donatus. The benefit of such a conservative method is that the resulting quantitative analysis will be based on what is known and certain. Moreover, hagiographical texts of uncertain historical veracity were not entirely lost from view, for many of them provide important insights into the attitudes, expectations, and beliefs of men and women in the later Roman empire. However, insofar as the database is meant to include only verifiably real men and women and what they actually did, it was necessary to omit "uncertain people" from unreliable sources.

In discussing my analysis of the evidence from the database, I have tried to take into account biases in the *PLRE* and its addenda and corrigenda, and in the first volume of the *PC*. The omission of aristocratic clergy noted above is an obvious bias. And the reliance on published works, archaeological as well as literary, is another sort of bias insofar as some areas are far better studied than others.[7] But there is one additional bias worth noting. The evidence for senatorial careers in the empire is generally biased in favor of the successful.[8] The aristocrat active in the world, whether in government, the church, or the military, tends to leave more of an imprint in life and in death than his disengaged contemporary. Thus evidence about such men will more often survive in the historical record.

Aside from the biases noted here, I found no other systematic bias in the survival of evidence on male aristocrats in the *PLRE* and in the *PC* that bears upon this database. Biases in the evidence on aristocratic women are discussed in Chapter 5. They include the greater survival of evidence on Christian rather than pagan women because of the differing epigraphic habits of Christians and pagans in relation to women, and the rhetorical role that women played in Christian texts.

Religion as a Marked Category

Sources vary in marking the religious affiliations of individuals. There are differences, too, over time and from region to region. In some sources, like Eusebius' *Vita Constantini*, religion was the most important category possible; in others, like Ammianus Marcellinus' history, it was not acknowledged openly. However, beginning with Constantine, the marking of aristocrats as

Christian was legal and in some ways desirable. Christians took up the epigraphic habit of their peers and identified themselves openly by their religion.[9] Although fewer Christians are attested epigraphically than pagans in this database, they do nevertheless appear so attested in significant proportions. I see little reason to think that, amidst the incentives to be identified with the emperor's religion, there were systematic biases or legal constraints that hindered aristocrats from marking themselves as Christian. To put it another way, I do not believe that the patterns discussed in this book are the result of changes in the marking of religious categories. Instead, they reflect evidence of behavior.

Self-identification or the testimony of a source that a certain individual was pagan or Christian was taken at face value. I did not attempt to judge the degree of a person's religious identification based on their religious activities or the views expressed about them by others.

Criteria for Inclusion in the Database

Analysis of these sources allowed me to gather 414 cases of senatorial aristocrats who fit the criteria I had established for inclusion in the database. The criteria fall into three general categories: aristocratic standing; geographic and chronological location; and religious affiliation.

ARISTOCRATIC STANDING. For the database, a senatorial aristocrat was defined as anyone who had attained the lowest senatorial rank, that of clarissimate, either by holding an office that conferred senatorial rank or by being born into the clarissimate (i.e., someone whose father was at the least a *clarissimus*).[10] Since the clarissimate was hereditary for men born after their father's promotion, the sons and grandsons of an original nonsenatorial office holder would be absorbed into the ranks of the senatorial aristocracy.[11] Although the laws only mention the passing of the clarissimate to male descendants, it was passed to women as well, either from their fathers or husbands. Titles such as *clarissima puella* and *clarissima femina* indicate this, but do not tell us if the title passed beyond one generation for women.[12]

Not all clarissimate families achieved high office or membership in the senate; admission to the senate had to be attained, according to the rule of the principate, upon election to the quaestorship. A. H. M. Jones, however, has argued that a senator's son was "obliged to take up his rank unless he—or his parents—obtained imperial permission to renounce it."[13] References to the senatorial aristocracy in this study must be understood as referring to the senatorial order in its widest sense, that is, as including both men and women of clarissimate rank even if their ancestors were not senatorial aristocrats by birth.

Moreover, membership in the senatorial aristocracy has to be distinguished from membership in the "nobility" *(nobilitas)*, who still formed a special group within the senatorial aristocracy and enjoyed a marked predominance over newcomers. The criteria for *nobilitas* in the fourth century is disputed; T. D. Barnes would stipulate that "at least after Constantine, a senator was a *nobilis* if he or a forebear had been either ordinary consul or prefect of the city or praetorian prefect."[14] However, testimony by other authors suggests that the term *nobilis* is based on somewhat less precise criteria in the fourth and fifth centuries.[15]

GEOGRAPHIC AND CHRONOLOGICAL LOCATION. Only those aristocrats attested as either living in or holding office that conferred senatorial rank in the western empire in the years 284–423 C.E. were incorporated into the database. The western empire was defined as including ancient Italia, Italia Suburbicaria, Galliae, Septem Provinciae (Viennensis), Britanniae, Hispaniae, and Roman Africa, the provinces shown by the *Notitia Dignitatum*.[16]

Although *PLRE* 1 covers the years 260–395, I began this study with the year 284 to coincide with the important reign of Diocletian. I extended the study to include those aristocrats whose careers were documented as beginning in the 390s but culminated in the first quarter of the fifth century since this is such a critical period for the conversion of the aristocracy. I also systematically analyzed all the high office holders in the western empire until 423, ending with the reign of Honorius.[17]

Office holders in the eastern empire were omitted. Only an aristocrat who lived or held one high office other than the consulship in the western empire was included. I did not include those eastern aristocrats who held only the honorific consulship in the West because such an honor did not indicate any residency in the West.[18]

As noted above, all people of doubtful or inexplicitly attested existence, rank, or geographic and chronological location were excluded, as were some people known only from hagiographical sources or the *Historia Augusta*. I also excluded all Augusti and Caesars—along with usurping Augusti or Caesars—and their wives, children, fathers, and mothers. By this latter exclusion I intended to distinguish between imperial and aristocratic families. The acquisition of imperial authority placed the emperor and his family in a different sphere from other aristocrats, and this omission acknowledged that reality even as it allowed me to maintain my focus on the aristocracy.

CRITERIA FOR RELIGIOUS AFFILIATION. Only those people for whom explicit evidence exists for religious preference or affiliation were included in the database. If the evidence for religious affiliation provided near certainty, the individual was included as probably pagan or probably Christian. A high degree of probability was required in such cases, as will be apparent from the discussion below. In assessing the evidence and determining if the individual met the stated criteria, I took a consistently conservative approach. When in doubt, I omitted the individual from the database. This degree of certainty compensates, I believe, for a smaller database than would have been possible if the criteria for religious affiliation had been relaxed.

By and large, the criteria for determining religious affiliation coincide with those in von Haehling's study.[19] Acceptable criteria included explicit epigraphic attestation, such as formulae specifically identifiable with pagan or Christian belief; Christian monograms and symbols on inscriptions, unless on the orders of an emperor; the dedication of a church, unless on the initiative of the emperor. Intervention in doctrinal disputes was acceptable if such intervention required knowledge of theological issues or if the person was a president of a church council where knowledge of theology was required. But if intervention in church affairs was simply a question of an official performing his duty, such intervention was not deemed sufficient as proof of religious affiliation unless additional information was available. Magistrates, as agents of the government, had little choice in accepting antipagan or pro-Christian laws or policies. Thus I did not take receipt of such a law or code as proof of religious affiliation. Nor did I take receipt of laws involving the regulation of church matters (e.g., property, privileges, use of the public post, etc.) as evidence for the religion of the recipient.

Several other types of evidence were deemed unacceptable. Names were not acceptable since even bishops had pagan theophoric names. Asylum was not acceptable since both pagans and Christians sought asylum in Christian holy places. Correspondence to or received by pagans or Christians was not adequate proof by itself, unless the letters include evidence of shared religious—not merely cultural—sentiments. Nor were all religious sentiments taken as significant; a formulaic phrase, the equivalent of saying "God bless you" when someone sneezes, was seen as neutral and hence insufficient, in and of itself, to indicate religious affiliation. Similarly, the dedication of a literary work was not acceptable as proof of the dedicatee's religion. Nor was the find site of an inscription (i.e., a pagan or Christian tomb) taken as proof of religious affiliation; since inscriptions could be moved or reused, and in some areas pagans and Christians were buried side by side, the find site and any evidence that an inscription provided had to be considered on a case-by-case basis.

In one area, however, the database was constructed in a markedly different way from that of von Haehling. Although von Haehling argued that family connections were of no value in determining religious affiliation in a period when religious affiliation often varied within families, he assumed in several instances that the religious preference of the children was probably the same as that of their parent or parents.[20] I tried, by contrast, to follow a consistently conservative approach, requiring independent verification of parental transmission of religious identity.

Moreover, although the criteria for the database coincide in many respects with those adopted by von Haehling, I did not come to the same conclusions as von Haehling in every case. For example, von Haehling considered Ulpius Limenius, the praetorian prefect of Italy from 347–349, as a possible pagan because he identified him as the pagan proconsul of Constantinople who prayed to Fortuna to kill Libanius. However, the identification of the western prefect Limenius with the eastern proconsul of a later date is not at all certain. Moreover, a quick prayer to "Good Luck" does not necessarily indicate paganism.[21] Thus Limenius was omitted from this database because I was not convinced that he met the religious and geographical criteria.

The importance of establishing fixed criteria as much as possible and holding to standards of explicit evidence for religious affiliation cannot be overemphasized; it is one of the areas, I believe, that distinguishes this book from other analyses. Admittedly, adopting such criteria has forced me to omit certain individuals. So, for example, I omitted the six *comites* who wrote to Athanasius in 345–346 at Constantius' bidding to urge Athanasius to return to Alexandria; since they wrote on the orders of the emperor, I did not use this text as proof of the religious affiliation of the six men.[22] Four of the men are not otherwise attested. And given the degree of religious change in the fourth century, family connections could not be assumed to make for probable shared religious affiliation. So, for example, I omitted certain individuals who, although members of Christian families and not holding pagan priesthoods, were nonetheless not otherwise attested, as, for example, the consul of 334, Anicius Paulinus.[23]

Difficulties arose, too, from the nature of the evidence concerning religious affiliation. Some of the texts are clearly polemical. Eusebius' claim that Constantine preferred Christians as provincial governors after 324 appears in a work that is clearly shaped by rhetorical ends and so could not be used for the religious affiliation of particular office holders unless they are otherwise attested.[24] Moreover, in assessing the textual evidence, I felt it important to keep in mind that religious differences did not necessarily divide the men and women of the fourth century. So, for example, when St. Augustine praises Septimius Acindynus, consul of 340, in a sermon as a moral man, I did not see this praise as explicit evidence that Septimius was a Christian, and consequently I omitted him from my database.[25] A recently discovered inscription to a certain Septimius A., identified as possibly a pagan priest, has been linked to this same Septimius Acindynus, consul of 340.[26] Although the identification is too uncertain for me to include Septimius Acindynus in the database, this new evidence clearly shows the problems of relying on assumptions and uncertain evidence, and of failing to set and consistently follow the criteria I established for certain or virtually certain attestation.

In some instances—67 out of 414—the evidence was overwhelmingly in favor of one or the other religious affiliation but absolute certainty was not possible. If there was, in my judgment, a 90% probability that the individual met the criteria for religious affiliation, he or she was included as probably pagan or probably Christian in this database.[27] So, for example, I included (A)cilius 1, App. 2, as a probable pagan because he appears on a list of senators who, in the view of the excavators, were probably members of a priestly college.[28] Another case where near certainty is possible is that of Proculus Gregorius. As praetorian prefect of Gaul in 383, Gregorius acted against the Priscillianists and gave refuge to Bishop Ithacius of Ossonoba. Since the bishop turned to Gregorius because he expected a favorable reaction and the prefect harbored him, Gregorius (whose name has also been linked with Christianity) was included as a probable Christian in this database.[29]

Since a high degree of probability was required for inclusion in the database, it seemed justifiable to consider probable Christians alongside Christians, and probable pagans alongside pagans in the tables I developed for Chapters 3 through 6. Differences between Christian sects were subsumed in the categories used for the quantitative analyses, largely because this study focuses on the differences between pagans and Christians, not between Christians. In combining these Christian groups, I do not mean to imply that differences within the Christian community were irrelevant to the social relations or to the politics of the day. Indeed, it is as true of the fourth century as of earlier centuries that there were "a fairly large number of Christianities."[30] These differences, however, are not the subject of this study.

In certain tables converts were included alongside pagans or Christians especially if this category was not highly relevant to the discussion at hand. Since the number of converts was so small in any one table, considering them alongside pagans and Christians clarified differences between the two major groups.

One religious group is absent from the database; I found no Jewish aristocrats in the sources on the western empire. This lacuna may be the result of the nature of the evidence and its survival, or it may reflect the realities of the composition of the aristocracy in the West in the years after Constantine.

Determining if any one aristocrat met the criteria for religious affiliation required judgment on a case-by-case basis. My assessment was based on the explicit criteria outlined here, applied as consistently as possible in all cases. Only in this way could the sources be approached in a critical yet systematic fashion in the hope that they would yield more certain and satisfying results.

Variables in the Database

Following the criteria outlined above, I constructed a database that included 414 men and women of the aristocracy who lived or held office in the western empire in the years 284–423 c.e. and about whom we have explicit evidence for religious affiliation. The men comprise 76% (315 out of 414) of the database, and the women 24% (99 out of 414). In terms of religious affiliation, 40% (166 out of 414) are pagan 56% (230 out of 414) are Christian, 3% (14 out of 414) are converts from paganism to Christianity, and 1% (4 out of 414) are converts from Christianity to paganism. For each aristocrat information was recorded about activities that might elucidate their religious choices. My goal was to test certain propositions, my own and those of other scholars, about social factors that may have influenced religious affiliation.

To organize information I created some eighty variables. Each variable was given a numerical value so that it could be considered quantitatively. The variables are outlined below. The reader will see that not all of the information gathered could be analyzed quantitatively, for there were lacunae in the biographies of individuals due to the nature of the sources. Hence for some variables, especially those pertaining to women, parents, and children, information could be collected in only a small number of cases. Even variables with considerable missing data are noted here for they may be of use to future scholars who may contact me for further information.

SEX.   Male and female aristocrats were recorded.

HIGHEST SENATORIAL RANK.   The senatorial rank—*illustris, spectabilis,* and *clarissimus*—was recorded where available. The largest proportion of male aristocrats (46%, 136 out of 295) were *illustres,* followed by *clarissimi* (40%, 117 out of 295) and then by *spectabiles* (14%, 42 out of 295) (see Table 3.5). This pattern reverses for aristocratic women in this study, with the largest proportion attested as *clarissimae* (86%, or 65 out of 76), followed by *illustres* (8%, or 6 out of 76) and by *spectabiles* (7%, 5 out of 76).

CHANGE OF STATUS.   A change of status occured under two conditions: (1) when an individual changed his aristocratic rank from *clarissimus* to *spectabilis* or from one of these to *illustris;* or (2) when an individual first moved into the aristocracy and became a *clarissimus.*

HIGHEST OFFICE; DATE OF HIGHEST OFFICE; EMPEROR AT HIGHEST OFFICE.   The first variable recorded the highest attested office held by the individual aristocrat.[31] A second variable recorded the date of the highest office held by that individual. A third variable recorded the emperor in the western empire at the time the individual held his highest office.[32] Since there was such a large number of categories (twenty-four) for this last variable that comparison was difficult, I collapsed the categories to make up longer time periods. These time periods took into account historical change and religious differences between emperors. For example, Table 4.3, Religious Identification of Men by Career Path and Time Period, which is based on the emperor ruling at the time of each individual's highest office, is divided into seven time periods. Each period reflects changes in political and religious policies that might be relevant to this study.

FIRST ATTESTED OFFICE; EMPEROR AT FIRST ATTESTED OFFICE.   The first variable recorded the aristocrat's first attested office.[33] The large number of variables led me to collapse categories; the goal was to arrive at roughly equal time periods that were also connected to relevant historical change. The second variable recorded the emperor under whom the individual held his first attested office.[34]

CURSUS.   Attested individuals were recorded in one of nine career paths: (1) a military career; (2) a senatorial civic career; (3) a career in the imperial bureaucracy; (4) a religious career; (5) a mixed but mainly military career; (6) a mixed but mainly senatorial civic career; (7) a mixed but mainly imperial bureaucratic career; (8) a mixed but mainly religious career; and (9) a career so mixed as to be indeterminate.[35] Religion is a career in the modern sense only for Christians (i.e., bishops, priests, or monks), since pagan priesthoods were not "full-time positions" in the same way that Christian ones were. Rather, pagan aristocrats generally held priesthoods along with their senatorial, civic, or imperial administrative posts. However, since some pagan aristocrats (seventeen in all) are known to us only as the holders of pagan priesthoods, I recorded these men under this category. I included only men in this analysis; women in the period could not be said to have had "career" paths in the same ways as men.[36]

Since the outlines of the different career paths were well established, it was generally possible to locate an individual in one or another career path even if only one office was attested and that one office was sufficiently distinctive. For example, a man attested as quaestor or praetor was located in the senatorial civic *cursus*. Again, I found it advisable to collapse the categories for certain analyses. Given the distinctive outlines of career paths, it was possible in the tables in Chapter 4 to analyze together men in a senatorial civic career path with those in a mainly senatorial civic career path, and so forth.

LOCATION OF POSTS.   The geographic locations of the offices that an aristocrat held were recorded.

EMPEROR DURING WHOSE REIGN THE MAJOR PART OF THE CAREER WAS UNDERTAKEN OR LIFE WAS LIVED.   Men and women were located in broad time periods: pre-Constantine; Constantine; from the death of Constantine to the death of Constantius II in 361; and then post-Constantius II.

RELIGION.   Individuals were recorded as pagan, Christian (including Christian heretical sects), converts to Christianity, converts to paganism, Neoplatonists (of pagan affiliation), probably pagan, and probably Christian.

In composing the tables in Chapters 3–6, these categories were merged into pagan and probably pagan and Christian and probably Christian, often including converts, as discussed above.

PAGAN RELIGIOUS ACTIVITIES.   Pagans who held official positions or priesthoods in one of the public state cults and/or the imperial cult were so noted. Pagans who held offices or priesthoods in private cults were also noted, along with their participation in the specific cults of Attis and the Magna Mater; Isis/Serapis/Osiris; Sol/Apollo/Mithras; or any mystery cult.

CHRISTIAN RELIGIOUS ACTIVITIES.   Christians were recorded as priest, bishop, or monk. I also recorded if the Christian was a member of one of the two most prominent heretical sects of the time, Arians or Donatists.

MARITAL STATUS; RELIGION AND RANK OF SPOUSE.   For the husbands and wives of the aristocrats in this study, the religious affiliation and rank of the spouse were recorded.

PARENTAL STATUS.   The following were recorded: if a parent was aristocratic or not, his/her rank, and if the parent was attested as senatorial before, during, or after Constantine's reign.

PARENTAL RELIGION.   The religious affiliation of the father and of the mother of each individual was recorded.

GEOGRAPHIC ORIGIN.   The origin for each aristocrat was recorded using the criteria cited above.

LOCATION OF FAMILY PROPERTY.   The area or areas in which a family held property was recorded.

CHILDREN.   Information about the children of aristocrats in the database was recorded, including how many children an aristocrat had; how many children were male or female; how many of the male and female children were attested for which religious affiliation; how many children followed the religion of the father or mother; and the religion of a child who did not follow the religion of one or the other parent.

Appendix 2:
Names and Religious Affiliation
of Aristocrats in the Study

A number after a name refers to the designation of that person in the *Prosopography of the Later Roman Empire,* volume 1. People are listed in alphabetical order in accord with the *PLRE*. The people who are derived from other sources are so indicated. For the works cited, see Appendix 3. Detailed analysis of individuals is available upon request from the author.

Fl(avius) Ablabius 4	Christian
Achantia	Christian
(A)cilius 1	Probably pagan
Adeodata (*PLRE* 2, p. 9)	Christian
Sextilius Agesilaus Aedesius 7	Pagan
Stefanilla Aemiliana 3	Christian
Aetheria 1 (*PLRE* 2, p. 18; Martindale, 1980)	Christian
Aurelius Agricolanus	Pagan
Alaric 1 (*PLRE* 2, pp. 43–48)	Christian
Albina 1 (the Elder)	Christian
Albina 2 (the Younger)	Christian
M. Nummius C(a)eionius Annius Albinus 7*	Pagan
Publilius C(a)eionius Caecina Albinus 8	Pagan
Caecina Decius Albinus Iunior 10	Pagan
Nummius Albinus 11	Pagan
C(a)eionius Rufius Albinus 14	Neoplatonist philosopher, pagan
C(a)eionius Rufius Albinus 15	Pagan

*I have adopted the convention of spelling C(a)eionius for members of the same family since variations in spelling this name (with or without the *a*) appear in documents and inscriptions.

Amanda (Mathisen, 1982, p. 366)	Christian
Ambrosius 3	Christian
Publius Ampelius 3	Pagan
Anapsychia (*PLRE* 2, p. 76)	Christian
Anastasia 1 (*PLRE* 2, p. 76)	Christian
Anatolius 3	Pagan
Postumia Antonia (Eck, 1972–1973, p. 334)	Christian
Antoninus 3	Pagan
C. Annius Anullinus 3	Pagan
Aper (Mathisen, 1982, p. 366)	Christian
Apollinaris 1 (*PLRE* 2, p. 113)	Convert to Christianity
Parecorius Apoll(inaris) 5	Christian
Petronius Apollodorus	Pagan
Apringius 1 (*PLRE* 2, p. 123)	Christian
Turcius Apronianus 8	Convert to Christianity
L. Turcius Apronianus 9	Probably pagan
L. Turcius Apronianus signo Asterius 10	Pagan
Arbogastes	Pagan
(Magnus?) Arborius 3	Probably Christian
Fl. Arcadius 4	Probably Christian
T. Cl. Aurelius Aristobulus	Probably pagan
Arsenius (St.) 4	Christian
Tullius Anatolius Artemius 3	Christian
Asella 1	Christian
Asella 2	Christian
Astania	Christian
Asterius 3 (*PLRE* 2, p. 171)	Christian
Asterius 4 (*PLRE* 2, p. 171)	Christian
Fl. Atticus 2	Pagan
Pontius Atticus 3	Probably pagan
(No)neius Tineius Tarrut(enius) Atticus 4	Pagan
Tamesius Olympius Augentius 1	Pagan
Aur. Victor Augentius 2	Pagan
Augustina	Christian
Decimius Magnus Ausonius 7	Christian
Petronia Auxentia	Christian
Avita	Christian
Baebianus	Christian
Arrius Balbinus	Pagan
Bassus 7	Christian
Anicius Auchenius Bassus 7 (*PLRE* 2, pp. 219–220)	Christian
Anicius Auchenius Bassus 11	Christian
Iunius Bassus signo Theotecnius 15	Christian
L. Caesonius Ovinius Manlius Rufinianus Bassus 18	Pagan

. . . us Bassus 22	Pagan
Flavius Bauto	Probably pagan
Benedictus 3	Christian
Benivolus	Christian
Blesilla 2	Christian
Caecilianus 1 (*PLRE* 2, pp. 245–247)	Christian
Claudius Hermogenianus Caesarius 7	Pagan
Roscia Calcedonia	Christian
Calvisianus	Pagan
Cassia 1	Christian
Flavius Iulius Catervius	Christian
Curtia Catiana (Martindale, 1980, p. 480)	Christian
Aco Catullinus signo Philomathius 3 or Aconius (Bagnall et al., 1987, p. 232)	Pagan
Celer 1 (*PLRE* 2, p. 275)	Christian
Marcia Romania Celsa (Martindale, 1980, p. 480)	Christian
Aurelius Celsinus 4	Pagan
Clodius Celsinus signo Adelphius 6	Probably Christian
Celsus (son of Paulinus 21 of Nola, *Carm.* 31.601–610; .619–620)	Christian
N(a)eratius Cerealis 2	Christian
Cethegus	Probably Christian
Chrysanthus	Christian
Flavius Insteius Cilo	Christian
Insteia Cilonis	Christian
Classicianus (*PLRE* 2, p. 298)	Christian
Claudia 4	Convert to Christianity
Coelia Claudiana	Pagan
Claudius Claudianus 5 (*PLRE* 2, pp. 299–300)	Probably pagan
Aurelius Prudentius Clemens 4	Christian
Clementinus 1	Pagan
Coelia Concordia	Pagan
Paulus Constantius 11	Christian
Maternus Cynegius 3	Christian
Dagalaifus	Probably pagan
Claudius Postumus Dardanus (*PLRE* 2, pp. 346–347)	Christian
Decens	Christian
Decentius 1	Pagan
Demetrianus (Eck, 1972–1973, p. 334)	Christian
Demetrias 2 (*PLRE* 2, pp. 351–352)	Christian
Nummius Aemilianus Dexter 3	Christian
Appius Claudius Tarronius Dexter 4	Pagan
Didyme	Christian
Cassius Dio	Probably pagan

L. Aelius Helvius Dionysius 12	Pagan
Donatus 1 (*PLRE* 2, p. 375)	Christian
Dorotheus (Aug. *Ep.* 14*, 15*)	Christian
Latinius Pacatus Drepanius	Pagan
Dulcitius 1 (*PLRE* 2, p. 381)	Christian
L . . . ia Aurelia Epi(ph)an(i)a	Probably pagan
Fl. Claudius Euangelus 2	Pagan
Iulius Eubulidas	Pagan
Eventius 1 (*PLRE* 2, p. 413)	Probably Christian
Flavius Eugenius 5	Christian
Eunomia (*PLRE* 2, p. 421)	Christian
Flavius Euodius 2	Christian
Eusebius 5 (*PLRE* 2, p. 429)	Christian
Eusebius of Reims (= Eusebius 2, Heinzelmann, 1982a, p. 602)	Christian
Fl. Eusebius 37	Pagan
Eustathius 2	Christian
Iulia Eustochium	Christian
Eustochius (Aug. *Ep.* 24*)	Christian
Eustolius	Christian
Eutherius 1 (a Eunuch)	Pagan
Eutropius 2	Probably pagan
Fabiola	Christian
Fabiola 2+3 (*PLRE* 2, p. 448)	Christian
Ulpius Egnatius Faventinus I	Pagan
Faustina 2 (*PLRE* 2, p. 449)	Probably Christian
A(ci)lius Faustinus 5	Probably pagan
Pompeius Appius Faustinus 7	Pagan
Anicius Faustus 6	Probably pagan
Sempronius Faustus 9	Probably pagan
Feliciana (Jerome *Ep.* 30.14)	Christian
Felix 2 (*PLRE* 2, pp. 458–459)	Pagan
Felix 3	Convert to paganism
Felix 7 (*PLRE* 2, p. 460)	Christian
Fl. Constantius Felix 14 (*PLRE* 2, pp. 461–462)	Christian
Rufius Festus 10	Pagan
Postumius Rufius Festus signo Avienius 12	Pagan
Flaccianus	Christian
Q. Clodius Flavianus 7	Pagan
Nicomachus Flavianus 14 (the Younger) (see J. O'Donnell, "The Career of Virius Nicomachus Flavianus," *Phoenix* 32 (1978), pp. 129–143; the evidence for his conversion to Christianity is not certain)	Probably pagan
Virius Nicomachus Flavianus 15 (the Elder)	Pagan

Clodius Insteius Flavius 3	Christian
Florentia	Christian
Flavius Florentius 10	Probably Christian
Astasius Fortunatus 2	Probably pagan
Furia	Christian
Caecilia Furia (*PLRE* 2, p. 488)	Christian
Galla (Mandouze, 1982, p. 519)	Christian
Galla 4 (*PLRE* 2, p. 491)	Christian
Naevia Galla 6 (*PLRE* 2, p. 491)	Christian
Gallicanus (*PLRE* 2, p. 492)	Christian
Ovinius Gallicanus 3 (Champlin, 1982, pp. 71–76)	Christian
Virius Gallus 2	Pagan
Gaudentius 5 (*PLRE* 2, pp. 493–494)	Probably Christian
Generidus (*PLRE* 2, pp. 500–501)	Pagan
Generosus 1 (*PLRE* 2, p. 501)	Christian
Germanus 1 of Auxerre (*PLRE* 2, pp. 504–505)	Christian
Acilius Glabrio 1	Pagan
Flavius Gorgonius 7	Christian
Gracchus 1 = Furius Maecius Gracchus 3 (*PLRE* 1, pp. 399–400)	Convert to Christianity
Annius Gratus (Eck, 1972–1973, p. 334)	Christian
Q. Sattius Fl. Vettius Gratus 3	Pagan
Gregorius 3	Probably Christian
Proculus Gregorius 9	Probably Christian
Hadrianus 2	Probably Christian
Helpidius 1 (*PLRE* 2, pp. 535–536)	Probably pagan
Helpidius 6	Convert to paganism
Decimius Hilarianus Hesperius 2	Probably Christian
Caelius Hilarianus 4	Pagan
Hilarius 2 (*PLRE* 2, p. 563)	Convert to Christianity
Hilarius 11 (*PLRE* 1, following Mathisen, 1979, pp. 160–169)	Convert to Christianity
Turrhenia Honorata 3	Christian
Honoratus 2	Christian
Honoratus (*SC* 235; of Arles)	Christian
Honoratus' father (*SC* 235; of Arles)	Christian
Honoria	Christian
Iulius Festus Hymetius	Pagan
Flavius Hypatius 4	Probably Christian
Iacobus 1 (*PLRE* 2, p. 581)	Christian
Flavius Ianuarinus 2	Christian
Innocentia (Aug. *C.D.* 22.8)	Christian
Flavius Iovinus 6	Christian
Iovius 2 (*PLRE* 2, pp. 622–623)	Probably Christian

Tanaucius Isfalangius	Probably Christian
Italica	Christian
Iulius Italicus 4	Pagan
Anicia Iuliana 2	Christian
Iuliane	Christian
Alfenius C(a)eionius Iulianus signo Kamenius 25	Pagan
M. C(a)eionius Iulianus signo Kamenius 26	Probably pagan
Flavius Iulianus 33	Christian
Sextilia Iusta 4	Christian
Iustus 2	Pagan
C. Vettius Aquilinus Iuvencus (Martindale, 1980, p. 487)	Christian
Laeta 2	Christian
Quintilius Laetus 2 (= Quintilius Laetus 3, *PLRE* 2, p. 654)	Christian
Postumius Lampadius 7 (*PLRE* 2, p. 656)	Probably Christian
Largus (*PLRE* 2, p. 657)	Christian
Lea	Christian
Leonas	Christian
Flavius Leontius 22	Christian
Cl(audius) Lepidus (*PLRE* 2, p. 675)	Christian
Licentius 2 (*PLRE* 2, p. 682)	Christian
Caecinia Lolliana	Pagan
Q. Flavius Maesius Egnatius Lollianus signo Mavortius 5	Pagan
Flavius Macrobius Longinianus (*PLRE* 2, pp. 686–687)	Christian
Lucceia (*ICUR n.s.*, vol. 5, no. 13355)	Christian
Lucilla	Christian
Plotius Acilius Lucillus 2	Pagan
Claudius Lupicinus 5	Christian
Flavius Lupicinus 6	Christian
Lycontius	Christian
Macedonius 3 (*PLRE* 2, p. 697)	Christian
Magnillus	Probably pagan
Fl. Magnus 10	Probably Christian
Claudius Mamertinus 2	Probably pagan
Virius Marcarianus	Pagan
Marcella 2	Christian
Marcellina 1	Christian
Flavius Marcellinus 10 (*PLRE* 2, pp. 711–712)	Christian
Marcellus 8	Christian
Marcianus 14	Convert to paganism
Marinianus 2	Probably pagan
Flavius Avitus Marinianus 3 (*PLRE* 2, pp. 723–724)	Christian

Marinus 1 (*PLRE* 2, p. 724)	Christian
Martinianus 5	Convert to Christianity
Iulius Firmicus Maternus Iunior 2	Convert to Christianity
Av(ianius?) Maximilianus 1	Probably pagan
Maximus (Barnes, 1984)	Probably pagan
Maximus 17	Probably pagan
Iun. Priscillianus Maximus 45	Pagan
Valerius Maximus signo Basilius 48	Pagan
Artorius Iulianus Megethius 3	Christian
Melania 1 (the Elder)	Christian
Melania 2 (the Younger)	Christian
Menander 3	Pagan
Messianus	Probably Christian
Rutilius Claudius Namatianus (*PLRE* 2, pp. 770–771)	Pagan
Flavius Nevitta	Pagan
Clodius Octavianus 2	Pagan
Furius Octavianus 4	Pagan
Anicius Hermogenianus Olybrius 2	Probably Christian
Q. Clodius Hermogenianus Olybrius 3	Christian
Olympius 2 (*PLRE* 2, pp. 801–802)	Christian
Olympius 3	Pagan
Aemilianus Corfo Olympius 14	Pagan
Aurelius Victor Olympius 17	Pagan
Nonius Victor Olympius 18	Pagan
Crepereius Optatianus 2	Pagan
Publilius Optatianus signo Porphyrius 3	Christian
L. Cornelius Scipio Orfitus 1	Pagan
Memmius Vitrasius Orfitus signo Honorius 3	Pagan
Orontius	Christian
Marcellus Orontius (or Arruntius)	Neoplatonist philosopher, pagan
Padusia (*PLRE* 2, p. 816)	Christian
Pammachius	Christian
Pascentius (*PLRE* 2, pp. 834–835)	Christian
(Ae)milius Florus Paternus 6	Christian
Paula (St.) 1	Christian
Paula 2	Christian
Paulina 3	Christian
Fabia Anconia Paulina 4	Pagan
Paulinus 5	Probably Christian
Paulinus of Pella 10	Christian
Anicius Paulinus 12	Christian
(I?)un(ius) Anicius P(aulinus) 13	Pagan
Sextus Anicius Paulinus 15	Christian

M. Iun. Caesonius Nicomachus Anicius Faustus Paulinus 17	Pagan
Meropius Pontius Paulinus 21 of Nola	Christian
Peregrinus (*PLRE* 2, p. 859)	Convert to Christianity
Perpetuus 1	Pagan
Petronia Petronilla (Aug. *C.D.* 22.8)	Christian
Petronius 1 (*PLRE* 2, pp. 862–863)	Convert to Christianity
Philagrius 2	Probably pagan
Flavius Philippus 7	Christian
Flavius Philippus 8	Christian
Valerius Pinianus 2	Christian
Placida 1	Probably pagan
Placidus 1	Probably pagan
M. Maecius Memmius Furius Baburius Caecilianus Placidus 2	Pagan
Polybius 2	Christian
Gabinius Barbarus Pompeianus 2 (*PLRE* 2, pp. 897–898)	Pagan
Insteius Pompeianus 6	Christian
Postumianus 2	Christian
Postumianus 2 (*PLRE* 2, p. 901)	Christian
Postumianus 3	Pagan
Iunius Postumianus 4	Pagan
Br(u)ttius Praesens	Pagan
Praetextata	Pagan
Vettius Agorius Praetextatus 1	Pagan
Brittius Praetextatus signo Argentius 2	Pagan
Vitrasius Praetextatus 3	Pagan
Principia (Jerome *Ep.* 65, 127)	Christian
Faltonia Betitia Proba 2	Christian
Anicia Faltonia Proba 3	Christian
Sextus Claudius Petronius Probus 5	Christian
Fl. Anicius Petronius Probus 11 (*PLRE* 2, pp. 913–914)	Christian
L. Aradius Valerius Proculus signo Populonius 11	Pagan
Q. Aradius Rufinus Valerius Proculus signo Populonius 12	Pagan
Proiecta	Christian
Numerius Proiectus	Probably pagan
Protadius 1	Probably pagan
Publicola 1	Christian
T. Flavius Iulian(i)us Quadratianus	Pagan
M. Aurelius Consius Quartus Iunior 2	Pagan
Flavius Richomeres	Pagan

Rogatianus 1	Neoplatonist philosopher, pagan
L. Crepereius Rogatus et qui Secundinus 2	Pagan
Flavius Pisidius Romulus 5	Probably Christian
Terentia Rufilla	Pagan
Rufina 2	Christian
Aradius Rufinus 10	Probably pagan
Aradius Rufinus 11	Convert to Christianity
C. Vettius Cossinius Rufinus 15	Pagan
Flavius Rufinus 18	Christian
Vulcacius Rufinus 25	Pagan
Flavius Rumoridus	Pagan
Ruptilius (Rutilius?) (Heinzelmann, 1982a, p. 683)	Probably Christian
Rusticiana	Probably pagan
Sabina 2	Pagan
Attusia Lucana Sabina 5	Christian
Sabinillus 2	Neoplatonist philosopher, pagan
Rufius C(a)eionius Sabinus 13	Pagan
Flavius Salia 2	Christian
Flavius Sallustius 5	Pagan
Uranius Satyrus	Christian
Saturninius Secundus Salutius 3	Pagan
Turcius Secundus 4	Probably Christian
L. Turcius Secundus signo Asterius 6	Pagan
Septiminus 1 (*PLRE* 2, p. 991)	Christian
Seranus (*PLRE* 2, p. 992)	Probably pagan
Severa (Delmaire, 1983, p. 86)	Christian
C. Magius Donatus Severianus 9	Pagan
C. Iulius Pomponius Pudens Severianus 10	Pagan
Septimia Severina 1	Christian
Severus (Delmaire, 1983, p. 86)	Christian
Acilius Severus 16	Probably Christian
Acilius Severus 17	Christian
Placidus Severus 28	Probably pagan
Sulpicius Severus 20 (*PLRE* 2, p. 1006)	Christian
Valerius Severus 29	Christian
Simplicius 5	Christian
Sophronia (Jerome *Ep.* 127)	Christian
Macrinius Sossianus 1	Pagan
Flavius Stilicho	Christian
Studius	Christian
(M)unatia Abita Susanna (= Egnatia, in *ILCV* 197a)	Christian
L. Aurelius Avianius Symmachus signo Phosphorius 3	Pagan

Q. Aurelius Symmachus signo Eusebius 4	Pagan
Q. Fabius Memmius Symmachus 10 (*PLRE* 2, pp. 1046–1047)	Probably pagan
Aurelius Valerius Tullianus Symmachus 6 (Barnes, 1989, p. 317)	Neoplatonist philosopher, pagan
Aulus Caecina Tacitus 2	Pagan
Taetradius	Convert to Christianity
C. Iulius Rufinianus Ablabius Tatianus 4	Pagan
Flavius Taurus 3	Christian
Annia Tertulla (Eck, 1972–1973, p. 334)	Christian
Tertullus 1 (*PLRE* 2, p. 1059)	Pagan
Tertullus 2	Pagan
M. Insteius Tertullus 8	Christian
Theodora 4	Christian
Flavius Mallius Theodorus 27	Christian
Therasia, wife of Paulinus 21 of Nola	Christian
Titiana	Christian
Celsinus Titianus 5	Pagan
Fabius Titianus 6	Pagan
T. Flavius Postumius Titianus 9	Pagan
Toxotius 1	Convert to Christianity
Trifolius	Christian
Accia Maria Tulliana	Christian
Tulliana Iunior	Christian
Turranius	Probably pagan
Valentinus = Avianius Valentinus 7 (recipient of Codex-Calendar of 354, following Salzman, 1990 = *PLRE* 1, p. 936)	Christian
Valerius 3 (*PLRE* 2, pp. 1143–1144)	Christian
T. Flavius Postumius Varus 3	Christian
Venantius (Honoratus' brother, *SC* 235)	Christian
Lucius Ragonius Venustus 3	Pagan
Vestina (*PLRE* 2, p. 1157)	Christian
M. Aur. Victor 12	Pagan
Sex. Aurelius Victor 13	Probably pagan
Fl. Vincentius 6 (*PLRE* 2, p. 1169)	Christian
Astius Vindicianus 3	Christian
Avianius Vindicianus 4	Pagan
Rufia Vo(lus)iana	Pagan
C(a)eionius Rufius Volusianus 3	Pagan
C. C(a)eionius Rufius Volusianus 4	Pagan
C. C(a)eionius Rufius Volusianus signo Lampadius 5	Pagan
Rufius Antonius Agrypnius Volusianus 6 (*PLRE* 2, pp. 1184–1185)	Convert to Christianity

Domitius Zenophilus	Pagan
. . . a [Female]	Probably Christian
. . . epus [Male]	Christian
(?Roma)nilla	Christian
. . . or (*Icur n.s.,* vol. 2, no. 5980)	Christian
P. Egn(atius) . . . s (*PLRE* 1, p. 1002; 4th century on basis of *D.* 3426 and *C.Th.* 8.5.46)	Pagan
. . . V (*PLRE* 1, p. 1002)	Pagan
Anonymus 18	Pagan
Anonymus 74	Pagan
Anonymus 79	Probably pagan
Anonymus 89	Pagan
Anonymus 108	Probably Christian
Anonymus (Martindale, 1980, p. 497)	Christian
Anonymus (suffect?) (Mathisen, 1986b, pp. 126–127)	Convert to paganism
Anonymus (Woods, 1993, p. 122)	Christian
Anonyma 8	Pagan
Anonyma 11	Christian
Anonyma 16	Christian
Anonyma 18	Pagan
Anonyma 20	Christian
Anonyma 22	Christian
Anonyma 23	Christian
Anonyma, daughter of Asterius 4 (Delmaire, 1983, pp. 83–84)	Christian
Anonyma, wife of Flavius Gorgonius 7 (ID no. 124; depicted on Christian Sarcophagus *CIL* 9.5897 = *D.* 1290)	Christian
Anonyma, wife of unnamed prefect (Eus. *HE* 8.14.16; *VC* 1.34)	Christian

Appendix 3:
Sources for the Database—
Addenda and Corrigenda to PLRE

Alföldy, G. Review of *Prosopography of the Later Roman Empire,* vol. 1. *Byzantinoslavica* 34 (1973): 234–243.

Bagnall, R. S. Review of *Prosopography of the Later Roman Empire,* vol. 2. *Classical Journal* 77 (1981–1982): 183–184.

Bagnall, R. S., A. Cameron, S. Schwartz, and K. Worp. *Consuls of the Later Roman Empire.* Atlanta, Ga., 1987.

Baldwin, B. "Some Addenda to the Prosopography of the Later Roman Empire." *Historia* 25 (1976): 118–121.

———. "Missing Persons: A Look at *PLRE,* II." *Medieval Prosopography* 2(2) (1981): 1–9.

———. "Some Addenda to the Prosopography of the Later Roman Empire." *Historia* 31 (1982): 97–111.

Barnes, T. D. "More Missing Names (A.D. 260–395)." *Phoenix* 27 (1973): 135–155.

———. "Another Forty Missing Persons (A.D. 260–395)," *Phoenix* 28 (1974), pp. 224–233.

———. *The New Empire of Diocletian and Constantine.* Cambridge, Mass., 1982, pp. 175–191.

———. "Christians and Pagans in the Reign of Constantius," in *L'Église et l'empire au IVe siècle,* ed. A. Dihle (*Entretiens sur l'antiquité classique* 34). Vandoeuvres-Geneva, 1989, pp. 301–343.

———. "Praetorian Prefects, 337–361." *ZPE* 94 (1992): 249–260.

———. "The Religious Affiliation of Consuls and Prefects, 317–361," in *From Eusebius to Augustine: Selected Papers, 1982–1993.* Aldershot, Hampshire, Great Britain, 1994, pp. 1–11.

———. "Statistics and the Conversion of the Roman Aristocracy." *Journal of Roman Studies* 85 (1995): 135–147.

Béranger, J. Review of *Prosopography of the Later Roman Empire,* vol. 1. *Museum Helveticum* 29 (1972): 302.

Birley, A. R. Review of *Prosopography of the Later Roman Empire,* vol. 1. *Journal of Roman Studies* 62 (1972): 185–186.

Burian, J. Review of *Prosopography of the Later Roman Empire*, vol. 1. *Listy Filologicke* 95 (1972): 53–54.

Callu, J.-P. Review of *Prosopography of the Later Roman Empire*, vol. 1. *Revue de Philologie* 46 (1972): 357.

Chadwick, H. Review of *Prosopography of the Later Roman Empire*, vol. 1. *Journal of Theological Studies* 23 (1972): 258–259.

Champlin, T. "Saint Gallicanus." *Phoenix* 36 (1982): 70–76.

Chastagnol, A. Review of *Prosopography of the Later Roman Empire*, vol. 1. *REL* 50 (1972): 382–384.

CIL VI, vol. 8.3: *Tituli magistratuum populi Romani*, ed. G. Alföldy. Berlin, 2000.

Clover, F. Review of *Prosopography of the Later Roman Empire*, vol. 2. *Classical Philology* 7–8 (1983): 162–166.

Criniti, N. "La nuova prosopografia dell'età tardo-imperiale romana." *Nuova Rivista Storica* 58 (1974): 133–152.

Delmaire, R. "Contribution des nouvelles lettres de saint Augustin à la prosopographie du Bas-Empire Romain *(PLRE),*" in *Les Lettres de Saint Augustin découvertes par J. Divjak.* Paris, 1983, pp. 83–86.

Demandt, A. Review of *Prosopography of the Later Roman Empire*, vol. 1. *Byzantinische Zeitschrift* 67 (1974): 170–173.

———. Review of *Prosopography of the Later Roman Empire*, vol. 2. *Byzantinische Zeitschrift* 76 (1983): 61–62.

Disselkamp, G. *"Christiani Senatus Lumina": Zum Anteil römischer Frauen der Oberschicht im 4 und 5. Jahrhundert an der Christianisierung der römischen Senatsaristokratie.* Bodenheim, Germany, 1977.

Eadie, J. Review of *Prosopography of the Later Roman Empire*, vol. 1. *American Classical Review* 2 (1972–1973): 50–51.

Eck, W. Review of *Prosopography of the Later Roman Empire*, vol. 1. *Zephyrus* 23 (1972–1973): 325–336.

———. "Sozialstruktur des römischen Senatorenstandes der hohen Kaiserzeit und statistische Methode." *Chiron* 3 (1973): 375–394.

———. Review of *Prosopographie de l'Afrique chrétienne*, by A. Mandouze. *Gnomon* 57 (1985): 719–725.

Fanning, S. Review of *Medieval Lives and the Historian: Studies in Medieval Prosopography*, by N. Bulst and J-P Genet. *Medieval Prosopography* 8 (1987): 49–54.

Frend, W. H. C. Review of *Prosopography of the Later Roman Empire*, vol. 1. *Journal of Ecclesiastical History* 23 (1972): 171–172.

Haehling, R., von. *Die Religionszugehörigkeit der hohen Amtsträger des römischen Reiches seit Constantins I. Alleinherrschaft bis zum Ende der Theodosianischen Dynastie.* Bonn, 1978.

Heinzelmann, M. "Gallische Prosopographie (260–527)." *Francia* 10 (1982a): 531–718.

———. "Neuerscheinungen der Jahre 1979–1980 zur Prosopographie des Frühmittelalters (5.-10.Jahrhundert)." *Medieval Prosopography* 3(1) (1982b): 113–140.

Hunt, E. D. Review of *Prosopography of the Later Roman Empire,* vol. 2. *Journal of Theological Studies* 33 (1982): 302–305.

ILCV, vols. 1–3: "Ordo senatorius, nobiles," nos. 56–275, ed. E. Diehl (1961; reprint, Dublin, 1970).

Laniado, A. "Some *Addenda* to the *Prosopography of the Later Roman Empire* (Vol. 2:395–527)." *Historia* 44(1) (1995): 121–128.

Lippold, A. Review of *Prosopography of the Later Roman Empire,* vol. 1. *Gnomon* 46 (1974): 268–273.

————. Review of *Prosopography of the Later Roman Empire,* vol. 2. *Gnomon* 54 (1982): 485–490.

Mandouze, A. *Prosopographie chrétienne du Bas-Empire,* vol. 1: *Prosopographie de l'Afrique chrétienne.* Paris, 1982.

Martindale, J. R. "*Prosopography of the Later Roman Empire:* Addenda and Corrigenda to Volume 1." *Historia* 23 (1974): 246–252.

————. "*Prosopography of the Later Roman Empire:* Addenda et Corrigenda to Volume 1." *Historia* 29 (1980): 474–497.

Masana, J. V. "El *ordo senatorius* en la *Hispania* de Teodosio," in *Actas Congreso Internacional: La Hispania de Teodosio,* vol. 1, ed. R. Teja and C. Pérez. Valladolid, Spain, 1997, pp. 293–306.

Mathisen, R. "Hilarius, Germanus and Lupus: The Aristocratic Background of the Chelidonius Affair." *Phoenix* 33 (1979): 160–169.

————. "Late Roman Prosopography in the West (A.D. 260–640): A Survey of Recent Work." *Medieval Prosopography* 2(1) (1981): 1–12.

————. "*PLRE* II: Suggested Addenda and Corrigenda." *Historia* 31 (1982): 364–386.

————. "Fifteen Years of PLRE: Compliments, Complaints, and Caveats." *Medieval Prosopography* 7(1) (1986a): 1–37.

————. "Ten Office-Holders: A Few Addenda and Corrigenda to *PLRE.*" *Historia* 35 (1986b): 125–127.

————. "A Survey of the Significant Addenda to *PLRE.*" *Medieval Prosopography* 8(1) (1987): 5–30.

————. "Medieval Prosopography and Computers: Theoretical and Methodological Considerations." *Medieval Prosopography* 9(1) (1988): 73–128.

Matthews, J. F. Review of *Prosopography of the Later Roman Empire,* vol. 1. *Classical Review* N.S. 24 (1974): 97–106.

Morgenstern, F. *Die Briefpartner des Augustinus von Hippo: Prosopographische, sozial- und ideologie-geschichtliche Untersuchungen (Bochumer historische Studien, Alte Geschichte Nr. 11).* Bochum, 1993.

Morris, J. "Prosopography of the Later Roman Empire." *Klio* 46 (1965): 361–365.

Pietri, C. "Appendice prosopographique à la Roma christiana (311–440)." *Mélanges d'archéologie et d'histoire de l'École française de Rome: Antiquité* 89 (1977): 371–415.

Roda, S. "Supplementi e correzioni alla *PLRE,* Vol. 1." *Historia* 29 (1980): 96–105.

Salzman, M. R. *On Roman Time: The Codex-Calendar of 354 and the Rhythms of Urban Life in Late Antiquity.* Berkeley, 1990, pp. 196–205.

Thébert, Y. "Le proconsul inconnu de Bulla Regia (ILAf 456): Une nouvelle hypothèse." *L'Africa Romana* 7 (1989): 879–885.

Vidman, L. Review of *Prosopography of the Later Roman Empire,* vol. 2. *Byzantinoslavica* 42 (1981): 58–59.

Wirth, G. Review of *Prosopography of the Later Roman Empire,* vol. 1. *Historische Zeitschrift* 216 (1973): 642–643.

Woods, D. "Some *Addenda* to the *PLRE.*" *Historia* 42(1) (1993): 122–125.

Appendix 4: High Office Holders

Dates for high office holders in the western empire are based on R. von Haehling (1978), A. Chastagnol (1960), and *PLRE* I and II. This appendix lists high office holders beginning in 324 with Constantine as sole ruler. The list of urban prefects begins in 312 with Constantine's defeat of Maxentius.

Name	*Dates*	*Religion*
Praetorian prefects—Italy		
Aco (or Aconius) Catullinus signo Philomathius 3	24.6.341–before 6.7.342	Pagan
M. Maecius Memmius Furius Baburius Caecilianus Placidus 2	342–28.5.344	Pagan
Vulcacius Rufinus 25	344(?)–28.12.349 12.6.365–19.5.367	Pagan
C. C(a)eionius Rufius Volusianus signo Lampadius 5	1.1.355–29.7.355	Pagan
Flavius Taurus 3	6.4.355–29.8.361	Christian
Q. Flavius Maesius Egnatius Lollianus signo Mavortius 5	25.7.356–Winter 356	Pagan
Claudius Mamertinus 2	Dec. 361–26.4.365	Prob. pagan
Sextus Claudius Petronius Probus 5	12.3.368–22.11.375 19.8.383–26.10.383 Summer 387	Christian
Decimius Hilarianus Hesperius 2	21.1.378–14.5.380	Prob. Christian
Flavius Hypatius 4	9.12.382–28.5.383	Prob. Christian
Vettius Agorius Praetextatus 1	21.5.384–9.9.384	Pagan

258

Name	Dates	Religion
Trifolius	388–389	Christian
Virius Nicomachus Flavianus 15	18.8.390–8.4.392 Apr. 393–5.9.394	Pagan
Nummius Aemilianus Dexter 3	18.3.395–1.11.395	Christian
Flavius Mallius Theodorus 27	31.1.397–20.1.399 13.9.408–15.1.409	Christian
Hadrianus 2	27.2.401–5.10.405 3.8.413–3.3.414	Prob. Christian
Caecilianus	21.1.409–ca. 1.2.409	Christian
Flavius Macrobius Longinianus	11.1.406–13.8.408	Christian
Postumius Lampadius 7	Dec. 409–July 410	Prob. Christian
Flavius Avitus Marinianus 3	3.11.422	Christian

Proconsuls—Africa

Name	Dates	Religion
M. C(a)eionius Iulianus signo Kamenius 26	ca. 326–333	Prob. pagan
Domitius Zenophilus	ca. 326–333	Pagan
L. Aradius Valerius Proculus signo Populonius 11	ca. 331–333	Pagan
Q. Flavius Maesius Egnatius Lollianus signo Mavortius 5	ca. 334–337	Pagan
Aurelius Celsinus 4	12.6.338–8.1.339	Pagan
M. Aurelius Consius Quartus Iunior 2	ca. 340–350 (?)	Pagan
Clodius Celsinus signo Adelphius 6	Before 351	Prob. Christian
Memmius Vitrasius Orfitus signo Honorius 3	Beginning 353	Pagan
Saturninius Secundus Salutius 3	Before 356	Pagan
Sextus Claudius Petronius Probus 5	23.6.358	Christian
Q. Clodius Hermogenianus Olybrius 3	19.5.361–3.8.361	Christian
Claudius Hermogenianus Caesarius 7	ca. 362/363–373	Pagan

Name	*Dates*	*Religion*
Clodius Octavianus 2	Spring 363–26.6.363	Pagan
Publius Ampelius 3	8.5.364	Pagan
Iulius Festus Hymetius	25.5.366–9.6.368	Pagan
Q. Aurelius Symmachus signo Eusebius 4	30.11.373	Pagan
Paulus Constantius 11	10.7.374–7.9.374	Christian
Decimius Hilarianus Hesperius 2	10.3.376–8.7.377	Prob. Christian
Valerius Severus 29	Autumn 381 (?)	Christian
Postumius Rufius Festus signo Avienius	middle or late 4th cent.	Pagan
Polybius 2	ca. 374–397	Christian
Messianus	17.9.385–386	Prob. Christian
(Ae)milius Florus Paternus 6	16.3.393	Christian
Flaccianus	7.10.393	Christian
Marcianus 14	393–394	Convert to paganism
Pammachius	Before 396	Christian
Seranus	Autumn 397–Apr. 398	Prob. pagan
Gabinius Barbarus Pompeianus 2	31.5.400–14.7.401	Pagan
Helpidius 1	402	Prob. pagan
Septiminus 1	20.2.403–13.9.403	Christian
Donatus 1	11.11.408–ca. 24.11.408	Christian
Rufius Antonius Agrypnius Volusianus 6	ca. 410	Convert to Christianity
Apringius 1	411	Christian
Largus	11.10.418–7.4.419	Christian

Praetorian prefects—Gaul

Fabius Titianus 6	Spring 341–12.11.349	Pagan
Vulcacius Rufinus 25	8.3.354	Pagan

Name	Dates	Religion
Q. Flavius Maesius Egnatius Lollianus signo Mavortius 5	End 354(?)–before 25.7.356	Pagan
Honoratus 2	356–357	Christian
Flavius Florentius 10	357–Feb. 360	Prob. Christian
Flavius Sallustius 5	361–Sept. 363	Pagan
Decimius Magnus Ausonius 7	23.5.376–28.7.377	Christian
Sextus Claudius Petronius Probus 5	380	Christian
Flavius Mallius Theodorus 27	ca. 382 (?)	Christian
Proculus Gregorius 9	Beginning of 383	Prob. Christian
Flavius Evodius 2	385–386	Christian
Hilarius 11	19.3.396–28.12.396	Convert to Christianity
Flavius Vincentius 6	18.12.397–9.12.400	Christian
Petronius 1	ca. 407	Convert to Christianity
Apollinaris 1	408	Convert to Christianity
Claudius Postumus Dardanus	7.12.412–413	Christian

Praetorian prefects—Africa

Gregorius 3	21.7.336–4.2.337	Prob. Christian

Urban prefects of Rome (PVR)

Aradius Rufinus 10	29.11.312–8.12.313	Prob. pagan
C. C(a)eionius Rufius Volusianus 4	8.12.313–20.8.315	Pagan
C. Vettius Cossinius Rufinus 15	20.8.315–4.8.316	Pagan
Ovinius Gallicanus 3	4.8.316–15.5.317	Christian
Valerius Maximus signo Basilius 48	1.9.319–13.9.323	Pagan
Acilius Severus 16	4.1.325–13.11.326	Christian
Publilius Optatianus signo Porphyrius 3	7.9.329–8.10.329 7.4.333–10.5.333	Christian

Name	*Dates*	*Religion*
Sextus Anicius Paulinus 15	12.4.331–7.4.333	Christian
M. C(a)eionius Iulianus signo Kamenius 26	10.5.333–27.4.334	Prob. pagan
C(a)eionius Rufius Albinus 14	30.12.335–10.3.337	Pagan
L. Aradius Valerius Proculus signo Populonius 11	10.3.337–13.1.338 18.12.351–9.9.352	Pagan
L. Turcius Apronianus 9	14.7.339–25.10.339	Prob. pagan
Fabius Titianus 6	25.10.339–25.2.341 27.2.350–1.3.351	Pagan
Aurelius Celsinus 4	25.2.341–1.4.342 1.3.351–12.5.351	Pagan
Q. Flavius Maesius Egnatius Lollianus signo Mavortius 5	1.4.342–6.7.342	Pagan
Aco Catullinus signo Philomathius 3	6.7.342–11.4.344	Pagan
M. Maecius Memmius Furius Baburius Caecilianus Placidus 2	26.12.346–12.6.347	Pagan
N(a)eratius Cerealis	26.9.352–8.12.353	Christian
Memmius Vitrasius Orfitus signo Honorius 3	8.12.353–13.6.356 (?) Before 28.4.357–25.3.359	Pagan
Flavius Leontius 22	10.11.356	Christian
Iunius Bassus signo Theotecnius 15	?–25.8.359	Christian
Tertullus 2	Autumn 359–Autumn 361	Pagan
Maximus 17	End 361–28.1.362	Prob. pagan
L. Turcius Apronianus signo Asterius 10	9.12.362–28.12.363	Pagan
L. Aurelius Avianius Symmachus signo Phosphorius 3	22.4.364–10.3.365	Pagan
C. C(a)eionius Rufius Volusianus signo Lampadius 5	4.4.365–17.9.365	Pagan
Vettius Agorius Praetextatus 1	18.8.367–20.9.368	Pagan

Name	Dates	Religion
Q. Clodius Hermogenianus Olybrius 3	Oct. 368–21.8.370	Christian
Publius Ampelius 3	1.1.371–5.7.372	Pagan
Tanaucius Isfalangius	ca. 372–375	Prob. Christian
Aradius Rufinus 11	?–after 13.7.376	Convert to Christianity
Furius Maecius Gracchus 3	1.12.376–4.1.377	Convert to Christianity
Martinianus 5	9.3.378	Convert to Christianity
Flavius Hypatius 4	Aug. 378(?)–5.4.379	Prob. Christian
(Magnus?) Arborius 3	13.1.380–15.2.380	Prob. Christian
Anicius Paulinus 12	24.4.380	Christian
Valerius Severus 29	1.4.382–1.8.382	Christian
Anicius Auchenius Bassus 11	22.11.382	Christian
Q. Aurelius Symmachus signo Eusebius 4	Summer 384–Jan. 385	Pagan
Sex. Aurelius Victor 13	388–389	Prob. pagan
C(a)eionius Rufius Albinus 15	17.6.389–24.2.391	Pagan
Flavius Philippus 8	18.11.391	Christian
Nicomachus Flavianus 14	393–5.9.394 6.6.399–8.11.400	Prob. pagan
Felix 2	6.3.398–29.3.398	Pagan
Quintilius Laetus 2	398–399	Christian
Protadius	401	Prob. pagan
Flavius Macrobius Longinianus	401–402	Christian
Caecina Decius Albinus Iunior 10	6.12.402	Pagan
Postumius Lampadius 7	ca. 403–407	Prob. Christian

Name	*Dates*	*Religion*
Flavius Pisidius Romulus 5	6.8.405–Spring 406	Prob. Christian
Hilarius 2	15.1.408	Convert to Christianity
Gabinius Barbarus Pompeianus 2	Dec. 408–Feb. 409	Pagan
Marcianus 14	409	Convert to paganism
Rutilius Claudius Namatianus	Summer 414	Pagan
Rufius Antonius Agrypnius Volusianus 6	4.11.417–before 24.12.418	Convert to Christianity

Abbreviations and Frequently Cited Works

Abbreviations for most of the ancient sources follow the conventions in the *Oxford Classical Dictionary*, 3d ed. (1996); the *PLRE;* or *Patrology*, vol. 4, trans. P. Solari, ed. A. di Berardino (Allen, Tex., 1986). Abbreviations for periodical titles follow the conventions of *L'Année Philologique*. Note also the following:

ACW	*Ancient Christian Writers*
AE	*Année épigraphique*
CCSL	*Corpus Christianorum, Series Latina.* Turnholt, 1954 to date.
Chron. Min.	*Chronica Minora,* ed. T. Mommsen. Monumenta Germaniae Historica, Auctores Antiquissimi. Berlin, 1892–1898.
CIL	*Corpus Inscriptionum Latinarum.* Berlin, 1863 to date.
C.J.	*Codex Justinianus*
CSEL	*Corpus Scriptorum Ecclesiasticorum Latinorum.* Vienna, 1886 to date.
C.Th.	*Codex Theodosianus*
D.	*Inscriptiones Latinae Selectae,* 5 vols., ed. H. Dessau. Berlin, 1892–1916; reprint, Chicago, 1979.
FHG	*Fragmenta Historicorum Graecorum,* 4 vols., ed. C. Müller. Paris, 1841–1870.
FIRA	*Fontes Iuris Romani Antelustiniani,* ed. S. Riccobono. Florence, 1940–1943.
FOTC	*The Fathers of the Church*
GCS	*Die griechischen christlichen Schriftsteller der ersten drei Jahrhunderte.* Leipzig and Berlin, 1897 to date.
HA	*Historia Augusta*
ICUR	*Inscriptiones Christianae urbis Romae septimo saeculo antiquiores,* 2 vols. ed. I. B. De Rossi. Rome, 1857–1915.
ICUR n.s.	*Inscriptiones Christianae urbis Romae: Nova series,* ed. I. B. De

	Rossi, A. Silvagni, A. Ferrua, D. Mazzoleni, and C. Carletti. Rome, 1922 to date.
ILCV	*Inscriptiones Latinae Christianae Veteres,* ed. E. Diehl. Berlin, 1925–1931.
LCL	*Loeb Classical Library*
MGH	*Monumenta Germaniae Historica*
NPNF	*A Select Library of Nicene and Post-Nicene Fathers of the Christian Church,* ed. P. Schaff and H. Wace. Second Series. Grand Rapids, Mich., 1952–1956.
OLD	*Oxford Latin Dictionary,* ed. P. G. W. Glare. Oxford, 1982.
PG	*Patrologiae cursus completus, series Graeca,* ed. J. P. Migne. Paris, 1857–1866.
PL	*Patrologiae cursus completus, series Latina,* ed. J. P. Migne. Paris, 1844–1864.
PLRE	*The Prosopography of the Later Roman Empire.* Vol. 1 (C.E. 260–395), ed. A. H. M. Jones, J. R. Martindale, and J. Morris. Cambridge, England, 1971. Vol. 2 (C.E. 395–527), ed. J. R. Martindale. Cambridge, England, 1980.
PLS	*Patrologia Latina: Supplementum,* ed. A. Hamman. Paris, 1958–1974.
SC	*Sources chrétiennes.* Paris, 1942 to date.
TLL	*Thesaurus Linguae Latinae.* Leipzig, 1900 to date.

In addition, certain modern works are regularly cited in an abbreviated form:

Arnheim, M. T. W. *The Senatorial Aristocracy in the Later Roman Empire.* Oxford: Clarendon Press, 1972.

Bagnall, R. S., et al., eds. *Consuls of the Later Roman Empire.* Atlanta, Ga.: Scholars Press, 1987.

Barnes, T. D. "Christians and Pagans in the Reign of Constantius," in *L'Église et l'empire au IVe siècle* (*Entretiens sur l'antiquité classique* 34), ed. A. Dihle. Vandouevres-Geneva: Fondation Hardt, 1989, pp. 301–343.

———. "Statistics and the Conversion of the Roman Aristocracy." *JRS* 85 (1995): 135–147.

Brown, P. "Aspects of the Christianization of the Roman Aristocracy." *JRS* 51 (1961): 1–11.

———. *The Body and Society: Men, Women, and Sexual Renunciation in Early Christianity.* New York: Columbia University Press, 1988.

———. *Authority and the Sacred: Aspects of the Christianisation of the Roman World.* Cambridge: Cambridge University Press, 1995.

Chastagnol, A. *La préfecture urbaine à Rome sous le Bas-Empire.* Paris: Presses universitaires de France, 1960.

————. *Les fastes de la préfecture de Rome au Bas-Empire.* Paris: Nouvelles Editions latines, 1962.

————. "La carrière sénatoriale du Bas-Empire (depuis Dioclétien)." *Epigrafia e ordine senatorio: Atti del Colloquio Internazionale AIEGL* 1 (Rome, 1982): 167–194.

————. *Le Sénat romain à l'époque impériale: Recherches sur la composition de l'Assemblée et le statut de ses membres.* Paris: Les Belles Lettres, 1992.

Clark, E. A., and D. Hatch. *The Golden Bough, the Oaken Cross: The Virgilian Cento of Faltonia Betitia Proba.* Chico, Calif.: Scholars Press, 1981.

Clark, G. *Women in Late Antiquity: Pagan and Christian Lifestyles.* Oxford: Oxford University Press, 1993.

Croke, B., and J. Harries. *Religious Conflict in Fourth-Century Rome: A Documentary Study.* Sydney, Australia: Sydney University Press, 1982.

Haehling, R., von. *Die Religionszugehörigkeit der hohen Amtsträger des römischen Reiches seit Constantins I. Alleinherrschaft bis zum Ende der Theodosianischen Dynastie (324–450 bzw. 455 n. Chr.).* Bonn: Habelt, 1978.

Heather, P. "Senators and Senate," in *The Cambridge Ancient History,* vol. 13: *The Late Empire,* A.D. *337–425,* ed. A. Cameron and P. Garnsey. Cambridge: Cambridge University Press, 1998, pp. 184–210.

Jacques, F. "L'ordine senatorio attraverso la crisi del III secolo," in *Società romana e impero tardoantico,* vol. 1: *Istituzioni, ceti, economie,* ed. A. Giardina. Roma-Bari: Laterza, 1986, pp. 81–225.

Jones, A. H. M. "The Social Background of the Struggle between Paganism and Christiantity," in *The Conflict between Paganism and Christianity in the Fourth Century,* ed. A. Momigliano. Oxford: Clarendon Press, 1963, pp. 17–37.

————. *The Later Roman Empire,* A.D. *284–602.* 2 vols. Oxford: Clarendon Press, 1964, 1986 reprint.

Kuhoff, W. *Studien zur zivilen senatorischen Laufbahn im 4. Jahrhundert n. Chr. Ämter und Amtsinhaber in Clarissimat und Spektabilität.* Frankfurt am Main: P. Lang, 1983.

Lane Fox, R. *Pagans and Christians.* Middlesex: Viking, 1986.

Lendon, J. *Empire of Honor: The Art of Government in the Roman World.* Oxford: Clarendon Press, 1997.

Löhken, H. *Ordines Dignitatum: Untersuchungen zur formalen Konstituierung der spätantiken Führungsschicht.* Cologne: Böhlau, 1982.

MacMullen, R. *Paganism in the Roman Empire.* New Haven: Yale University Press, 1981.

————. *Christianizing the Roman Empire:* A.D. *100–400.* New Haven: Yale University Press, 1984.

Mathisen, R. *Roman Aristocrats in Barbarian Gaul.* Austin: University of Texas Press, 1993.

Matthews, J. *Western Aristocracies and Imperial Court* A.D. *364–425.* Oxford: Clarendon Press, 1975.

Momigliano, A., ed. *The Conflict between Paganism and Christianity in the Fourth Century.* Oxford: Clarendon Press, 1963.

Näf, B. Senatorisches Selbstandesbewusstsein in spätrömischer Zeit (*Paradosis* 40). Freiburg: Universitätsverlag, 1995.

Salzman, M. R. "Aristocratic Women: Conductors of Christianity in the Fourth Century?" *Helios* 16(2) (1989): 207–220.

————. *On Roman Time: The Codex-Calendar of 354 and the Rhythms of Urban Life in Late Antiquity.* Berkeley: University of California Press, 1990.

————. "How the West Was Won: The Christianization of the Roman Aristocracy in the West in the Years after Constantine." *Latomus* 217 (1992): 451–479 (*Studies in Latin Literature and Roman History* 6, ed. Carl Deroux).

————. "The Evidence for the Conversion of the Roman Empire to Christianity in Book 16 of the Theodosian Code." *Historia* 42(3) (1993): 362–378.

Schlinkert, D. *Ordo senatorius und nobilitas: Die Konstitution des Senatsadels in der Spätantike* (*Hermes Einzelschriften* 72). Stuttgart: Franz Steiner Verlag, 1996.

Sivan, H. *Ausonius of Bordeaux: Genesis of a Gallic Aristocracy.* London: Routledge, 1993.

Stark, R. *The Rise of Christianity: How the Obscure, Marginal Jesus Movement Became the Dominant Religious Force in the Western World in a Few Centuries.* San Francisco: Harper Collins, 1996.

Symmachus, *Epistulae, Orationes,* and *Relationes,* in *Q. Aurelii Symmachi quae supersunt* (*MGH: auctores antiquissimi VI.1*), ed. O. Seeck, Berlin, 1883.

Van Dam, R. *Leadership and Community in Late Antique Gaul.* Berkeley: University of California Press, 1985.

Notes

Preface

1. D. Praet, "Explaining the Christianization of the Roman Empire: Older Theories and Recent Developments," *Sacris Erudiri: Jaarboek voor Godsdienstwetenschappen* 33 (1992–1993), pp. 7–119, gives a survey of the field.
2. A. D. Nock, *Conversion: The Old and the New in Religion from Alexander the Great to Augustine of Hippo* (Oxford, 1933), pp. 7, 211.
3. See J. Gager, *Kingdom and Community* (Englewood Cliffs, N.J., 1975).
4. See, for example, Van Dam (1985), pp. 141ff., on Germanus of Auxerre and Paulinus of Pella.
5. P. Fredriksen, "Paul and Augustine: Conversion Narratives, Orthodox Traditions, and the Retrospective Self," *JTS* n.s. 37(1) (1986), pp. 21–37.
6. See L. M. White, "Adolf Harnack and the 'Expansion' of Early Christianity: A Reappraisal of Social History," *The Second Century* 5(2) (1985–1986), p. 101, on the influential work of A. Harnack, *The Mission and Expansion of Christianity in the First Three Centuries,* 2d ed., trans. James Moffatt (London, 1908; reprint, Gloucester, Mass., 1972).
7. See, for example, A. Fitzgerald, *Conversion through Penance in the Italian Church of the Fourth and Fifth Centuries* (Lewiston, N.Y., 1988).
8. Stark (1996), pp. 211–212.
9. Lane Fox, (1986), pp. 266ff., 330; see also E. A. Judge, *The Conversion of Rome: Ancient Sources of Modern Social Tensions* (Sydney, 1980), pp. 1–28.
10. P. Hadot, *Marius Victorinus: Recherches sur sa vie et ses oeuvres* (Paris, 1971), pp. 31–32, is one of the few.
11. For example, MacMullen (1984), pp. 29, 32–38, 50; Lane Fox (1986), pp. 590ff.; Barnes (1989), p. 306; Barnes (1995).
12. On Constantine's role in Christianizing the empire, see, for example, Lane Fox (1986), pp. 609ff., who reflects the influence of the important book by N. H. Baynes, *Constantine the Great and the Christian Church* (London, 1931).
13. A. Alföldi, *The Conversion of Constantine and Pagan Rome,* trans. H. Mattingly (Oxford, 1948; reprint, 1969), pp. 1ff. Cf. Chastagnol (1960), p. 402; Arnheim (1972), pp. 72–73, 76–82.

14. See, for example, Chastagnol (1960), p. 402.
15. Von Haehling (1978), pp. 569–575; Barnes (1989) pp. 301–337. Barnes (1995), pp. 135–147, claimed that conversion occurred a good deal earlier than is generally assumed, starting in the third century and culminating in the years under Constantine (306–337) and his son, Constantius (337–361).
16. Matthews (1975), pp. 146ff., 211–220, 254ff.
17. Lane Fox (1986), pp. 623–624; Salzman (1993); D. Hunt, "Christianizing the Roman Empire: The Evidence of the Code," in *The Theodosian Code,* ed. J. Harries and I. Wood (Ithaca, N.Y., 1993), pp. 143–158. On the emperor as patron, see, for example, MacMullen (1984), pp. 48–54.
18. Jones (1963), pp. 17–37.
19. Brown (1961), pp. 1–11; Brown (1988).
20. See, for example, J. Matthews, "Continuity in a Roman Family: The Rufii Festi of Volsinii," *Historia* 16 (1967), pp. 484–509.
21. See, for example, N. Moine, "Melaniana," *Recherches Augustiniennes* 15 (1980), pp. 3–79; A. E. Hickey, *Women of the Roman Aristocracy as Christian Monastics* (Ann Arbor, Mich., 1987).

1. Approaches to a Paradox

1. Zos. *New History* 4.59, trans. R. T. Ridley (Canberra, Australia, 1982; reprint, 1984).
2. Prud. *C. Symm.* 1.506–523. For the circumstances of this poem, see T. D. Barnes and R. W. Westall, "The Conversion of the Roman Aristocracy in Prudentius' *Contra Symmachum,*" *Phoenix* 45 (1991), pp. 50–61.
3. Zos. *New History* 4.59.
4. See Zos. *New History,* trans. R. T. Ridley, pp. 202–203. N. McLynn, *Ambrose of Milan: Church and Court in a Christian Capital* (Berkeley, 1994), pp. 311–313, assumes the historicity of the visit.
5. A. Chastagnol, "L'évolution de l'ordre sénatorial aux IIIe et IVe siècles de notre ère," *Rev. Hist.* 244 (1970), pp. 305–314. Chastagnol (1992), pp. 201–258, 324–344; Heather (1998), pp. 184–187.
6. The epitaph for the noble Praetextatus claims that he deemed trivial the coveted secular honors and offices that he had achieved compared to wearing "priestly headbands" and serving the gods; *CIL* 6.1779 = *D.* 1259, vv.18–21. This attitude is traditional. R. Gordon, "The Veil of Power: Emperors, Sacrificers and Benefactors," and "Religion in the Roman Empire: The Civic Compromise and Its Limits," in *Pagan Priests: Religion and Power in the Ancient World,* ed. M. Beard and J. North (Ithaca, 1990), pp. 201–231, 235–255.
7. See, for example, the Anonymous *Carmen contra paganos,* ed. D. R. Shackleton-Bailey, *Anthologia Latina* 1.1 (Leipzig, 1982), pp. 17–23; the Pseudo-Cyprian, *Carmen ad senatorem, (CSEL* 3.3.302–305 = *CSEL* 23.1.227–230); Salzman (1990), passim. I use paganism as a synonym for polytheism throughout this book, following the conventions of most ancient historians who, like G. W.

Bowersock, *Hellenism in Late Antiquity* (Ann Arbor, 1990), p. 6, use it to signify an "alternative expression of piety." Although "pagan" is a label crafted by Christians to denigrate polytheists, I do not intend it negatively.

8. P. Brown, "The Problem of Christianization," Magie Lecture, delivered at Princeton University, May 9, 1991.

9. W. Eck, "Das Eindringen des Christentums in den Senatorenstand bis zu Konstantin d. Gr.," *Chiron* 1 (1971), pp. 381–406. The attempts of Barnes (1995), pp. 135–137, to add to this group are flawed; see Appendix 1.

10. See Preface.

11. Lendon (1997), p. 37.

12. While I recognize problems in using the term aristocracy—a term with medieval associations—to describe a social stratum in Roman society, I will give reasons for my choice in Chapter 2 that justify its use.

13. For example, see MacMullen (1984), especially pp. 29–33; N. H. Baynes, *Constantine the Great and the Christian Church* (London, 1931), p. 3; Lane Fox (1986), pp. 590–610; Barnes (1989), p. 306; Barnes (1995).

14. Barnes (1989), p. 306, well describes the traditional view.

15. Among the few is Barnes (1989), pp. 301–337; cf. F. Millar, *The Emperor in the Roman World, 31* B.C.–A.D.*337* (London, 1977), pp. 551ff. For Christians as a larger percentage of the population, see especially Stark (1996); K. Hopkins, "Christian Number and Its Implications," *JECS* 6(2) (1998), pp. 185–226.

16. R. von Haehling's 1978 study, in many ways exemplary, is limited in this regard.

17. G. Clemente, "Cristianesimo e classi dirigenti prima e dopo Costantino," in *Mondo Classico e Cristianesimo* (Rome, 1982), pp. 51–64.

18. The figure of 36,000 is a rough estimate, based in part on Heather (1998), pp. 189–195. Heather sees some 3,000 public officers in the West as possessing or receiving senatorial rank by 400 C.E. Since, in some cases, such as *agentes in rebus,* only senior members had senatorial status, and in others, such as notaries, they acquired this right only after 381, over the course of the century some 2,000 offices offered clarissimate rank every generation. If we posit a twenty-five-year generation for a 150-year period, there were then some 12,000 *clarissimi,* with an equal number of women, and probably some 6,000 surviving children. There were far fewer military aristocrats; 1,000 per generation would add another 6,000.

19. For a more detailed discussion of the database, see Appendix 1. For a list of the senatorial aristocrats in the study and their religious identifications, see Appendix 2.

20. A man or woman could be born into this rank, since rank was hereditary for three generations, or a man could attain this rank through holding a sufficiently high office; see Chapter 2.

21. Lib. *Ep.* 70; P. Heather, "New Men for New Constantines? Creating an Imperial Elite in the Eastern Mediterranean," in *New Constantines: The Rhythms of Imperial Renewal in Byzantium, 4th-13th Centuries,* ed. P. Magdalino (Hampshire, U.K.,

1994), pp. 11–33; A. Skinner, "The Birth of a Byzantine Senatorial Perspective," *Arethusa* 33(3) (2000), pp. 363–378.

22. Lib. *Or.* 42.23–25.

23. R. MacMullen, "Women in Public in the Roman Empire," *Historia* 29 (1980), pp. 208–209, 217–218; A. Arjava, *Women and Law in Late Antiquity* (Oxford, 1996), pp. 244–245; S. Elm, *Virgins of God* (Oxford, 1994), p. 58, note 80.

24. I define the western empire as including ancient Italia, Italia Suburbicaria, Galliae, Septem Provinciae, Britanniae, Hispaniae, and Roman Africa, as shown by the *Notitia Dignitatum* (ca. C.E. 400). See A. H. M. Jones, *The Decline of the Ancient World* (London 1966), pp. 100–101; and Jones (1964, 1986 reprint), vol. 2, Map 2 (at pp. 1069–1070) and App. 3.

25. See Appendix 1 for specific criteria used.

26. K. Hopkins (1998), p. 187, makes a similar point about the "different Christianities" in the early church. Similarly, acknowledging the "diversity of its core," I use the category "Christian" to mark a boundary between it and paganism.

27. See Appendix 1, note 7.

28. Ambr. *Ep.* 72[17].9 (*CSEL* 82.3.14–15).

29. Cf. Symm. *Ep.* 3.30–37 to Ambrose. All citations to Symm. *Epistulae, Orationes,* and *Relationes* are to the O. Seeck edition (1883), unless otherwise noted.

30. Cf. Symm. *Ep.* 1.57, 1.97, and 2.58.

31. See especially P. Fredriksen, "Paul and Augustine: Conversion Narratives, Orthodox Traditions and the Retrospective Self," *JTS* n.s. 37(1) (1986), pp. 21–37.

32. Ibid., p. 20; and Aug. *C. Acad.* 2.2.5 (*CC* 29.20–21).

33. A. Segal, *Paul the Convert* (New Haven, 1990), p. 294. One fascinating study, J. A. Beckford, "Accounting for Conversion," *British Journal of Sociology* 29(2) (1978), pp. 249–262, examined the language of conversion accounts by Jehovah's Witnesses as reflections of socially elicited responses.

34. Chapter 2, note 158.

35. M. Le Glay, "Nouveaux documents, nouveaux points de vue sur Saturne africaine," *Studia Phoenicia VI, Carthago* ed. E. Lipinski (1988), pp. 209–211.

36. Chapter 3, note 126.

37. J. M. Roquette, "Trois nouveaux sarcophages chrétiens de Trinquetaille (Arles)," *Comptes rendus de L'Académie des Inscriptions et Belles-lettres* (1974), pp. 254–273.

38. J. P. Caillet, *L'évergétisme monumental chrétien en Italie et à ses marges d'après l'épigraphie des pavements de mosaïque (IV-VII s.), CEFT* 175 (1993).

39. M. Weber, "Class, Status, Party," in *From Max Weber: Essays in Sociology,* trans. and ed. H. H. Gerth and C. Wright Mills (New York, 1946), p. 187.

40. Cf. Lendon (1997), pp. 30–106.

41. Chapter 2, note 111.

42. Matthews (1975), pp. 146–172, and passim, and Jones (1963), pp. 17–35, are among those scholars who posit the importance of provincial provenance but do not demonstrate it in a systematic way; see Chapter 3.

43. See, for example, Brown (1961), pp. 1–11; J. Matthews, "Continuity in a Roman Family: The Rufii Festi of Volusinii," *Historia* 16 (1967), pp. 484–509; A. Chastagnol, "Le sénateur Volusien et la conversion d'une famille de l'aristocratie romaine au Bas-Empire," *REA* 58 (1956), pp. 241–253.

44. R. Stark and W. Bainbridge, "Networks of Faith: Interpersonal Bonds and Recruitment to Cults and Sects," *American Journal of Sociology* 85 (1980), pp. 1376ff. and 1381; Stark (1996), pp. 16ff.

45. R. Stark and W. Bainbridge (1980), p. 1377; cf. J. G. Gager, *Kingdom and Community: The Social World of Early Christianity* (Englewood Cliffs, N.J., 1975), p. 130.

46. Symm. *Ep.* 3.30–37. The favors continued, despite any possible tension in their relationship; N. McLynn, (1994), pp. 272–276. For the ideal of friendship, see, for example, Sid. Ap. *Ep.* 4.1.1, 4.4.1 ("amicus animorum similitudine"); and C. White, *Christian Friendship in the Fourth Century* (Cambridge, U.K., 1992).

47. See Chapter 5.

48. Symm. *Ep.* 1.51: "nunc aris deesse Romanos genus est ambiendi."

49. See Chapter 4.

50. Ambr. *Ep.* 36[2].3–5 (*CSEL* 82.2.4–5); *De Off.* 1.100–104 (ed. M. Testard [Paris, 1984–1992], 1.144–146).

51. Cf. Jerome *Ep.* 118.5 (*CSEL* 55.441–443). On *nobilitas*, see Chapter 7 and, more broadly treated, M. R. Salzman, "Competing Claims to '*Nobilitas*' in the Western Empire of the Fourth and Fifth Centuries," *JECS* 9(3) (2001), pp. 359–385.

52. Constantius of Lyons, *Vita Germani* 22 (*SC* 112.164): "natalibus nobilis, religione nobilior." See Mathisen (1993), p. 90.

2. Defining the Senatorial Aristocracy

1. M. Weber, "Class, Status, Party," in *From Max Weber: Essays in Sociology*, trans. and ed. H. H. Gerth and C. Wright Mills (Oxford, 1946), pp. 185–187. Weber's discussion is a classic statement of the status-group concept in sociological theory. His analysis provides insight into the Roman aristocracy.

2. Symm. *Ep.* 1.52: "pars melior humani generis."

3. Jones (1964, 1986 reprint), p. 523, note 1, cites Symm. *Ep.* 1.52 and *Pan. Lat.* 10[4].35.2 as criteria. The speech of Constantius II recommending Themistius for adlection to the senate of Constantinople (*Demegoria Constantii,* in Them. *Or.,* ed. W. Dindorf [1832; reprint, Hildesheim, Germany, 1961], pp. 21–27), cites wealth, property, state service, rhetorical skills, and virtue (*arête*), but fittingly omits noble birth, since Themistius lacked it. See also Symm. *Rel.* 5; *Or.* 5, 6, 7.

4. *C.J.* 12.1.2 (313–315 c.e.); *C.J.* 12.1.6 also excludes men in discredited professions or who have made their money in dishonorable ways, such as money-changers, bankers, and artisans.

5. As early as the time of the emperor Gaius, a very distinctive "senatorial class"—the *laticlavii*—existed. K. Hopkins and G. Burton, "Ambition and Withdrawal: The Senatorial Aristocracy under the Emperors," in *Death and Renewal:*

Sociological Studies in Roman History, ed. K. Hopkins (Cambridge, 1983), pp. 176–193; R. J. A. Talbert, *The Senate of Imperial Rome* (Princeton, 1984), pp. 11–13. See Jones (1964, 1986 reprint), pp. 547ff.

6. Arnheim (1972), pp. 3–19; S. J. B. Barnish, "Transformation and Survival in the Western Senatorial Aristocracy, A.D. 400–700," *PBSR* 56 (1988), p. 121. Rank was probably inherited for three generations.

7. Chastagnol (1992), pp. 295–296, citing *C.Th.* 2.1.7, notes that a woman born in the senatorial order did not lose her rank if she married below her, but a woman who acquired clarissimate status by marriage would lose that rank if she remarried below her; cf. Arnheim, (1972), p. 9.

8. R. J. A. Talbert (1984), p. 12.

9. Ibid., pp. 15–16; Chastagnol (1992), Chapters 8, 9, and 15; A. Chastagnol, "Les modes de recrutement du Sénat au IVe siècle," in *Recherches sur les structures sociales dans l'antiquité classique,* ed. C. Nicolet (Paris, 1970), pp. 190–201. Chastagnol notes that in the fourth century adlections *inter praetores* or *inter consulares* were the norm at Rome, but at Constantinople, where no quaestors are attested (Jones [1964, 1986 reprint], p. 532), praetorship was the norm for adlection and perhaps for admission to the senate; only praetorian games were required there by Constantius (*C.Th.* 6.4.5 [340 C.E.]).

10. A. Chastagnol (1970), pp. 190–201. By 359 the praetorship could take the place of the quaestorship as a qualification for membership in the senate at Constantinople (*C.Th.* 6.4.15), but at Rome, as Symm. *Or.* 8, implies, entry into the senate was still based on the quaestorship.

11. Jones (1964, 1986 reprint), p. 531 and note 19; Symm. *Or.* 8. Fortunatus' mother renounced his rank because of the expense of the quaestorship.

12. *C.Th.* 6.2.13; Chastagnol (1992), pp. 298–299.

13. Jones (1964, 1986 reprint), p. 541; *C.Th.* 6.4.7; Chastagnol (1992), p. 298.

14. Jacques (1986), pp. 121–125 and notes 132–135. For Constantine's changes, see Zos. 2.40, and W. Ensslin, "Der Konstantinische Patriziat und seine Bedeutung im 4. Jh.," in *Mélanges Bidez* 2 (1934), pp. 361–376.

15. T. D. Barnes, "Who Were the Nobility of the Roman Empire?" *Phoenix* 28 (1974), p. 446.

16. S. J. B. Barnish (1988), p. 123 and note 11; Schlinkert (1996), pp. 177–187.

17. Symm. *Or.* 8.3: "agitur in votum recuperandi, quod genere quaesiverat, inpulsu fortasse boni sanguinis, qui se semper agnoscit."

18. Mathisen (1993), p. 12, observed: "It is this collective acceptance as an aristocrat by other aristocrats that perhaps was the most important criterion of all of aristocratic status."

19. Lendon (1997), pp. 37–38; B. D. Shaw, "Among the Believers," *Échos du monde classique/Classical Views* 28 (1984), pp. 453–479. Despite such qualifications, historians still use the term "aristocracy"; for example, *The Cambridge Ancient History.* vol. 13, ed. Averil Cameron and P. Garnsey (Cambridge, 1998), passim, especially A. Marcone, "Late Roman Social Relations," pp. 354–356.

20. For fuller discussions of "elite," "class," and "order," see the *International Ency-*

clopedia of the Social Sciences, vol. 5, ed. D. Sills (New York, 1968). The need to differentiate elites is well stated there by S. Keller, and elaborated as well by G. Marcus, "Elite as a Concept, Theory and Research Tradition," in *Elites: Ethnographic Issues*, ed. G. Marcus (Albuquerque, N.M., 1983), pp. 3–27. For problems with "class," see Näf (1995), pp. 1–11, whose analysis of individual authors leads him to discern common elements of senatorial self-understanding that lends further support to my using the term "senatorial aristocracy."

21. For the elite's disdain for commerce, see, for example, Cic. *De Off.* 1.150–151. See also the *Oxford Classical Dictionary*, 3d ed. (1996), s.v. "Trade."

22. See A. Chastagnol, "Observations sur le consulat suffect et la préture du bas-empire," *Rev. hist.* 219 (1958), pp. 221–253, with corrections by Bagnall et al. (1987), p. 2, note 14; and Kuhoff (1983), pp. 20–28.

23. This situation encouraged widespread bribery; see R. MacMullen, *Corruption and the Decline of Rome* (New Haven, 1988), pp. 148–170.

24. For military landowners, see Gratian, father of the emperor Valentinian, with an estate in Pannonia: Amm. Marc. 30.7.2 ff., Symm. *Or.* 1.1 ff.; Flavius Promotus, with estates on the Bosporus and in Constantinople: Aus. *Ep.* 5.39–40, John Chrys. *Ep.* 207 (*PG* 52.726–727); and Flavius Theodosius, with estates in Spain: *Pan. Lat.* 12[2].9.1ff.; cf. Matthews (1975), pp. 34–40, 120–121.

25. Claudius Postumus Dardanus, App. 2 (of this book) = *PLRE* 2.346–347, is illustrative; probably from humble origins, Dardanus enjoyed a successful career in law and state service that provided the wealth with which he acquired a large estate in Narbonensis Secunda. Military landowners are cited above in note 24.

26. Olymp. *Frag.* 44 (*FHG* 4.67–68).

27. Matthews (1975), p. 30 and note 1. Since senators were traditionally prohibited from direct involvement in trade, agents generally handled their transactions. D. Vera, "Strutture agrarie e strutture patrimoniali nella tarda antichità: L'aristocrazia romana fra agricoltura e commercio," *Opus* 2 (1983), pp. 489–533.

28. D. Vera "Simmaco e le sue proprietà: struttura e funzionaménto di un patrimonio aristocratico del quarto secolo d.C.," in *Colloque Genevois sur Symmaque*, ed. F. Paschoud (Paris, 1986), pp. 243ff. Following Trajanic policy, Marcus Aurelius required senators of non-Italian origin to invest one-quarter of their capital in Italy; *HA Marcus* 11.8. This policy probably lapsed for there is little evidence of ownership of Italian land by provincial aristocrats in the fourth century.

29. Symm. *Ep.* 6.11, 6.12, 6.66, 7.66, 9.32, 9.52[49], ed. O. Seeck (Berlin, 1883), pp. xlv–xlvi; D. Vera (1986), pp. 234–239. Paulinus of Pella owned lands not only near Bordeaux and Marseilles but also in Achaea and in Old and New Epirus; Paul. of Pella *Euch.* 498ff., 570ff., 413ff., and 516ff.

30. D. Vera (1986), p. 251.

31. Jones (1964, 1986 reprint), pp. 781–788. Estates could be larger than towns, as was Melania's estate near Tagaste; see *The Life of Melania the Younger* 21, trans. E. A. Clark (New York, 1984), p. 44 and note 27.

32. K. Dunbabin, *The Mosaics of Roman North Africa* (Oxford, 1978); Palladius *De Re*

Rustica 1.6; Sid. Ap. *Ep.* 8.12.5 and *Carm.* 22. The urban residences of aristocrats could also be self-sufficient; Olympiodorus *Frag.* 43 (*FHG* 4.67) describes houses at Rome as "cities within cities."

33. *C.Th.* 5.17.1.1.
34. Matthews (1975), p. 24; Arnheim (1972), pp. 142ff.
35. Matthews (1975), pp. 25–26; Heather (1998), pp. 204–209.
36. Arnheim (1972), p. 152.
37. See R. MacMullen (1988), pp. 150–153, on *suffragium* won through "customary" bribes, described as such in law (e.g., *C.Th.* 6.30.11).
38. Jones (1964, 1986 reprint), p. 537.
39. Ibid., pp. 535–536; reiterated for *illustres* again in 409.
40. Lendon (1997), pp. 176–236; Arnheim (1972), pp. 49–102.
41. *C.Th.* 6.3.4 indicates abuses in this system, which probably lie behind the new fourth-century office of *defensor civitatum* or *plebis;* see also *C.Th.* 1.29.1; R. M. Frakes, "Late Roman Social Justice and the Origin of the *Defensor Civitatis,*" *CJ* 89(4) (1994), pp. 337–348; Lendon (1997), pp. 176–177, 222–236.
42. *C.Th.* 8.15.1 (334); Arnheim (1972), p. 159. The *N. Val.* 32.1 of 451 revoked this ban in accord with a lost law of Honorius.
43. See, for example, Symm. *Ep.* 3.34 on Magnillus' outstanding abilities as vicar of Africa ("publice privatimque").
44. Matthews (1975), p. 29.
45. Symm. *Ep.* 1.2.3, v.3; 6.5; 9.67[62].
46. Ibid., *Ep.* 1.3.3–4.
47. Jones (1964, 1986 reprint), pp. 490–491, note 47. The lower senatorial orders lost this privilege at the end of the century, but the *illustres* retained it into the fifth century; see Chastagnol (1992), pp. 321ff.; Symm. *Rel.* 48.
48. *C.Th.* 12.1.57–58, 12.1.83, 12.1.93 for curials; 11.16.14–16, 11.16.18, 11.16.19 for public service. See F. Millar, "Empire and City, Augustus to Julian: Obligations, Excuses, and Status," *JRS* 73 (1983), pp. 76–96.
49. Arnheim (1972), pp. 21–48; Jones (1964, 1986 reprint), p. 525.
50. This is the conventional view; see, for example, P. Brown, *The World of Late Antiquity* (London, 1971), pp. 22–48, and Averil Cameron, *The Later Roman Empire* (London, 1993), pp. 1–12.
51. Jacques (1986), pp. 81–225. He argues against scholars like Arnheim (1972) and Jones (1964, 1986 reprint), pp. 525ff., who see a "fossilization" because they believe the senate at the beginning of the fourth century contained only families already *clarissimi* at the beginning of the third century. Similarly, Jacques criticizes C. Lécrivain, *Le sénat romain depuis Dioclétien à Rome et à Constantinople* (Paris, 1888), pp. 3–23, who had argued that the ancient senatorial families had been eliminated but were later revived.
52. Jacques (1986), pp. 113–125. Although Jacques, p. 121, estimates that patrician families represented at most 10 percent of the senate, their monopoly of certain priesthoods forced them to replace extinct families, creating a semblance of continuity.

53. Ibid., especially pp. 89–108, 127–130. According to Jacques, p. 91, based on the *Fasti* of Cales in Campania, dated 289, the number of adlections remained small over the course of the third century, with no more than fifty to seventy-five senators out of a senate of probably only 600 men (pp. 87–89); see also F. Jacques, "Le nombre de sénateurs au IIe et IIIe siècles," in *Epigrafia e ordine senatorio*, vol. 1, *Atti del coll. internazionale AIEGL* (Rome, 1982), pp. 137–142. But the senatorial order did increase after Diocletian, even if the senate did not; see Chastagnol (1992), pp. 261–265, and my discussion below.

54. Jacques (1986), pp. 124–127.

55. Arnheim (1972), pp. 39–73.

56. Jacques (1986), pp. 133–134.

57. Jones (1964, 1986 reprint), p. 525.

58. Aur. Vict. *Caes.* 37.5–6. Scholars debate whether this text indicates a new policy or the formulation of existing precedents; see A. Chastagnol, "Constantin et le Sénat," in *Accademia Romanistica Costantiniana, Atti* (Rimini, Italy, 1976), pp. 51–52; H. G. Pflaum, "Zur Reform des Kaisers Gallienus," *Historia* 25 (1976), pp. 109ff.; M. Christol, "Les réformes de Gallien et la carrière sénatoriale," *Epigrafia e ordine senatorio*, vol. 1 (Rome, 1982), pp. 143–166. Some provinces, such as Syria Coele, still had senatorial governors, but they no longer performed military duties.

59. Arnheim (1972), pp. 32–48.

60. K. Hopkins and G. Burton (1983), p. 183.

61. M. Christol, *Essai sur l'évolution des carrières sénatoriales dans la seconde moitié du IIIe siècle* (Paris, 1986), pp. 61–66.

62. Ibid., pp. 66, 143–166. See also C. Lepelley, "Fine dell'ordine equestre: Le tappe dell'unificazione della classe dirigente Romana nel IV secolo," in *Società romana e impero tardoantico*, vol.1: *Istituzioni, ceti, economie*, ed. A. Giardina (Rome, 1986), pp. 229–231; and papers by H. Devijver, S. Demougin, and K. P. Johne in *Prosopographie und Sozialgeschichte: Studien zur Methodik und Erkenntnismöglichkeit der kaiserzeitlichen Prosopographie, Kolloquium Köln, 1991*, ed. W. Eck (Cologne, 1993), pp. 206–259.

63. *HA Gord. Tres*, especially section 14; *Maximus et Balbinus*, especially sections 1–3. In *HA Probus*, section 10, the senate refused to choose the next emperor, but in section 11 Probus turns to the senate for recognition.

64. Zos. 1.37.

65. Jacques (1986), pp. 91–92.

66. Aur. Vict. *Caes.* 41.18; the populace were upset at news of the death of Constantine because "armis legibus clementi imperio quasi novatam urbem Romam arbitrarentur." At 41.12, Victor notes that Constantine reorganized the "militiae ordo," including military and administrative service. See also *C.Th.* 15.14.4; G. Dagron, *Naîssance d'une capitale: Constantinople et ses institutions de 330 à 451* (Paris, 1974), p. 121; Eus. *VC* 1. 39–40 (*GCS* 7.36–37); *Pan. Lat.* 9[12].20; Lact. *De mort. pers.* 44.

67. A. Chastagnol (1976), pp. 52–69, but he overemphasizes Constantine's role.

68. Them. *Or.* 34.13, dated to the 380s, states that Constantius II increased the senate at Constantinople to 2,000 members, presumably to equal the senate at Rome. Chastagnol (1992), pp. 261–265, dates the increase to 357–359, but Constantine presumably contributed to this, for he certainly increased the order; Eus. *VC* 4.1 (*GCS* 7.118). Others are probably right to see a gradual increase from 357 to 387. See A. Chastagnol, "Les modes de recrutement" (1970), pp. 187–211; Aus. *Professores* 1.9; Jones (1964, 1986 reprint), p. 527; Heather (1998), p. 187, note 7.

69. Two were adlected *inter consulares:* C. Caelius Saturninus signo Dogmatius = Saturninus 9, *PLRE* 1.806, adlected ca. 325–326, and C. Iulius Rufinianus Ablabius Tatianus = Tatianus 4, *PLRE* 1.875–876, adlected after 324. Two were adlected *inter praetorios:* L. Papius Pacatianus = Pacatianus 2, *PLRE* 1.656, adlected between 309/310–329, and Iulius (or Ionius) Iulianus = Iulianus 35, *PLRE* 1.478–479, adlected probably in 324–325. For Iulianus' name, see Bagnall et al. (1987), pp. 629–630. For Saturninus and Pacatianus, see also von Haehling (1978), pp. 334, 289–290. For adlections, see A. Chastagnol (1976), pp. 53–55.

70. New senatorial posts included the *praefecti annonae* and *praefecti vigilum* at Rome, as well as certain praetorian prefectures; see A. Chastagnol, *Recherches sur l'Histoire Auguste* (Bonn, 1970), pp. 58–59; Chastagnol (1992), pp. 233–259; Kuhoff (1983), pp. 47, 232ff.

71. A. Chastagnol, "Les consulaires de Numidie," in *Mélanges d'archéologie, d'épigraphie et d'histoire offerts à J. Carcopino* (Paris, 1966), pp. 215–218; Jones (1964, 1986 reprint), pp. 106–107, who also notes that *correctores* were replaced by senatorial consulars in several provinces; Kuhoff (1983), pp. 50–78; Chastagnol (1992), pp. 233–258; and G. A. Cecconi, *Governo imperiale e élites dirigenti nell'Italia tardoantica* (Como, Italy, 1994), pp. 21–82.

72. For *comites* outside of court (*comites provinciarum* or *comites qui per provincias constituti sunt*), see Jones (1964, 1986 reprint), pp. 104–105, 333–337; Kuhoff (1983), pp. 112–117, 118–119.

73. Jones (1964, 1986 reprint), p. 106 and note 62, pp. 533–537 and note 28. See also note 14 above.

74. See A. Chastagnol (1976), pp. 58–59; Kuhoff (1983), pp. 20–39, 76–78; and Bagnall et al. (1987), pp. 2, 21, on the suffect consulship.

75. For provincials, see Nazarius in 321, *Pan. Lat.* 10[4].35.2; for equestrians, see *HA Alex. Sev.* 19.4: "adserens seminarium senatorum equestrem locum esse." See also A. Chastagnol, *"Latus clavus et Adlectio:* l'access des hommes nouveaux au sénat romain sous le haut-empire," *Revue Historique de Droit Français et Etrangier* 53 (1975), pp. 375–394.

76. *Sent. Pauli* 1.7 = *Dig.* 50.1.22.6; *Dig.* 1.9.11. Paul in the early third century first states the principle of "double domicile." A. Chastagnol, "Le problème du domicile légal dans sénateurs romains à l'époque impériale," in *Mélanges offerts à Léopold Sédar Senghor* (Dakar, 1977), pp. 43–54; A. Chastagnol (1976), pp. 57–58.

77. A. Chastagnol (1976), pp. 57–58, attributes this change to Constantine, although no extant legislation states this; cf. A. Chastagnol (1977), pp. 51–54, who notes that Ausonius never came to Rome, and Paulinus of Nola came to Rome only briefly for his suffect consulship.
78. Symm. *Ep.* 4.8; *Rel.* 23.2.
79. Only under Theodosius II were all *spectabiles* and *clarissimi,* but not *illustres,* released from obtaining permission to leave the capital. See *C.J.* 12.1.15 (426/442); Jones (1964, 1986 reprint), pp. 536–537 and note 34.
80. Amm. Marc. 21.10.8: "eum aperte incusans, quod barbaros omnium primus ad usque fasces auxerat et trabeas consulares."
81. Flavius Arbitio 2, *PLRE* 1.94–95.
82. A. Demandt, "Der spätrömische Militäradel," *Chiron* 10 (1980), pp. 609–636, especially p. 610 and note 11, opines that Germans were probably regular consuls; Alan Cameron, "The Roman Friends of Ammianus," *JRS* 54 (1964), pp. 15–28, argued convincingly against interpreting this passage as evidence for barbarian suffect consuls.
83. Jones (1964, 1986 reprint), p. 105.
84. Soz. 2.3.4 (*GCS* 50.52); Heather (1998), pp. 185–186.
85. A. Chastagnol (1976), p. 61, notes that not one name can be indisputably transferred from Rome to Constantinople under Constantine, where senators were *clari* rather than *clarissimi;* see also Anonymus Valesianus 6.30. However, A. Skinner, "The Birth of a 'Byzantine' Perspective," *Arethusa* 33 (2000), pp. 363–378, argues for equal status under Constantine.
86. Lib. *Ep.* 70.
87. P. Heather, "New Men for New Constantines: Creating an Imperial Elite in the Eastern Mediterranean," in *New Constantines: The Rhythms of Imperial Renewal in Byzantium, 4th—13th Centuries,* ed. P. Magdalino (Aldershot, 1994), pp. 11–33.
88. A. Chastagnol (1976), pp. 66–69; A. Chastagnol, "Les modes de recrutement" (1970), pp. 197–201; Chastagnol (1992), Chapters 9 and 15. The dating of this innovation depends on *CIL* 6.1708 = 31906 = *D.* 1222: "Ceionium Rufium Albinum v.c. cons. [ord] . . . / philosophum, Rufi Volusiani bis ordinarii cons . . . / fi[l]ium, senatus ex consulto suo quod eius liberis . . . / post Caesariana tempora id est post annos CCCLXXX et I . . . / auctoritatem decreverit/ [Constantinus]."
89. O. Seeck, "Die Inschrift des Ceionius Rufius Albinus," *Hermes* 19 (1884), pp. 186–187; A. Chastagnol (1976), pp. 66–67 and notes 48–50.
90. C. Caelius Saturninus signo Dogmatius was adlected *petitu senatus inter consulares* around 325–326; *CIL* 6.1704 = *D.* 1214.
91. *C.Th.* 6.4.10 (356): "allectionis quaerendus est honor."
92. *C.Th.* 6.4.12 and .13 (361), 6.4.14 and .15 (359).
93. Flavius Severus in Symm. *Or.* 6 and *PLRE* 1.835–836; Synesius in *Or.* 7 and *PLRE* 1.871–872. For those not running for office, see Celsus, Symm. *Rel.* 5, and Dynamius, Symm. *Ep.* 7.96.1–2.
94. See Jones (1964, 1986 reprint), pp. 530–531; and Libanius, in his speech on

behalf of his friend Thalassius who had sought admission to the senate in Constantinople, *Or.* 42.6.

95. Chastagnol (1992), pp. 312–316.

96. *C.Th.* 6.4.8, .9, .10, and 6.4 passim. Similarly, for the senate of Constantinople, see G. Dagron (1974), pp. 125ff.

97. Amm. Marc. 21.16.2.

98. See Zon. 13.22C for Constantius; Lib. *Or.* 18.158 for Julian; and W. H. V. Harris, *Ancient Literacy* (Cambridge, Mass., 1989), pp. 313–314.

99. Amm. Marc. 21.10.7, 28.1.23.

100. See Salzman (1990), pp. 185–186.

101. See Symm. *Or.* 2.1–2 on consulting the senate, and C. Ando, *Imperial Theology and Provincial Loyalty in the Roman Empire* (Berkeley, Calif., 2000), pp. 152–174 and 404–405, on the role of the senate in building consensus.

102. Symm. *Rel.* 3.

103. Ibid., *Or.* 4.6.26–27; Heather (1998), p. 198.

104. Amm. Marc. 28.1.24–25.

105. Jones (1964, 1986 reprint), p. 143 and note 15; *C.Th.*, especially 6.5.2 (384), 6.6.1 (382), 6.7.1 (372), and 6.7.2 (380).

106. Heather (1994), pp. 19–20.

107. *C.Th.* 6.35.7 (367).

108. See Löhken (1982), pp. 135–147; Näf (1995), pp. 15ff.; and my discussion below of aristocrats at work.

109. Amm. Marc. 28.1.1–56; Matthews (1975), pp. 56–59; P. Brown, "Sorcery, Demons and the Rise of Christianity," in *Witchcraft Confessions and Accusations (Association of Social Anthropologists Monographs, No. 9)* (1970), pp. 17–45.

110. Amm. Marc. 28.1.6; cf. 27.3.1 and 28.1.42; Matthews (1975), pp. 39–41.

111. Jones (1964, 1986 reprint), p. 143 and note 15; Heather (1998), pp. 184–210.

112. Symm. *Ep.* 9.112[102] suggests this identification; see O. Seeck, (1883), p. xxv, note 49.

113. The two exceptions were Sextus Petronius Probus and Vulcacius Rufinus.

114. Matthews (1975), pp. 37–40. For Viventius, see *PLRE* 1.972.

115. Löhken (1982), Chapter 2.

116. Matthews (1975), pp. 231–238. Virius Nicomachus Flavianus was *quaestor sacri palatii* under Theodosius.

117. S. J. B. Barnish (1988), pp. 121–127; Arnheim (1972), pp. 101–102.

118. P. Heather (1998), pp. 184–210, and Heather (1994), p. 19, although this number includes perfectissimate posts that only late in the century conferred clarissimate rank.

119. For privileges for *illustres*, see *C.Th.* 12.1.187 (436); *C.J.* 12.1.15 (426) and 12.1.16 (442–443); Jones (1964, 1986 reprint), pp. 466–467 and note 133, p. 550 and note 47. For diminished privileges of *clarissimi* and *spectabiles*, see *C.Th.* 11.16.15 and 12.1.187 (436); *C.J.* 12.2.1 (450).

120. Jones (1964, 1986 reprint), pp. 527–532, and A. Chastagnol, "Sidoine Apollinaire et le sénat de Rome," *Acta Antiqua Academiae Scientiarum Hungaricae*

26 (1978), pp. 57–70, argued that the senate in 450 still included all three senatorial ranks, but only the *illustres* had the *ius sententiae dicendi*. However, S. J. B. Barnish (1988), p. 121, note 10, has shown that the "devaluation of the *clarissimus* title was not marked until the mid sixth-century."

121. *C.Th.* 6.2.16 (395).
122. Löhken (1982), pp. 107ff.; Chastagnol (1992), pp. 316ff.
123. *FIRA* 1.2, 64.
124. See note 77 above; see also Augustine *Civ. Dei* 5.17.2.
125. S. J. B. Barnish (1988), pp. 130ff.; Chastagnol (1992), pp. 316ff.
126. Jones (1964, 1986 reprint), pp. 528–529, 741–743.
127. Flavius Theodosius 3, *PLRE* 1.902–904. His brother, Flavius Eucherius 2, *PLRE* 1.288, was an imperial administrator; Matthews (1975), pp. 107ff.
128. Hugh Elton, *Warfare in the Roman Empire*, A.D. *350–425* (Oxford, 1996), p. 142.
129. Zos. 5.20 on Fravitta.
130. Matthews (1975), p. 120.
131. R. MacMullen, *Soldier and Civilian in the Later Roman Empire* (New Haven, 1963), pp. 49ff., 180.
132. Julian *Or.* 2.58C; see also R. S. O. Tomlin, "Notitia Dignitatum Omnium, Tam Civilium Quam Militarium," in *Aspects of the Notitia Dignitatum*, ed. R. Goodburn and P. Bartholomew, *British Archaeological Reports* 15 (Oxford, 1976), pp. 189–209.
133. Amm. Marc. 25.5.1–3, on Saturninius Secundus Salutius 3, App. 2.
134. Symm. *Ep.* 3.60, 3.61, 3.65 for Flavius Richomeres, App. 2. Richomeres introduced a mutual friend to his nephew Arbogastes; R. S. O. Tomlin (1976), pp. 192–195.
135. See Chapter 4; A. Demandt (1980), especially pp. 614–615 and notes 28–29, amplified in A. Demandt, "The Osmosis of Late Roman and Germanic Aristocracies," in *Das Reich und die Barbaren*, ed. E. K. Chrysos and A. Schwarcz (Vienna-Cologne, 1989), pp. 75–85.
136. H. Elton (1996), pp. 143ff.
137. Amm. Marc. 30.9.4; *Epit. de Caes.* 45.5–6; H. Elton (1996), pp. 136–154.
138. Ausonius, Symm. *Ep.* 1.13–43; Bauto, Symm. *Ep.* 4.15–16; Richomeres, Symm. *Ep.* 3.54–69.
139. Lib. *Ep.* 70 for evidence of geographic split; *Or.* 42.11, .22–25.
140. P. Heather (1994), pp. 11–33, especially p. 14 and note 13.
141. Symm. *Ep.* 1.1.2: "libet enim non minus otii quam negotii praestare rationem." See L. Cracco Ruggini, "Simmaco: *Otia* et *Negotia* di classe, fra conservazione e rinnovamento," in *Colloque Genevois sur Symmaque*, ed. F. Paschoud (1986), p. 98; P. Bruggisser, *Symmaque ou le rituel épistolaire de l'amitié littéraire: Recherches sur le premier livre de la correspondance* (Freibourg, Switzerland, 1993), pp. 53–55.
142. J. Aymard, *Essai sur les chasses romaines* (Paris, 1951), Chapters 23 and 24.
143. Symm. *Ep.* 5.67, .68.1.
144. Paul. of Pella *Eucharisticos* 149–153. Ausonius teases Theon, *Ep.* 18.28–51, about the dangers of the hunt.
145. Amm. Marc. 28.4.18.

146. Symm. *Ep.* 8.2 and 4.18; for representations of hunting parties, see notes 149 and 150 below.
147. Paul. of Pella *Eucharisticos* 113–154.
148. See Symm. *Ep.* 4.18.2; Ambr. *De Nabuthae* 13.54 (*CSEL* 32.2.499).
149. See K. Dunbabin (1978), pp. 54ff.
150. Y. Thébert, "Private Life and Domestic Architecture in Roman Africa," in *History of Private Life,* vol. 1, ed. P. Veyne (Cambridge, Mass., 1987), p. 403; cf. Aug. *De doctr. Christ.* 2.25 (*CC* 32.60–61).
151. K. Dunabain (1978), pp. 55ff., on the basis of extant mosaics; S. Ellis, "Power, Architecture and Decor: How the Late Roman Aristocrat Appeared to His Guests," in *Roman Art in the Private Sphere* (Ann Arbor, Mich., 1991), ed. E. Gazda and A. Haeckl, especially pp. 124–132 and notes 35–36.
152. S. Ellis (1991), pp. 126–128.
153. Symm. *Ep.* 1.30–37.
154. Amm. Marc. 14.16.1 describes the aristocrats who held "whirlpools of dinners" *(mensarum voragines).*
155. Ibid., 28.4.13.
156. Y. Thébert, "Private and Public Spaces: The Components of the Domus," in *Roman Art in Context,* ed. E. D'Ambra (Englewood Cliffs, N.J., 1993), p. 225, as in the House of the Hunt at Bulla Regia.
157. Amm. Marc. 28.4.13; Y. Thébert (1993), pp. 227ff., notes as well the prophylactic symbolism of this scene. Cf. K. Dunbabin (1978), p. 250, note 2.
158. S. Ellis (1991), pp. 120ff.
159. Symm. *Ep.* 7.15.
160. Ibid., 3.23.
161. Ibid., 6.32.
162. Ibid., 8.23.3.
163. L. Cracco Ruggini (1986), especially p. 105 and note 23.
164. Aug. *De doctr. Christ.* 2.25 (*CC* 32.60–61).
165. Amm. Marc. 14.6.9.
166. Ibid., 28.4.8.
167. *C.Th.* 16.2.27 (390); women intending to be deaconesses were required to give their jewelry to their families.
168. Amm. Marc. 28.4.19.
169. Symm. *Ep.* 1.53; cf. *Ep.* 4.18 (396) to Protadius and *Ep.* 3.23 to Marinianus.
170. *CIL* 6.1779 = *D.* 1259. See L. Cracco Ruggini (1986), p. 106 and note 26, for Praetextatus as a source for Boethius, *Comm. in librum Aristotelis de interpr.,* 2nd ed., vol. 1, pp. 3–4, ed. K. Meiser (Leipzig, 1877–1880), 1.2 (*PL* 64.393); and Ps. Augustine (*PL* 32.1422).
171. Sid. Ap. *Ep.* 8.3.1; see also L. Cracco Ruggini (1986), p. 106, note 26.
172. J. E. G. Zetzel, "The Subscriptions in the Manuscripts of Livy and Fronto and the Meaning of *Emendatio,*" *CPh* 75 (1980), pp. 38–59.
173. See the *Epigrammata Bobiensia,* no. 65, ed. W. Speyer (Berlin, 1963); L. Cracco Ruggini (1986), p. 112. For Symmachus as a poet, see L. Cracco Ruggini,

"Simmaco e la poesia," *La poesia toardoantica: tra retorica, teologia e politica, Atti del V corso della Scuola Superiore di Archeologia e Civiltà Medievali* (Messina, 1984), pp. 477–521.

174. For example, Arusianus Messius, an orator and an aristocrat, dedicated his work *Exempla elocutionum ex Virgilio, Sallustio, Terentio, Cicerone digesta* to the brothers Olybrius and Probinus of the influential famly of the Probi (associated with the Petronius Probianus eulogized by Avianius) sometime before 387; Arusianus Messius, *PLRE* 1.600; cf. Iulius(?) Naucellius, *PLRE* 1.617–618.

175. Pliny *Ep.* 5.3.5; Lendon (1997), pp. 38–42.

176. H. I. Marrou, *A History of Education in Antiquity,* trans. G. Lamb (1948; reprint, Madison, Wis., 1982), pp. 242–298; R. Kaster, *Guardians of Language* (Berkeley, 1988), pp. 11–96; Lendon (1997), pp. 36–58.

177. Amm. Marc. 21.16.4 on Constantius; on the schoolmaster, see Dio 75.5.1–3 (*LCL* 76), pp. 204–207. See also Lendon (1997), pp. 36–47.

178. Symm. *Ep.* 1.20.1; cf. 10.2.5; D. Nellen, *Viri litterati: Gebildetes Beamtentum und spätrömisches Reich im Westen zwischen 284 und 395 nach Christus* (Bochum, Germany, 1977), pp. 19–97.

179. L. Cracco Ruggini (1986), pp. 97–118, especially p. 101; S. Roda, "Simmacho nel gioco politico del suo tempo," *SDHI* 39 (1973), pp. 53–114.

180. Amm. Marc. 14.6.18; cf. 28.4.14–15. Ammianus' critique still stands, even though some scholars doubt his residency in Rome; for an overview of this issue, see T. D. Barnes, *Ammianus Marcellinus and the Representation of Historical Reality* (Ithaca, N.Y., 1998), pp. 54–64.

181. Amm. Marc. 14.6.1: "splendore liberalium doctrinarum minus quam nobilem decuerat institutus."

182. A. Momigliano, "Pagan and Christian Historiography in the Fourth Century A.D.," in Momigliano, ed. (1963), pp. 79–99.

183. Amm. Marc. 27.11.3.

184. Matthews (1975), pp. 9ff., especially note 4, citing *Expositio Totius Mundi et Gentium* 55 (*SC* 125), p. 194.

185. Sid. Ap. *Ep.* 8.8.2: "parce tantum in nobilitatis invidiam rusticari"; cf. 8.8.3.

186. Q. Flavius Maesius Egnatius Lollianus signo Mavortius, App. 2 = Lollianus 5, *PLRE* 1.512–514. J. Matthews (1975), pp. 11ff., sees as typical one year in office followed by several years in private life. Others would attribute this pattern to evidentiary problems, as did A. Giardina, "Review of J. Matthews, *Western Aristocracies and Imperial Court* A.D. *364–425,*" in *Dialoghi di archeologia* 9–10 (1976–1977), pp. 668–678.

187. Bagnall et al. (1987), pp. 2ff. and note 14; Kuhoff (1983), pp. 20–28.

188. Amm. Marc. 27.3.2–10.

189. Symm. *Ep.* 8.5 and 8.20; 3.34 praises Magnillus as vicar in Africa.

190. See note 186 above.

191. R. H. Barrow, *Prefect and Emperor: The Relationes of Symmachus* A.D. *384* (Oxford, 1973), pp. 1ff.

192. Amm. Marc. 19.10.1ff.

193. Jones (1964, 1986 reprint), pp. 50–51, 100–103, 370–372; Kuhoff (1983), pp. 237–238; T. D. Barnes, "Praetorian Prefects, 337–61," *ZPE* 94 (1992), pp. 249–260.

194. Symm. *Ep.* 1.2.7; see also Locrius Verinus 2, *PLRE* 1.951–952. Although A. D. Lee, "The Army," in *The Cambridge Ancient History,* vol. 13 (1998), ed. A. Cameron and P. Garnsey, p. 229, emphasizes the division between military and civil spheres, R. S. O. Tomlin (1976), pp. 195–203, lists several instances of civilian officials exercising military duties.

195. Symm. *Ep.* 9.67.

196. Lendon (1997), p. 181.

197. Constantine upgraded a number of provinces and gave their governors the title of *consularis* rather than the lower-status *praeses* to attract candidates; see Jones (1964, 1986 reprint), p. 106.

198. Lendon (1997), pp. 181–201.

199. Lendon (1997), pp. 36–47, 192–194; see also Men. Rhet. *Treatise* 415–417, ed. D. A. Russell and N. G. Wilson (Oxford, 1981).

200. *C.Th.* 11.24.2; Arnheim (1972), pp. 151ff.

201. Symm. *Ep.* 7.66; D. Vera (1986), pp. 255ff.

202. D. Vera (1986), pp. 237, 254ff.; Symm. *Ep.* 1.10, 7.2.

203. See Chapter 5.

204. Ambr. *De Exc. Sat.* 26 (*PL* 16.1298); D. Vera (1986), pp. 231–276.

205. S. Roda, "Polifunzionalità della lettera commendaticia: teoria e prassi nell'epistolario Simmachiano," in *Colloque Genevois sur Symmaque,* ed. F. Paschoud (Paris, 1986), p. 177; Symm. *Ep.* 1.40 and 1.41.

206. See S. Roda, *Commento storico al libro IX dell'epistolario di Q. Aurelio Simmaco* (Pisa, Italy, 1981), pp. 219–220, on *Ep.* 9.88 as the beginning of their relationship; Symm. *Ep.* 1.14.4 on court life; Symm. *Ep.* 1.35, a polite apology for a delay in correspondence. See also Sivan (1993), pp. 205ff.

207. Matthews (1975), p. 3.

208. Symm. *Ep.* 1.14; cf. Symm. *Ep.* 1.18.

209. See Symm *Ep.* 1.32.3 for Ausonius' fulsome compliments. Symm. *Ep* 1.13–31, 1.33–43.

210. S. Roda, "Alcune ipotesi sulla prima edizione dell'epistolario di Simmaco," *La Parola del Passato* 134 (1979), pp. 35–54; L. Cracco Ruggini (1986), p. 103; J. P. Callu, ed., *Symmaque Lettres: Livres I-II* (Paris, 1972), pp. 33ff.

211. Symm. *Ep.* 1.16.2; P. Bruggisser (1993), pp. 28–29. Symmachus used the parent-child metaphor for Attalus, *Ep.* 7.15; Romulus, *Ep.* 8.57[56]; and Auxentius, *Ep.* 9.7.1. He addressed several young protégés as *filius:* Protadius, *Ep.* 4.47; Valentinus, *Ep.* 6.44; Caecilianus, Symm. *Ep.* 4.41. This term was generally used for young men whom one counseled or taught; *TLL,* s.v. "filius."

212. P. Bruggisser (1993), pp. 140–143, cites twelve out of thirty recommendations, including Ausonius' response; Symm. *Ep.* 1.32.

213. Symm. *Ep.* 1.37.2; see also 1.25 on envy and flattery as the enemies of friendship.

214. Ibid., *Ep.* 3.17, .72; 5.51, .52, .63; 7.44.

215. S. Roda (1986), pp. 177–208.

216. Symm. *Ep.* 4.28.

217. Sid. Ap. *Ep.* 7.9.22; cf. 3.2.4, 7.12.4. Roman aristocrats traditionally called themselves *boni;* see *OLD*, s.v. *"bonus";* Lendon (1997), p. 41; G. Achard, "L'emploi de *boni, boni viri, boni cives* et leur formes superlatives dans l'action politique de Cicéron," *EC* 41 (1973), pp. 207–221.

218. S. Roda (1986), pp. 177–203, especially pp. 183–184; Symm. *Ep.* 9.46.

219. *D.* 1264, cited in part in *CIL* 6.31902; Alfenius C(a)eionius Iulianus signo Kamenius 25, App. 2 = Iulianus 25, *PLRE* 1.474–475.

220. M C(a)eionius Iulianus signo Kamenius 26, App. 2 = Iulianus 26, *PLRE* 1.476. The phrase "a parentibus patronus" in *CIL* 8.25525 is formulaic. For Nicomachus Flavianus 14, App. 2 = Flavianus 14, *PLRE* 1.345–347, see *D.* 8985.

221. Symm. *Ep.* 6.5.

222. Ibid., *Ep.* 6.3, .44; 7.120; 9.7, .43, .49, .133. Symmachus was involved in his daughter's marriage to Nicomachus Flavianus the Younger in 388 and Galla's to Memmius Symmachus in 401; A. Marcone, *Commento Storico al libro VI dell'epistolario di Q. Aurelio Simmaco* (Pisa, Italy, 1981), p. 20, note 13; p. 24, note 28; p. 65.

223. Amm. Marc. 14.6.24.

224. Symm. *Ep.* 6.35; A. Marcone (1981), p. 110.

225. *C.Th.* 2.1.7; *C.J.* 12.1.13.

226. *CIL* 6.1754 = *D.* 1269: "Aniciae Faltoniae Probae, Amnios Pincios Aniciosque decoranti." See Lendon (1997), pp. 45–46 and note 76, citing as evidence Sid. Ap. *Ep.* 2.8.3 and *HA Aelius* 5.11.

227. These elements of womanly behavior are frequently cited by authors urging asceticism; cf. Jer. *Ep.* 77.2, 127.3 (*CSEL* 55.38 and 56.147).

228. Amm. Marc. 14.6.16.

229. On Paulina, see note 255 below. On women priests, see Chapter 5.

230. Aug. *Sol.* 1.10.17 (*PL* 32.878); see also John Chrys. *De Virg.* 58 (*PG* 48.579–580).

231. Suet. *Aug.* 44; presumably, this practice continued into the fourth century. On women at public baths, see Jerome *Ep.* 77.4 (*CSEL* 55.40–42).

232. See G. Clark (1993), pp. 120–126, on inferiority; A. Arjava, *Women and Law in Late Antiquity* (Oxford, 1996), pp. 76–156.

233. See, for example, John Chrys. *De Virg.* 57 (*PG* 48.577–579).

234. G. Nathan, *The Family in Late Antiquity* (London, 2000), pp. 17–20.

235. Amm. Marc. 14.6.17; P. Veyne, "The Roman Empire," in *A History of Private Life*, vol. 1, ed. P. Veyne (Cambridge, Mass., 1987), pp. 72ff.

236. John Chrys. *De non iter. coniugio* 4 (*PG* 48.615–616); Ambrose *De vid.* 9.58 (*PL* 16.252).

237. See, for example, Paul. of Nola *Ep.* 44.4 (*CSEL* 29.372–376). Aper gave control of his estate to his wife, Amanda.

238. John Chrys. *De Virg.* 75.3 (*PG* 48.588–589).
239. Cf. G. Nathan (2000), pp. 15–27; 185–187. Although Nathan, p. 19, sees wives as valued for their managerial role, his evidence indicates only an appreciation for their frugality.
240. K. Bradley, "The Nurse and the Child at Rome," *Thamyris* 1(2) (1994), pp. 137–156; G. Clark (1993), p. 19 and note 6.
241. Jer. *Ep.* 14.3 (*CSEL* 54.47–49) suggests that the relative physical distance of aristocratic mothers might lead to a certain degree of psychological removal, leaving the nurse or tutor to fill the vacant emotional space; cf. K. Bradley (1994), pp. 137–156.
242. On women as guardians, see A. Arjava (1996), pp. 84–94, who cites the law of Theodosius (*C.Th.* 3.17.4 [390]) and notes that there is disagreement as to whether this law is an innovation or whether Theodosius is placing a restriction (i.e., vowing not to remarry) on a preexisting law that allowed widows to gain guardianship over minor children. See also R. Saller, "Men's Age at Marriage and Its Consequences in the Roman Family," *CP* 82 (1987), pp. 21–34; G. Nathan (2000), pp. 155–158.
243. Symm. *Ep.* 1.2.5, vv.1–2: "Cuius opes aut nobilitas aut tanta potestas, / Cedenti cui non praeluxerit Amnius unus?"
244. Ibid., *Ep.* 1.2.5, vv.3–4: "cunctisque adcommodus idem / Hic et carus erat, conferre iuvare paratus"; cf. 2.3.3, vv.3–4.
245. Ibid., *Ep.* 1.2.5, vv.5–6: "illis / Grandior, aeterno conplebat nomine Romam."
246. Amnius Anicius Iulianus 23, *PLRE* 1.473–474, is plausibly identified as the son of Anicius Faustus 6, *PLRE* 1.329, urban prefect in 299–300 and twice consul. Amnius Anicius Iulianus' son, Amnius Manius Caesonius Nicomachus Anicius Paulinus Junior signo Honorius = Paulinus 14, *PLRE* 1.679, was urban prefect in 334–335, consul in 334, and was honored by the people and senate of Rome with a gilded statue (*CIL* 6.1683 = D. 1221). As this son's names indicate, the Anicii married well.
247. Symm. *Ep.* 1.2.4, vv.1–3; Paul. of Nola *Carm.* 21.218–224 (*CSEL* 30.165); Rut. Nam. 1.271–272.
248. Jacques (1986), pp. 131–133; P. Bruggisser (1993), pp. 102–107.
249. Symm. *Ep.* 1.2.4, vv.4–5.
250. Cf. Näf (1995), pp. 276–295.
251. *CIL* 6.1756.4–5 ("dives opum clarusque genus praecelsus honore / Fascibus inlustris, consule dignus avo"), trans. Croke and Harries (1982), p. 117.
252. Sid. Ap. *Ep.* 8.7.3, trans. W. B. Anderson (*LCL*), pp. 435–437.
253. *CIL* 6.1751 = D. 1265 ("nobilitatis culmini, litterarum et eloquentiae lumini, auctoritatis exemplo, provisionum ac dispositionum magistro, humanitatis auctori, moderationis patrono"), trans. Croke and Harries (1982), pp. 115–116.
254. Sid. Ap. *Ep.* 4.1.1 and 4.4.1; Mathisen (1993), pp. 14–16. For the classical background to this concept, see C. White, *Christian Friendship in the Fourth Century* (Cambridge, U.K., 1992), pp. 1–43.

255. *CIL* 6.2145 = *D.* 1259.7–8 ("pietate matris, coniugali gratia, nexu sororis, filiae modestia"), trans. Croke and Harries (1982), pp. 106–107.
256. Sid. Ap. *Ep.* 2.8.3, trans. W. B. Anderson *(LCL),* p. 449.
257. Lendon (1997), pp. 45–47.
258. John Chrys. *De non iter. coniugio* 5 (*PG* 48.616–617).
259. J. Scheid, "The Priest," *The Romans,* ed. A. Giardina, trans. L. G. Cochrane (Chicago, 1993), pp. 68ff. On public rites, see Festus 284L; Macrobius *Sat.* 1.16.4–10. For the provinces, see *D.* 6087 = *FIRA* 1.177–198, the Urso Charter from Spain; and J. B. Rives, *Religion and Authority in Roman Carthage from Augustus to Constantine* (New York, 1995), pp. 29–40.
260. R. MacMullen, "Women in Public in the Roman Empire," *Historia* 29 (1980), reprinted in MacMullen, *Changes in the Roman Empire: Essays on the Ordinary* (Princeton, 1990), p. 166.
261. *CIL* 6.1690= *D.* 1240; *CIL* 6.1691 and 6.1693 = *D.* 1241. These record the Roman corporations of swine drivers and slaughterers and the people of Puteoli as Proculus' clients; cf. Symm. *Ep.* 1.2.4, vv.1–2.
262. Aug. *Ep.* 16.1 (*CSEL* 34.1, .37): "At vero nostrae urbis forum salutarium numinum frequentia possessum nos cernimus et probamus." Cf. Nectarius of Calama's letter to Augustine, *Ep.* 103.2 (*CSEL* 34.2.579), and Aug. *Ep.* 90, 91, 103, 104, discussed by C. Lepelley, *Les cités de l'Afrique romaine au bas-empire* (Paris, 1979–1981), p. 358.
263. Symm. *Rel.* 3.3: "repetimus igitur religionum statum, qui reip. diu profuit . . . quis ita familiaris est barbaris, ut aram Victoriae non requirat!" See also *Rel.* 3.5, .9, .18.
264. Macr. *Sat.* 3.13.1; R. Gordon, "The Veil of Power," in *Pagan Priests: Religion and Power in the Ancient World* (Ithaca, N.Y., 1990), p. 223 and note 65; G. Wissowa, *Religion und Kultus der Römer* (Munich, 1912), p. 474.
265. Jones (1964, 1986 reprint), pp. 537–538; Olymp. *Frag.* 44, in *FHG* 4.67–68. In some cities, as the Urso Charter from Spain indicates (note 259 above), the state stipulated the minimum amount the presiding magistrate paid but he or the city could augment that; see also J. H. W. G. Liebeschuetz, *Antioch: City and Imperial Administration in the Late Roman Empire* (Oxford, 1972), p. 146.
266. For spending restictions, see, for example, *C.Th.* 6.4.24, .25. In 354 Constantius ordered all senators who were due to give games to return to Rome. *C.Th.* 6.4.4 (354); 6.4.7 (354); 6.4.18 (365); cf. 6.4.1 (329–330). A. H. M. Jones (1964, 1986 reprint), p. 537, note 37, follows O. Seeck (1883) and argues (on the basis of Symm. *Or.* 8.2 and *Rel.* 8) that the poorest senators at Rome might be let off with only the quaestorian games; at Constantinople, Constantius required only praetorian games (*C.Th.* 6.4.5).
267. See the Urso Charter from Spain, *D.* 6087 = *FIRA* 1.177–198; J. B. Rives (1995), pp. 30–31; A. Chastagnol, *Le Sénat romain sous le règne d'Odoacre: Recherches sur l'épigraphie du Colisée au Ve siècle (Antiquitas* R.3, B.3) (Bonn, 1966), pp. 1ff.; R. Gordon (1990), p. 228; J. Scheid (1993), pp. 61ff.

268. *CIL* 6.45 = *D.* 3222. I take "aedem providit" as a temple dedication rather than mere maintenance; as urban prefect Praetextatus also restored the Portico of the Consenting Gods in Rome. See B. Nieddu, "Il portico degli Dei Consenti," *Bolletino D'Arte* 71 (1986), pp. 37–52. *C.Th.* 15.1.1–53 are addressed to governors; see Y. Janvier, *La législation du bas-empire sur les édifices publics* (Aix-en-Provence, 1969), pp. 1ff.

269. L. Cornelius Scipio Orfitus, presumably an ancestor, had dedicated an altar to Sol/Sarapis earlier in the century in Rome; *CIL* 6.402 = *D.* 4396. Proculus 11, *PLRE* 1.747–749, as proconsul restored the temple of Magna Mater and Attis in Carthage: *CIL* 8.24521. His family may have had ties to this cult.

270. *Carmen contra paganos* 112–114, ed. D. R. Shackleton-Bailey, *Anthologia Latina* 1.1 (Leipzig, 1982), pp. 17–23. B. Ward-Perkins, *From Classical Antiquity to the Middle Ages: Urban Public Building in Northern and Central Italy.* A.D. *300–850* (Oxford, 1984), views the building of temples by individuals as rare after 300.

271. See, for example, the dedication of a statue to Venus by Tyrrania Anicia Iuliana, probably the aristocratic Iuliana 3, *PLRE* 1.468. For wills, see Symm. *Rel* 3.13; for temple maintenance, see *Dig.* 50.4.18.10. See also J. B. Rives (1995), p. 37.

272. R. Gordon (1990), p. 224.

273. J. North, "The Development of Religious Pluralism," in *The Jews among Pagans and Christians,* ed. J. Lieu, J. North, and T. Rajak (1992), pp. 174–193, on voluntary religious acts; see also J. B. Rives (1995), pp. 181ff.

274. See R. Duthoy, *The Taurobolium: Evolution and Terminology* (Leiden, 1969), notes 1–34, for aristocrats. For the costly bull sacrifice, see also Salzman (1990), pp. 167–169. Cost may have been a factor in what some scholars have seen as a decline in blood sacrifice in the eastern empire of the fourth century; see S. Bradbury, "Julian's Pagan Revival and Blood Sacrifice," *Phoenix* 49 (1995), pp. 331–356.

275. N. McLynn, "The Fourth Century *Taurobolium,*" *Phoenix* 50 (3–4) (1996), pp. 312–330.

276. *C.Th.* 16.10.20; Aug. *Civ. Dei* 2.4, 7.26.

277. Aur. Victor Augentius 2, *PLRE* 1.125, and his sons, Tamesius Olympius Augentius 1, *PLRE* 1.124–125, and Aemilianus Corfo Olympius 14, *PLRE* 1.646.

278. Cf. Paulina and Praetextatus, *CIL* 6.1779 = *D.* 1259.

279. P. Athanassiadi-Fowden, *Julian and Hellenism* (Oxford, 1981), p. 184; D. Bowder, *The Age of Constantine and Julian* (London, 1978), p. 228; J. B. Rives (1995), pp. 173–249; D. Ladage, *Staatische Priester und Kultämter im lateinischen Westen des Imperium Romanum zur Kaiserzeit* (Köln, 1971), pp. 121–125.

280. F. Jacques, *Le privilège de liberté: Politique impériale et autonomie municipale dans les cités de l'*Occident romain *(161–244)* (Rome, 1984), p. 36, note 38, cites G. Barbieri, *L'albo senatorio da Settimio Severo a Carino (193–285)* (Rome, 1952), pp. 479ff; see also Jacques (1986), p. 121.

281. See G. Halsberghe, *The Cult of Sol Invictus* (Leiden, 1972), p. 163, note 1, for

dated inscriptions of priests of the cult of Sol, many of whom were aristocrats, such as *CIL* 6.1778 (387 C.E.). For *pontifex Solis* associated with a family, see T. Flavius Postumius Titianus 9 and Celsinus Titianus 5, *PLRE* 1.919–920 and 1.917–918, respectively; and Rufius Caeionius Sabinus 13, *PLRE* 1.793, associated with the family of C. C(a)eionius Rufius Volusianus signo Lampadius 5, *PLRE* 1.978–980.

282. Firm. Mat. *Mathesis* 2.30.2–7. The author is discussed under Maternus 2, *PLRE* 1.567–568.

283. Firm. Mat. *Mathesis* 3.7.19.

284. A. Chastagnol, *L'Album municipal de Timgad* (Bonn, 1978). H. Horstkotte, "Heidnische Priesterämter und Dekurionat im vierten Jahrhundert n. Chr.," in *Religion und Gesellschaft in der römischen Kaiserzeit*, ed. W. Eck (Cologne, 1989), pp. 165–184, sees some local variation. *C.Th.* 12.1.75 (371) assures privileges.

285. *CIL* 6.1779 = *D.* 1259, Rome.

286. Orosius 7.42.8 (*CSEL* 5.557); see note 287 below.

287. Symm. *Ep.* 1.51. D. Vera, *Commento storico alle Relationes di Quinto Aurelio Simmaco* (Pisa, Italy, 1981), p. 28, doubts this unwillingness was widespread.

288. Attacks on pagan priests were seen as a sign of vitality by R. Dodaro, "*Christus sacerdos:* Augustine's Preaching against Pagan Priests in the Light of S. Dolbeau 26 and 23," in *Augustin Prédicateur (395–411), Actes du Colloque International de Chantilly*, ed. G. Madec (Paris, 1998), pp. 373–379.

289. R. J. A. Talbert (1984), p. 72; Amm. Marc. 16.10.5.

290. S. MacCormack, *Art and Ceremony in Late Antiquity* (Berkeley, Calif., 1981), pp. 106–109; L. Cracco Ruggini, "Apoteosis e politica senatoria nel IV secolo d.c.," *Rivista storica italiana* 89 (1979), p. 431.

291. Tacitus *Ann.* 1.76, 2.86, 4.16, 6.12, 15.44; Gell. 1.12.12. These duties probably continued into the fourth century. See Rut. Nam. 2.52, .55; J. Geffcken, *The Last Days of Greco-Roman Paganism*, trans. and with updated notes by S. MacCormack (Amsterdam, 1978), pp. 226–227.

292. A. Chastagnol (1978), pp. 100–101, and *D.* 6122; J. B. Rives (1995), pp. 39ff.

293. Loss of prestige may explain two violent outbursts against Christians in Africa involving local elites, ca. 399 and 408; see C. Lepelley (1979–1981), pp. 355ff., and Aug. *Ep.* 50 (*CSEL* 34.2.143).

294. Stark (1996), pp. 55–59.

3. Aristocratic Men: Social Origins

1. The basis for membership in the fourth-century nobility is disputed, but family pedigree was still of great import; see Chapters 2 and 7, and Schlinkert, (1996), pp. 177–188, pp. 220–233.

2. The late empire's definition of *novus homo* differs from that of the principate, yet the term is of use; see Chapter 2.

3. Jacques (1986), pp. 131–133.

4. Although these titles were somewhat fluid in the early fourth century, at-

tempts to stabilize and correlate them to fixed offices especially under Valentinian I led to a more rigid system of titulature. See Chapter 2; Jones (1964, 1986 reprint), pp. 528–530.

5. See, for example, Barnes (1995), pp. 135–147, and MacMullen (1984), pp. 29–33.

6. Men. Rhet. *Treatise* 369.17–371.3, ed. D. A. Russell and N. G. Wilson (Oxford, 1981); Näf, (1995), pp. 278–283.

7. Symm. *Ep.* 6.52; Flavius Mallius Theodorus, App. 2 (of this book) = Theodorus 27, *PLRE* 1.900–902.

8. Maternus Cynegius, App. 2 = Cynegius 3, *PLRE* 1.235–236.

9. Petronius Probianus 3, *PLRE* 1.733–734, consul in 322 and urban prefect in 329–331. If his daughter is Faltonia Betitia Proba 2, *PLRE* 1.732, then she wed the aristocratic Clodius Celsinus signo Adelphius 6, *PLRE* 1.192–193, urban prefect of 351. Probianus' grandson, Sextus Claudius Petronius Probus 5, *PLRE* 1.736–740, wed Anicia Faltonia Proba 3, *PLRE* 1.732–733. For family property, see *CIL* 6.1751 = *D.* 1265: "Veneti adque Histri peculiares eius"; *HA Probus* 24.1–2.

10. A. Giardina, "Review of J. Matthews, *Western Imperial Aristocracies and Imperial Court* A.D. *364–425*," in *Dialoghi di archeologia* 9–10 (1976–1977), pp. 670–671; Matthews (1975), pp. 25–28.

11. See Chapter 2, notes 76 and 77. Moreover, provincial senators could celebrate their games in absentia; see *C.Th.* 6.4.2 (327 c.e.), 6.4.7 (354), and 6.4.18 (365). The codes of 340 and 354 state that senators were once more expected to come to Rome to furnish games; see *C.Th.* 6.4.6 (340), 6.4.4 and 6.4.7 (354); cf. 6.2.16 (395). However, this was not always the case; see *C.Th.* 6.4.11 (357).

12. *C.J.* 12.1.15; cf. *C.Th.* 6.2.16 (395).

13. Arnheim (1972), pp. 152–154; Jones (1964, 1986 reprint), p. 553. R. J. A. Wilson, *Sicily under the Roman Empire* (Wiltshire, England 1990), pp. 234–236, adds archaeological evidence from Sicily to support the view that senatorial aristocrats built more lavish country estates and spent more time on their provincial properties. For Gaul, see K. F. Stroheker, *Der senatorische Adel im spätantiken Gallien* (Darmstadt, 1970 reprint), pp. 38ff.; and Matthews, (1975), pp. 77–80, 349–351.

14. G. Wissowa, *Religion und Kultus der Römer,* 2d ed. (Munich, 1912), pp. 262ff.; P. Merlat, *Jupiter Dolichenus* (Paris, 1960); and J. Geffcken, *The Last Days of Greco-Roman Paganism* (Amsterdam, 1978), pp. 10–11 (translation by S. MacCormack of *Der Ausgang des griechisch-römischen Heidentums,* 1929). Similarly, Diana was assimilated with Hecate, with the Celtic Arduinna, and with Abnoba from the Black Forest; J. Geffcken, p. 10, note 114. See also MacMullen, (1981), pp. 3ff., 113ff.; J. B. Rives, *Religion and Authority in Roman Carthage from Augustus to Constantine* (New York, 1995), pp. 4–13.

15. See for northern Italy, Martin Connell, "The Liturgical Year in Northern Italy (365–450)," (Ph.D. dissertation, University of Notre Dame, 1994), pp. 1–21, 285–307.

16. Aug. *Conf.* 6.2.

17. Salzman (1990), pp. 116–131.

18. Symm. *Rel.* 3.7.

19. Libanius *Or.* 30.33–34.

20. Barnes (1995), pp. 134–138, lists scholars who take this view, as did von Haehling (1978), p. 611; Averil Cameron, *The Later Roman Empire* (Cambridge, Mass., 1993), p. 157; Alan Cameron and J. Long, *Barbarians and Politics at the Court of Arcadius* (Berkeley, 1993), p. 14; J. Geffcken (1978 trans.), pp. 117ff., 124, 225–248; and H. D. Altendorf, "Römische Senatsaristokratie und Christentum am Ende des 4. Jahrhunderts," *Kirchengeschichte als Missionsgeschichte*, vol. 1 (Munich, 1974), pp. 227–243.

21. Symm. *Rel.* 3. For bibliography, see Croke and Harries (1982), pp. 80ff. Gratian's edict is referred to in *C.Th.* 16.10.20 (415). N. McLynn, *Ambrose of Milan: Church and Court in a Christian Capital* (Berkeley, 1994), pp. 151–152, believes Ambrose's claim that he was not responsible for the measures and proposes Christian careerists instead.

22. Symm. *Rel.* 3.1–2.

23. Ambr. *Ep.* 72[17] and 73[18] (*CSEL* 82.3.11–53); Prud. *C. Symm.*, Books 1 and 2. See also Salzman (1990), p. 233.

24. Matthews (1975), pp. 210–211.

25. J. J. O'Donnell, "The Demise of Paganism," *Traditio* 35 (1979), pp. 43–88.

26. Ambr. *Ep.* 10[57].6 (*CSEL* 82.3.205–211); Paul. of Milan, *V. Ambrosii* 26 (*PL* 14.38).

27. J. J. O'Donnell (1979), pp. 137–140.

28. E. Türk, "Les 'Saturnales' de Macrobe, source de Servius Danielis," *REL* 41 (1963), p. 348; the quotation is from the introduction to *Macrobius: The Saturnalia*, trans. P. V. Davies (New York, 1969), p. 4.

29. Alan Cameron, "The Date and Identity of Macrobius," *JRS* 56 (1966), pp. 25–38.

30. See von Haehling (1978), pp. 610–613, who discusses the active careers of Roman pagan aristocrats.

31. Symm. *Rel.* 3.5, trans. Croke and Harries (1982), p. 36.

32. Salzman (1990), pp. 184–188.

33. Averil Cameron (1993), p. 156.

34. Amm. Marc. 28.1.23; cf. 28.1.52. On fears about attacking nobility, cf. A. Alföldi, *A Conflict of Ideas in the Late Roman Empire* (Oxford, 1952), pp. 48–95.

35. G. Clemente, "Cristianesimo e classi dirigenti prima e dopo Costantino," in *Mondo classico e cristianesimo* (Atti del Convegno su "Mondo greco-romano e cristianesimo") (Rome, 1982), pp. 51–64.

36. P. Bruggisser, *Symmaque ou le rituel épistolaire de l'amitié littéraire: recherches sur le premier livre de la correspondance* (Freibourg, Switzerland, 1993), pp. 102–107; D. Vera, *Commento storico alle Relationes di Quinto Aurelio Simmaco* (Pisa, 1981), pp. 81, 85; L. Cracco-Ruggini, *Simboli di battaglia ideologica nel tardo ellenismo* (Pisa, 1972), pp. 70–71.

37. C. C(a)eionius Rufius Volusianus, urban prefect 313–315, App. 2 = Volusianus 4, *PLRE* 1.976–978; C. C(a)eionius Rufius Volusianus signo Lampadius, App. 2 = Volusianus 5, *PLRE* 1.978–980; his son C(a)eionius Rufius Volusianus, App. 2 = Volusianus 3, *PLRE* 1.976; his daughter, Rufia Volusiana, App. 2 = *PLRE* 1.975; Petronius Apollodorus, App. 2 = *PLRE* 1.84. I have adopted the convention of spelling C(a)eionius for members of the same family since variations in spelling this name (with or without the *a*) appear in documents and inscriptions. Cf. A. Chastagnol, "Le sénateur Volusien et la conversion d'une famille de l'aristocratie au Bas-Empire," *REA* 58 (1956), pp. 241–253; Matthews (1975), pp. 25–30. N. McLynn, "The Fourth-Century *Taurobolium*," *Phoenix* 50 (3–4) (1996), pp. 312–330, sees in this cult's popularity a polemical position.

38. Provenance and landholdings were based on the provinces of the *Notitia Dignitatum;* see Jones (1964, 1986 reprint), vol. 2, Map II (at pp. 1069–1070) and Appendix 3. I grouped aristocrats from Italy into areas, separating Rome and its environs from Italia Suburbicaria (which included southern Italy, Sicily, Sardinia, and Corsica) and from Italy north of Rome, Tuscia and Umbria. I combined these groups in Table 3.1.

39. A. H. M. Jones, "Ancient Empires and the Economy: Rome," in *The Roman Economy: Studies in Ancient Economic and Administrative History,* ed. P. Brunt (Oxford, 1974), p. 137; Jones (1964, 1986 reprint), pp. 554–557; Matthews (1975), pp. 25–28.

40. *Expositio Totius Mundi et Gentium,* in R. Valentini and G. Zuchetti, *Codice topographico della città di Roma,* vol. 1 (1942) p. 265: "Colunt autem et deos ex parte Iovem et Solem."

41. Matthews (1975), pp. 25–31. See L. Harmand, *Le Patronat sur les collectivités publiques* (Paris, 1957), pp. 304–305; Jens-Uwe Krause, *Spätantike Patronatsformen im Westen des römischen Reiches* (Munich, 1987), pp. 25ff.

42. Nicomachus Flavianus, App. 2 = Flavianus 14, *PLRE* 1.345–347, was probably a pagan; see App. 2. For patron of Naples, see *D.* 8985.

43. Anicius Auchenius Bassus, App. 2 = Bassus 11, *PLRE* 1.152–154; for his career, see *CIL* 6.1679 = *D.* 1262.

44. Matthews (1975), p. 26; Symm. *Ep.* 1.51 suggests property in Etruria. For the governorship of Vettius Agorius Praetextatus, see *CIL* 6.1777–1779 = *D.* 1258–1259; for that of the man identified by *PLRE* as his father, C. Vettius Cossinius Rufinus, see *D.* 1217; both are in Appendix 2.

45. Ovinius Gallicanus, App. 2, and Sextus Anicius Paulinus, App. 2 = Paulinus 15, *PLRE* 1.679–680. See D. M. Novak, "Constantine and the Senate: An Early Phase of the Christianization of the Roman Aristocracy," *Ancient Society* 10 (1979), p. 293.

46. Barnes (1995), pp. 135–147. My assessment of pagan and Christian high office holders differs from that of T. D. Barnes in part because his statistics are based on inconsistent criteria for religious affiliation and hypothesized family ties; see Appendix 1.

47. Brown (1961), pp. 1–11.
48. Three were from Rome: Q. Clodius Hermogenianus Olybrius, App. 2 = Olybrius 3, *PLRE* 1.640–642; Iunius Bassus signo Theotecnius, App. 2 = Bassus 15, *PLRE* 1.155; N(a)eratius Cerealis, App. 2 = Cerealis 2, *PLRE* 1.197–199. Sextus Claudius Petronius Probus = Probus 5, *PLRE* 1.736–740, was from Verona.
49. K. Rosen, "Ein Wanderer zwischen zwei Welten: *Carmen ad quendam senatorem ex Christiana religione ad idolorum servitutem conversum*," in *Klassisches Altertum, Spätantike und frühes Christentum: Adolf Lippold zum 65. Geburtstag gewidmet*, ed. K. Dietz, D. Hennig, and H. Kaletsch (Würzburg, 1993), pp. 393–408, cites Aug. *Conf.* 8.2.3.
50. Matthews (1975), p. 206, cites Ambr. *Ep.* 72[17].10 (*CSEL* 82.3.15–16); von Haehling (1978), pp. 569–575.
51. Jer. *Ep.* 66.4 to Pammachius (379 C.E.), trans. W. H. Fremantle *(NPNF)*, pp. 135–136.
52. Brown (1988), pp. 342–345.
53. G. Clemente (1982), pp. 51–64.
54. MacMullen (1984), pp. 81–83.
55. A. Marcone, "La fine del paganesimo a Roma: per un'interpretazione politica," in *Studi offerti ad Anna Maria Quartiroli e Domenico Magnino* (Pavia, 1987), pp. 53–59.
56. S. Mazzarino, "La conversione del Senato," in *Il basso impero: Antico, tardoantico ed èra costantiniana*, vol. 1, ed. S. Mazzarino (Rome, 1974), pp. 378–397.
57. Von Haehling (1978), pp. 571–575. My study included women and Roman aristocrats who did not hold high office or held only low office, and did not include eastern high-office-holding aristocrats. Hence my study population is significantly different from that gathered by von Haehling and from my earlier work, Salzman (1992), pp. 451–479.
58. L. Turcius Secundus = Secundus 5, *PLRE* 1.817; his son was L. Turcius Apronianus, App. 2 = Apronianus 9, *PLRE* 1.88, and was probably pagan. The latter's sons, L. Turcius Secundus signo Asterius, App. 2 = Secundus 6, *PLRE* 1.817–818, and L. Turcius Apronianus signo Asterius, App. 2 = Apronianus 10, *PLRE* 1.88–89, certainly were pagan; *CIL* 6.1768 = *D.* 1229; *CIL* 6.3118.
59. Amm. Marc. 23.1.4.
60. *CIL* 6.1772 = *D.* 1230. For the *correctores* of Flaminia-Picenum, see *PLRE* 1.1094; and for ties to aristocrats, see G. Cecconi, *Governo imperiale e élites dirigenti nell'Italia tardoantica* (Como, 1994), pp. 51–67.
61. The man is Turcius Secundus, App. 2 = Secundus 4, *PLRE* 1.817; see Proiecta, App. 2 = *PLRE* 1.750, for the chest.
62. *ILCV* 3446, Rome; I follow the dating of Alan Cameron, "The Date and Owners of the Esquiline Treasure," *AJA* 85 (1985), pp. 135–145, not that of K. Shelton, "The Esquiline Treasure: The Nature of the Evidence," *AJA* 89 (1989), pp. 147–155.
63. Turcius Apronianus, App. 2 = Apronianus 8, *PLRE* 1.87.
64. *Hist. Laus.* 54.4; his wife was Avita, App. 2 = *PLRE* 1.126.

65. Fl. Turcius Rufius Apronianus Asterius = Asterius 11, *PLRE* 2.173–174.
66. See Matthews (1975), pp. 182, 183ff., for bibliography.
67. Jer. *Chron.* (374 C.E.) (*GCS* 47.247).
68. R. Lizzi, "Ambrose's Contemporaries and the Christianization of Northern Italy," *JRS* 80 (1990), pp. 156–173; p. 162, note 37, cites Zeno *Tract.* 1.25.10 (*CC* 22.75).
69. R. Lizzi (1990), p. 173; ibid., pp. 166–173, cites, for example, Max. Taur. *Sermo* 107.32–40 (*CC* 23.420).
70. Jones (1964, 1986 reprint), vol. 2, Map II (at pp. 1069–1070). No aristocrats from Britanniae are in this database; one British *clarissima* (*ILCV* 185) and one British *clarissimus* (Gerontius, *PLRE* 2.508) are attested but both lacked evidence for religious affiliation.
71. H. Horstkotte, "Heidnische Priestämter und Dekurionat im Vierten Jahrhundert nach Chr.," in *Religion und Gesellschaft in der römischen Kaiserzeit*, ed. W. Eck (Kolen, Vienna, 1989), pp. 165–183; cf. *C.Th.* 12.1.21 (335) and 12.1.77 (372). Horstkotte's argument that priesthoods did not bring entrance into the curia is only possibly demonstrated for Antioch and not for other areas in the West, which he admits are different.
72. See note 162 below Cf. Ausonius, a Gaul and a new man, who tried to build ties to aristocrats in Rome, to men like Symmachus and Sextus Petronius Probus; see Sivan (1993), pp. 113–115; Aus. *Ep.* 12.
73. Jones (1964, 1986 reprint), p. 378; F. D. Martino, *Storia della costituzione romana* 5 (Naples, 1967), p. 332; A. Giardina (1976–1977), p. 674.
74. K. Hopkins, "Elite Mobility in the Roman Empire," *Past and Present* 32 (1965), pp. 23–24.
75. See Chapter 2, note 48.
76. Jones (1964, 1986 reprint), pp. 140–144, 528–529, 541; A. Chastagnol, "Les modes de recrutement du sénat au IVe siècle après J. C.," *Recherches sur les structures sociales dans l'antiquité classique*, ed. C. Nicolet (Paris, 1970), pp. 194–206.
77. *Pan. Lat.* 10[4].35.2.
78. Salvian, *De Gub. Dei* 8.2.12 (*CSEL* 8. 195–196).
79. Aug. *Conf.* 8.2.
80. Apollinaris, App. 2 = Apollinaris 1, *PLRE* 2.113. Felix, who served the pagan Julian, was apparently so influenced by that emperor that he converted from Christianity to paganism; Felix, App. 2 = Felix 3, *PLRE* 1.332. His origins are unknown.
81. See, for example, J. B. Rives (1995), p. 176, on Carthage.
82. D. Fishwick, *The Imperial Cult in the Latin West* (Leiden, 1987), p. 93 (*Études préliminaires aux religions orientales dans l'empire romain* 108); J. B. Rives (1995), pp. 86ff.
83. Salzman (1990), pp. 131–146; A. Chastagnol, N. Duval, L. Cerfaux, and J. Tondriau, *Un concurrent du christianisme: Le culte des souverains dans la civilisation gréco-romaine* (Tournaie, 1957), pp. 379ff. See also I. Gradel, *Heavenly Honors: Roman Emperor Worship, Caesar to Constantine* (Oxford, forthcoming).
84. Cf. J. B. Rives (1995), p. 98.

85. *CIL* 11.5265; not until 386 did emperors prohibit Christians from holding the chief priesthoods of the imperial cult, but even after that date, and continuing into the mid-fifth century, Christian provincials continued to hold the flaminate and lower imperial cult priesthoods, as did the Christian Astius Vindicianus, App. 2 = Vindicianus 3, *PLRE* 1.968. See also A. Chastagnol and N. Duval, "Les survivances du culte impérial dans l'Afrique Nord à l'époque Vandale," *Mélanges à W. Seston* (Paris, 1974), pp. 89–118.

86. Sivan (1993), p. 11, note 43; J. F. Drinkwater, *The Gallic Empire* (Stuttgart, 1987) and *Roman Gaul* (London, 1983), p. 202.

87. In W. Held's survey of fourth-century Gallic nobles, forty-three out of sixty-nine, or more than 60%, held either state or provincial offices. "Die gallische Aristokratie im 4. Jahrhundert hinsichtlich ihrer Siedlungsstandorte und ihrer zentralen Stellung zur römischen Provinzial bzw. Zentraladministration," *Klio* 58 (1976), pp. 121–140. Although I do not agree with Held's attribution of Gallic origins in all cases, his survey is still useful. Cf. Matthews (1975), pp. 32ff.

88. Sivan (1993), p. 14.

89. M. Labrousse, *Toulouse antique* (Paris, 1968), pp. 567–572; C. Stancliffe, *St. Martin and His Hagiographer* (Oxford, 1983), pp. 3–6; "Gallula Roma Arelas," Aus. *Ordo* 10.

90. Saturninius Secundus Salutius, App. 2 = Secundus 3, *PLRE* 1.814–817; Julian *Or.* 8.252A–B.

91. See Flavius Bauto, App. 2 = *PLRE* 1.159–160, and Flavius Richomeres, App. 2 = *PLRE* 1.765–766, for the careers of each.

92. This study includes only those for whom we have evidence of family origin; many other aristocrats lived, died, and even owned property in Gaul, but such activity does not necessarily indicate family origin. For example, Crispinus 4, *PLRE* 1.233, governor of an unknown province in 353, may have belonged to a family who held land in Gaul, but that does not prove that his family is of Gallic origin; W. Held (1976), p. 137, and M. Heinzelmann, "Gallische Prosopographie 260–527," *Francia* 10 (1982), p. 588, however, call him Gallic. See also Sivan (1993), p. 14.

93. Von Haehling (1978), p. 611.

94. See Chapter 6, Table 6.2. See also von Haehling (1978), pp. 569–570.

95. W. Held (1976), pp. 121–140.

96. Claudius Postumus Dardanus, App. 2 = Dardanus, *PLRE* 2.346–347. His brother, Lepidus, also benefited from imperial proximity and Dardanus' success; Cl(audius) Lepidus, App. 2 = *PLRE* 2.675. Dardanus' wife was Naevia Galla, App. 2 = Galla 6, *PLRE* 2.491. Dardanus probably acquired his training from good Gallic professors, like those cited by Aus. *Professores;* see also K. Hopkins, "Social Mobility in the Later Roman Empire: The Evidence of Ausonius," *CQ* 11 (1961), pp. 239–249.

97. Sid. Ap. *Ep.* 3.12.5: "ruris militiae forique cultor." See also J. Harries, *Sidonius Apollinaris and the Fall of Rome* (Oxford, 1992), pp. 26–28; Matthews (1975), pp. 307–313; Apollinaris, App. 2 = Apollinaris 1, *PLRE* 2.113.

98. W. Held (1976), p. 139; Sivan (1993), pp. 18–20. We cannot be certain how

many Gallic aristocrats served earlier, nor do we know how many of these men were new to the aristocracy. But the increased number of Gallic aristocrats after 350 indicates the advantages of proximity to a resident imperial court where legal and rhetorical skills were most needed; see F. D. Martino (1967), p. 332; A. Giardina (1976–1977), p. 674.

99. Jer. *Chron.* (*GCS* 47.230); N. Gauthier, *L'évangélisation des pays de la Moselle, IIIe-VIIIe siècles* (Paris, 1980), pp. 81–110.

100. Amm. Marc. 21.2.5

101. These areas were home not only to the Christian Sulpicius Severus but also to Ausonius and Ausonius' relations, including his son Decimius Hilarianus Hesperius, App. 2 = Hesperius 2, *PLRE* 1.427–428, his wife Attusia Lucana Sabina, App. 2 = Sabina 5, *PLRE* 1.788–789, and a probable cousin (Magnus?) Arborius, App. 2 = Arborius 3, *PLRE* 1.97–99. Also from this area (and included in Appendix 2) were Flavius Rufinus 18, Meropius Pontius Paulinus 21 of Nola, and Claudius Lupicinus 5, patron of Maxima Senonia. Aquitaine was the home of aristocratic pagans as well, notably the orator Latinius Pacatus Drepanius, App. 2 = Drepanius, *PLRE* 1.272, and Saturninius Secundus Salutius, App. 2 = Secundus 3, *PLRE* 1.800.

102. Decimius Magnus Ausonius, App. 2 = Ausonius 7, *PLRE* 1.140–141; for his estate, see Aus. *Dom.* 1.

103. Meropius Pontius Paulinus of Nola, App. 2 = Paulinus 21, *PLRE* 1.681–683; Paul. of Nola, *Carm.* 10.93–96 (*CSEL* 30.28). See also Matthews (1975), pp. 56–87.

104. Therasia, App. 2 = *PLRE* 1.909; Aper and Amanda, Paul. of Nola *Ep.* 39, 44 (*CSEL* 29.334–339, .369–378). See D. Trout, *Paulinus of Nola* (Berkeley, 1999), pp. 59–60, 142–158.

105. K. F. Stroheker (1970 reprint), p. 69: "Der Umschwung vollzog sich in Gallien allerdings reibungsloser und unter weniger heftigen Zusammenstössen als etwa in Rom."

106. Protadius, App. 2 = Protadius 1, *PLRE* 1.751–752. Chastagnol (1962), pp. 235–255, asserted Protadius was pagan because of his interest in classical texts, noted by Symm. *Ep.* 4.17–34. Since such interests are not certain indicators of paganism, I omitted Protadius' two brothers, Florentius 2 and Minervius 2 in *PLRE* 1, because they are known as pagan by their cultural pursuits alone. But Symm. *Ep.* 4.18.2 states that Protadius celebrated the *natales canum dies* and *venatica festa*, holidays associated with the Ides of August and the Ambarvalia of Diana of Aricia (Stat. *Silv.* 3.1.57–58; Grat. *Cyn.* 484–485; Arrian, *Cyn.* 34). Celebrating these pagan rituals, which Ambrose (*De Nabuthae* 13.54, *CSEL* 32.2.499) decries, suggests that Protadius was probably pagan. Von Haehling (1978), p. 400, cites Rut. Nam. 1.542–558 as evidence for Protadius' paganism, but this passage only adds to the probability without making for certainty.

107. K. F. Stroheker (1970 reprint), pp. 69–71, noted that the grandfather of Sidonius Apollinaris converted ca. 400. For arguments against Gratian's influence as decisive, see W. Held (1976), pp. 121–140.

108. See R. Mathisen, *Ecclesiastical Factionalism and Religious Controversy in Fifth Century Gaul* (Washington, D.C., 1989), pp. 7–9, for bibliography; Van Dam (1985), especially p. 154 and Chapter 10; K. F. Stroheker (1970 reprint), p. 9. Sidonius Apollinaris tells of one family who chose to serve the church rather than the court. Sid. Ap. *Ep.* 7.2.3; R. von Haehling (1978), p. 613; Matthews (1975), pp. 56–87.

109. The numbers are small, but all thirteen Christians as compared to seven out of nine pagans are from the period 367–423.

110. Aristocrats like Paulinus of Nola respected Martin's religiosity, even if the story of the proconsul Taetradius' conversion at the hands of Martin is suspect; Sulp. Sev. *Mart.* 17 (*CSEL* 1.126–127).

111. Paul. of Nola *Ep.* 18.4 (*CSEL* 29.130–132).

112. C. Stancliffe (1983), p. 332.

113. W. Held (1976), pp. 121–140.

114. Gregory *Hist. Fr.* 1.31.

115. S. T. Loseby, "Arles in Late Antiquity: *Gallula Roma Arelas* and *Urbs Genesii*," in *Towns in Transition: Urban Evolution in Late Antiquity and the Early Middle Ages*, ed. N. Christie and S. T. Loseby (Aldershot, Hants, England, 1996), pp. 71–98; Sivan (1993), pp. 19–25.

116. Endelechius, "De mortibus boum," *Anth. Lat.* 1.2.893, ed. F. Buecheler and A. Riese (Leipzig, 1906), vv. 106–107: "Magnis qui colitur solus in urbibus,/ Christus." See also C. Stancliffe, "From Town to Country: The Christianisation of the Touraine 370–600," in *The Church in Town and Countryside: Studies in Church History*, vol. 16, ed. D. Baker (Oxford, 1979), pp. 43–59, but it is too optimistic to say that this was already the case by 360 as claimed by C. Stancliffe (1983), p. 5.

117. See J. Geffcken (1978 trans.), pp. 230–232, and Van Dam (1985), Chapter 7, for an overview of the problem.

118. W. Klingshirn, *Caesarius of Arles: Life, Testament, Letters* (Liverpool, 1994), pp. 201–244.

119. Matthews (1975), pp. 146ff.; Van Dam (1985), pp. 88–117; K. F. Stroheker, "Spanische Senatoren der spätrömischen und westgotischen Zeit," *Madrider Mitt.* 4 (1963), pp. 107–132; P. de Palol, "La conversion de l'aristocratie de la péninsule ibérique au IVe siècle," pp. 47–72, and M. C. Diáz y Diáz, "L'expansion du christianisme et les tensions épiscopales dans la péninsule ibérique," pp. 84–94, in *Miscellanea Historiae Ecclesiasticae* 6 (Brussels, 1983) (= *Bibl. de la revue d'histoire ecclésiastique* 6).

120. K. F. Stroheker (1963), pp. 107–132, often uses criteria for Spanish origin too loosely. See also A. Chastagnol, "Les Espagnols dans l'aristocratie gouvernementale à l'époque de Théodose," in *Les empereurs romains d'Espagne*, Colloque international du Centre National de la Recherche Scientifique (Madrid-Italica, 1964), pp. 269ff.; J. V. Masana, "El *ordo senatorius* en la *Hispania* de Teodosio," in *Actas Congreso Internacional: La Hispania de Teodosio*, vol. 1, ed. R. Teja and C. Pérez (Valladolid, Spain, 1997), pp. 293–306.

121. I. Rodà, "Hispania from the Second Century A.D. to Late Antiquity," in *The Archaeology of Iberia*, ed. M. Díaz-Andreu and S. Keay (London, 1997), pp. 219–227.

122. Acilius Severus, App. 2 = Severus 16, *PLRE* 1.834; and C. Vettius Aquilinus Iuvencus, App. 2 (Martindale, 1980, App. 3).

123. Marinianus, App. 2 = Marinianus 2, *PLRE* 1.559–560. Marinianus was a native of Gallaecia, now part of Portugal. Symm. *Ep.* 3.25. *PLRE* 1 ascribes paganism to Marinianus because he is identified with a vicar who favored the Priscillianist heretics. Sulp. Sev. *Chron.* 2.49 (*CSEL* 1.101–103). This is not compelling evidence, but Symmachus' assertion, *Ep.* 3.24.1, that the *iugales deos* joined Marinianus to a *materfamilias* and gave a child to them makes him a probable pagan, as is also proposed by J. V. Masana (1997), p. 301, note 3, on the evidence of *Ep.* 3.23.2.

124. See Nummius Aemilianus Dexter, App. 2 = Dexter 3, *PLRE* 1.251, for his career. He was the dedicatee of Jerome's *De Vir. Ill.* (*GCS* 14.1), but there is no reason to think that his father, the bishop Pacianus, was a *clarissimus*, as stated by I. Rodà, "Hispania," in *The Archaeology of Iberia*, ed. M. Díaz-Andreu and S. Keay (London, 1997), pp. 222–224.

125. Maternus Cynegius, App. 2 = Cynegius 3, *PLRE* 1.235–236; Lib. *Or.* 30.46. Cynegius' family status is unknown.

126. D. Fernández-Galiano, "The Villa of Maternus at Carranque," *Ancient Mosaics at Bath, 1987*, in *Journal of Roman Archaeology*, supplementary series, vol. 9(1) (Ann Arbor, Mich., 1994), pp. 119–227.

127. Aurelius Prudentius Clemens, App. 2 = Clemens 4, *PLRE* 1.214.

128. P. de Palol (1983), pp. 47–72.

129. See, for example, Matthews (1975), pp. 160–169, and Van Dam (1985), pp. 88ff.

130. *Conc. Caesaraug.* Canons 1–3, 7 (*PL* 84.315–317); Sulp. Sev. *Chron.* 2.24ff., 2.50 (*CSEL* 1.79–80). See also relevant texts in B. Vollmann, *Studien zum Priscillianismus: Die Forschung, die Quellen, der fünfzehnte Brief Pabst Leos des Grossen* (St. Ottilien, 1965), pp. 51–85.

131. Van Dam (1985), pp. 88–113; cf. Sulp. Sev. *Chron.* 2.48 (*CSEL* 1.101), 2.50.4 (*CSEL* 1.103).

132. See Sulp. Sev. *Chron.* 2.51 (*CSEL* 1.104–105); Jer. *De Vir. Ill.* 123 (*GCS* 14.53) for Tiberianus; Sulp. Sev. *Chron.* 2.48 (*CSEL* 1.101). See also *PLRE* 1.289 for Euchrotia; 1.744 for Procula; and 1.246 for Attius Tiro Delphidius.

133. Sulp. Sev. *Chron.* 2.49.1 (*CSEL* 1.101) says that Volventius was corrupted ("corrupto"), that is, bribed.

134. Aug. *Ep.* 11*; R. Delmaire, "Contribution des nouvelles lettres de Saint Augustin à la prosopographie du Bas-Empire Romain," in *Les lettres de Saint Augustin découvertes par J. Divjak*, ed. C. Lepelley (Paris, 1983), p. 186.

135. *C. Th.* 12.1.111, .113, .114.

136. Scholars have turned to other sources to study the conversion of the Spanish aristocracy. J. Matthews (1975), pp. 147–148, and T. D. Barnes and R. W. Wes-

tall, "The Conversion of the Roman Aristocracy in Prudentius's *Contra Symmachum*," *Phoenix* 45 (1991), pp. 50–61, have focused on the writings of Spanish Christians, Prudentius in particular. P. de Palol (1983), pp. 47–69, compiled a survey of excavated sites in Spain that showed that wealthy Christians lived in urban and rural contexts beginning with the reign of Constantine, but this survey did not verify the intensity of the process among *clarissimi;* many wealthy Christians were part of the provincial elite, such as those in the Priscillianist movement, but were not *clarissimi.* Subsequent archaeological work about fourth-century Spain has not significantly changed our knowledge of Spanish aristocratic families See, for example, M. I. L. Garcia, "La difusión del cristianesimo en los medios rurales de la Península Iberica a fines del impero Romano," *SHHA* 4–5 (1986–1987), pp. 195–204, and S. J. Maloney and J. R. Hale, "The Villa of Torre de Palma (Alto Alentejo)," *JRA* 9 (1996), pp. 275–294. A recent study by K. Bowes, "Villa-Churches, Rural Piety, and the Priscillianist Controversy," in *Urban Centers and Rural Contexts in Late Antiquity,* ed. T. S. Burns and J. W. Eadie (East Lansing, Mich., 2001), pp. 323–348, presents a good discussion of recent archaeological work on villas that pertains to Christianization and lends further support for my suggested association of local elites and Priscillianism.

137. See, for example, Lane Fox (1986), pp. 272–276, and W. H. C. Frend, *The Donatist Church,* 2d ed. (Oxford, 1972), pp. 87ff. The bibliography on the Christianization of North Africa is vast, but most of it has focused on ecclesiastical texts to highlight Donatism or Saint Augustine's thought and has obscured the presence of pagan aristocrats and paganism. Attempts to shift this focus by C. Lepelley, *Les cités de l'Afrique romaine au Bas-Empire,* 2 vols. (Paris, 1979–1981), and T. Kotula, *Les principales d'Afrique* (Wroclaw, 1982), as well as by MacMullen (1984), have been partially successful. For recent work on Roman Africa, see D. J. Mattingly and R. B. Hitchner, "Roman Africa: An Archaeological Review," *JRS* 85 (1995), pp. 165–213, and J. B. Rives (1995).

138. J. Geffcken (1978 trans.), pp. 228–229.

139. G. Charles-Picard, *La Carthage de Saint Augustin* (Paris, 1965), p. 211.

140. Aug. *Sermo* 359.8 (*PL* 39.1596).

141. M. Overbeck, *Untersuchungen zum afrikanischen Senatsadel in der Spätantike* (Kallmünz, Germany, 1973), pp. 39ff.

142. M. C(a)eionius Iulianus signo Kamenius, App. 2 = Iulianus 26, *PLRE* 1.476, was probably pagan, given his offices, the paganism of his uncle, Tarracius Bassus = Bassius 21, *PLRE* 1.158, and his inherited patronage ties; see von Haehling (1978), p. 367. Certainty exists for Alfenius C(a)eionius Iulianus signo Kamenius, App. 2 = Iulianus 25, *PLRE* 1.474–475, whose career and paganism are recorded by *D.* 1264.

143. C. Lepelley, "Les limites de la Christianisation de l'État romain sous Constantin et ses successeurs," *Christianisme et pouvoirs politiques* (Lille, 1973), pp. 25–41; cf. Y. Thébert, "À propos du 'triomphe du Christianisme,'" *Dialogues d'histoire ancienne* 14 (1988), pp. 277–345, and D. Riggs, "The Continuity of Pa-

ganism between the Cities and Countryside of Late Roman Africa," in *Urban Centers and Rural Contexts in Late Antiquity,* ed. T. S. Burns and J. W. Eadie (East Lansing, Mich., 2001), pp. 285–300.

144. C. Lepelley (1973); MacMullen (1984), pp. 82–83.
145. S. Panciera, "Ancora sulla famiglia senatoria 'africana' degli Aradii," *L'Africa Romana* 4(2) (1986), pp. 547–571, especially pp. 558–559.
146. Aradius Rufinus, App. 2 = Rufinus 10, *PLRE* 1.775; Symm. *Ep.* 1.2.3.
147. L. Aradius Valerius Proculus signo Populonius, App. 2 = Proculus 11, *PLRE* 1.747–749; Q. Aradius Rufinus Valerius Proculus signo Populonius, App. 2 = Proculus 12, *PLRE* 1.749.
148. S. Panciera (1986), pp. 554ff., discusses the inscription.
149. The son, L. Aradius Valerius Proculus signo Populonius, was urban prefect in 337–338 and 351–352; see *CIL* 6.1690 = *D.* 1240 and Proculus 11, *PLRE* 1.747–749. The father, Aradius Rufinus, was urban prefect ca. 304 and twice more in 312–313; see Rufinus 10, *PLRE* 1.775.
150. L. Aradius Valerius Proculus held several offices in Africa, culminating with the proconsulship of Africa before 333 (*CIL* 6.1693 = *D.* 1241), and Q. Aradius Rufinus Valerius Proculus was a *praeses* as well as patron of several African towns (*CIL* 6.1684–1689 = *D.* 611A-C).
151. Symm. *Ep.* 1.2.4, vv. 4–5: "simplex / Caelicorum cultus."
152. Aradius Rufinus, App. 2 = Rufinus 11, *PLRE* 1.775–776. His conversion is indicated if he is the "sanctissimus senes" referred to by Ambr. *De Off.* 3.7.48 (ed. M. Testard [Paris, 1984–1992], 2.104); see S. Panciera (1986), p. 558, and von Haehling (1978), pp. 382–384.
153. Four of the Christians from Africa and none of the pagans are attested in the period from 392 through 423; see Table 3.4.
154. Salvian, *De Gub. Dei* 8.2.12, 8.3.14 (*CSEL* 8.195–196).
155. Aug. *Ep.* 112 (*CSEL* 34.2.657–659) to Donatus, App. 2 = Donatus 1, *PLRE* 2.375–376. Another African Christian landowner, Celer, proconsul of Africa in 429, wrote to Augustine about his conversion to orthodoxy from Donatism; Celer, App. 2 = Celer 1, *PLRE* 2.275. Since Celer's career fell before 425 he is included in my database. See C. Lepelley "L'aristocratie lettrée païenne: une menace aux yeux d'Augustin," in *Augustin Prédicateur (395–411),* ed. G. Madec (Paris, 1998), pp. 327–342.
156. M. Overbeck (1973), pp. 50–53.
157. H. Montgomery, "Decurions and Clergy: Some Suggestions," *Opuscula Romana* 15 (1985), pp. 93–95; T. Klauser, "Bischöfe als staatliche Prokuratoren im dritten Jahrhundert?," *JAC* 14 (1971), pp. 140–149; Lane Fox (1986), pp. 265–335; K. Torjesen, "Christianity as Culture Critique" (unpublished paper, Claremont Graduate University, 1998).
158. W. Eck, "Das Eindringen des Christentums in den Senatorenstand bis zu Konstantin d. Gr.," *Chiron* 1 (1971), pp. 381–406; Barnes (1995), pp. 135–136.
159. For the Fabii, Jerome *Ep.* 77.2; for the Julii, *Ep.* 108.4; Marcella *Ep.* 127.1 (*PL*

22.691, .879, .1087). See also Jacques (1986), pp. 131–133; Arnheim (1972), pp. 107–108.

160. See note 1 above.

161. Symm. *Or.* 7.4.

162. Symmachus patronized many a new man, supporting for the senate Flavius Severus (*Or.* 6) and the son of Julianus Rusticus (*Or.* 7); see also Arnheim (1972), p. 19.

163. *C.Th.* 6.35.7; *C.J.* 12.19; Jones (1964, 1986 reprint), p. 541. See also A. Chastagnol (1970), pp. 194–206. For social mobility, see A. Demandt, "Der spätrömische Militäradel," *Chiron* 10 (1980), especially pp. 628ff; K. Hopkins (1965), pp. 21ff.

164. See Salzman (1990), pp. 149–153, for Aurelian and Sol.

165. Salvian, *De Gub. Dei* 8.2.12, .3.14 (*CSEL* 8.195–196).

166. Jones (1963), pp. 17–37; Chastagnol (1982), pp. 167–194. See also Sivan (1993), pp. 11–12, 110–111, and K. Hopkins, "Social Mobility in the Later Roman Empire: The Evidence of Ausonius," *CQ* n.s. 11 (1961), pp. 239–249, who suggest a link between new men and Christianity.

167. The Christians tended to omit their rank from inscriptions and only gradually incorporated it over the course of the fourth century. C. Carletti, "'Epigrafia cristiana,' 'epigrafia dei cristiani': alle origini della terza età dell'epigrafia," in *La terza età dell'epigrafia,* ed. A. Donati (Faena, 1988), pp. 115–136. This habit made it more difficult to find new men.

168. Eusebius *VC* 4.1 (*GCS* 7.120), trans. E. C. Richardson (*NPNF* 1), p. 540; "no one could request a favor from the emperor and fail of obtaining what he sought . . . some obtained the Praetorian Prefecture, others senatorial, others again consular rank; many were appointed provincial governors." See also Jones (1964, 1986 reprint), p. 106.

169. Eutropius 10.7; Zosimus 2.38. See also A. Chastagnol, "Zosime 2.38 et *l'Histoire Auguste,*" *Bonner H. A. Colloquium 1964/65* (Bonn, 1966), pp. 43–78, and Jul. *Symp.* 335B.

170. Amm. Marc. 21.10.8, .12.25.

171. C. Caelius Saturninus signo Dogmatius = Saturninus 9, *PLRE* 1.806; C. Iulius Rufinianus Ablabius Tatianus, App. 2 = Tatianus 4, *PLRE* 1.875–876; L. Papius Pacatianus = Pacatianus 2, *PLRE* 1.656; and Iulius (or Ionius) Iulianus. These men may have been of provinicial origin. See also Chapter 2, note 69.

172. A. Demandt (1980), pp. 611–612, note 16, cites the *comes* Gratianus and *dux* Arbitio as coming from low-status families, as were the Franks Bonitus and Ursicinus. Of unknown descent are the *comes* Leontius and the *duces* Ursacius, Ursinus, and Rometalca. Only Flavius Arbitio 2, *PLRE* 1.94–95, and Ursicinus 2, *PLRE* 1.985–986, held sufficiently high offices to have certain aristocratic status, but neither met the geographic and religious criteria for inclusion in my study.

173. See note 169 above.

174. Eusebius *VC* 2.44 (*GCS* 7.66); Theod. *HE* 1.2.3 (*GCS* 44.5); Sozomen *HE* 1.8.5 (*GCS* 50.17–18).
175. Von Haehling (1978), pp. 520–521.
176. See Chapter 4 and von Haehling (1978), pp. 514–515.
177. See Appendix 2. Appendix 4 lists office holders active in the West beginning with Constantine as sole ruler in 324; only the urban prefects of Rome begin in 312, with Constantine's victory over Maxentius.
178. Fl(avius) Ablabius, App. 2 = Ablabius 4, *PLRE* 1.3–4, was apparently praetorian prefect in Italy, and hence received *C.Th.* 11.27.1. As *PLRE* notes, he was probably with Constantius Caesar in Italy in 329, then consul in 331. He seems to have been attached to the emperor (and hence is listed in Appendix 4). For this type of prefect, see T. D. Barnes, "Himerius and the Fourth Century," *CP* 82 (1987), p. 217, note 51. Ablabius was one of a small number of easterners who held high offices in the West, as did Ulpius Limenius 2, *PLRE* 1.510, Hermogenes 3, *PLRE* 1.423, and Eustathius, App. 2 = Eustathius 2, *PLRE* 1.310–311.
179. The four Christian appointees with fathers of unknown status include (1) Publilius Optatianus signo Porphyrius, App. 2 = Optatianus 3, *PLRE* 1.649. An African by birth, he was already a senator when Constantine recalled him and appointed him as urban prefect of Rome twice, in part in recognition for his poetic abilities. *PLRE* 1.912 suggests that C. Iunius Tiberianus 8 may have been Optatianus' father, but this identification is uncertain. (2) Acilius Severus, App. 2 = Severus 16, *PLRE* 1.834, was a Spaniard and probably a new man; cf. Jerome *De Vir. Ill.* 111 (*GCS* 14.50). (3) Flavius Ianuarinus, App. 2 = Ianuarinus 2, *PLRE* 1.453. Following *PLRE* 1.453, I take Ianuarinus 2 to be identified with Ianuarinus 1. Hence he was vicar in Rome in 320 and consul in 328. (4) Gregorius, App. 2 = Gregorius 3, *PLRE* 1.403.
180. Neither man is known to have been Christian before his appointment. Sextus Anicius Paulinus has been identified as the first of the high-ranking Anicii to publicly adopt Christianity, but Sextus' identification with the "generosus Anicius" mentioned by Prud. *C. Symm.* 1.552–553 has been rightly criticized by Barnes (1995), pp. 135–147.
181. The nine pagan aristocrats listed in Appendix 2 are Q. Flavius Maesius Egnatius Lollianus signo Mavortius 5; Aurelius Valerius Tullianus Symmachus 6; C(a)eionius Rufius Albinus 14; L. Aradius Valerius Proculus signo Populonius 11; Valerius Maximus signo Basilius 48; M. C(a)eionius Iulianus signo Kamenius 26; C. C(a)eionius Rufius Volusianus 4; Aco Catullinus signo Philomathius 3; and Aradius Rufinus 10. I included Aradius Rufinus because his third urban prefectureship, 312 Nov. 29–313 Dec. 8, indicates that he served under Constantine as well as Maxentius; Symm. *Ep.* 1.2.3. The three from unknown families were Fabius Titianus 6, Domitius Zenophilus, and C. Vettius Cossinius Rufinus 15. The origin of C. Vettius Cossinius Rufinus 15 is still uncertain; see also Anonymus 12, *PLRE* 1.1006 1008, which identification

is contested by T. D. Barnes, "Two Senators under Constantine," *JRS* 65 (1975), pp. 40–49, suggesting instead C(a)eionius Rufius Albinus 14.

182. M. C(a)eionius Iulianus signo Kamenius, App. 2 = Iulianus 26, *PLRE* 1.476. C(a)eionius may be an Etruscan name in origin, but his Italian provenance is not attested.

183. In this study aristocrats whose parents were attested in the clarissimate before the rule of Constantine (284–312) were more likely to be pagan than Christian. Twenty-seven percent (6 out of 22) of the aristocrats in my study population who were Christian had parents of the clarissimate rank or higher in this time period as compared to 73% (16 out of 22) of the aristocrats who were pagan (see Table 3.6).

184. Fl(avius) Ablabius, App. 2 = Ablabius 4, *PLRE* 1.3–4; Acilius Severus, App. 2 = Severus 16, *PLRE* 1.834.

185. This approach elucidates the continuing senatorial support for Constantine, evidenced by, among other things, the senate's dedication of a statue to him, *Pan. Lat.* 9(12).25.4.

186. Libanius *Or.* 1.39. In *Or.* 1.74 Libanius says that after his panegyric on Constans and Constantius at court (*Or.* 59), some pagans attacked him for having good relations with Christian courtiers.

187. Datianus 1, *PLRE* 1.243–244; Lib. *Or.* 42.24–25.

188. H. C. Teitler, *Notarii and Exceptores* (Amsterdam, 1985), pp. 54–72.

189. Flavius Taurus, App. 2 = Taurus 3, *PLRE* 1.879–880. Two easterners who came west and served Constantius are included in Appendix 2, namely Flavius Ablabius and Flavius Philippus. Two other easterners who came west were omitted due to evidentiary problems. Ulpius Limenius 2, *PLRE* 1.510, and Hermogenes 3, *PLRE* 1.423, lack evidence for religious affiliation. Limenius' identification with the proconsul of Constantinople in Lib. *Or.* 1.45–47 is not certain.

190. *AE* 1934, p. 159.

191. The two easterners of nonsenatorial background were Flavius Taurus = Taurus 3, *PLRE* 1.879, and Helpidius = Helpidius 6, *PLRE* 1.415, who later converted to paganism. The three from unknown parentage were Flavius Florentius = Florentius 10, *PLRE* 1.365, Flavius Leontius = Leontius 22, *PLRE* 1.503, and Honoratus = Honoratus 2, *PLRE* 1.438–439 (perhaps from Bithynia; von Haehling [1978], p. 115). The five from aristocratic families were N(a)eratius Cerealis = Cerealis 2, *PLRE* 1.197; Iunius Bassus signo Theotecnius = Bassus 15, *PLRE* 1.155; Sextus Claudius Petronius Probus = Probus 5, *PLRE* 1.736–740; Q. Clodius Hermogenianus Olybrius = Olybrius 3, *PLRE* 1.640–642; and Flavius Hypatius = Hypatius 4, *PLRE* 1.448–449. All are in Appendix 2.

192. *CIL* 6.1158 = *D.* 731.

193. Of uncertain parentage are Saturninius Secundus Salutius = Secundus 3, *PLRE* 1.814–817, and Tertullus = Tertullus 2, *PLRE* 1.882–883. The remaining four are Q. Flavius Maesius Egnatius Lollianus signo Marvortius = Lollianus 5,

PLRE 1.512–514; Memmius Vitrasius Orfitus signo Honorius = Orfitus 3, *PLRE* 1.651–653; Vulcacius Rufinus = Rufinus 25, *PLRE* 1.782–783; and C. C(a)eionius Rufius Volusianus signo Lampadius = Volusianus 5, *PLRE* 1.978–980. All the men are in Appendix 2.

194. For Gratian, see Sivan (1993), pp. 14ff. For appointments exemplary of Gratian's policy, see note 195 below. Matthews (1975), pp. 47ff., minimizes too much the friction between Valentinian's Pannonian appointees and the old aristocracy; see A. Giardina (1976–1977), pp. 672–673.

195. The three Christian appointees from nonsenatorial families are Decimius Magnus Ausonius, App. 2 = Ausonius 7, *PLRE* 1.140–141; (Magnus?) Arborius, App. 2 = Arborius 3, *PLRE* 1.97–98; and Flavius Mallius Theodorus = Theodorus 27, *PLRE* 1.900–902. The three Christian appointees from unknown families are the convert Martinianus, App. 2 = Martinianus 5, *PLRE* 1.564; Proculus Gregorius, App. 2 = Gregorius 9, *PLRE* 1.404; and Valerius Severus, App. 2 = Severus 29, *PLRE* 1.837. Decimius Hilarianus Hesperius, App. 2 = Hesperius 2, *PLRE* 1.427–428, is the son of a new man, the poet Ausonius.

196. Sivan (1993), pp. 19–20.

197. The seven men from senatorial origins, all listed in Appendix 2, were Flavius Hypatius = Hypatius 4, *PLRE* 1.448–449; Sextus Claudius Petronius Probus = Probus 5, *PLRE* 1.736–740; Gracchus = Furius Maecius Gracchus 3 = Gracchus 1, *PLRE* 1.399–400; Anicius Paulinus = Paulinus 12, *PLRE* 1.678; Anicius Auchenius Bassus = Bassus 11, *PLRE* 1.152–154; Q. Clodius Hermogenianus Olybrius = Olybrius 3, *PLRE* 1.640–642; and Aradius Rufinus = Rufinus 11, *PLRE* 1.640–642. Decimius Hilarianus Hesperius = Hesperius 2, *PLRE* 1.427–428, was the son of a new man. All but Hypatius 4 were from Rome; I considered Aradius Rufinus as a Roman since he was born in Rome (Lib. *Ep.* 1493), even though his family has African roots (see my discussion above and notes 147–150).

198. Aug. *Sermo* Morin I.3 (*PLS* 2.657–660); C. Lepelley (1979–1981), pp. 215ff.; Aug. *En. in Psalm.* 7.9 (*CC* 38.42–43); and Symm. *Ep.* 1.51.

199. Provincials, successful in their quest for clarissimate status, were required to first meet their obligations to their home cities; after 360, every ennobled curial family was required to leave at least a branch to meet these obligations. *C.Th.* 12.1.57 and 12.1.58 (364); applied to all senators by 377, *C.J.* 12.1.11. See also Valens' law, *C.Th.* 12.1.74 (371).

200. Flavius Mallius Theodorus, App. 2 = Theodorus 27, *PLRE* 1.900–902. See Claudian, *Pan. dict. Manlio Theodoro* (of 399); cf. similar rhetoric for Flavius Severus, Symm. *Or.* 6.

201. Matthews (1975), pp. 216–219; Claudian *Pan. dict. Manlio Theodoro* 61–112.

202. Nummius Aemilianus Dexter, App. 2 = Dexter 3, *PLRE* 1.251; *CIL* 2.4512.

203. See C. Iulius Rufinianus Ablabius Tatianus, App. 2 = Tatianus 4, *PLRE* 1.875–876; *CIL* 10.1125 = *D.* 2942.

204. See Appendix 1. For this same reason, we know more about converts who were *illustres*.

4. Aristocratic Men: Career Paths

1. Diocletian and Constantine turned back to aristocrats for government service, thus reinvigorating the traditional senatorial civic *cursus honorum*. T. D. Barnes, *Constantine and Eusebius* (Cambridge, Mass., 1981), p. 43, attributed this change primarily to Constantine, as did Arnheim (1972), p. 5, and Jones (1964, 1986 reprint), pp. 523–524. For senatorial career paths, see Chastagnol (1982), pp. 167–194, and my discussion in Chapter 2.
2. Symm. *Ep.* 1.51: "nunc aris deese Romanos genus est ambiendi."
3. Aug. *Conf.* 8.6.
4. The two remaining in secular service were probably Christian since they congratulated the former on their decision; Aug. *Conf.* 8.6.
5. Aurelius Celsinus, App. 2 (of this book) = Celsinus 4, *PLRE* 1.192; *CIL* 8.12272. See also Chastagnol (1960), pp. 112–114.
6. R. Stark (1996), p. 56, observed: "accepting a new religion is part of conforming to the expectations and example of one's family and friends."
7. Typical is A. Demandt, "Der spätrömische Militäradel," *Chiron* 10 (1980), pp. 609–636, who showed the importance of networks for the military aristocracy but summarily dismissed religion, as did Chastagnol (1982), pp. 167–192, and Kuhoff (1983).
8. Jones (1963), pp. 17–37, especially p. 35.
9. Ibid., pp. 29–37.
10. For example, Eusebius *VC* 4.54.2 (*GCS* 7.142); Sozomen *HE* 2.5.6 (*GCS* 50.57), trans. C. D. Hartranft *(NPNF)*, p. 262: "Others, envious of the honor in which Christians were held by the emperor [Constantine], . . . were convinced that it was better to become Christians." See also Jones (1963), p. 36.
11. For criticism of von Haehling's influence, see Barnes (1995), pp. 135–147.
12. See von Haehling (1978), pp. 507–619, for imperial appointments. Anecdotes support this: Amm. Marc. (20.8.14) stated that the *mores* and *voluntates* of appointees (i.e., religion) were critical to Julian; Prud. *C. Symm.* 1.616–621 notes that what makes Theodosius a good emperor is that he ignores the paganism of his appointees.
13. Symm. *Ep.* 3.34.
14. Ibid., *Ep.* 9.67: "macte igitur primi honoris auspiciis et ad honorem et gloriam felices tende conatus, ut et tibi ad celsiores gradus ianuam pandas."
15. Ibid., *Ep.* 1.58; cf. 1.61. Translation by Matthews (1975), p. 11.
16. Amm. Marc. 27.11.3.
17. Sid. Ap. *Ep.* 1.3.2, 1.4.2, 3.6.2; *Carm.* 7.464–468; Paul. of Nola *Ep.* 8.3, 25.3 (*CSEL* 29.47–52, 232–233).
18. For methodology, see Appendix 1. With the exception of the religious career,

these career paths correspond roughly to those cited by Ausonius *Grat. Actio.* 4 (see Chapter 4 epigraph). For the codification of career steps, see Chastagnol (1982), p. 176. I omitted the consulship from the senatorial civic *cursus* since it was rarely held by senatorial aristocrats in the fourth century; see Bagnall et al. (1987), pp. 4–6, 97ff. Kuhoff (1983), p. 255, argued for a single mixed cursus of traditional and newly created posts by the late fourth century. Although there was some overlap between court and extra-court careers (see Chastagnol [1982], pp. 177, 189), there was no noticeable decline in traditional senatorial civic office holders. Hence the categories adopted in this study differ from Kuhoff's.

19. Kuhoff (1983), pp. 255ff.
20. Ibid., pp. 11ff.
21. (Ae)milius Florus Paternus, App. 2 = Paternus 6, *PLRE* 1.671–672.
22. Chastagnol (1982), pp. 167–194; the titles (*clarissimi, spectabiles, illustres*) attached to these offices are attested toward 363 and were codified in laws of Valentinian I, Gratian, and Valens in 372. See *C.Th.* 6.7.1, .9.1, .11.1, .14.1.
23. Symm. *Rel.* 3, passim. Symm. *Ep.* 7.50 underscores the demands that come with the honor *(praemium)* of high office.
24. Jones (1964; 1986 reprint), pp. 381–382.
25. Clodius Octavianus, App. 2 = Octavianus 2, *PLRE* 1.637; Amm. Marc. 23.1.4.
26. See note 22 above.
27. T. D. Barnes, "Pretorian Prefects 337–361," *ZPE* 94 (1992), pp. 249–260; Kuhoff (1983), pp. 248ff.
28. Jones (1963), pp. 333, 528–529, 534; cf. Vulcacius Rufinus, App. 2 = Rufinus 25, *PLRE* 1.782–783, who was *comes ordinis primi intra consistorium, CIL* 6.32051 = *D.* 1237.
29. Kuhoff (1983), pp. 195–205, 238–247.
30. For Valentinian's laws, see *C.Th.* 6.7.1, .9.1, .11.1, .14.1. For Gratian's laws, see *C.Th.* 6.9.2 (380), 26.2 (381). Cf. Chastagnol (1982), pp. 184ff., and Kuhoff (1983), passim.
31. Publius Ampelius, App. 2 = Ampelius 3, *PLRE* 1.56–57; Kuhoff (1983), pp. 254–255.
32. Jones (1964, 1986 reprint), pp. 142–143, 527. The *comes rei militaris* Marinus (App. 2 = Marinus 1, *PLRE* 2.724) was *spectabilis.*
33. D. Hunt, "The Church as a Public Institution," in *The Cambridge Ancient History,* vol. 13 (Cambridge, U.K., 1998), ed. Averil Cameron and P. Garnsey, pp. 238–276, also discusses the church "as a career."
34. *CIL* 6.499 = *D.* 4147; Claudius Hermogenianus Caesarius, App. 2 = Caesarius 7, *PLRE* 1.171–172.
35. *HA Sev. Alex.* 21.8.
36. Jones (1964, 1986 reprint), pp. 390–392.
37. Chapter 2, notes 89 and 90. An emperor could step in and appoint a man to a low office, as did Julian when he made the historian Sextus Aurelius Victor, App. 2 = Victor 13, *PLRE* 1.960, consular governor of Pannonia Secunda,

Amm. Marc. 21.10.6, but this was rare. Victor was probably a pagan, given his occupation, Julian's support, and Ammianus' praise of his *sobrietas,* an attribute ascribed by Ammianus (31.10.19) to that good pagan, Marcus Antonius.

38. Symm. *Or.* 6, 7, 8; *Ep.* 7.96 and 3.38 are exemplary.

39. Ibid., *Rel.* 17. On merit, see Lendon (1997), p. 187, especially note 57.

40. See note 1 above and Chapter 2, notes 70–73.

41. *Pan. Lat.* 4[10].35.2; see also Symm. *Ep.* 1.52.

42. Symm. *Ep.* 1.2.

43. Sid. Ap. *Ep.* 1.3.1.

44. This path included men whose careers were entirely senatorial civic and those that were mixed but mainly senatorial civic.

45. Amm. Marc. 27.3.5; C. C(a)eionius Rufius Volusianus signo Lampadius, App. 2 = Volusianus 5, *PLRE* 1.978–980. I have adopted the convention of spelling C(a)eionius for members of the same family since variations in spelling this name (with or without the *a*) appear in documents and inscriptions.

46. See note 80 below. Consider too the legally trained senatorial civic careerist, Ragonius Vincentius Celsus 9, *PLRE* 1.195–196, who was omitted from my database because he lacks attestation of religious affiliation.

47. C. Iulius Rufinianus Ablabius Tatianus, App. 2 = Tatianus 4, *PLRE* 1.875–876, and Nummius Aemilianus Dexter, App. 2 = Dexter 3, *PLRE* 1.251.

48. Each man was dated by his highest office; see Appendix 1.

49. Symm. *Rel.* 3.1–3.

50. The father, Aco Catullinus 2, *PLRE* 1.187, was omitted from this study since his religion is not attested. For the career of his son, see Aco Catullinus signo Philomathius 3, *PLRE* 1.187–188. Since he is attested as pagan (*CIL* 2.2635), he is included in Appendix 2 as Aco Catullinus, as he is listed in the *Codex-Calendar of 354;* but T. D. Barnes (1992), p. 257, prefers Aconius because of its attestation in *CIL* 6.1780.

51. Fabia Aconia Paulina, App. 2 = Paulina 4, *PLRE* 1.675; daughter of Catullinus signo Philomathius (*CIL* 6.1780); wed to Praetextatus (*CIL* 6.1779 = D. 1259).

52. Q. Aurelius Symmachus signo Eusebius, App. 2 = Symmachus 4, *PLRE* 1.865–870; career noted (*CIL* 6.1699 = D. 2946).

53. Symm. *Ep.* 1.68. See also Celsinus Titianus, App. 2 = Titianus 5, *PLRE* 1.917–918.

54. This pattern coincides with that found by von Haehling (1978), pp. 284ff. and 416ff., for the praetorian prefects of Italy. For *consulares* and *correctores* of Campania, see G. Clemente, *Governo imperiale e élites dirigenti nell'Italia tardoantica* (Como, 1994), pp. 61–67. Of the forty-nine *consulares* and *correctores* of Campania recorded by *PLRE* 1.1092–1093 and included in Appendix 2, thirteen were pagan, five were Christian, and thirty-one were missing religious affiliation. Pagans clearly predominate among those with attested religion.

55. See Chapter 3; Jones (1964, 1986 reprint), pp. 537–538; Olymp. *Frag.* 44 in *FHG* 4.67–68; Salzman (1990), pp. 184–188.

56. *CIL* 6.102 = D. 4003. The aristocrat Volusianus 5, *PLRE* 1.978–980, had his

name carved on buildings he restored in Rome as if he had built them himself;
Amm. Marc. 27.3.7. See also G. Clemente (1994), pp. 225–228.

57. Tertullian *Idol.* 17.3.

58. Zosimus 2.29; Eusebius *VC* 1.48 (*GCS* 7.40); J. Straub, *Vom Herrscherideal in der Spätantike* (Stuttgart, 1939; reprint, Darmstadt, 1964), pp. 98 ff., 175–204; and J. Straub, "Konstantins Verzicht auf den Gang zum Kapitol," *Historia* 4 (1955), pp. 297–303.

59. *C.Th.* 16.10.3; M. R. Salzman, "*Superstitio* in the *Codex Theodosianus* and the Persecution of Pagans," *Vigiliae Christianae* 41 (1987), pp. 172–188.

60. *C.Th.* 16.10.3, .8, .17; Salzman (1990), pp. 235–246; R. Lim, "People as Power: Games, Munificence and Contested Topography," *JRA Supplement* no. 33 (1999), pp. 265–281.

61. Lib. *Or.* 30.33–34.

62. P. Sabbatini Tumolesi, *Epigrafia anfiteatrale dell'occidente romano I: Roma* (Rome, 1988), pp. 96–103.

63. See also von Haehling (1978), pp. 416–452.

64. Amm. Marc. 27.3.13; von Haehling (1978), pp. 614–615.

65. See Chapter 2 and notes 89 and 90.

66. Symm. *Or.* 5, *Pro Trygetio; Or.* 6, *Pro Flavio Severo; Or.* 8, *Pro Valerio Fortunato.*

67. Paul. of Nola *Ep.* 8.3 (*CSEL* 29.47–52), trans. P. G. Walsh *(FOTC)*, vol. 1, pp. 78–80.

68. *Carmen contra paganos* 80–85, trans. Croke and Harries (1982), p. 82, who note the various identifications for the consul as Praetextatus, Pompeianus, or Nicomachus Flavianus the Elder.

69. *C.Th.* 16.10.10 (391) and .10.11, as N. McLynn, *Ambrose of Milan: Church and Court in a Christian Capital* (Berkeley, 1994), pp. 331ff., argued.

70. *C.Th* 16.1.1.

71. *C.Th.* 16.10.2, 16.10.3; Salzman (1990), pp. 205–209.

72. Ambr. *Ep.* 72[17].9 and 73[18].31 (*CSEL* 82.3.14–15, 50).

73. Ambr. *Ep.* 27[58].3 (*CSEL* 82.1.181), trans. Sister Mary Melchior Beyenka *(FOTC)*, p. 144; see also Paul. of Nola *Ep.* 8 (*CSEL* 29.45–52).

74. Aug. *Ep.* 94.2 (*CSEL* 34.2.499): "quia necdum illum desuerat senatoriae dignitatis ambitio."

75. For attestation as patron, see Anicius Paulinus, App. 2 = Paulinus 12, *PLRE* 1.678.

76. *CIL* 6.1756, lines 5–12. Sextus Claudius Petronius Probus, App. 2 = Probus 5, *PLRE* 1.736–740.

77. Chastagnol (1982), pp. 184–185. Men in imperial bureaucratic careers sometimes did, beginning with Constantius II, hold an office in the senatorial civic career path, such as provincial governor or proconsul.

78. See the Preface and Chapter 6.

79. For differing opinions on the role of the imperial quaestor, see J. Harries, "The Roman Imperial Quaestor from Constantine to Theodosius II," *JRS* 78 (1988), pp. 148–172, and T. Honoré, "The Making of the Theodosian Code," *ZSS Röm. Abt* (1986), pp. 133–222.

80. Decimius Magnus Ausonius, App. 2 = Ausonius 7, *PLRE* 1.140–141; Claudius
    Postumus Dardanus, App. 2 = *PLRE* 2.346–347. For mobility via law, see Jones
    (1964, 1986 reprint), pp. 370ff.; via rhetoric, see K. Hopkins, "Social Mobility
    in the Later Roman Empire: The Evidence of Ausonius," *CQ* 11 (1961),
    pp. 239–249; R. Kaster, *Late Antique Grammarians* (Berkeley, 1988); and D.
    Nellen, *Viri Litterati: Gebildetes Beamtentum und spätrömisches Reich im Westen
    zwischen 284 und 395 nach Christus* (Bochum, 1977), pp. 117–127.
81. Lib. *Or.* 2.44, .46, .58; 18.131–134; 42.23–25; 62.10–11; 115.51.
82. The status of notaries in the West rose so high that by 381 the highest notaries
    ranked with proconsuls. See *C.Th.* 6.10.2; H. C. Teitler, *Notarii and Exceptores*
    (Amsterdam, 1985), pp. 54–72.
83. Felix, App. 2 = Felix 3, *PLRE* 1.332; Amm. Marc. 20.9.5; *C.Th.* 9.42.5a.
84. Decentius, App. 2 = Decentius 1, *PLRE* 1.244; Lib. *Ep.* 1505, 1507, 1521.
85. Flavius Eugenius, App. 2 = Eugenius 5, *PLRE* 1.292; this cites Ath. *Apol. Const.*
    3 (*PG* 25.597–600).
86. *C.Th.* 6.10.1, associated with Ausonius; similarly, 6.22.5, 6.28.2; see Sivan
    (1993), pp. 135—138.
87. Maternus Cynegius, App. 2 = Cynegius 3, *PLRE* 1.235–236.
88. Eusebius *VC* 2.12.1 (*GCS* 7.53), trans. E. C. Richardson *(NPNF)*, p. 503.
89. Sozomen *HE* 2.5.2 (*GCS* 50.56), trans. C. Hartranft *(NPNF)*, p. 262.
90. Lib. *Or.* 30.7.
91. Felix, App. 2 = Felix 3, *PLRE* 1.332; Libanius *Or.* 14.36; Helpidius, App. 2 =
    Helpidius 6, *PLRE* 1.415; Philost. *HE* 7.10; Theod. *HE* 3.12.
92. *C.Th.* 16.5.42, trans. C. Pharr, *The Theodosian Code and Novels and the Sirmondian
    Constitutions* (Princeton, 1952). Zosimus 5.46 notes that Honorius withdrew
    this law.
93. Sextilius Agesilaus Aedesius, App. 2 = Aedesius 7, *PLRE* 1.15–16, which lists
    his career (*CIL* 6.510) and pagan activities, including the *taurobolium*, a cult
    popular among the Roman elite.
94. Ambr. *Expos. ps.* 118.20.49 (*CSEL* 62.469): "venit quis in ecclesiam, dum
    honorem affectat sub imperatoribus christianis, simulata mente orationem
    deferre se fingit, inclinatur et solo sternitur qui genu mentis non flexerit."
95. Aug. *Sermo* 1.3 (ed. G. Morin [Rome, 1930–1931]), *PLS* 2:657–660 (ed. A.
    Hamann [Paris, 1957]): "Ut maiores pagani non sint, ut non dominentur
    pagani christianis." Cf. Aug. *En. in psalm.* 7.9 (*CCSL* 38.42).
96. The conversions of imperial bureaucrats could be heartfelt; the apostate
    Helpidius, App. 2 = Helpidius 6, *PLRE* 1.415, remained a pagan although he
    served the Christian Jovian, according to Lib. *Ep.* 1120.
97. Generidus, App. 2 = *PLRE* 2.500–501; Zos. 5.46.5. See also H. Elton, *Warfare in
    Roman Europe* (Oxford, 1996), pp. 234–264.
98. R. MacMullen, *Soldier and Civilian in the Later Roman Empire* (Cambridge, Mass.,
    1963), pp. 49–76.
99. Gaudentius, App. 2 = Gaudentius 5, *PLRE* 2.493–494, was wed to an Italian
    noble woman who lacks explicit religious attestation; Greg. Tur. *HF* 2.8 (*PL*
    71.202).

100. Zos. 5.21.3; Elton (1996), pp. 142–144.
101. Aurelius Victor *Caes.* 37.5–7.
102. R. MacMullen (1963), pp. 171–172, although civilians took to wearing the *cingulum* to gain status. For imperial policy, see Amm. Marc. 21.16.3; Jones (1964, 1986 reprint), p. 161.
103. A. Demandt (1980), pp. 609–636.
104. Amm. Marc. 14.10.4.
105. See Flavius Eusebius 39, *PLRE* 1.307–308, with the evidence for this marriage.
106. Philost. *HE* 11.6 on Bauto; see Flavius Stilicho, App. 2 = *PLRE* 1.853–858, for the relevant sources for these matches.
107. Symm. *Ep.* 4.15–16, 3.54–69. See R. S. O. Tomlin, "Notitia dignitatum omnium, tam civilium quam militarium," in *Aspects of the Notitia Dignitatum,* ed. R. Goodburn and P. Bartholomew *(BAR Supplementary Series 15)* (Oxford, 1976), pp. 189–210.
108. A. Demandt (1980), pp. 615ff., updated by "The Osmosis of Late Roman and Germanic Aristocracies," in *Das Reich und die Barbaren,* ed. E. Chrysos and A. Schwarcz (Böhlau, 1989), pp. 75–86.
109. Von Haehling (1978), pp. 453ff., 495. Up until 423, he cites eleven Christians or Arians and seven pagans; after 423, ten Christians and one pagan.
110. A. Demandt (1980), pp. 609–636 and 613, note 25; E. Gabba, "I cristiani nell'esercito romano del quarto secolo d.C." in E. Gabba, *Per la storia dell'esercito romano in età imperiale* (Bologna, 1974), pp. 75–109; R. Tomlin, "Christianity and the Late Roman Army," in *Constantine,* ed. S. N. C. Lieu and D. Montserrat (London, 1998), pp. 21–51.
111. See MacMullen (1984), pp. 44–47, 80, on the origins of military recruits; R. Tomlin (1998), pp. 35–51, on tolerance.
112. MacMullen (1984), pp. 44–47, 80; R. Tomlin (1998), pp. 21–51. For Christians in the fourth-century military, see also K. L. Noethlichs, "Kirche, Recht und Gesellschaft in der Jahrhundertmitte," in *L'Église et L'empire au IVe siècle,* ed. A. Dihle *(Entretiens sur l'antiquité classique* 34) (Vandoeuvres-Geneva, 1989), pp. 251–299; and J. Helgeland, R. J. Daly, and J. P. Burns, *Christians and the Military* (Philadelphia, 1985), pp. 67–72, 73–86.
113. This study population includes all military men, not only the *magistri militum* analyzed by von Haehling. I omitted men directly tied to the imperial house or pretenders to the throne, however, since these men had crossed from aristocratic to imperial dynastic networks. Orthodox and Arian Christians were grouped together for the purposes of this study. See Appendix 1.
114. For Constantius, see E. D. Hunt, "Did Constantius II Have Court Bishops?" *Studia Patristica* 19 (1989), pp. 86–90. As caesar, Julian attended Easter services; Amm. Marc. 21.2.5. When Julian became emperor, Lib. *Or.* 18.168 noted that he "persuaded the man that took up a spear to take up a libation and incense as well . . . and, if reason did not avail, gold and silver combined to persuade" (trans. R. Tomlin [1998], p. 33).
115. In the East Julian kept the Christian *magistri militum* Hormisdas, Flavius

Arintheus, and Victor, and in the West he had Christian *magistri militum,* Flavius Iovinus, App. 2 = Iovinus 6, *PLRE* 1.462–463, and Flavius Nevitta, App. 2 = *PLRE* 1.626–627. I considered Iovinus a Christian, contra to von Haehling (1978), pp. 250–51, because Iovinus' dedication of a church at Rheims (*ILCV* 61) does not appear to have been compelled by a Christian emperor. Similarly, two groups of officers—one of Gallic origin and thus likely pagan, and another group of Constantius' favorites, thus likely Christian—chose as a successor to Julian first a pious pagan; then, after this man refused, they turned to a Christian. See Amm. Marc. 25.5; MacMullen (1984), p. 47.

116. Flavius Bauto, App. 2 = *PLRE* 1.159–160; Generidus, App. 2 = *PLRE* 2.500–501; Zos. 5.46 on *C.Th.* 16.5.42.

117. Amm. Marc. 26.5.14; for Cretio, *comes* of Africa, *PLRE* 1.231; for Masaucio, *PLRE* 1.566. Similarly, St. Martin's father is said to have put him in the military guard; Sulp. Sev. *Mart.* 2 (*CSEL* 1.110–112).

118. Jer. *C. Ioa. Hierosol.* 8: "facite me Romanae urbis episcopum et ero protinus Christianus." See also for such competition, R. Lim (1999), pp. 265–281. Damasus was no aristocrat; see A. Ferrua, *Epigrammata Damasiana* (Vatican City, 1942), pp. 59–77.

119. The four are Ambrose, Paulinus of Nola, Sulpicius Severus, and Petronius (Appendix 2). For Petronius, bishop of Verona by 432, once praetorian prefect of Gaul, see R. Mathisen, "Petronius, Hilarius and Valerianus," *Historia* 30 (1981), pp. 106–112. For Sulpicius Severus as, if not an ordained priest, at the least an ascetic leader, see Gennadius *De Vir. Ill.* 19 (*GCS* 14.69); C. Stancliffe, *St. Martin and His Hagiographer* (Oxford, 1983), p. 16, note 5. Not included here are individuals who were privately devoted to asceticism, such as Valerius Pinianus, *PLRE* 1.702, and Christian careerists whose clarissimate status was not certain. F. Giliard, "Senatorial Bishops in the Fourth Century," *HTR* 77.2 (1984), pp. 153–175, demonstrates this uncertainty for Reticius and Simplicius from Autun; Petilian, the Donatist bishop from Africa; and for the Gallic bishops Maximinus (Trier), Maxentius (Poitiers), Urbicus (Clermont), and Hilary (Poitiers). I included Claudius Lupicinus in the senatorial civic career path because his identification as bishop of Vienne by M. Henzelmann, *Bischofsherrschaft in Gallien: Zur Kontinuität römischer Führungsschichten vom 4. bis 7. Jahrhundert (Beiheft, Francia 5)* (Munich, 1976), pp. 224–226, is only tentative.

120. Ambr. *Ep.* 27[58].3 (*CSEL* 82.1.181).

121. Van Dam (1985), pp. 308–310.

122. Aug. *Ep.* 124–126 (*CSEL* 34.3.1–18).

123. Paulinus of Pella, *Euch.* 293–296, 455ff.; Paulinus of Pella, App. 2 = Paulinus 10, *PLRE* 1.677–678.

124. N. McLynn (1994), pp. 31–52.

125. Ambr. *De off.* 1.14 (ed. M. Testard [Paris, 1984–1992], 1.119–122). Ambrose was allegedly pressured into the bishopric, although the sources allow for political maneuvering; see N. McLynn (1994), pp. 1–52.

126. Marcellus, App. 2 = Marcellus 8, *PLRE* 1.552; C. Vettius Aquilinus Iuvencus, App. 2, discussed by J. R. Martindale, "*Prosopography of the Later Roman Empire:* Addenda et Corrigenda to Volume I," *Historia* 29 (1980), pp. 474–497; see Jerome *De Vir. Ill.* 84 (*PL* 23.729–730).

127. One Christian aristocrat was a priest (*flamen*) in the imperial cult; Astius Vindicianus, App. 2 = Vindicianus 3, *PLRE* 1.968.

128. See Hilarius, *Vita Honorati* 9–12 (*SC* 235.90–102).

129. See Arsenius, App. 2 = Arsenius 4, *PLRE* 1.111, for his career.

130. Sulp. Sev. *Chron.* 2.32 (*CSEL* 1.86–87).

131. Van Dam (1985), pp. 115ff.; R. Mathisen, *Ecclesiastical Factionalism and Religious Controversy in Fifth Century Gaul* (Washington, D.C., 1989), pp. 7–9; Mathisen (1993), passim.

132. For Hilarius, bishop of Arles, see Mathisen (1993), pp. 93–119; for Petronius, see Petronius 3, *PLRE* 2.86. For accusation, see Zosimus *Ep.*, "Exigit dilectio" (*PL* 20.669ff.).

133. P. Brown, *The World of Late Antiquity* (London, 1971; reprint, New York, 1989), p. 131; C. Piétri, "Aristocratie et société clericale dans l'Italie chrétienne au temps d'Odoacre et de Théodoric," *Mélanges d'archéologie et d'histoire de l'école française de Rome: Antiquité* 93 (1981), pp. 417–467.

134. If a pagan held a priesthood and an office in another career path, he was recorded under the other career path.

135. Lucius Ragonius Venustus, App. 2 = Venustus 3, *PLRE* 1.948; see *CIL* 6.503 = D. 4151.

136. For discussion and bibliography of these two positions, see C. W. Hedrick, Jr., *History and Silence: The Purge and Rehabilitation of Memory in Late Antiquity* (Austin, 2000), Chapter 3. See also Salzman (1992), pp. 451–479.

137. This confluence and the willingness of Christians to pursue careers led me to conclude that these offices retained their appeal for Christians of the fourth and early fifth centuries, contrary to the view of Näf (1995), pp. 83–116.

138. K. Shelton, *The Esquiline Treasure* (London, 1981), pp. 63–68; Alan Cameron, "Paganism and Literature in Late Fourth Century Rome," in *Christianisme et formes littéraires de l'antiquité tardive en Occident,* ed. M. Fuhrmann (Fondation Hardt, Entretiens sur l'antiquité classique no. 23) (Vandoeuvres-Geneva, 1977), pp. 1–40; Salzman (1990), pp. 196–231.

5. Aristocratic Women

1. See K. Hopkins, "Elite Mobility in the Roman Empire," *Past and Present* 32 (1965), pp. 12–26, for the term "salon culture." Jerome *Ep.* 22 (*CSEL* 54.143–211) and Amm Marc. 14.6 provide satirical accounts yet they fit with what we know about aristocratic women's lives at Rome.

2. A. Harnack, *The Mission and Expansion of Christianity in the First Three Centuries,* vol. 2, 2d ed., trans. James Moffatt (London, 1908), pp. 64–84, 324–337.

3. L. M. White, "Adolf Harnack and the Expansion of Early Christianity: A Reappraisal of Social History," *The Second Century* 5(2) (1985–1986), pp. 111–127.

4. Elisabeth Schüssler Fiorenza's pioneering study, *In Memory of Her: A Feminist Theological Reconstruction of Christian Origins* (New York, 1983), has spawned a vast literature. For surveys, see E. A. Clark, "Early Christian Women: Sources and Interpretation," in *That Gentle Strength: Historical Perspectives on Women in Early Christianity,* ed. L. L. Coon, K. J. Haldane, and E. W. Sommer (Charlottes-ville, Va., 1990), pp. 19–35; and E. A. Castelli, "Gender, Theory, and the *Rise of Christianity:* A Response to Rodney Stark," *JECS* 6(2) (1998), pp. 227–258, es-pecially notes 1–3.

5. For example, J. Laporte, *The Role of Women in Early Christianity* (New York, 1982); Jo Ann McNamara, "Sexual Equality and the Cult of Virginity in Early Christian Thought," *Feminist Studies* 3 (1976), pp. 145–158.

6. See, for example, R. Ruether, "Mothers of the Church: Ascetic Women in the Late Patristic Age," in *Women of Spirit,* ed. R. Ruether and E. McLaughlin (New York, 1979), pp. 72ff.; A. Ewing Hickey, *Women of the Roman Aristocracy as Chris-tian Monastics* (Ann Arbor, Mich., 1987); M. Raub Vivian, "Escaping Women: Paradox and Achievement in Late Roman Asceticism," in *The Formulation of Christianity by Conflict through the Ages,* ed. K. B. Free (Lewiston, 1995), pp. 101–125.

7. See, for example, E. A. Clark, "Ascetic Renunciation and Feminine Advance-ment: A Paradox of Late Ancient Christianity," *Anglican Theological Review* 63 (1981), pp. 240–257; R. S. Kraemer, "The Conversion of Women to Ascetic Forms of Christianity," *Signs* 6 (1980), pp. 298–307; Lane Fox (1986), pp. 306–311; G. Cloke, *"This Female Man of God": Women and Spiritual Power in the Patris-tic Age* A.D. *350–450* (London, 1995), pp. 57–81; G. Clark, "Women and Asceti-cism in Late Antiquity: The Refusal of Status and Gender," in *Asceticism,* ed. V. Wimbush and R. Valantasis (Oxford, 1995), pp. 33–48.

8. Brown (1961), pp. 1–11.

9. For example, N. Moine, "Melaniana," *Recherches Augustiniennes* 15 (1980), pp. 1–79; A. Yarbrough, "Christianization in the Fourth Century: The Example of Roman Women," *Church History* 45 (1976), pp. 149–165; W. Eck, "Das Eindringen des Christentums in den Senatorenstand bis zu Konstantin d. Gr.," *Chiron* 1 (1971), pp. 381–406; Stark (1996), pp. 99–101; and G. Disselkamp, *"Christiani Senatus Lumina"* in *Zum Anteil römischer Frauen der Oberschicht im. 4 und 5. Jahrhundert an der Christianisierung der römischen Senatsaristokratie* (Bodenheim, Germany, 1997), pp. 1–11 and 228–232.

10. Jer. *Ep.* 133.3 (*CSEL* 56.246) alludes to Melania as a woman "cuius nomen nigredinis testatur perfidiae tenebras" because she has supported his enemy, Rufinus. Although Jerome praised Melania earlier (*Ep.* 3.3, 4.2, 39.5, 45.4–5; *CSEL* 54.15, .20, .305, .325), he omits her from his discussion of the C(a)eionian family, to which she is nearly related (*Ep.* 107; *CSEL* 55.290–305), and erased her name from his *Chronicle* after his fight with Rufinus (Rufinus *Apologia contra Hieronymum* 2.29; *CCSL* 20.105).

11. See also B. Feichtinger, *Apostolae apostolorum: Frauenaskese als Befreiung und Zwang bei Hieronymus* (Frankfurt am Main, 1995), pp. 209ff.

12. A. Arjava, *Women and Law in Late Antiquity* (Oxford, 1996), pp. 111–156, and

"Paternal Power in Late Antiquity," *JRS* 88 (1998), pp. 147–165. I use patriarchal to indicate subordination, including as well the idea, expressed by R. Saller, "*Pater Familias, Mater Familias* and the Gendered Semantics of the Roman Household," *CPh* 94(1) (1999), pp. 192–193, that "the husband-wife and father-child relationships were believed by (male) authors to be unequal."

13. The first part of this chapter is based in part on earlier studies, Salzman (1989), pp. 207–220, and (1992), pp. 451–479. My initial work has been augmented by research, and the database used here has been improved; see Appendix 1.

14. The stony silence of pagan women in my study population concerning religious affiliation is parallel to the findings of other scholars, such as MacMullen (1981), pp. 116–117, and S. K. Heyob, *The Cult of Isis among Women in the Greco-Roman World* (Leiden, 1975), pp. 86ff. and 110.

15. Even in inscriptions that indicate family ties (which are largely funerary), husband-to-wife dedications predominate in the early empire. R. P. Saller and B. D. Shaw, "Tombstones and Roman Family Relations in the Principate: Civilians, Soldiers and Slaves," *JRS* 74 (1984), pp. 336–355.

16. B. D. Shaw, "Latin Funerary Epigraphy and Family Life in the Later Roman Empire," *Historia* 33 (1984), pp. 457–497.

17. Ibid., p. 467.

18. Men were dated by the time of their lowest office; women were dated by calculating when they reached age twenty. See Appendix 1.

19. For example, Jer. *Ep.* 22.20 (*CSEL* 54.170): "Laudo nuptias, laudo coniugium, sed quia mihi virgines generant"; cf. *Ep.* 107.1 (*CSEL* 55.290–291). On Laeta, see A. Yarbrough (1976), pp. 162–164.

20. This number is derived from G. Stoico, *L'epistolario di S. Girolamo* (Naples, 1972), pp. 69ff., who omitted the unnamed virgins of Emona. See Jer. *Ep.* 107.1 (*CSEL* 55.290–291) for Toxotius, App. 2 (of this book) = Toxotius 1, *PLRE* 1.921. One other case of a conversion in the group of women attested by Jerome's letters is alleged by Gerontius, *Vie de Sainte Mélanie* 50–55, ed. D. Gorce (*SC* 90.224–238): the brother of Albina the Younger, Volusianus, App. 2 = Volusianus 6, *PLRE* 2.1184–1185, remained a pagan until his deathbed conversion in 437 by his niece, Melania the Younger.

21. Hippolytus, *Refut. omnium haeresium* 9.12.24 (*GCS* 26.250); see Lane Fox (1986), pp. 308ff.

22. Justinian, *Dig.* 23.2.44 (*Lex Iulia et Papia, Book 1,* Paul) and 1.9.12 (Ulpian). *C.Th.* 4.12 reiterates Claudian's strictures against freedwomen and senatorial women marrying slaves in 314, 362, and 366. This prohibition remained into the fifth century; see *The Novels of Anthemius* 1.1, 1.2, and 1.3, and S. Mazzarino, *The End of the Ancient World,* trans. G. Holmes (New York, 1966), pp. 120ff.

23. Julia Soaemias wed the equestrian Varius Marcellus, H. Dessau, *ILS* 478; Cass. Dio. 78.3.2–3. Julia Mamaea, another niece of Julia Domna, also wed an equestrian and retained her rank, but her husband was not elevated; thus is explained a ruling of Caracalla, *Dig.* 1.9.12 (*Census, Book 2,* Ulpian), that al-

lowed the emperor's kinswomen to retain their rank even if married to nonsenators.

24. Julia Soaemias (*HA Elagabulus* 4.3–4) was associated with a *senaculum* whose duties had included preventing the loss of nobility by aristocratic women who married nonsenators. Although the veracity of this *senaculum* has been disputed, the wording is so similar to the formula of the Edict of Pope Callistus that S. Mazzarino (1966), pp. 131–132, conjectured a direct connection between the two documents. W. Eck (1971), pp. 389–391, cites five senatorial women married to nonsenatorial men who kept their rank.

25. Aug. *De fid. et op.* 19.35 (*CSEL* 41.80); *De adult. coniug.* 1.21, .25, .26 (*PL* 40.465ff.); B. A. Pereira, *La doctrine du mariage selon S. Augustin*, 2d ed. (Paris, 1930), pp. 165–171. Church councils did not declare intermarriage illicit; at most they adopted canonic sanctions. See M. Bianchini, "Disparità di culto e matrimonio; orientamenti del pensiero cristiano e della legislazione imperiale nel IV secolo D.C.," *Serta Historica Antiqua* 15 (1986), pp. 233–246.

26. R. S. Kramer (1980), pp. 298–307.

27. The infrequency of intermarriage in this study accords with the absence of legislation in the Theodosian Code against pagans marrying Christians. This is especially striking since the intermarriage of Christians and Jews is expressly prohibited (*C.Th.* 3.7.2 = *C.Th.* 9.7.5 [388 C.E.]; see also *C.Th.* 16.8.6 [339]) and since there is a good deal of law on married life (e.g., *C.Th.* 3.5–16, 4.12).

28. This number omits the marriage of the poetess Proba to Clodius Celsinus signo Adelphius, both of whom I considered as Christians. Although Proba had some sort of religious change of heart, her poetry leaves it uncertain if her conversion (*Cento* 45–55, 415–428, 594; *CSEL* 16.571), was from paganism or from a disinterested Christianity to sincere belief. See Clark and Hatch (1981), pp. 97–102. Similarly, her husband's Christianity is attested (*Cento* 689–694; *CSEL* 16.609) but not his conversion.

29. Toxotius, App. 2 = Toxotius 1, *PLRE* 1.921.

30. This is the account found in Palladius *Hist. Laus.* 54 (ed. C. Butler [Hildesheim, Germany, 1967 reprint], p. 146). See also Paul. of Nola. *Carmen* 21.211–260, 313–325 (*CSEL* 30.165–166, .168) on the baptism of Turcius Apronianus, App. 2 = Apronianus 8, *PLRE* 1.87–88.

31. Publilius C(a)eionius Caecina Albinus, App. 2 = Albinus 8, *PLRE* 1.34–35; C(a)eionius Rufius Albinus, App. 2 = Albinus 14, *PLRE* 1.37.

32. The tradition appears in Theodoret, *HE* 1.18 (*GCS* 44.63–65), who is followed by, among others, Gelasius of Cyzicus, *HE* 3.6.1 (*GCS* 28.144–145); see T. D. Barnes, *Constantine and Eusebius* (Cambridge, Mass., 1981), p. 49.

33. The sons were Caecina Decius Albinus Iunior, App. 2 = Albinus 10, *PLRE* 1.35–36, and Rufius Antonius Agrypnius Volusianus, App. 1 = Volusianus 6, *PLRE* 2.1184–1185.

34. As P. Brown (1961), p. 7, argued. See also A. Chastagnol, "Le sénateur Volusien et la conversion d'une famille de l'aristocratie romaine au bas-empire," *REA* 68 (1956), pp. 241–253.

35. Turcius Apronianus, App. 2 = Apronianus 8, *PLRE* 1.87–88, father of a Christian son Asterius and a Christian daughter, Eunomia; Toxotius, App. 2 = Toxotius 1, *PLRE* 1.921, had no son, only a Christian daughter, Paula 2, App. 2 = Paula 2, *PLRE* 1.675.

36. Laeta, App. 2 = Laeta 2, *PLRE* 1.492; Albina, App. 2 = Albina 2, *PLRE* 1.33; Avita, App. 2 = Avita, *PLRE* 1.126; and Paula, App. 2 = Paula 2, *PLRE* 1.675, were daughters of Christian mothers in mixed marriages.

37. Eus. *VC* 3.47 (*GCS* 1.1.103); cf. T. G. Elliott, "Constantine's Conversion: Do We Really Need It?" *Phoenix* 41 (1987), p. 421.

38. Aug. *Quaest. in Hept.* 1.153 (*CCSL* 33.59); cf. Aristotle *Politics* 1.2.12.

39. B. D. Shaw, "The Family in Late Antiquity: The Experience of Augustine," *Past and Present* 115 (1987), p. 28 and note 104, citing Aug. *Serm.* 332.4 (*PL* 38.1463): "'You are the master, she is the slave,' those are the terms of the *tabellae matrimoniales.*"

40. John Chrys. *Hom.* 20.2 on *Ephesians* (*PG* 62, 135–138). See also B. D. Shaw (1987), pp. 28–29; A. Arjava (1996), pp. 127–133.

41. A. Arjava, "Women in the Christian Empire: Ideological Change and Social Reality," *Studia Patristica* 24, ed. E. Livingstone (1993), pp. 6–7, cites Aug. *Quaest. in Hept.* 1.153 (*CCSL* 33.59) and Jer. *In Tit.* 2.3–5 (*PL* 26.617). See also A. Arjava (1996), pp. 127–133.

42. Ambrosiaster *Comm. ad Eph.* 5.24 (*CSEL* 81.3.118); Ambrosiaster *Comm. ad 1 Tim.* on Adam and Eve, at 2.11–14 (*CSEL* 81.3.263).

43. Ambrosiaster, *Comm. ad 1 Cor.* 14.34–35 (*CSEL* 81.2.163–164); cf. for the East, John Chrys. *Hom.* 20.1 on *Ephesians* (*PG* 62.135–136).

44. On women as guardians, see *C.Th.* 3.17.4 (390), and A. Arjava (1996), p. 174; on wealthy wives, ibid., p. 129. On demographics, see R. Saller, "Men's Age at Marriage and Its Consequences in the Roman Family," *CP* 82 (1987), pp. 21–34, and G. Nathan, *The Family in Late Antiquity* (London, 2000), pp. 155–158.

45. Melania the Elder, App. 2 = Melania 1, *PLRE* 1.592–593; Paul. of Nola *Ep.* 29.5–11 (*CSEL* 29.251–258); Pall. *Hist. Laus.* 46 (ed. C. Butler, pp. 134–136); Jer. *Ep.* 39.5 (*CSEL* 54.305).

46. Aug. *Ep.* 262.3–9 (*CSEL* 52.623–629). On Roman women in control of property, see A. Arjava (1996), pp. 73–75, 132–156.

47. Soz. *HE* 5.15 (*PG* 67.1260B); cf. J. M. G. Barclay, "The Family as the Bearer of Religion in Judaism and Early Christianity," in *Constructing Early Christian Families,* ed. H. Moxnes (London, 1997), pp. 75–78.

48. *C.Th.* 16.10.12 (392); 16.10.13 (395). This is also in accord with Roman law on *patria postestas;* A. Arjava (1998), 155–165. See also Maximus of Turin, *Sermo.* 106.1.13–18, 107.1.14–21 (*CSEL* 23.417, .420); and Zeno *Trac.* 1.25.10, 1.35.1–3 (*CSEL* 22.75, .89).

49. The anonymous fourth-century *Homily on Virginity,* in V. W. Wimbush, *Ascetic Behavior in Greco-Roman Antiquity: A Sourcebook* (Minneapolis, 1990), pp. 33–44.

50. Sid. Ap. *Ep.* 3.12 = *CIL* 13.2352.

51. Prudentius *C. Symm.* 1.558–560 (*CSEL* 61.240), trans. H. J. Thomson (*LCL*), p. 393. Other prominent families are then noted by their male converts, such

as the consul and heir of the Olybrian family, 1.553–555, and Sextus Petronius Probus' family, 1.552ff.

52. Brown (1988), pp. 13–14.
53. H. Dessau, *ILS* 1259.9–11, trans. Brown (1988), p. 15.
54. Ambr. *Ep.* 14[63].107 (*CSEL* 82.3.293).
55. Ambr. *De Abraham* 1.5.37 (*CSEL* 32.1.530.15–18), trans. W. J. Dooley; see W. J. Dooley, *Marriage according to Ambrose* (Washington, D.C., 1948), p. 25; pp. 25–30, for a discussion of Ambrose's notion of marriage as salvation, but the texts do not demonstrate equality in marriage.
56. R. MacMullen, "Woman in Public in the Roman Empire," *Historia* 29 (1980), pp. 208–218; E. Forbis, "Women's Public Image in Italian Honorary Inscriptions," *AJPh* 111 (1990), pp. 502–504; J. Scheid, "The Religious Roles of Roman Women," in *A History of Women in the West*, vol. 1, ed. P. Schmitt Pantel (Cambridge, Mass., 1992), pp. 377–408; R. S. Kraemer, *Her Share of the Blessings: Women's Religions among Pagans, Jews and Christians in the Greco-Roman World* (Oxford, 1992), pp. 80–93; and A. Richlin, "Carrying Water in a Sieve," in *Women and Goddess Traditions in Antiquity and Today*, ed. K. L. King (Minneapolis, Minn., 1997), p. 341.
57. Paul. of Nola *Ep.* 44.4 (*CSEL* 29.375–376), trans. P. G. Walsh (*ACW* 36), p. 240; see also *Ep.* 38, 39, 44 (*CSEL* 29.323–334, .334–339, .369–378). Aper and Amanda are in Appendix 2.
58. Cf. Paul. of Nola *Ep.* 51 (*CSEL* 29.423–425) for Eucherius and Galla, although neither are included in my sample for neither were known to be *clarissimi;* and for Paulinus and Therasia, discussed by P. G. Walsh (*ACW* 36), pp. 1–3. Wives who encouraged their husbands to enter monastic life became so common that in sixth-century Gaul canonical regulations were placed on the husbands' behavior. See Council of Turin, *Can.* 20(19) (*CCSL* 148a.183–184).
59. Paul. of Nola *Ep.* 44.6 (*CSEL* 29.377), trans. P. G. Walsh (*ACW* 36), pp. 241–242.
60. Clark and Hatch (1981), p. 109.
61. *Vie de Sainte Mélanie* 1–6, ed. D. Gorce (*SC* 90.130–139).
62. Aug. *Ep.* 262.4–8 (*CSEL* 57.624–628), trans. W. Parsons (*FOTC* 5), pp. 261–262.
63. Jerome *Ep.* 127.4 (*CSEL* 56.148–149), trans. F. A. Wright (*LCL*), p. 449.
64. *Vie de Sainte Mélanie* 1, ed. D. Gorce (*SC* 90.130), trans. E. A. Clark, *The Life of Melania the Younger* (New York, 1984), p. 27. See J. Harries, "'Treasure in Heaven': Property and Inheritance among Senators of Late Rome," in *Marriage and Property*, ed. E. M. Craik (Aberdeen, 1984), pp. 65–69.
65. *Vie de Sainte Mélanie* 7, ed. D. Gorce (*SC* 90.139–140).
66. *Vie de Sainte Mélanie* 8–12, ed. D. Gorce (*SC* 90.140–152). The conflict between Severus and the younger Melania's relatives fueled a slave revolt, leading the urban prefect and Roman senate to try to confiscate the couple's property: see ibid., 10, 19 (*SC* 90.144–146, 90.162–168). The *Vie* 12, 19 (*SC* 90.148–152, 90.162–168) attributes the resolution to the Empress Serena and to God. For the animal imagery, see Pall. *Hist. Laus.* 54 (ed. C. Butler, pp. 146–148).
67. Ambr. *De virg.* 1.11.66 (*PL* 16.207–208).

68. Ambr. *Ep.* 62[19].2 (*CSEL* 82.2.121–122), and see note 25 above for church leaders' opposition to betrothing pagans and Christians even as they acknowledge the limits of their influence.
69. Aug. *De fide et operibus* 19.35 (*CSEL* 41.80).
70. Aug. *Conf.* 9.9; Salzman (1993), pp. 362–378, note 54.
71. R. MacMullen (1980), pp. 208–218. Here I disagree with Brown (1988), pp. 16–17; the much-praised *parrhésia* of second-century women does not fit the widespread fourth-century womanly ideal, nor did Christianity change the expectation that married women be subordinate to men, whatever else it may have changed.
72. John Chrys. *Hom.* 31 on *Rom* 16.5 (*PG* 60.668–669); cf. John's emphasis on Priscilla's role as atypical in *Hom.* 10 on 2 *Tim.* 4.9–13 (*PG* 62.657–658). A woman may serve the church and speak, but public teaching is not acceptable; see John Chrys. *Hom.* 30 and 31 on *Rom.* 16.5 (*PG* 60.661–676); J. Lang, *Ministers of Grace: Women in the Early Church* (Slough, England, 1989), pp. 73–92. Chrysostom does not support a role for women in the ministry, as seen by G. Gould, "Women in the Writings of the Fathers: Language, Belief and Reality," in *Women in the Church,* ed. W. J. Sheils and D. Wood (Oxford, 1990), pp. 1–14.
73. Pelagius *Expos. XIII ep. Pauli, Comm. 1 Tim.* 2.12; Pelagius *Comm. 1 Cor.* 11, 5 (ed. A. Souter [Cambridge, U.K., 1926] pp. 482, 188).
74. Jer. *Ep.* 122.4 (*CSEL* 56.70), trans. W. H. Fremantle (*NPNF* 6), p. 229.
75. A. Arjava (1996), pp. 177–192; J. Evans Grubbs, *Law and Family in Late Antiquity* (Oxford, 1995), pp. 225–260; G. Nathan (2000), pp. 107–116.
76. John Chrys. *De non iter. conj.* 5 (*PG* 48.616). For divorce, see A. Arjava (1996), pp. 177–192.
77. J. Goody, *The Development of the Family and Marriage in Europe* (Cambridge, U.K., 1983), pp. 89ff.; J. M. G. Barclay (1997), pp. 66–80; G. Cloke (1995), pp. 153ff.
78. Pelagius to Celantia, *CSEL* 56.329–356; Augustine to Ecdicia, *Ep.* 262.4–8 (*CSEL* 57.624–628); G. Cloke (1995), pp. 150ff.
79. B. D. Shaw (1987), pp. 32ff. J. Gardner, *Women in Roman Law and Society* (London, 1986), pp. 146ff.; G. Cloke (1995), pp. 134ff.
80. Pub. Syr. *Max.* 105, ed. R. A. H. Bickford-Smith (London, 1895), p. 7: "Casta ad virum matrona parendo imperat."
81. A. Arjava (1996), pp. 48–52; A. Arjava (1998), pp. 147–165.
82. Symm. *Ep.* 6.67, 6.40. Symmachus' admonitions may have been more rhetorical than real, but they exemplify the parental role.
83. Cato *De Agr.* 143; D. Harmon, "The Family Festivals of Rome," *ANRW* II, part 16.2, pp. 1592–1603.
84. Prud. *C. Symm.* 1.197–214 (*CSEL* 61.226–227). The cult of the Genius was a fourth-century reality; it was expressly forbidden by *C.Th.* 16.10.2.
85. Prud. *C. Symm.* 1.205–208 (*CSEL* 61.226). See note 96 below.
86. J. Scheid (1992), p. 380.
87. Servius *Ad Aen.* 1.730; parodied by Petronius *Sat.* 60.
88. Fronto *Vol.* 1.180, ed. C. R. Haines *(LCL).*

89. Aeneas' roles as father and son are paradigmatic. Virg. *Aeneid* 5.97–103; Ovid *Fasti* 2.533ff.; W. Eisenhut, "Parentalia," *RE Suppl.,* Bd. XII (1970), cols. 979–982. For third- and fourth-century Africa, see B. D. Shaw (1987), p. 28, note 102.

90. Aug. *En. Psalm.* 127.2 (*CCSL* 40.1869). Augustine notes that the duty of maintaining and setting up the *monumentum* for the deceased fell upon the parents, if they were alive, or on "filii aut quicumque cognati vel amici" if they were not. *De cur. mort.* 4.6 (*CSEL* 41.630–631); B. D. Shaw (1987), p. 27.

91. J. Scheid (1992), pp. 377–408.

92. T. Wiedemann, *Adults and Children in the Roman Empire* (New Haven, 1989), pp. 155ff.

93. Macrobius *Sat.* (Praef.); Martianus Capella *De Nuptiis Phil. et Merc.* 1.2, trans. W. H. Stahl, *Martianus Capella and the Seven Liberal Arts* (New York, 1971), vol. 2, pp. 4, 8–12. Aulus Gellius apparently wrote his *Noctes Atticae* for his children as well (*Praef.* 1–2).

94. See MacMullen (1981), p. 11, note 50, and pp. 46–48, note 21, for second-century inscriptions that show how a chorus might have been organized. See also Cassius Dio 75.4.5 (193 C.E.); Herodian 4.2.5 (211).

95. B. D. Shaw (1987), p. 33; R. S. Kraemer (1992), pp. 66ff. For women tied to their natal families (i.e., women buried in father's, not husband's, tombs), see B. Rawson, "The Roman Family," in *The Family in Ancient Rome,* ed. B. Rawson (London, 1986), pp. 20ff., and A. Arjava (1996), pp. 123–133.

96. Prud. *C. Symm.* 1.197–214 (*CSEL* 61.226–227) describes a mother worshipping Fortuna at a family rite. Fortuna is identified by her cornucopia. If Prudentius confused Fortuna with the Genius of the household (who also held a cornucopia), then he is depicting the mother participating in the husband's family cult, leading B. Rawson (1986), p. 20, to question the extent of the wife's exclusion from her husband's ancestral religion.

97. J. Scheid (1992), p. 405.

98. Salzman (1990), pp. 159–161. For private rites, see ibid., p. 159, note 159; Ovid *Fasti* 6.309–318; see also Virg. *Aen.* 5.744 and cf. Serv. *Comm. ad Ecl.* 8.82. On the *Matralia,* reserved only for *matronae,* see R. S. Kraemer (1992), pp. 66–70; Salzman (1990), pp. 128, 131.

99. A. Richlin (1997), p. 336, note 37, cites Paulus 472L for priestesses and virgins who used a sacrificial knife; see ibid., p. 342, for artifacts such as the tombstone of a woman *sacerdos* of Venus and Ceres that depicts a woman sacrificing. For sacrifice to the *Bona Dea,* see H. S. Versnel, "The Festival for Bona Dea and the Thesmophoria," *Greece and Rome* 39 (1992), pp. 31–55.

100. J. Scheid (1992), p. 405.

101. Jer. *Ep.* 54.15 (*CSEL* 54.482).

102. Aus. *Ep.* 24 (ed. H. G. Evelyn White, *LCL,* vol. 2, p. 86) = *Ep.* 18 (ed. R. P. H. Green [Oxford, 1991], p. 217); Aus. *Ep.* 27.9–12 (ed. White, *LCL,* vol. 2, p. 100) = *Ep.* 27.8–12 (ed. Green, p. 217). For the age of Paulinus, see D. Trout, *Paulinus of Nola: Life, Letters and Poems* (Berkeley, 1999), p. 287.

103. John Chrys. *De inani gloria* (*SC* 188.39–40).
104. Ibid. (*SC* 188.41).
105. Ibid. (*SC* 188.88).
106. Ibid. (*SC* 188.19).
107. John Chrys. *Adversus oppug. vit. monast. Lib.* 3 (*PG* 47.386); see also ibid., 47.370, .383.
108. John Chrys. *De inani gloria* (*SC* 188.90); cf. *PG* 51.240.
109. Although this speech is prescriptive in nature, we know much about the attitudes of Chrysostom and his contemporaries from other sources; cf. B. D. Shaw (1987), pp. 4–13. Thus K. Holum, *Theodosian Empresses* (Berkeley, 1982) p. 78, may be right that though John's prejudices against women were "out of date" where the empress was concerned, his views won the support of many in his aristocratic audience in the East and West.
110. Eus. *HE* 6.2.7–10.
111. *Acta Martyrum, PL* 8, col. 699. The proconsul asks the boy Hilarianus, "Did you follow your father or your brothers?" The boy answers, "I am a Christian and of my own free will I assembled with my father and brothers."
112. Eus. *VC* 4.51 (*GCS* 1.1.141).
113. Julian, *Ep.* 23, 38; *Ep. ad Ath.* 271B-C; Soz. 5.2 (*PG* 67.1213).
114. Arsenius 4, *PLRE* 1.111.
115. Jer. *Ep.* 128.4 (*CSEL* 56.160), trans. F. A. Wright (*LCL*), p. 477.
116. Jer. *Ep.* 107.4 (*CSEL* 55.294–295). Jerome owes much of his educational program to Quintilian's *Institutes;* see J. M. Petersen, "The Education of Girls in Fourth-Century Rome," pp. 29–38, and G. Clark, "The Fathers and the Children," p. 20, in *The Church and Childhood,* ed. D. Wood (Oxford, 1994).
117. Jer. *Ep.* 107.6 (*CSEL* 55.297). John Chrysostom shares Jerome's view that the father is responsible for the salvation of his dependents, his wife, and children. John Chrys. *Hom. 21 ad Eph.* 6.4 (*PG* 62.154) and *Adversus oppug. vit. monast. Lib.* 3.3–4 (*PG* 47.351–356). See G. Gould, "Childhood in Eastern Patristic Thought: Some Problems of Theology and Theological Anthropology," in *The Church and Childhood,* ed. D. Wood (Oxford, 1994), pp. 39–52. Similary, Paulinus, *Ep.* 44.5–6 (*CSEL* 29.376–377) views the parents, but especially the father, even the ascetic Aper, as responsible for the religiosity of the children. See also Gaudentius, in V. M. Wimbush (1990), pp. 33–44.
118. Jer. *Ep.* 107.6 (*CSEL* 55.297) quotes 1 *Tim.* 2.15 but uses *pudicitia* instead of *sophrosyne.*
119. See, for example, Tertullian *De virg. vel.* 9.6 (*CSEL* 76.93), speaking to a nonaristocratic audience, and G. Nathan (2000), pp. 142–154, whose emphasis on the mother as primary religious educator runs counter to my evidence.
120. Clark and Hatch (1981), pp. 7, 97ff.; H. Sivan, "Anician Women, the *Cento* of Proba, and Aristocratic Conversion in the Fourth Century," *Vig. Chr.* 47 (1993), pp. 140–157.
121. Claudian 10, *Epith. Hon. et Mariae* 229–237. Although some girls did go to school, there is no evidence of this for the fourth century. The one case that is

cited, the grandparents of Ausonius, were not aristocrats at the time they attended school; see A. C. Dionisotti, "From Ausonius' Schooldays," *JRS* 72 (1982), p. 102, who notes Aus. *Protr. ad nep.* 33–34 and Jer. *Ep.* 107.4 as showing the more typical situation of home education.

122. Jer. *Ep.* 128.1 (*CSEL* 56.156–157). For an education similar to Paula's, see *Ep.* 107.9, .12 (*CSEL* 55.300, .302–303), and to Macrina's, Gregory of Nyssa, *Vie de Sainte Macrine* 3 (*SC* 178.148–150) and *De anima et resurr.* (*PG* 46.21). Cf. Symmachus' reminder that his daughter spin; *Ep.* 6.67. In a senator's villa in fifth-century Gaul, Sid. Apoll. (*Ep.* 2.9.4) describes a library with "devotional style" books for ladies and books "distinguished by the grandeur of Latin eloquence" for men. Cf. A. Momigliano, "The Life of St. Macrina by Gregory of Nyssa," in *The Craft of the Ancient Historian*, ed. J. Eadie and J. Ober (Lanham, Md., 1985), pp. 443–582.

123. It was exceptional for a mother like Saint Paula to study Hebrew as well as exegesis with her daughters under Jerome's guidance; see J. N. D. Kelly, *Jerome* (London, 1975), pp. 91ff.; G. Cloke (1995), pp. 134ff.; and J. M. Petersen (1994), pp. 29–31. Similarly exceptional were Melania the Elder and Melania the Younger; see Palladius *Hist. Laus.* 54 (ed. C. Butler, pp. 146–148); *Vie de Sainte Mélanie* 26, ed. D. Gorce (*SC* 90.178–180).

124. W. Harris, *Ancient Literacy* (Oxford, 1989), pp. 304ff., cites John Chrys. *Hom in Ioann.* 32.3 (*PG* 59.187–188) and *De Lazaro* 3.1–4 (*PG* 48.991–996). Chrystostom's condemnation of the lazy literary habits of aristocrats may be a literary trope; cf. Amm. Marc. 14.6.18.

125. G. Cloke (1995), pp. 139ff.

126. Ambr. *Expos. ad Luc.* 10.157 (*CCSL* 14.390).

127. A. Arjava (1993), p. 7; A. Arjava (1996), pp. 230–256.

128. R. Nürnberg, "Non decet neque necessarium est, ut mulieres doceant," *JAC* 31 (1988), pp. 51–73.

129. Jer. *Ep.* 127.7 (*CSEL* 56.151), trans. F. A. Wright (*LCL*), p. 455.

130. This incident was recorded in the Latin version of Melania's life. In what may be a significant difference between East and West, only in the Greek version did her audience include men of learning. See G. Clark, *Women in Late Antiquity* (Oxford, 1993), p. 128; and *The Life of Melania the Younger*, ed. E. A. Clark (New York, 1984), p. 22–23.

131. G. Clark (1993), p. 128; cf. V. Burrus, *The Making of a Heretic: Gender, Authority, and the Priscillianist Controversy* (Berkeley, 1995), pp. 7–9, 33–34.

132. Jer. *Ep.* 54.3 (*CSEL* 54.468); Jerome could point to statements in the New Testament (e.g., *Matthew* 10.37) for support.

133. J. Goody (1983), p. 88.

134. Jer. *Ep.* 38.5, 40.2, 39.6 (*CSEL* 54.292–293, .310–311, .306–307).

135. Clark and Hatch (1981), pp. 97–121; Clodius Celsinus signo Adelphius, App. 2 = Celsinus 6, *PLRE* 1.192–193; Faltonia Betitia Proba 2, App. 2 = Proba 2, *PLRE* 1.732.

136. Clark and Hatch (1981), p. 111.

322   Notes to Pages 163–167

137. *Cento* 477–479 (*CSEL* 16.597); Clark and Hatch (1981), pp. 111–112.

138. *Cento* 524–526 (*CSEL* 16.600); Clark and Hatch (1981), p. 112.

139. *Cento* 522 (*CSEL* 16.600); Clark and Hatch (1981), pp. 118–121.

140. *Cento* 205 (*CSEL* 16.581): "animum subita dulcedine movit" just as Venus urges Juno to persuade her husband Jupiter. See *Cento* 132–146, *Cento* 183–203 (*CSEL* 16.577, .580–581); *Cento* 194 (*CSEL* 16.580), which echoes *Aen.* 4.113; Clark and Hatch (1981), pp. 151–159.

141. *Cento* 693 (*CSEL* 16.609); Clark and Hatch (1981), pp. 116–119, note that this line echoes *Aen.* 2.777.

142. G. Clark (1993), pp. 102–103; G. Jenal, *Italia ascetica atque monastica: Das Asketen und Mönchtum in Italien von den Anfängen bis zur Zeit der Langobarden* (Stuttgart, 1995), vol. 1, pp. 12–143.

143. J. Goody (1983), p. 89, and J. Evans Grubbs, *Law and Family in Late Antiquity: The Emperor Constantine's Marriage Legislation* (Oxford, 1995), have questioned how "Christian" these legal changes were.

144. *C.Th.* 8.16.1.

145. H. J. W. Drijvers, "Virginity and Asceticism in Late Roman Western Elites," in *Sexual Asymmetry,* ed. J. Blok and P. Mason (Amsterdam, 1987), pp. 353–354.

146. S. Treggiari, *Roman Marriage* (Oxford, 1991), pp. 176–180.

147. G. Clark (1993), p. 15, on legal status; A. Arjava (1996), pp. 167–177.

148. M. Lightman and W. Zeisel, "Univira: An Example of Continuity and Change in Roman Society," *Church History* 46 (1977), pp. 19–32.

149. J. Evans Grubbs (1995), pp. 118–131.

150. B. D. Shaw and P. Saller, "Close Kin Marriage in Roman Society?" *Man* n.s. 19 (1984), pp. 432–444. Cf. A. Arjava, (1996), pp. 164–167; J. Evans Grubbs (1995), pp. 118–131.

151. Basil *Ep.* 199.18 (*PG* 32.719) and Jerome, discussed by G. Clark (1993), p. 53.

152. Aug. *Ep.* 3*.1.3 (*CSEL* 88.22), ed. J. Divjak (Vienna, 1981).

153. *C.Th.* 8.16.2.

154. G. Clark (1993), pp. 140, 124, and 50–56. See also G. Gould (1990), pp. 10ff., on Gregory's portrait of Gorgonia.

155. Paul. of Nola *Ep.* 29.9 (*CSEL* 29.255–257); Palladius *Hist. Laus.* 46 (ed. C. Butler, pp. 134–136); J. Harries (1984), p. 59; and E. A. Clark, "Ascetic Renunciation and Feminine Advancement: A Paradox of Late Ancient Christianity," in *Ascetic Piety and Women's Faith,* ed. E. A. Clark (New York, 1986), pp. 175–208.

156. See Brown (1961), pp. 9–10, and Brown (1988), especially pp. 343ff., on the impact of upper-class ascetic women in the West. Neither he nor J. Harries (1984), pp. 54–70, sees the class as threatened by asceticism.

157. G. Clark (1993), pp. 139–140.

158. K. Cooper, "Insinuations of Womanly Influence: An Aspect of the Christianization of the Roman Aristocracy," *JRS* 82 (1992), pp. 150–164.

159. For a similar reaction in the fifth and sixth centuries, see K. Cooper, *The Virgin and the Bride: Idealized Womanhood in Late Antiquity* (Cambridge, Mass., 1996), pp. 116–143.

160. See notes 6 and 7 above; and J. Simpson, "Asceticism in the Fourth Century: A Question of Interpretation," *Journal of Religious History* 15 (1988), pp. 38–60; H. J. W. Drijvers (1987), pp. 241–273.

161. G. Clark (1993), p. 127; Averil Cameron, "Virginity as Metaphor: Women and the Rhetoric of Early Christianity," in *History as Text*, ed. Averil Cameron (Chapel Hill, N.C., 1989), pp. 181–205; A. Arjava (1996), pp. 157–164.

162. E. A. Clark (1984), p. 93, notes 3–7. Marcella, App. 2 = Marcella 2, *PLRE* 1.542–543, refused remarriage to the elderly N(a)eratius Cerealis, probably after his consulship in 358. Although Jerome (*Ep.* 127.5; *CSEL* 56.149–150) dates Marcella, the first aristocratic ascetic woman, as interested in asceticism in 340 C.E., that is probably too early: she lived until 410 and would have been a child in 340.

163. Ambrose's sister, Marcellina, was consecrated to virginity by Pope Liberius in Rome sometime after 353, but Ambrose, *De virg.* 3.1 (*PL* 16.231–233), does not tell if the "many virgins" who were present were aristocrats. Pope Damasus' sister Irene may have lived an ascetic life around 360, but she was not aristocratic. Asella and Lea, probably aristocrats, were older female ascetics in Rome when Jerome arrived in the 380s, but we do not know how long Lea had practiced asceticism; Jerome *Ep.* 23.2 (*CSEL* 54.212). Asella, about age fifty in 384, had been dedicated to virginity at age twelve, therefore ca. 346 C.E.; Jer. *Ep.* 24.2–3 (*CSEL* 54.215–216).

164. *Cento* 45–55 (*CSEL* 16.572); Clark and Hatch (1981), pp. 97–102. The editors date the poem to ca. 362.

165. Theodoret *HE* 2.14 (*GCS* 44.125–128), trans. B. Jackson *(NPNF)*, p. 79.

166. Clark and Hatch (1981), p. 110. R. Lizzi, "Ascetismo e monachesimo nell'Italia tardoantica," *Codex Aquilarensis* 5 (1991), pp. 56–61, suggests that ascetic withdrawal at Rome was a means of expressing resistance to Constantius' religious policies.

167. Brown (1988), p. 344.

168. Jer. *Ep.* 54.18, 127.2 (*CSEL* 54.485, 56.146–147). Melania the Younger, App. 2, another celibate widow, came from a family already Christian under Constantius II. Lea, a prominent Christian widow, converted to asceticism. Jerome *Ep.* 23.3, 24.1 (*CSEL* 54.213–214).

169. Asella 1, App. 2 = Asella 1, *PLRE* 1.117, identified as the "possible" sister of Marcella.

170. Brown (1988), pp. 366–386.

171. Amm. Marc. 28.1, 28.47–56.

172. See G. Clark (1993), p. 131 and note 4, for bibliography.

173. See D. Hunter, "Resistance to the Virginal Ideal in Late Fourth-Century Rome: The Case of Jovinian," *Theological Studies* 48 (1987), pp. 45–67. Cf. in Milan, Brown (1988), pp. 341–365.

174. Jer. *Ep.* 23.3 (*CSEL* 54.213); A. Yarbrough (1976), pp. 149–165; A. Arjava (1996), pp. 157–167; Averil Cameron (1989), pp. 181–205.

175. A. Yarbrough (1976), pp. 149–165. Cf. Ambr. *De virg.* 1.11.65–66 (*PL* 16.207–

208), who underscores the widespread sense among Christians that the ascetic needs to win family approval first.

176. D. Hunter (1987), pp. 45–64.

177. V. Burrus (1995), p. 1–22; Brown (1988), p. 372.

178. K. Cooper (1992), pp. 150–164; K. Cooper (1996), pp. 92–115.

179. K. Cooper (1992), p. 151.

180. Ibid., p. 158.

181. Ibid., p. 162.

182. See, for example, the *Liber ad Gregoria* and *Gesta Martyrum,* discussed by K. Cooper (1996), pp. 92–147.

183. For a more theoretical justification of this view, see E. A. Clark, "Holy Women, Holy Words: Early Christian Women, Social History, and 'the Linguistic Turn,'" *JECS* 6(3) (1998), pp. 413–430.

184. Averil Cameron (1989), p. 199.

185. On women in paganism, see J. Nichols, "*Patrona Civitatis:* Gender and Civic Patronage," in *Latomus: Studies in Latin Literature and Roman History,* vol. 5, ed. C. Deroux (Brussels, 1989), pp. 117–142; L. Cracco Ruggini, "Juridical Status and Historical Reality of Women in Roman Patriarchal Society," *Klio* 71(2) (1989), pp. 616–617; R. Van Bremen, "Women and Wealth," in *Images of Women in Antiquity,* ed. A. Cameron and A. Kuhrt (London, 1983), pp. 223–243; and R. MacMullen (1980), pp. 208–218. On women in church office, see notes 188, 192, 195, and 205 below, and K. Torjesen, *When Women Were Priests: Women's Leadership in the Early Church and the Scandal of Their Subordination in the Rise of Christianity* (San Francisco, 1993), pp. 5–6.

186. R. S. Kraemer (1992), p. 182.

187. M. Alexandre, "Early Christian Women," in *A History of Women,* vol. 1, ed. P. Schmitt Pantel, trans. A. Goldhammer (Cambridge, Mass., 1992), p. 432.

188. *C.Th.* 16.2.27 and 16.2.28 were directed to the praetorian prefect of the East, Tatian. In Constantinople aristocratic women like Olympias and her sisters were deaconesses; Soz. *HE* 8.9.1–2 (*GCS* 50.361); John Chrys. *Lettres à Olympias,* 2d ed.: *Vie Anonyme d'Olympias* 7 (*SC* 13 BIS, p. 420).

189. I owe this information to Professor Brent Shaw who with Katherine Eldred made a computerized search of *ICUR n.s.* through Volume 10, cataloging all funerary stones and stones that had date-of-death evidence on them. In this huge number, there were some deacons but not a single deaconess.

190. *CCSL* 148, p. 50. F. Cardman, "Women, Ministry and Church Order in Early Christianity," in *Women and Christian Origins,* ed. R. S. Kraemer and M. R. D'Angelo (New York, 1999), pp. 318–320, believes that Ambrosiaster (*Comm. on 1 Tim* 3.11 [*CSEL* 81.3.268]), like the members of later councils, associated deaconesses with heretical groups. A fifth-century council in Orange explicitly opposed deaconesses (*CCSL* 148, p. 184) as did later western councils; see A. G. Martimort, *Deaconesses: An Historical Study,* trans. K. D. Whitehead (San Francisco, 1986), pp. 187–205.

191. See A. Arjava (1996), pp. 245–246; R. MacMullen (1980), pp. 208–209, 217–218, for veils.

192. For the formal renunciation, see Ambrosiaster *Comm. on 1 Tim.* 5.6 and *1 Tim.* 5.11 (*CSEL* 81.3.280.6–7, 81.3.281.12, .14). For the order, see *1 Tim.* 5.4 (*CSEL* 81.3.279.8); R. Gryson, *Le ministère des femmes dans l'Église ancienne* (Gembloux, Belgium, 1972), pp. 157–158. Widowhood was considered an irrevocable choice. Ambrosiaster *Comm. on 1 Tim.* 5.16 (*CSEL* 81.3.284.3–6); M. Alexandre (1992), pp. 409–444. Evidence from the West often notes widows but does not generally indicate if they were enrolled in the order, as, for example, the widow Marcella, App. 2 = Marcella 2, *PLRE* 1.542–543.

193. Ambr. *De viduis* 2.11–12 (*PL* 16.251), trans. H. De Romestin (*NPNF* 10), p. 393.

194. On honor, see Ambrosiaster *Comm. on 1 Tim.* 5.3, 5.4, and 5.13 (*CSEL* 81.3.278.24–279.2, .279.10, .282.8–9, respectively); on material aid, see Ambrosiaster *Comm. on 1 Tim.* 5.4–5 (*CSEL* 81.3.279.3–25); and on women taken in, see Ambrosiaster *Comm. on 1 Tim.* 5.5 (*CSEL* 81.3.279.21), 5.9–10 (*CSEL* 81.3.281.9–10).

195. For Tertullian, see B. Thurston, *The Widows: A Women's Ministry in the Early Church* (Minneapolis, Minn., 1989), pp. 76–81; *Apostolic Constitutions* 3.6 (*SC* 239.132–134).

196. Jer. *Ep.* 54.16 (*CSEL* 54.483); see also Ambr. *De viduis* 9.52–54 (*PL* 16.263–264).

197. Ambrosiaster *Comm. on 1 Tim.* 5, 9–10 (*CSEL* 81.3.281.6–7).

198. *C.Th.* 3.17.4 (390). Cf. G. Clark (1993), pp. 56–62, and A. Arjava (1996), pp. 84–94.

199. See, for example, Jer. *Ep.* 54.12, 54.14 (*CSEL* 54.478–479, .481); Ambr. *De viduis* 2.11, 5.29 (*PL* 16.251, .256).

200. Jer. *Ep.* 54.12 (*CSEL* 54.478), following *Luke* 6.30 and Paul *Galatians* 6.10.

201. For constraints on women in eastern documents, see C. Methuen, "Widows, Bishops, and the Struggle for Authority in the *Didascalia Apostolorum*," *JEH* 46 (1995), pp. 197–213; *Didascalia et Constitutiones Apostolorum* 3.5.3–6, 6.1–2, 8.1–3 (ed. F. Funk [Turin, 1964], vol. 1, pp. 188–190); *Apostolic Constitutions* 3.5, 3.6 (*SC* 329.128–134).

202. Paul, *Epistle to Titus* 2:3–5.

203. See Jer. *Ep.* 130 (*CSEL* 56.175–201), especially Chapter 14; M. Alexandre (1992), p. 430, on virgins. The quotation is no. 1700 (*ILCV*, ed. E. Diehl), on Manlia Daedalia, an upper-class woman but not an attested *clarissima*.

204. Jer. *Ep.* 22 (*CSEL* 54.143–211) to Eustochium; *Ep.* 130 (*CSEL* 56.175–201).

205. J. E. Salisbury, *Church Fathers, Independent Virgins* (London, 1991), p. 33. see Ambr. *Ep.* 56[5].16 (*CSEL* 82.2.93): "what is more excellent (especially in a maiden whose private parts demand modesty) than . . . retirement?"

206. F. E. Consolino, "Il monachesimo femminile nella tarda antichità," *Codex aquilarensis* 2 (1988), pp. 33–45; G. D. Gordini, "Origine e sviluppo del monachesimo a Roma," *Gregorianum* 37 (1956), pp. 220–260; R. Lorenz, "Die Anfänge des abendländischen Mönchtums im 4. Jahrhundert," *Zeitschrift für Kirchengeschichte* 77 (1966), pp. 12ff.

207. J. E. Salisbury (1991), p. 33; Jerome *Ep.* 130.2 (*CSEL* 56.176–177).

208. Jer. *Ep.* 130.6 (*CSEL* 56.182).

209. Brown (1988), p. 344; I. Bremmer, "Pauper or Patroness? The Widow in the Early Christian Church," in *Between Poverty and the Pyre: Moments in the History of Widowhood,* ed. I. Bremmer and L. van den Bosch (New York, 1995), pp. 31– 57.
210. *Vie de Sainte Mélanie* 19, ed. D. Gorce (*SC* 90.162–169).
211. Ibid., 17 (*SC* 90.160).
212. Brown (1988), p. 345.
213. *Vie de Sainte Mélanie* 29, ed. D. Gorce (*SC* 90.182–184), trans. E. A. Clark, *The Life of Melania the Younger* (New York, 1984), pp. 47–48.
214. *Vie de Sainte Mélanie* 56, 68, ed. D. Gorce (*SC* 90.238).
215. Ibid., 11, 20 (*SC* 90.146–148, .168–170).
216. Jer. *Ep.* 77.6–10 (*CSEL* 55.42–47).
217. Brown (1988), p. 345.
218. E. A. Clark, *The Origenist Controversy: The Cultural Construction of an Early Christian Debate* (Princeton, N.J., 1992), Chapter 1.
219. A. Arjava (1996), pp. 249–250; I. Bremmer (1995), pp. 31–57; J. Nichols (1989), pp. 117–142; R. van Bremen (1983), pp. 23–42; R. MacMullen (1980), pp. 208–218.
220. Fabia Aconia Paulina, App. 2 = Paulina 4, *PLRE* 1.675, and *CIL* 6.2145 = *D.* 1261. The fourth-century Turrania Anicia Iuliana 3, *PLRE* 1.468, may possibly be identified with or related to the Turrania Anicia who dedicated a statue of Venus, *CIL* 6.5665, although I omitted this woman from my study population for lack of secure identification.
221. See F. E. Consolino, "Sante o patrone? Le aristocratiche tardoantiche e il potere della carità," *Studi storici* 30 (1989), pp. 969–991.

6. The Emperor's Influence on Aristocratic Conversion

1. Quotation is from N. H. Baynes, *Constantine the Great and the Christian Church* (London, 1931), p. 3. See for representatives of this view, Barnes (1995), pp. 135–147; MacMullen (1984), pp. 43–51, 86–120; and E. Gibbon, *The History of the Decline and Fall of the Roman Empire,* vol. 1, ed. J. B. Bury (reprint, New York, 1946), pp. 347–400, 560–584.
2. See Symm. *Or.* 1.10, 4.9, and 4.12 for the emperor as noble; *Or.* 1.7 for change-of-clothes metaphor; F. Millar, *The Emperor in the Roman World* (Ithaca, N.Y., 1977), pp. 3–12, and passim, and H. Löhken, (1982), pp. 112–147, for imperial ties to the aristocracy.
3. *C.Th.* 9.2.1: "The rights of senators and the authority of that order in which we number ourselves also must be defended."
4. See H. Löhken (1982), pp. 135–147, and the review by J. F. Drinkwater, *Latomus* 44 (1985), pp. 421–427.
5. Symm. *Ep.* 1.2.3, vv.5–6. On the need for emperors to gain the support of the senate and create a consensus among the aristocracy, see also C. Ando, *Imperial Ideology and Provincial Loyalty in the Roman Empire* (Berkeley, 2000), pp. 131–175.

6. *C.Th.* 16.5.42; Zos. 5.46; Generidus, App. 2 = (of this book) *PLRE* 2.500–501.
7. Amm. Marc. 16.10.13.
8. J. R. Martindale, in his review of R. von Haehling (1978), *JRS* 69 (1979), p. 196, wondered with good reason if all emperors had conscious religious policies.
9. Eus. *HE* 10.5.15–17; *C.Th.* 16.2, 16.2.4 (321) (e.g., bequeathing funds to the church).
10. Eus. *HE* 10.5.18–20, .6.1–5 on Donatists; *VC* 3.4–24 (*GCS* 7.82–94) on Nicaea.
11. Eus. *VC* 3.24; 4.24, .29, .32, .55 (*GCS* 7.94, .128, .130–131, .132, and .143, respectively).
12. Eus. *VC* 4.32. *The Oration to the Saints* is, in my view, rightly attributed to Constantine and dated to Good Friday, April 325; see R. Lane Fox, *Pagans and Christians* (New York, 1987), pp. 642–653.
13. W. H. C. Frend, "Mission, Monasticism and Worship (337–361)," in *L'Église et l'empire au IVe siècle,* ed. A. Dihle (Geneva, 1989), pp. 73–112.
14. T. D. Barnes, *Athanasius and Constantius: Theology and Politics in the Constantinian Empire* (Cambridge, Mass., 1993), pp. 165–176.
15. Amm. Marc. 21.16.18.
16. *C.Th.* 16.2.16 ("scientes magis religionibus quam officiis et labore corporis vel sudore nostram rem publicam contineri"), trans. C. Pharr, *The Theodosian Code and Novels and the Sirmondian Constitutions* (Princeton, 1952).
17. Salzman (1990), pp. 208–209; S. Bradbury, "Constantine and the Problem of Anti-pagan Legislation in the Fourth Century," *CPh.* 89 (1994), pp. 120–139.
18. *C.Th.* 16.10.20 (415); Symm. *Rel.* 3; Zos. 4.36. See also A. Cameron, "Gratian's Repudiation of the Pontifical Robe," *JRS* 58 (1968), pp. 96–99; Salzman (1990), p. 233, note 3.
19. J. Matthews (1975), pp. 131 and 107ff., and Matthews, "A Pious Supporter of Theodosius I: Maternus Cynegius and His Family," *JThS* n.s. 18 (1967), pp. 438–446. Some archaeologists would identify a recently excavated villa from Toledo, Spain, as belonging to Maternus; see D. Fernández-Galiano, "The Villa of Maternus at Carranque," *Ancient Mosaics at Bath, 1987,* in *Journal of Roman Archaeology,* supplementary series, vol. 9(1) (Ann Arbor, Mich., 1994), pp. 119–227.
20. On the violence surrounding the Serapeum, see R. MacMullen (1984), pp. 99–100; G. Fowden, "Bishops and Temples in the Eastern Roman Empire A.D. 320–435," *JThS* n.s. 29 (1978), pp. 53–78.
21. See Chapter 1, notes 1–4.
22. *C.Th.* 16.10.10, 16.10.12.
23. See Alan Cameron, *Claudian: Poetry and Propaganda at the Court of Honorius* (Oxford, 1970), pp. 189–190, who also sees the visit as historically true. N. McLynn, *Ambrose of Milan: Church and Court in a Christian Capital* (Berkeley, 1994), pp. 311–313, emphasizes Theodosius' desire to build bonds with the Roman aristocracy.
24. H. Drake, *Constantine and the Bishops: The Politics of Intolerance* (Baltimore, 2000), pp. 192–272, 393–440.

25. *C.Th.* 16.10.2; Barnes (1995), p. 144.

26. *C.Th.* 16.10.3.

27. Firm. Mat. *De err. prof.* 16.4–5, 20.7, 29.1–2. On church affairs, see T. D. Barnes (1993), pp. 165–175.

28. Much has been written about Julian's religious goals; for bibliography, see G. Fowden, "Polytheist Religion and Philosophy," *The Cambridge Ancient History,* vol. 13, ed. Averil Cameron and P. Garnsey (Cambridge, U.K., 1998), pp. 538–548.

29. *C.Th.* 12.1.50.

30. Amm. Marc. 22.10.6, 25.4.20; *C.Th.* 13.3.5.

31. Them. *Or.* 5.70B.

32. Although *H. Aceph.* 12 alleges that Jovian declared Christianity the official religion of the empire, that seems erroneous; for Jovian in internal affairs, see Ath. *Ep. ad Jov.* (*PG* 36.83ff.).

33. Amm. Marc. 30.9.5.

34. Ibid.

35. Lib. *Or.* 30.7; *C.Th.* 9.16.8 (370).

36. On Manichees, see *C.Th.* 16.5.3; on clerics, *C.Th.* 16.2.20.

37. J. Curran, "From Jovian to Theodosius," *Cambridge Ancient History,* vol. 13 (Cambridge, U.K., 1998), pp. 78–100.

38. I followed the offices selected by von Haehling (1978) and then reanalyzed by Barnes (1995).

39. Imperial influence may help to explain the presence of two converts to paganism from Christianity under the pagan Julian: Helpidius, App. 2 = Helpidius 6, *PLRE* 1.415; Felix, App. 2 = Felix 3, *PLRE* 1.332.

40. The importance of the 367–383 period is also underscored by von Haehling (1978), pp. 571–580. Moreover, this date cannot be attributed to a greater frequency of epigraphic material for Christians.

41. My findings agree with those of von Haehling (1978), pp. 576–580, although he included eastern and western high officials.

42. Ibid., pp. 576–577.

43. Chastagnol (1960), pp. 439ff.

44. R. von Haehling (1978), pp. 583ff.; Ambr. *De obitu Theodosii* 34 (*CSEL* 73.346); Rufinus 11.18; Aug. *Civ. dei* 5.26.

45. Often the lowest attested office was also the first; aristocratic careers are known largely from funeral or honorific inscriptions that list all the offices of the deceased.

46. Lendon (1997), p. 117.

47. See Chapter 2, note 137.

48. Symm. *Rel.* 3.7.

49. Lendon (1997), pp. 108–129.

50. *Pan. Lat.* 12[2].47.3.

51. Aur. Vict. *Caes.* 40.12ff.; Amm. Marc. 29.3.6; Zos. 3.36.

52. Amm. Marc. 26.1.4; Flavius Equitius 2, *PLRE* 1.282.

53. *Epistula Porfyrii,* ed. G. Polara (Turin, 1973), p. 6: "inter / tot divinae maiestatis insignia, quibus et invictus semper et primus es." Although Polara thinks the *Epistula Porfyrii* a forgery, I think it authentic, agreeing with T. D. Barnes, *Constantine and Eusebius* (Cambridge, Mass., 1981), p. 48, and "Publilius Optatianus Porfyrius," *AJP* 96 (1975), pp. 173–186. Hence I included Publilius Optatianus signo Porphyrius as a Christian in my study (Appendix 2), contrary to the view of his religiosity expressed by *PLRE* 1.649.

54. Bemarchius, *PLRE* 1.160; Lib. *Or.* 1.39; J. Bidez, *La vie de l'empereur Julien* (Paris, 1930–1948), p. 365.

55. Flavius Mallius Theodorus, App. 2 = Theodorus 27, *PLRE* 1.900–902. I consider Claudian, App. 2 = Claudius Claudianus 5, *PLRE* 2.299–300, a probable pagan because of Aug. *Civ. Dei* 5.26 and Orosius 7.35.21 (*CSEL* 5.531–532); cf. Matthews (1975), pp. 216–219.

56. Amm. Marc. 28.1.24–25.

57. R. Étienne, "La démographie des familles impériales et sénatoriales au IVe siècle après J. C.," in *Transformation et conflits au quatrième siècle après J. C.,* ed. A. Alföldi and J. Straub (Bonn, 1978), pp. 133–168.

58. Constantia 1, *PLRE* 1.221; Aur. Vict. *Epit.* 41.7; Lact. *Mort. Pers.* 43; Eutropia 2, *PLRE* 1.316; Virius Nepotianus 7, *PLRE* 1.625.

59. Stilicho, App. 2 = *PLRE* 1.853–858.

60. Flavius Bauto, App. 2 = *PLRE* 1.159–160; Eudoxia 1, *PLRE* 2.410 (omitted from this study because she was a member of the imperial household). Bauto was probably pagan; Ambr. *Ep.* 57[10].3 (*CSEL* 82.3.206–207) suggests a Frankish religiosity, and most Franks were still pagan.

61. Eunapius, *Frg.* 60 (*FHG* 4.40–41); A. Demandt, "The Osmosis of Late Roman and Germanic Aristocracies," in *Das Reich und Die barbaren,* ed. E. K. Chrysos and A. Schwarcz (Vienna-Cologne, 1989), pp. 75–85.

62. Alan Cameron, "Orfitus and Constantius: A Note on Roman Gold-Glasses," *JRA* 9 (1996), pp. 295–301.

63. F. Millar (1977), pp. 133ff.

64. *Pan. Lat.* 12[2].16.2–3, trans. C. E. V. Nixon (Liverpool, 1987).

65. J. Lendon (1997), pp. 63–73, 107–175.

66. M. Maecius Memmius Furius Baburius Caecilianus Placidus, App. 2 = Placidus 2, *PLRE* 1.705–706; Fabius Titianus, App. 2 = Titianus 6, *PLRE* 1.918–919.

67. P. Sabbatini Tumolesi, *Epigrafia anfiteatrale dell'occidente romano,* vol. 1: *Roma* (Rome, 1998) p. 130; G. Clemente, "Cristianesimo e classi dirigenti prima e dopo Costantino," in *Mondo Classico e Cristianesimo* (Rome, 1982), pp. 51–64.

68. See Appendix 4; cf. von Haehling (1978), pp. 284–330.

69. See Appendix 4; cf. von Haehling (1978), pp. 331–353.

70. *C.Th.* 16.10.24 (June 423) seems to contradict *C.Th.* 16.10.22 (April 423), which states the imperial "belief" that there were no longer any pagans; by June it was clear there were.

71. Ambr. *Ep.* 17[72].4 (*CSEL* 82.3.12–13): "those privileges were ones by which

even Christians were often led astray," for "some [Christians] through the wish to avoid the trouble of expenditure on public needs [had] lapsed [back into paganism] even under Christian emperors." Trans. Croke and Harries (1982), p. 31. Constantine exempted clerics from certain compulsory public services and from serving as tax receivers (*C.Th.* 16.2.1 and 16.2.7 [330]). Constantius II (*C.Th.* 16.2.9 [349]) extended exemptions to deacons and their sons, but this was retracted because so many men took advantage of this privilege (*C.Th.* 16.2.11). Valentinian I restored these exemptions (*C.Th.* 16.2.18 [370]; cf. *C.Th.* 16.2.24 and .26). For exemptions from compulsory public services of a menial nature, see *C.Th.* 16.2.10 (346); 16.2.14 (356); 16.2.15 (360); 16.2.16 (361).

72. For exemptions for pagan priests, see Chapter 2, note 284.

73. D. Hunt, "Christianising the Roman Empire," in *The Theodosian Code,* ed. J. Harries and I. Wood (Ithaca, New York, 1993), p. 151.

74. *C.Th.* 16.2.10. The translator, C. Pharr (1952), p. 442, notes that this constitution may be dated to 320; if so, it would be among the privileges granted by Constantine.

75. Although Eusebius claims that Constantine legislated against pagan sacrifice as early as 324, that Constantinian law is not extant; if it existed, it probably was only of local import in the eastern empire. M. R. Salzman, "*Superstitio* in the *Codex Theodosianus* and the Persecution of Pagans," *Vig. Chris.* 41(1987), pp. 172–188. Penalites included fines, confiscation of property, and even capital punishment. *C.Th.* 16.10.4, 16.10.6.

76. Gratian's law, not extant, is cited in *C.Th.* 16.10.20 (415); cf. Symm. *Rel.* 3.

77. Symm. *Rel.* 3.11–14.

78. See for examples Salzman (1990), pp. 193–246.

79. Imperial concern for apostasy may have been justified; see Ambr. *Ep.* 17[72].4 (*CSEL* 82.3.12–13); K. Rosen, "Ein Wanderer zwischen zwei Welten: *Carmen ad quendam senatorem ex Christiana religione ad idolorum servitutem conversum,*" in *Klassisches Altertum, Spätantike und frühes Christentum: Adolf Lippold zum 65. Geburtstag gewidmet;* ed. K. Dietz, D. Hennig, and H. Kaletsch (Würzburg, 1993), pp. 393–408.

80. *C.Th.* 16.5.42; Zos. 5.46.

81. Although the compilers of the Theodosian Code might have omitted some earlier code on this point, there is no reference to it in the 416 code nor, to my knowledge, in any other source.

82. Imperial views are forcefully stated. The Theodosian Code refers to pagan practices in derogatory terms, calling sacrifices polluting (*polluat: C.Th.* 16.10.10); abominable (*abominanda sacrificia: C.Th.* 16.10.13); or insane (*sacrificiorum . . . insania: C.Th.* 16.10.2). Those who perform pagan sacrifices are criminals (*sceleratae mentis paganae: C.Th.* 16.10.25) or mad and sacrilegious (*vesanus ac sacrilegus: C.Th.* 16.10.7). Paganism is branded a "*superstitio*" (*C.Th.* 16.10.2); M. R. Salzman (1987), pp. 172–188.

83. M. McCormick, *Eternal Victory: Triumphal Rulership in Late Antiquity, Byzantium, and the Early Medieval West* (Cambridge, Mass., 1986), pp. 106–107; ibid., note 118, cites Ambr. *Ep.* 61[2].4 (*CSEL* 82.3.181).

84. Eus. *VC* 2.45–46 (*GCS* 7.66–68); F. Millar (1977), pp. 551ff. Typical was the action of the emperor Valens who gave land to Bishop Basil of Caesarea from his private estates; Theodoret *HE* 4.16 (*GCS* 44.237–238).

85. P. Brown, *Power and Persuasion in Late Antiquity: Towards a Christian Empire* (Madison, Wis., 1992), pp. 95ff. For one such aristocratic donation by Boniface, see Augustine *Ep. 7**, in *Lettres 1*-29**, ed. J. Divjak (Paris, 1987).

86. Eus. *VC* 4.24 (*GCS* 7.128).

87. Eus. *VC* 4.17 (*GCS* 7.126); T. D. Barnes (1981), pp. 48–49.

88. *Pan. Lat.* 12[2].15.1 (1987).

7. The Aristocrats' Influence on Christianity

1. For example, Jerome *Ep.* 66.8 (*CSEL* 54.656–658) advises Pammachius to aim for perfection through total poverty, yet he proudly proclaims the nobility of Pammachius and his family. As R. Van Dam (1985), p. 139, observed, Jerome's view of monasticism was "a way of elevating aristocratic retirement into Christian respectability."

2. See my discussion in Chapter 1, especially note 26.

3. For an excellent discussion of this phenomenon, see Averil Cameron, *Christianity and the Rhetoric of Empire: The Development of Christian Discourse* (Berkeley, 1991), pp. 1–47.

4. P. Hadot, *Marius Victorinus: Recherches sur sa vie et ses oeuvres* (Paris, 1971); A. D. Nock, *Conversion: The Old and the New in Religion from Alexander the Great to Augustine of Hippo* (Oxford, 1933).

5. See especially G. Bardy, *La Conversion au Christianisme durant les premiers siècles* (Paris, 1949), pp. 32–58, 233 284, especially note 23, on theology's import; A. Fitzgerald, *Conversion through Penance in the Italian Church of the Fourth and Fifth Centuries* (Lewiston, N.Y., 1988), for salvationism and sin; and G. Fowden, *Empire to Commonwealth: Consequences of Monotheism in Late Antiquity* (Princeton, 1993), for monotheism. These approaches are related to the views of E. R. Dodds on the second and third centuries in *Pagan and Christian in an Age of Anxiety: Some Aspects of Religious Experience from Marcus Aurelius to Constantine* (Cambridge, Mass., 1965).

6. For conversion as radical reorientation, see A. D. Nock (1933). R. Stark (1996), p. 55, observed, "People are more willing to adopt a new religion to the extent that it retains cultural continuity with conventional religion(s) with which they already are familiar." This same logic applies here.

7. *CIL* 6.1756 = *ILCV* 63, vv.5–24, trans. Croke and Harries (1982), p. 116, with my translation of line 9: "Transcendis senior donatus munere Christi." Sextus Claudius Petronius Probus, App. 2 (of this book) = Probus 5, *PLRE* 1.736–740. Cf. Matthews (1975), pp. 195–197.

8. Van Dam (1985), p. 155.

9. Meropius Pontius Paulinus, App. 2 = Paulinus 21, *PLRE* 1.681–683; for his life, see Paul. of Nola *Carmen* 21 (*CSEL* 30.158–186); Prud. *C. Symm.* 1.558–560

(*CCSL* 126.205); Jerome *Ep.* 118.5.5–14 (*CSEL* 55.441). See Sulp. Sev. *Vita Mart.* 25.4–5 (*SC* 133.310) for Martin's high regard for Paulinus. See also D. Trout, *Paulinus of Nola: Life, Letters and Poems* (Berkeley, 1999).

10. Ambr. *Ep.* 27[58].3 (*CSEL* 82.1.181).

11. Van Dam (1985), p. 308 and notes 17–19.

12. Paul. of Nola *Carmen* 21.458–459 (*CSEL* 30.173), trans. P. G. Walsh, *The Poems of St. Paulinus of Nola* (New York, 1975), pp. 187–188.

13. J. Fontaine, "Valeurs antiques et valeurs chrétiennes dans la spiritualité des grands propriétaires terriens à la fin du IVe siècle occidental," in *Epektasis: Mélanges patristiques offerts au Cardinal Jean Daniélou,* ed. J. Fontaine and C. Kannengiesser (Paris, 1972), pp. 571–595.

14. Van Dam (1985), p. 309.

15. Paul. of Nola *Ep.* 8.12–16 (*CSEL* 29.48).

16. Jer. *Ep.* 66.7.2–3, .10–13 (*CSEL* 54.655), trans. W. H. Fremantle (*NPNF,* 2d series), vol. 6, p. 137.

17. Jer. *Ep.* 66.7.18–20 (*CSEL* 54.655), trans. W. H. Fremantle (*NPNF,* 2d series), vol. 6, p. 137.

18. Siricius *Ep.* 10.5 (*PL* 13.1190A) is dated to 388. See also C. Pietri, *Roma christiana: Recherches sur l'Église de Rome, son organisation, sa politique, son idéologie de Miltiade à Sixte III (311–440)* (Paris, 1976), pp. 764–772.

19. Siricius *Ep.* 1.10 (*PL* 13.1138C–1139B); see A. Rousselle, "Aspects sociaux du recrutement ecclésiastique au IVe siècle," *Mélanges d'archeologie et d'histoire de l'école française de Rome: Antiquité* 89 (1977), pp. 331–370.

20. Paul. of Nola *Carmen* 21.395–396, 21.376 (*CSEL* 30.171, .170).

21. Siricius *Ep.* 6.1 (*PL* 13.1164A-B); Innocent, *Ep* 2.2 (*PL* 20.470A-B).

22. N. McLynn, *Ambrose of Milan: Church and Court in a Christian Capital* (Berkeley, 1994), pp. 298–315.

23. Jer. *C. Ioh. Hierosol.* 8 (*PL* 23.361C): "[Praetextatus] Homo sacrilegius et idolorum cultor, solebat ludens beato Papae Damaso dicere: Facite me Romanae urbis episcopum, et ero protinus Christianus."

24. Sid. Ap. *Ep.* 7.12.4: "sic absque conflictatione praestantior secundum bonorum sententiam computatur honorato maximo minimus religiosus." Cf. Mathisen (1993), p. 90.

25. H. C. Kee, "Rich and Poor in the New Testament and in Early Christianity," in *Through the Eye of a Needle,* ed. E. Albu Hanawalt and C. Lindberg (Kirksville, Mo., 1994), pp. 29–42.

26. Clement of Alexandria, *Quis dives salvetur?* 11, 14 (*GCS:* Clemens Alexandrinus 3, pp. 166–169), ed. O. Stahlin (1905–1909; reprint, Leipzig, 1970), pp. 159–191; see also L. W. Countryman, *The Rich Christian in the Church of the Early Empire: Contradictions and Accommodations* (New York, 1980), pp. 197ff.

27. Cyp. *De op. et eleem.* 2 (*CSEL* 3.374); and in the early fourth century, cf. Lactantius *Div. inst.* 6.11–12 (*CSEL* 19.1.2.519–532).

28. Ambr. *Exp. evang. sec. Luc.* 8.85 (*CCSL* 14.330).

29. Aug. *Serm.* 48.8 (*CCSL* 41.610, trans. *FOTC*); cf. *Serm.* 61.3.3 (*PL* 38.410). On

this same theme, see Pelagius *De divitiis* 19.4 (*PL Suppl.* 1.1414); cf. Ambr. *De Nabuthae* 12.52 (*CSEL* 32.2.497–498).

30. See, for example, Petrus Chrysologus *Serm.* 124 (*CCSL* 24A.747–752); Zeno *Tract.* 1.2.4.9 (*CCSL* 22.17). Ambr. *De off.* 1.9.29 (ed. M. Testard [Paris, 1984–1992], 1.109) contrasts Lazarus and the rich man but not charity; that is suggested by Ambr. *De interpellatione Iob et David* 2.5 and 3.3 (*CSEL* 32.2.243–247 and 32.2.251–254), and *De Nabuthae* 12.52–53 (*CSEL* 32.2.497–498). See also B. Ramsey, "Almsgiving in the Latin Church: The Late Fourth and Early Fifth Centuries," *Theological Studies* 43 (1982), pp. 226–259.

31. Ambr. *De Helia et ieiunio* 20, 76 (*CSEL* 32.2.458).

32. Ambr. *De off.* 2.21.111 (ed. M. Testard 2.59); Jer. *Comm. in Esaiam* 58.6–7 (*CCSL* 73A.666); Aug. *Serm.* 61.11.12 (*PL* 38.414). Cf. B. Ramsey (1982), pp. 233–235.

33. Aug. *Serm.* 85.4.5 (*PL* 38.522).

34. Aug. *Serm.* 61.11.12 (*PL* 38.414).

35. Ambr. *De off.* 1.30.149 (ed. M. Testard 1.167–168).

36. The injunction to give with the right—that is, humble—attitude became a commonplace. See Ambr. *De off.* 1.30 (ed. M. Testard 1.164–172); Aug. *Ep.* 157 (*CSEL* 44.449–488). See also Jerome, *Tract. in ps.* 133.164–174 (*CCSL* 78.288) for charity as self-pity; Aug. *In Ep. Ioann.* 8–9 (*PL* 35.2040) for charity as pride.

37. Ambr. *Exp. in ps.* 119[118].17.4 (*CSEL* 62.379); Aug. *Enarr. in ps.* 46.5 (*CCSL* 38.532). Jer. *Ep.* 120.1 (*CSEL* 55.475–476) contradicts his views in *Comm. in Eccl.* 11.1 (*CCSL* 72.344).

38. Ambr. *De off.* 1.30.150 (ed. M. Testard 1.168); Jer. *Ep* 120.1 (*CSEL* 55.477); Aug. *Ep* 243.12 (*CSEL* 57.578–579); cf. Ambrosiaster *Comm. on 1 Tim.* 5.16 (*CSEL* 81.3.283–284), and J. Harries, "'Treasure in Heaven': Property and Inheritance among Senators of Late Rome," in *Marriage and Property,* ed. E. M. Craik (Aberdeen, 1984), pp. 54–70.

39. Aug. *Ep.* 262 (*CSEL* 57.623). Cf. criticism of Celantia by Pelagius; *Ep. ad Celantiam* (*CSEL* 56.329–356).

40. Ambr. *Exp. in ps.* 119[118].17.4 (*CSEL* 62.379).

41. Ambr. *De viduis* 5.27–32 (*PL* 16.256–257); Aug. *De bono viduitatis* 21.26 (*CSEL* 41.337–338).

42. Ambr. *Ep.* 36[2].26 (*CSEL* 82.2.17), written ca. 379. Ambrose influenced Vigilius, bishop of Tridentum; Chromatius, bishop of Aquileia; Gaudentius, bishop of Brescia; and Zeno, bishop of Verona; see R. Lizzi, "Ambrose's Contemporaries and the Christianization of Northern Italy," *JRS* 80 (1990), pp. 156–173.

43. On avarice, see especially Ambrose's *De Nabuthae* (*CSEL* 32.2.467–516), *De Helia et ieiunio* (*CSEL* 32.2.409–465), and *De Tobia* (*CSEL* 32.2.517–573), treatises based on sermons against avarice; and cf. his *Ep.* 10[38] (*CSEL* 82.1.73–78) to the priest Simplicianus; Bishop Zeno's treatises, *De avaritia* 1.5 (*CCSL* 22.38–42), 1.14 (*CCSL* 22.57–59), and 1.21 (*CCSL* 22.68); and L. Padovese, *L'originalità cristiana: Il pensiero etico-sociale di alcuni vescovi norditaliani del IV secolo*

(Rome, 1983), pp. 77–92 on Zeno, pp. 114–118 on Gaudentius, and pp. 169ff. on Chromatius.

44. Chromatius *Serm.* 12.7 (*CCSL* 9A.56).

45. Traditional criticism found in Sallust *Rep.* 2.8.4; Cicero *De off.* 2.6.4; Juv. *Sat.* 14.18.

46. R. Lizzi (1990), p. 167 and note 82, citing Max. of Turin *Serm.* 61.2.23–34 (*CCSL* 23.244–245).

47. Max. of Turin *Serm.* 71.3.44–54, .56–74 (*CCSL* 23.298–299); cf. L. Padovese (1983), pp. 223–234.

48. Aug. *Serm.* 60.7.7 (*PL* 38.405); see also "laturarii" in Aug. *Serm.* 38.9 (*CCSL* 41.484–485). B. Ramsey (1982), p. 248, note 110, notes that only Augustine uses this word in this period to refer to the poor; cf. investment imagery in Max. of Turin *Serm.* 96 (*CCSL* 23.383) and Aug. *Enarr. in ps.* 121.11 (*CCSL* 40.1812).

49. Paul. of Nola *Ep.* 34.10.16–23 (*CSEL* 29.311). Although classified as a letter, it is almost certainly a sermon.

50. S. A. Harvey, "The Holy and the Poor: Models from Early Syrian Christianity," in *Through the Eye of a Needle,* ed. E. Albu Hanawalt and C. Lindberg (Kirksville, Mo., 1994), p. 44, summarized the alleged differences between pagan and Christian views of charity but omitted the aristocratic interests studied here.

51. B. Ramsey (1982), pp. 251–252. For criticism of a donor as eager for popularity, see Jer. *Comm. in Esaiam* 58.6–7 (*CCSL* 73A.666); cf. Aug. *Ep.* 157 to Hilarius (*CCSL* 44.449–488).

52. Aug. *Serm.* 39.6 (*CCSL* 41.491–492); cf. *Serm.* 11.2 (*CCSL* 41.161–163), 85.7 (*PL* 38.523); *Enarr. in ps.* 124.2 (*CCSL* 40.1836–1837). Cf. also Optatus *De schismate Donatistarum* 3.39 (*CSEL* 26.74–75); Peter Chrysologus *Serm.* 124 (*CCSL* 24A.747–752).

53. Gaudentius *Ad Benivolum Praef.* 21–22 (*CSEL* 68.7): "Non malitiose, sed providenter te Deus divitem fecit, ut per opera misericordiae invenires peccatorum tuorum vulneribus medicinam." Cf. Paul. of Nola *Ep.* 34.6 (*CSEL* 29.307–308).

54. For public basilicas, see R. Lizzi (1990), pp. 157–166. In Aquileia, for example, no less than three churches attributed to the Bishop Chromatius were planned and started. For martyrs' shrines, see Paul. of Nola *Carm.* 21.367–394 (*CSEL* 30.170–171); see also R. Van Dam (1985), pp. 305–308.

55. H. I. Marrou, *A History of Education in Antiquity,* trans. G. Lamb (1948; reprint, Madison, Wis., 1982), pp. 314–329.

56. Jer. *Ep.* 22.30 (*CSEL* 54.189–191); for acceptance, see Aug. *De doctr. chris.* 4.27.59 (*CCSL* 32.163–164). For discussion and bibliography, see Averil Cameron, "Education and Literary Culture," *Cambridge Ancient History,* vol. 13, ed. Cameron and P. Garnsey (Cambridge, U.K., 1998), pp. 665–673, and the still fundamental study by H. Haggendahl, *Latin Fathers and the Classics (Studia Graeca et Latina, Gothoburgensia, 6)* (Göteborg, 1983).

57. For the scriptures recast into epic, see M. Roberts, *Biblical Epic and the Rhetorical Paraphrase in Late Antiquity* (Liverpool, 1985); for Paulinus of Nola's fusion of

Christian scripture and asceticism within a wedding hymn, see *Carm.* 21 (*CSEL* 30.158–186) and D. Trout (1999), pp. 198–251.

58. M. Mann, *The Sources of Social Power* (Cambridge, U.K., 1986), vol. 1, p. 316; cf. H. Gamble, *Books and Readers in the Early Church* (New Haven, 1997), pp. 1–41. Aristocrats were so deeply associated with literate culture that at the end of the sixth century, when offical rank had disappeared, Sidonius Apollinaris (*Ep.* 8.2.2) feared that learning alone would remain the sole indicator of *nobilitas*.

59. Ambr. *De off.* 1.22.101 (ed. M. Testard 1.145), trans. H. D. Romestin *(NPNF),* vol. 10, p. 18. See also Ambr. *Ep.* 36[2].3–4 (*CSEL* 82.2.4–5).

60. Ambr. *De off.* 1.22.100–1.23.104 (ed. M. Testard 1.144–146), trans. H. D. Romestin *(NPNF),* vol. 10, p. 18. See also Ambr. *Ep.* 36[2].5 (*CSEL* 82.2.5).

61. Ambr. *Ep.* 5[4].7 (*CSEL* 82.1.38).

62. Aug. *Ep.* 136.1 (*CSEL* 44.93–94).

63. A. Ferrua, *Epigrammata Damasiana* (Rome, 1942), pp. 7–13, 181–263.

64. Aug. *Conf.* 3.5, 6.3–5.

65. So, for example, the *Life of St. Antony,* a biography in a "simple" style, colored by Origenist theology, appealed to Augustine and to elite women in Rome; see Averil Cameron (1998), pp. 667–670, note 23. See also Jer. *Ep.* 52.8 (*CSEL* 54.428–430).

66. C. White, *Christian Friendship in the Fourth Century* (Cambridge, U.K., 1992), pp. 3, 164–184.

67. See, for example, Ambr. *De off.* 3.21.125–22.126 (M. Testard 2.140–141).

68. C. White (1992), p. 4.

69. Ibid., pp. 118ff.; for the classical notion of friendship, see D. Konstan, *Friendship in the Classical World* (Cambridge, U.K., 1997), pp. 122–148, 157–160.

70. Ambr. *De off.* 3.21.125 (ed. M. Testard 2.140–241) and Cicero *Laelius* 13.44C.

71. Paul. of Nola *Ep.* 1.5 (*CSEL* 29.4–5); cf. Cicero *Laelius* 6.20: "omnium divinarum humanarumque rerum cum benevolentia et caritate consensio."

72. Paul. of Nola *Ep.* 11.1–6, 13.2 (*CSEL* 26.60–64). Cf. C. White (1992), pp. 156ff.; see D. Trout (1999), pp. 198–251, for bibliography.

73. Paul. of Nola *Ep.* 11.1 (*CSEL* 29.60), trans. P. G. Walsh *(ACW),* vol. 1, p. 90; cf. 13.2 (*CSEL* 29.85–86).

74. Paul. of Nola *Ep.* 11.6 (*CSEL* 29.64–65); Aug. *Conf.* 4.4, 9.3. See J. Lienhard, "Friendship in Paulinus of Nola and Augustine," *Collectanea Augustiniana: Mélanges à T. J. van Bavel* (Leuven, Holland, 1990), pp. 279–296.

75. Even a casual perusal of the letters of other bishops indicates how widespread was the expectation that a bishop would act in this way; see C. White (1992), pp. 146–163, 185–217.

76. For example, Sulpicius Severus, Delphinus, Amandus of Bordeaux, and Vitricius of Rouen, along with his newer African friends, Augustine and Alypius; see P. Fabre, *Saint Paulin de Nole et l'amitié chrétienne = Bibl. des écoles fr. d'Athènes et de Rome* (Paris, 1949), vol. 167, Chapter 3.

77. Paul. of Nola *Ep.* 1, 5, 11, 17, 22 (*CSEL* 29.1–10, .24–39, .60–73, .125–128, .154–156).

78. Ambr. *Ep.* 61[89] (*CSEL* 82.2.119–120) to Alypius, *Ep.* 60[90] (*CSEL* 82.2.118–119) to Antonius, and *Ep.* 42[88] (*CSEL* 82.2.41) to Atticus all end with this formula. Trans. M. M. Beyenka *(FOTC)*, vol. 26, pp. 399–400. Cf. the conventional references to shared love at the close of letters. Cicero *Ep. ad fam.* 2.1; Fronto to Marc. Aurelius 4.1. See also S. K. Stowers, *Letter Writing in Greco-Roman Antiquity* (Philadelphia, 1986), pp. 58–76; ibid., p. 186, provides an index of Selected Epistolary Commonplaces, which includes "Longing for or to be with a loved one."

79. See Aul. Gell. 20.5.13 for etymology; hence *nobilitas* could be applied to notable cities, as in Ausonius' *Ordo Urbium Nobilium*, or to rivers, people, horses, and so on.

80. M. Gelzer, *Die Nobilität der römischen Republik* (Berlin, 1912), pp. 1ff.; D. C. Earl, *The Moral and Political Tradition of Early Rome* (Ithaca, N.Y.: 1967), pp. 11–43.

81. Cicero *Off.* 2.44; M. Gelzer (1912), pp. 1ff. The technical restriction of *nobilitas* to men of consular ancestry cannot be shown to have persisted in fourth- and fifth-century usage; see Chapter 2, notes 15 and 16.

82. At times the term was extended to men of local distinction and to members of the immediate entourage of foreign kings, such as the "nobility" of Germanic tribesmen. See J. Harries, "Bishops, Aristocrats and Their Towns: Some Influences on, and Developments in, the Role of Churchmen from Gaul from Paulinus of Nola to Sidonius Apollinaris" (Unpublished dissertation, Oxford University, 1981), pp. 43–63, 73.

83. No one Roman author includes all these, but analysis of the texts supports these characteristics; see *"nobilitas," OLD*; J. Harries (1981), pp. 43ff.; D. C. Earl (1967), pp. 11ff.; and *"nobilitas," TLL*.

84. J. Harries (1981), p. 59.

85. This is part of a larger change whereby the church came to "absorb what had previously been 'secular,' indifferent from a religious point of view, into the realm of the 'sacred.'" R. Markus, *The End of Ancient Christianity* (Cambridge, U.K., 1990), pp. 1–18, 213–229. For an expanded discussion of *nobilitas*, see M. R. Salzman, "Competing Claims to *'Nobilitas'* in the Western Empire of the Fourth and Fifth Centuries," *JECS* 9(3) (2001), pp. 359–385.

86. Fourth-century Christians were not the first to attempt to redefine *nobilitas*. In the late republic upwardly mobile non-nobles *(novi homines)* sought to substitute personal virtue for ancestry as the truest source of *nobilitas*. Cicero *In Pis.* 2; *In Verr.* 2.3.7, 2.5.180; *Pro Mur.* 17; D. C. Earl (1967), pp. 44–58. Efforts continued in the empire. Seneca *Ep.* 44.5, 66.3; *De brevitate vitae;* Juvenal *Sat* 8.20. But such attempts were not successful in dislodging traditional criteria.

87. The terms *nobilis and nobilitas* and the verb *nobilitaret* occur more often—474 times—in Jerome's work than in any other work that I have examined for this study. I examined Jerome's texts and those of the other authors via the *Patrologia Latina Database,* and I examined the writings of Ambrose and Augustine via the *Cetedoc* database. Augustine, whose body of work is larger than Jerome's, used *nobilis* or *nobilitas* 360 times, according to *Cetedoc.*

88. Jer. *Ep.* 66.6.1–2 (*CSEL* 54.654); 57.12.1–2 (*CSEL* 54.524).

89. Jer. *Ep.* 66.4.14–19 (*CSEL* 54.651), trans. W. H. Fremantle *(NPNF),* vol 6, p. 136.

90. Jer. *Ep.* 118.5.11 (*CSEL* 55.441): "nobilis es: et illi, sed in Christo nobiliores."

91. Pelagius *Expos. XIII ep. Pauli* ascribes "true glory" to Christians, and he chooses as his examples those who are already noble. See, for example, "sic autem vos de generis nobilitate iactatis," *Prologus ep. ad Rom.* (ed. A. Souter [Cambridge, U.K., 1922], p. 7, line 16); J. Harries (1981), pp. 58ff.

92. Paul. of Nola *Ep.* 13.15 (*CSEL* 29.96–97).

93. Ibid.; cf. Paul. of Nola *Carm.* 21.202–224 (*CSEL* 30.164–165).

94. Jer. *Ep.* 108.1.5–6 (*CSEL* 55.306): "nobilis genere, sed multo nobilior sanctitate."

95. Jer. *Ep.* 130.1 (*CSEL* 56.175–176).

96. Jer. *Ep.* 22 to Eustochium uses *nobilis* no less than six times, four times in reference to women, 22.11, .15, .27, 32 (*CSEL* 54.158, .162, .183, .193), and twice for the houses of noble families, 22.16, .28 (*CSEL* 54.163, .185); for Melania possessing *vera nobilitas,* see *Ep.* 39.5 (*CSEL* 54.305); for Ageruchia, her grandmother Matronia, her mother Benigna, and her aunt, *Ep.* 123.1 (*CSEL* 56.72–73); for Proba, *Ep.* 130.7 (*CSEL* 56.182); for Fabiola, *Ep.* 77.2 (*CSEL* 55.38). See K. Torjesen, "In Praise of Noble Women: Asceticism, Patronage and Honor," *Semeia* 57 (1992), pp. 41–64.

97. Jer. *Ep.* 130.6.5–6 (*CSEL* 56.181): "nobilem familiam virgo virginitate sua nobiliorem faceret."

98. See, for example, Ambrose on the noble virgin martyr Sotheris. Ambr. *Exhor. virg.* 12.82 (*PL* 16.360) and *De virg.* 3.38 (*PL* 16.232). Sotheris was not included in my database because there is no evidence that she was a *clarissima;* Ambrose presents her as "noble" for rhetorical purposes. See N. McLynn (1994), pp. 34–35. On noble virgin martyrs, see also Ambr. *Ep.* 2.7[37].36 (*CSEL* 82.1.61).

99. Cf. Paul. of Nola *Ep.* 29.6 (*CSEL* 29.252) to Melania ("consulibus avis nobilis, nobiliorem se contemptu corporeae nobilitatis dedit"). Cf. also 29.7, .10 (*CSEL* 29.252–53, 257), and *Carm.* 21.836–844 (*CSEL* 30.185). See K. Torjesen (1992), pp. 50–51, and E. A. Clark, "Authority and Humility: A Conflict of Values in Fourth-Century Female Monasticism," *Byzantinische Forschungen* 9 (1985), pp. 17–33, for the ascetic evidence.

100. Aug. *Ep.* 150.10–13 (*CSEL* 44.381) to Proba and Iuliana, trans. W. Parsons *(FOTC),* vol. 20 (1953), p. 267; cf. *Ep.* 188.1.9–15 (*CSEL* 57.120).

101. Avitus *In ord. episc. I (MGH: Auct. Ant.)* 6.2.124: "vera et intera nobilitas." Later, Venantius Fortunatus, *Carm.* 1.15.32–33, referred to the episcopate as an "altera nobilitas."

102. C. Pietri, "Aristocratie et société clericale dans l'Italie chrétienne au temps d'Odoacre et de Theodoric," *Mélanges d' archéologie et d'histoire de l'école française de Rome: Antiquité* 93 (1981), pp. 417–467.

103. See, for example, Constantius of Lyons, *Vita Germani* 4.22 (*SC* 112.164): "natalibus nobilis, religione nobilior." See also Mathisen, (1993), p. 90.

104. Prud. *Peristephanon* 10.123–125 (*CCSL* 126.334), trans. H. J. Thomson *(LCL),* vol. 2 (1953), p. 237.

105. Prud. *Peristephanon* 10.112 (*CCSL* 126.334) claims Romanus was a noble. Else-

where, Prudentius uses *nobilitas* to refer to alleged nobles who attain a higher spirituality through Christ. See, for example, Eulalia, *Peristephanon* 3.1–2 (*CCSL* 126.278), and *Peristephanon* 2.521–522 (*CCSL* 126.275).

106. Hilarius *Sermo* 16.2 (*SC* 235.112).
107. Hilarius *Sermo* 4.1 (*SC* 235.76).
108. Valerian *Hom.* 14.3 (*PL* 52.736).
109. Frank Abate, editor in chief of the U.S. Dictionaries Program for Oxford University Press, observed, "When people's attitudes change, that changes the language." *New York Times*, July 25, 1999, sec. 4, p. 2.
110. M. Mann (1986), vol. 1, pp. 301–302.
111. Ambr. *Exameron* 6.8.51 (*CSEL* 32.1.243); cf. Aug. *Sermo* 61.8.9 (*PL* 38.412).

Appendix 1

1. *PLRE* 1, p. vi. As this Appendix indicates, I have augmented and developed this database after publishing initial studies: Salzman (1989), pp. 207–220, and (1990), pp. 451–479.
2. Numbers are from W. Eck's review of A. Mandouze, *Prosopographie de l'Afrique chrétienne (305–533)*, vol. 1 (Paris, 1982), in *Gnomon* 57 (1985), pp. 719–725.
3. R. Mathisen, "A Survey of the Significant Addenda to PLRE," *Medieval Prosopography* 8(1) (1987), pp. 5–30; cf. R. Mathisen, "Fifteen Years of PLRE: Compliments, Complaints, and Caveats," *Medieval Prosopography* 7(1) (1986), pp. 1–37.
4. For the numbers in Mandouze (1982), see W. Eck (1985), pp. 719–725. Unfortunately, Part II of the *Prosopographie chrétienne du Bas-Empire—Prosopographie de L'Italie chrétienne*, vols. 1 and 2, ed. C. Pietri and L. Pietri (*École française de Rome*, Rome, 1999–2000)—was not available for inclusion in this study. However, a large number of the Christian clergy contained in it and certainly the most conspicuous members of the aristocracy could be located through the sources that I used.
5. T. D. Barnes, "More Missing Names (A.D. 260–395)," *Phoenix* 27 (1973), pp. 135–155.
6. T. D. Barnes, *The New Empire of Diocletian and Constantine* (Cambridge, Mass., 1982), pp. 175–191.
7. For example, subsequent patterns of habitation may affect the excavation of certain sites, or Christian veneration of the dead may have preserved Christian funeral sites better than pagan ones in certain areas. See also on the biases of *PLRE*, W. Eck, "Sozialstruktur des römischen Senatorenstandes der hohen Kaiserzeit und statistische Methode," *Chiron* 3 (1973), pp. 375–394.
8. K. Hopkins, *Death and Renewal* (Cambridge, 1983), pp. 164ff., noted this bias for the early empire.
9. C. R. Galvao-Sobrinho, "Funerary Epigraphy and the Spread of Christianity in the West," *Athenaeum* 83(2) (1995), pp. 431–466.
10. Jones (1964, 1986 reprint), pp. 547ff.
11. Arnheim (1972), pp. 3–19; S. J. B. Barnish, "Transformation and Survival in the Western Senatorial Aristocracy, A.D. 400–700," *PBSR* 56 (1988), p. 121. The clarissimate was probably hereditary for three generations.

12. Arnheim (1972), p. 9.
13. Jones (1964, 1986 reprint), p. 531 and note 19.
14. T. D. Barnes, "Who Were the Nobility of the Roman Empire?" *Phoenix* 28 (1974), p. 446.
15. On this point, I am in agreement with S. J. B. Barnish, (1988), p. 123 and his note 11.
16. The provinces of the *Notitia Dignitatum* (ca. 400 C.E.) are based on Jones (1964, 1986 reprint), vol. 2, Map 2. I did not include Illyricum as a separate area in the western empire since I agree with von Haehling (1978), pp. 97–99, who located the administration of this area under the eastern empire, in part because this area was disputed and divided, passing between the eastern and western emperors during the period under consideration.
17. All the holders of major offices recorded by von Haehling (1978) and by Barnes (1989), and again by Barnes (1995), pp. 135–147, were analyzed, as well as any cited by *PC* or in R. Mathisen's articles (listed in Appendix 3).
18. Bagnall et al. (1987), pp. 1–12.
19. Von Haehling (1978), pp. 19–48, 308.
20. Von Haehling (1978), pp. 370–371, for example, sees Petronius Probinus, urban prefect of 345–346 and consul of 341, as a probable Christian because of his family ties (his sister and his son were Christian or Christian converts). I omitted him.
21. Von Haehling (1978), p. 292, cites Lib. *Or* 1.46 and *PLRE* 1.510. Barnes (1995), p. 146, and (1989), p. 318, also sees Limenius as a probable pagan.
22. Athan. *Hist. Arian.* 22.1 (*PG* 25.717). Here I differ from Barnes (1995), pp. 135–147, who in general has identified more Christian aristocrats than met my criteria for inclusion in my database.
23. Amnius Manius Caesonius Nicomachus Anicius Paulinus iunior signo Honorius 14 = Paulinus 14, *PLRE* 1.679. My unwillingness to read silence as evidence for religious affiliation distinguishes my study of women from others, such as that of G. Disselkamp, *"Christiani Senatus Lumina": Zum Anteil römischer Frauen der Oberschicht im. 4 und 5. Jahrhundert an der Christianisierung der römischen Senatsaristocratie* (Bodenheim, Germany, 1997), pp. 19–23.
24. Barnes (1989), pp. 318–319, views Flavius Constantius, Valerius Maximus, and Gregorius as probable Christians on the basis of Eusebius *VC* 2.44 (*GCS* 1.1, p. 66). But Eusebius only states Constantine's preference to promote Christians as provincial governors, not mentioning Constantius and Maximus. Only Gregorius has any evidence for probable Christian affiliation.
25. Augustine *De sermone domini in monte* 1.50; Septimius Acindynus 2, *PLRE* 1.11.
26. J. C. Saquette would restore the inscription to this unidentified Septimius A. to read "XV vir(o) [s(acris) f(aciundis)]" or "XV vir[o sac(ris) faciundis]." See Saquette, "Septimius Acindynus, Corrector Tusciae et Umbriae: Notes on a New Inscription from Augusta Emerita (Mérida, Spain)," *ZPE* 129 (2000), pp. 281–286.
27. This resulted in 35 probable pagans, 27 probable Christians, and 5 Neoplatonist philosophers, also identified as probably pagan; see Appendix 2.

28. *Not. Scav.* (1917), 22 = *Bull. Comm.* (1917), 225 Rome; considered an early fourth-century senator by *PLRE* 1.10.

29. Proculus Gregorius, App. 2 (of this book) = Gregorius 9, *PLRE* 1.404; Sulp. Sev. *Chron.* 2.49.2–3 (*SC* 441.338–340). I. Kajanto, *Onomastic Studies in the Early Christian Inscriptions of Rome and Carthage: Acta Instituti Romani Finlandiae,* vol. 2, part 1 (Helsinki-Helingfors, 1963), p. 86, considers Gregorius a Christian name, and so von Haehling (1978), p. 343, cites him as a probable Christian. Similarly, Acilius Severus 16, App. 2, consul in 323, was also included as a probable Christian; Jerome *De Vir. Ill.* 111 (*PL* 23.745–746) sent him two books of letters and praised him in this work that celebrates Christians.

30. K. Hopkins, "Christian Number and Its Implications," *JECS* 6(2) (1998), p. 187, takes a similar position.

31. Thirty-eight positions were recorded. The second consulship and the second urban prefectureship were distinguished from the first holding of those offices and were considered the higher offices. The offices that were coded were (in order of their coding and not of their importance) second consulship; first consulship; pretorian prefect; urban prefect; proconsular; vicar; governor of a province (title not attested); consular; *corrector; praeses;* praetor; quaestor; count of the consistory; *quaestor sacri palatii; magister officiorum;* bureau chief (unspecified); *magister equitum (et peditum); comes rei militaris; magister militum; magister officiorum* (in the military); *dux* (military); *dux* (not military); *comes* (military); - *comes* (not military); suffect consul; *pontifex maximus* or *quindecemvir s.f.;* second urban prefectureship; *praepositus sacri cubiculi,* prefect of the *annona;* prefect of Egypt; *duodecemvir;* prefect of Constantinople; *sacerdos* or *augur; praefectus vigilum; curator;* legate; *tribunus;* and *notarius.* At times it was difficult to determine what was the highest office, as, for instance, deciding that a *dux* in the military was "lower" than a *dux* outside of the military context. However, these sorts of problems were relatively few, since most individuals tended to stay within particular career paths and, within these, the highest office reached was apparent.

32. Men were recorded in twenty-four categories: Carinus (283–285); Maximian (286–305, 307–310); Constantius I (305–306); Severus (306–307); Maxentius (307–312); Constantine (306–324); Constantine as sole ruler (324–337); Constantine II (including the first three years of Constans) (337–340); Constans (340–350); Constantius II, eastern emperor (337–350); Magnentius and Constantius II (350–353); Constantius II as sole ruler (353–361); Julian (361–363); Jovian (363–364); Valentinian I (sole, 364–367); Valentinian I with Gratian (367–375); Gratian with Valentinian II (375–383); Magnus Maximus (383–388); Valentinian II (383–392); Eugenius (392–394); Theodosius I (394–395); Honorius (395–423); Valentinian III (425–455); and a category for those who held office in the years 423–430, but for whom it was not possible to determine when and consequently under whom the individual held his highest office. All others for whom one could not tell the emperor at time of highest office were omitted from this variable. Dates based on Croke and Harries (1982), pp. xiv–xv.

33. Thirty-two different positions were coded; they are listed here by order of their coding as consul, pretorian prefect, urban prefect, *proconsular*, provincial governor (title not attested), vicar, *consular, praeses*, count of the consistory, *quaestor sacri palatii, magister officiorum*, bureau chief (unspecified), *magister militum* or *magister equitum, comes* (undetermined), *comes* (military), *comes* (domestic or court), *dux, corrector, praepositus* or tribune (military), honorary office of prefect, *prefect of the annona, curator*, legate, suffect consul, *comes Orientis, praefectus vigilum*, prefect of Egypt, urban praetor or *tutelaris, notarius* or *rationalis*, quaestor, *magister scrinii*, and *tribunus* or *notarius*.

34. There were twenty-two different categories for the emperors under whom one held first attested office. These are the same as those recorded for highest office in note 32 above, with the omission of Valentinian III (425–455) and the broad category 423–430. Obviously, those individuals who held lowest office in these time periods would not meet the chronological criteria for this study. The first category included those who held their lowest office before Maximian, that is, ca. 260–286, including the period of Carinus that I held distinct in determining highest office.

35. With the exception of the religious career, these career paths correspond roughly to the categories cited by Ausonius *Grat. Actio.* 4. See Chastagnol (1982), p. 176. I omitted the consulship from the traditional senatorial *cursus* since it was rarely held by senatorial aristocrats in the fourth century. Bagnall et al. (1987), pp. 4–6, 97ff. These categories differ somewhat from those of Kuhoff (1983), p. 255, who argues for a single mixed *cursus* of traditional and newly created posts by the late fourth century. There was some of this, as well as an overlap between court and extra-court careers (Chastagnol, 1982, pp. 177, 189) by then, but the different tracks remained distinctive into the fifth century.

36. The possible exceptions, Vestal Virgins and female heads of monastic communities, were few, and the degree to which these were career paths is arguable.

Index

Ablabius, Fl(avius), 100, 101, 302n178, 303n189

Achantia, 71

Acindynus, Septimius, 238

Adlection: as basis for membership in the senatorial aristocracy, 21–22, 34, 121, 274n10; as source of status for senatorial patrons, 34

Aedesius, Sextilius Agesilaus, 127

Africa. *See* Roman Africa

Albina, the Elder, 152

Albina, the Younger, 314n20

Albinus, C(a)eionius Rufius, 145, 146

Albinus, Publilus C(a)eionius Caecina, 145, 146

Alexander, Severus (emperor), 114

Alypius (friend of Augustine), 213

Amanda (wife of Aper), 88, 151, 285n237

Ambrose: on almsgiving, 206, 207; on appeal of Christianity to the wealthy, 218; career of, 133, 311n125; on Christian literary style, 210; claims about Christian majority in the Senate, 79, 122; connections with pagans, 15; criticism of opportunism as motive in conversion, 128; criticism of women's subordination, 152–153; on friendship, 212; influence on Gratian, 74; influence on other Christian bishops, 333n42; intervention in worldly affairs, 205; on marriage, 317n55; and Monica (mother of Augustine), 72; on *nobilitas* and aristocratic

women, 216; opposition to return of the altar of Victory, 74; on Paulinus of Nola's devotion to the church, 132; property disputes and financial dealings of, 52; recommendation on style appropriate to aristocratic audiences, 17; on religious concordance of husbands and wives, 150; statements by, as evidence of aristocrats' conversion, 11; on the virgin martyr Sotheris, 337n98; on uses of wealth, 206, 209; on widows, 172

Ambrosiaster, 148, 172

Ammianus Marcellinus, 19, 69, 178, 233; on aristocratic status, 19; on aristocratic status pride, 69; on barbarians raised to consulships under Constantine, 33, 99–100; depiction of emperor Valentinian I, 37, 189; on hunting among Roman aristocrats, 44–45; on Julian's policies toward Christianity, 184; on the lifestyle of Roman aristocrats, 44, 47, 48, 49, 56; praise for Constantius II, 36; praise of Sextus Aurelius Victor, 306–307n37; on Valentinian I's religious toleration, 185; on the zealousness of Constantius II, 182

Anicii family, 183–184

Antoninus Pius (emperor), 156

Antony (Christian monk), 108

Aper (husband of Amanda), 88, 151, 285n237

Apocryphal Acts of the Apostles, 145

Apollos, in New Testament, 153

342

Polytheism, vitality in third and fourth
centuries, 3
Pompeianus, 55
Ponticianus, 108, 126
Praetextatus, Vettius Agorius, 60, 75, 118,
119, 132, 190, 205, 270n6, 288n268; lit-
erary activities of, 47; on religious con-
cordance of husbands and wives, 150;
religious offices of, 65
Pragmatic concerns, as basis for coopera-
tion between emperors and aristocrats,
192–193
Priscilla, 153, 318n72
Priscillian, 175
Priscillianist movement, 92–93, 169, 238,
298–299n136
Private cults of aristocrats, 63–64
Proba, Anicia Faltonia, 56
Proba, Faltonia Betitia (poet), 136, 160,
163–164, 168, 315n28
Probianus, Petronius, 283n174
Probinus, Petronius, 339n20
Probus, Sextus Claudius Petronius, 49,
102, 110–111, 123, 137, 280n113; epi-
taph of, 59–60, 202–203, 214–215
Probus, Sextus Petronius. See Probus,
Sextus Claudius Petronius
Procula, 92
Proculus, L. Aradius Valerius signo
Populonius, 59, 76, 95
Proculus, Q. Aradius Rufinus Valerius
signo Populonius, 95
Proiecta, 81, 136
Promotus, Flavius, 275n24
Prosopographie chrétienne du Bas-Empire 1,
Prosopographie de l'Afrique chrétienne, 231–
232
Prosopographie chrétienne du Bas-Empire 2,
Prosopographie de l'Italie chrétienne, 232,
338n4
Prosopography of the Later Roman Empire,
231, 235
Protadius, 54, 88, 296n106
Provincial elites: advancement of, under
Constantine, 32–33; as members of sen-

atorial order, 39–40; and obligations to
home cities, 304n199
Prudentius, 91, 216, 217, 319n96,
338n105; on conversion of prominent
Roman families, 149; on the role of men
in religious rites, 155–156, 157; story
concerning Theodosius, 1, 2–3
Public office-holding, as source of status,
50–52
Public service, exemptions from, 329–
330n71

Ramsey, B., 208
Recommendations, system of, 114–115,
127, 137, 192, 193, 194
Religious career paths, 132–135
Richomeres, Flavius, 86, 130, 281n134;
friendship with established families, 42
Roman Africa, aristocracy of: and conversion of, 93–96; and ties to Rome-based
aristocrats, 93–94. See also Aristocracy
Romanus, 216–217
Rome and Italy, aristocracy of, 39, 43; as
centers of aristocratic paganism, 73–83;
and dating of conversion of, 78–80; impact of fall of Rome on, 134; and quantitative evidence for conversion of, 77–78;
as symbolic center of the empire, 73. See
also Aristocracy
Rosen, K., 78
Rufinus (ascetic), 174, 175
Rufinus, Aradius, 95, 302n181
Rufinus, Vulcacius, 178–179, 280n113

Sabbatini Tumolesi, P., 120
Salvian, 96
Saquette, J. C., 339n26
Saturn, cult of, in Africa Proconsularis, 13
Saturnalia. See Macrobius
Satyrus, Uranius, property disputes and
financial dealings of, 52
Secundus, L. Turcius, 80, 81
Secundus, L. Turcius signo Asterius, 80, 81
Secundus, Saturninius Salutius, 42, 86,
102